Neck and Neck
to the White House

Neck and Neck to the White House

The Closest Presidential Elections, 1796–2000

ROBERT E. KELLY

McFarland & Company, Inc., Publishers
Jefferson, North Carolina, and London

ALSO BY ROBERT E. KELLY AND FROM MCFARLAND

Baseball's Offensive Greats of the Deadball Era: Best Producers Rated by Position, 1901–1919 (2009)

The National Debt of the United States, 1941 to 2008 (2d ed., 2008)

Baseball for the Hot Stove League: Fifteen Essays (1989)

Baseball's Best: Hall of Fame Pretenders Active in the Eighties (1988)

LIBRARY OF CONGRESS CATALOGUING-IN-PUBLICATION DATA

Kelly, Robert E., 1926–
    Neck and neck to the White House : the closest presidential elections, 1796–2000 / Robert E. Kelly.
        p.   cm.
    Includes bibliographical references and index.

    ISBN 978-0-7864-4484-7
    softcover : 50# alkaline paper ∞

    1. Presidents— United States— Election — History.   2. United States— Politics and government.   I. Title.
    JK524.K35   2011
    324.973 — dc22   2010048330

BRITISH LIBRARY CATALOGUING DATA ARE AVAILABLE

Front Cover images © 2011 Shutterstock

Manufactured in the United States of America

McFarland & Company, Inc., Publishers
Box 611, Jefferson, North Carolina 28640
www.mcfarlandpub.com

Acknowledgments

This book could not have been produced without the patience exhibited and the editorial assistance provided by my wife, Margaret Rodden Kelly.

Table of Contents

Preface

The election of 2000, a win for George Bush in a most unique way, immediately grabbed my imagination. Was it unique in its closeness and its bitterness? Were there others? How many? Who were involved? Time and opportunity to explore those questions finally appeared. That's why you are holding this book in your hands today — because you're as curious about the answers as I am.

The election of 2000 was conducted in a bitterly partisan atmosphere. The political left hoped it would be the final challenge to its ability to govern the nation according to legal and political precepts established under Woodrow Wilson, Franklin Roosevelt and Lyndon Johnson that had, over decades, changed the face of America. Yes, legal concepts were involved in those elections too, as you will see in this book. One does not rule on such things as slavery, voting rights, desegregation, affirmative action, pornography, abortion and the freedom to pray without causing a stir in the body politic, without changing a vote here and there.

Victory belonged to the political left in 1992 when President Clinton rose to power because, more than any other, he represented the liberated man of his generation, one who would represent the giants of the progressive movement and its modern-day constituency well. And if Vice President Gore were elected president for eight more years, their ideas would be so deeply cemented into the federal edifice that no opposing force could ever unseat them. Only George Bush stood between them and the continuation of the bright, new world they envisioned for the nation that would, under their supervision, become better for all Americans and for the world.

Unfortunately for the dreamers, President Clinton's second term was filled with lurid stories of his sexual meanderings. He was impeached for lying about them, but he survived a Senate trial. Now, survival is a condition much admired by Darwinians. But it isn't greeted with equivalent respect in the everyday world of politics and society where other values, more specifically human, are held in higher esteem. Clinton took the blows associated with his behavior, and for that he deserves respect. But he lost the admiration of others, some argue, because of the disrespect he brought to the nation's most exalted institution, the presidency. It wasn't so much the generally unacceptable nature of

1

Clinton's behavior that bothered many Americans as who he was and where he was when he did what he did and, from a legal standpoint, how he explained what he did.

Clinton energized those on the political right to an extraordinary extent. They, and many independent voters, saw the election as a chance to restore dignity to a White House that had been deflowered before their eyes. They said, "Enough! We need fresh air in Washington." Those on the political left defended their hero and argued that his successes as president, not his lapses as a human being, should be his heritage.

Al Gore, vice president throughout the Clinton era, was burdened with the reputation of his predecessor during the presidential contest with Republican nominee Governor George W. Bush from Texas. Considering the circumstances, Gore did remarkably well at selling the usual liberal agenda to a nation that, for a half century, had shown itself to be increasingly willing to value security over liberty.

Arguably, absent the burden of the Clinton heritage Gore would have won the election; and the world for good or ill would have been a different place today, because he and Bush are driven by entirely different agendas. Gore was fifty-two and Bush fifty-four in the year 2000 — about the same age. On that basis one might think both men would be regarded as laudable examples of their generation, at least by their peers. Not so. Gore — whether he liked it or not — was regarded as Clinton's successor, a man who would continue to carry the torch of the progressives to its final end. Clinton had been adopted by the Woodstock generation as one of their own and Gore (who was and remains absolutely nothing like Clinton) had become his political heir.

Bush was regarded by Gore supporters as more than a political opponent — he was a threat to their social revolution and a traitor to his generation. He would overturn the social progress made over four decades; he would restore to acceptance the old-fashioned values of an earlier generation. He was an enemy; he had to be stopped. Simply by being what he was, Bush inherited a level of animosity customarily reserved for the nation's most dangerous enemies. The election, through that prism, had the tone of a religious battle: New versus old; absolute freedom versus self-control.

Given these prevailing attitudes, it isn't surprising that Bush's narrow victory caused an emotional and political uproar made worse by the fact that he won the electoral vote but lost the popular vote. And the fierce unyielding partisan politics of the 1980s that had surfaced under President Reagan, when he reinstalled a Republican presidency for eight years, blossomed once again to new intensity during Bush's eight years in the Oval Office.

But was the 2000 election unusually close or ill-tempered? Was it really a new phenomenon in American politics? Or had that road been traveled before? The latter is the case. There have been many close presidential elections, and it's the purpose of this book to show most of them to you.

Introduction

What Is a Close Presidential Election?

From the beginning, presidents have been selected under the electoral vote system, with each state given a number of electoral votes. Candidates in most states engage in winner-take-all elections; electoral votes are counted; the winner is president. It can be said, therefore, that a close election obviously exists when the electoral vote is extremely close. Such a conclusion is true. But it is the view of the writer that the electoral measure is not enough to totally define a close election. More is needed. Why? Because successful administrations need one essential property — unity. Without it, they move from crisis to crisis and have little success in turning agendas into law or common practice.

Obviously, not all close elections are super-competitive and few are a real presidential dogfight but, for the purposes of context and continuity, even the pacific ones are briefly summarized in this book.

The Central Importance of Unity

Slavery flourished in the United States during the administrations of its first fifteen presidents. Many disapproved of it (even as they profited by it), and they had something to say about it, especially the Founding Fathers:

- George Washington: There is not a man living who wishes more sincerely than I do, to see a plan adopted for the abolition of it.[1]
- John Adams: I have throughout my whole life held the practice of slavery in ... abhorrence.[2]
- Thomas Jefferson: Nothing is more certainly written in the book of fate that these people are to be free.[3]
- James Madison: [T]hey should be considered ... in the light of human beings and not as mere property.[4]

Despite these sentiments, slavery continued throughout the early presidencies until, finally, the cancer exploded into a civil war that pitted American

3

against American, friend against friend and relative against relative in a bloody conflict that killed or injured about a half-million men. Finally, Abraham Lincoln, the sixteenth president, called a halt to the inhumane practice. Slaves were freed. Abraham Lincoln said, "Whenever I hear anyone arguing for slavery, I feel a strong impulse to see it tried on him."[5]

Why did it take so long? Why did men who personally abhorred the practice, allow other humans to be traded like cattle? No doubt there was selfishness, greed and racism involved in the mix, but the political reason for the tolerance of the intolerable was the value placed by the early presidents on unity. These men were nation builders, forming out of the formless a new nation — one that had never been seen before. Freedom was the prize within a framework of order.

But an enemy to success lurked within. The south was married to a system of slavery. Its economy was based on it; its citizens wanted to protect their way of life and refused to accept the moralizing of the north. To press the south too hard would cause a breach in the union — would make America vulnerable to predatory European nations that would reclaim old holdings or try to establish new ones.

The highest value of the day? Protect the union. The cost? Slavery! And to protect the former people accepted the moral stigma of the latter for the better part of a century. A property of government valued so highly by the Founders and the early builders of the nation is not to be idly dismissed. And that notion leads to the following definition of a close presidential election: It exists when election results reflect a serious lack of unity that will affect the future ability of the new administration to govern.

The Symptoms of a Close Presidential Election

The basic measurement for electing a president is the electoral vote. The closeness of it is a harbinger of things to come.* But the supremacy of the electoral vote over the popular vote does not mean the popular vote is irrelevant. On the contrary, new presidents must lead the whole nation and nobody would deny that a popular chief executive has an easier time of it. The closeness of the popular vote, therefore, also foretells of a president's success.

The Selection of the Closest Presidential Elections

All presidential elections have been examined. Selected for detailed investigation are those that have one or both of the following characteristics: A close electoral vote — a four-vote spread or less; a close popular vote — less than 51

*The smallest states (2008) have three electoral votes.

percent of votes cast for the two leading candidates. When these thresholds are not met it is probable the new president will have difficulty governing. Failure to meet both thresholds is a clear indicator of major trouble ahead for the new administration.

Under these thresholds of eligibility twelve of the fifty-five elections for president of the United States were, to some degree, very close. One of the most interesting that did not qualify as a close election was that of President George H.W. Bush versus William J. Clinton. Absent the presence of H. Ross Perot in the race, which was much more of a blow to the elder Bush than it was to Clinton, the case could be made that Bush would have won. Apart from Clinton's home state of Arkansas and Washington, D.C., Clinton didn't get 50 percent or more of the vote in any state.

What Causes Close Presidential Elections?

Many believe close presidential races exist when it becomes exceedingly difficult to choose between two experienced, attractive and articulate candidates. That is rarely the case. Usually external events (war, recession, controversial legislation, legal rulings, personal behavior, etc.) and the public's reaction to them trigger the voting action toward the candidate who seems to reflect a similar response.

For that reason, each chapter that deals with a close election will include national, international and legal material that describes the environment before and after the election so that the reasons behind the sometimes bitter tone of campaigns are clear.

Undramatic Elections

Twelve close elections will be discussed in depth in the chapters that follow. The forty-three other elections were rather one-sided, the outcome, in most cases, almost obvious from the beginning.

Since every president has had an impact on what happens in a future election, the regimes of all presidents are mentioned; and those that had an obvious impact on a featured election are highlighted in the relevant chapter.

1

1796: John Adams
vs. Thomas Jefferson

(Electoral Votes, 138; Majority, 70)

Introduction

George Washington led the nation through its formative eight years, during which the first ten amendments (1791, the Bill of Rights) and Amendment Eleven were added to the Constitution, the government was formed, fundamental relations with foreign powers were established and three new states (Vermont, Kentucky, Tennessee) were added to the Union, bringing the total to sixteen.[1]

Such was the quality of Washington's leadership that John Adams, in addition to his own prodigious personal qualifications, gained incalculable prestige by serving at Washington's side as vice president. This made him the unquestioned favorite in the 1796 election.

But Washington was not without critics, and nothing stimulated those critics more than the John Jay Treaty with England,[2] which he had supported and approved, and the Tariff Act of 1791.[3] The former was regarded by Thomas Jefferson and his followers as a sellout to England; the latter stimulated the Whiskey Rebellion (1794), which Washington put down by mobilizing 13,000 troops to enforce the law — the first test of the power of the federal government.[4] Jeffersonians in general feared and resisted centralized power.

The Fugitive Slave Act (1793)[5] became law during Washington's administration, and made escaped slaves fugitives for life, fined those who helped them escape and required all captured slaves to be returned to their owners. Since northerners were generally opposed to slavery, being associated with this law was a liability to Adams as he approached the 1796 election. Another action that drew political fire was the establishment in 1791 of the Bank of the United States.[6] The idea of a central bank, the brainchild of Alexander Hamilton, was abhorred by Jeffersonians and remained a contested issue for decades thereafter.

Washington completed his two terms unopposed. His stature among the highly intelligent men around him was unique. He was their undisputed leader — no small accomplishment when the quality of the competition is considered. Had he wanted a third term, it would have been his. But he didn't want it. And in turning his back on the opportunity he may have preserved the presidency; he certainly established the standard of behavior for future presidents, until Franklin D. Roosevelt decided to change it.

These few examples of Washington's baggage did not destroy the luster of his reputation, which Adams shared, but they did become issues in the upcoming election sufficiently controversial to stimulate much more opposition to Adams' election than was expected. Adams, the heir apparent, was a formidable man, but he did not have the stature of Washington. There would be competition in this election and, most likely, in all that would follow.

Electoral Process, Caucuses

Political parties in 1796 did not exist.[7] The office was bestowed on the man; the man did not overtly seek it. Washington, a man of the times, was unopposed during the first two elections. Not so with Adams. He had opposition and it was nasty.

Each elector cast two votes for two men who were on the list of candidates— no mention was made of vice president, or of a first or second choice. The man with the highest vote count became president and second highest vice president. Under that system the man allegedly competing for second place (vice president) behind some obvious front runner could hit it lucky and emerge the winner. Also the election could — as it did in 1796 — produce two men to serve together as president and vice president who disagreed on almost everything.

When two men shared a majority vote, the House of Representatives would choose the president; the other man would serve as vice president. When nobody got a majority vote, the House chose the president from the top five candidates; the vice president would be the one in the remaining group who had the most electoral votes. If, in such a case, there was a tie vote, the Senate would break the tie.

There were no political parties, but humans, being what they are, naturally split into factions initially separated by their views on the strength of the central government versus state governments and the people. Adams, like Washington, believed in a strong central government, a position, which at the time was appropriate for a young nation of states with disparate interests who were trying to unite as a whole governmental body. Central discipline was needed to herd the states into the federal corral. This group were called Federalists.[8] Jefferson, as experienced and as well known as Adams, feared centralized power. He believed that as a concept it contradicted the aims of the war. His group were called Democratic-Republicans.[9]

The issue of a standing army serves as a useful example of the fundamental difference between the two factions. Federalists, led by Alexander Hamilton and hyper-aware of dangers from Europe, believed a standing army controlled by the central government was prudent as a matter of homeland defense. Democratic-Republicans regarded it as a danger to liberty. Ironically, although a fervent supporter of a formidable navy, Adams did not support a standing army. But, as a Federalist, he was associated with the belief that it was necessary to maintain one.[10]

Both sides made sense; both sides attracted followers. And without difficulty, Jefferson emerged from political conferences as the principal nominee of one group, with Aaron Burr also running, presumably hoping to win the vice presidency. On the Federalist side, Alexander Hamilton, the master manipulator behind the scenes, was no friend of John Adams. Hamilton saw to it that Adams had competition in the form of Thomas Pinckney of South Carolina, who was presumably seeking the vice presidency but, if Hamilton could swing it, would be a surprise winner for the Federalists.

Thumbnail Sketches of Top Candidates

John Adams and Thomas Jefferson were among the best known Americans. Voters knew who and what they were; respect for both men was high. But their ideas were different; factions were formed and the foundation for political parties was unwittingly formed by both men — once friends, now political enemies.

JOHN ADAMS, FEDERALIST

Born: 1735, Massachusetts; **Education:** Local schools; Harvard; studied law; **Wife:** Abigail Smith, Weymouth, Massachusetts; **Children:** Five (he buried three); **Died:** 1826.[11]

Soon after completing the study of law, Adams built a successful career as a lawyer; he also became a political activist. He openly opposed, for example, the Stamp Act of 1765 that so enraged the colonists. He also showed early on his lifelong adherence to principle and his indifference to popularity when he decided to defend eight British troops who were involved in the so-called Boston Massacre of 1770. Six were exonerated; two, who were charged with murder, were found guilty of manslaughter.

Adams' reputation is largely national in character. But it's important to recognize that his sense of patriotism, which also drove him to the doorstep of the Declaration of Independence, had deep roots in Massachusetts. He had served in the legislature as an outspoken activist; he was a supporter of the Boston Tea Party and the primary author in 1780 of the Massachusetts constitution, a document that still lives as a model that many have followed. National politics soon drew Adams' attention. He clearly recognized that freedom from British rule could be achieved only if the colonies could unite in a common cause.

He became a delegate to the Continental Congress (1774–77) and gained a broad reputation as a patriot. It was he who nominated George Washington as commander-in-chief of the colonial army. Also, he assigned to Thomas Jefferson the composition of the Declaration of Independence and eagerly signed the approved version of it. Thereafter his career as a diplomat began.

Adams was assigned in 1778[12] to France to join Benjamin Franklin and Arthur Lee[13] in their pre–Revolution diplomatic missions. The trip was a failure. Franklin was idolized by the French; Adams was not well received. His straightforward, abrupt mannerisms weren't appreciated and his relationship with Franklin soured, all of which led to his return to Massachusetts.

Soon after, Adams was back on the Atlantic headed for Britain, there to serve as minister plenipotentiary to negotiate peace. His duties led him to peace talks in Paris and to the same lack of success that had characterized his earlier dealings with the French. His continued inability to reach a compatible relationship with their diplomats cost him the support of Congress, which revoked his commission to negotiate the peace treaty alone.

Due to the slowness of communications in those days, Franklin was unaware of congressional attitudes when he undertook his journey to the Netherlands in search of financial backing. His aim was to reduce the dependence of the colonists on France for support during the Revolutionary War. He was successful — a major coup.

Adams then returned to Paris and the peace talks that were designed to end the war. This again brought him into direct contact with Ben Franklin and the French. But this time John Jay, who agreed with Adams on the peace terms, was a member of the negotiating team. Both were surprised to learn that Franklin would abandon his usual pro–French position and join them in a united front. The treaty was signed on September 3, 1783. Thereafter, for the next five years, Adams served as the first minister to Britain with his wife, Abigail, at his side. They returned in 1788 to Massachusetts. Four years later, Adams, as vice president of the United States, worked shoulder to shoulder with the man he had, years before, launched into a military career that had matured into a new one as the first president of the United States of America.

The practice of the time was for each elector to cast two votes for president. In the first and second elections, the choice of George Washington was unanimous.[14] In both prior elections, Adams had the second-highest vote count, which under the system in play made him vice president.

Now it was his turn. Now it was time to step from the covering shadows of George Washington and assume the mantle of leadership. He was ready to be president; no man was more experienced.

THOMAS PINCKNEY, FEDERALIST

Born: 1750, South Carolina; **Education:** Westminster, Oxford, England; French Military College; law school, London; **Wife:** Elizabeth Motte; **Children:** Six (he buried two); **Died:** 1828.[15]

It was no act of false ego that led Pinckney to become a candidate in the 1796 election — he was highly qualified. Educated in England, Pinckney, after his return to his home in Charleston, South Carolina, was admitted to the bar. Because his education included training at a French military college, he was put to good use as an officer during the American Revolution. In the battle of Camden he was wounded and held prisoner for over a year. After the war, Pinckney became governor of his state (1787–89) and remained active in local politics until again his European training influenced Washington to make him ambassador to Great Britain (1792–96). As an additional duty during those same years, he negotiated the 1795 Treaty of Lorenzo (Pinckney's Treaty), which established borders between Florida and Mississippi.

Upon his return from Great Britain, Pinckney served in the U.S. House of Representatives (1797–1801), after which he retired again to private life. Then, once more duty called and he served as a major general in the War of 1812.

By education and training, Pinckney was an aristocrat with pro–British leanings, yet he took great risks and made great sacrifices for the cause of America, all the more reason to admire his actions when the strain at times must have been difficult.

THOMAS JEFFERSON, DEMOCRATIC-REPUBLICAN

Thomas Jefferson was in another close election in 1800, which he won. In chapter two of this book his biographical material will be more fully presented. For the limited purposes of the subject analysis it is sufficient to say that Adams could not have had a more worthy opponent.

Jefferson, author of the Declaration of Independence and one of the great intellects of the age, had separated ideologically from his former ally. He conducted a fierce campaign through surrogates. Out of their battle the outlines of the two political parties that exist today came into being.

AARON BURR, DEMOCRATIC-REPUBLICAN

Born: 1756, New Jersey; **Education:** Princeton (College of New Jersey); **Wives:** Theodosia Bartow Prevost (1782–94); Eliza Bowen Jumel (for four months); **Children:** Two daughters (one survived to adulthood); **Died:** 1836.[16]

Aaron Burr's college education was behind him at sixteen. As a major in theology, he thereafter switched to the field of law and was so engaged when in 1775, at nineteen, he joined the Continental Army. He was assigned to General Washington's staff in 1776, but shortly thereafter (allegedly because of a clash of personalities) he was transferred and became aide-de-camp to General Putnam.

Throughout his military career, Burr saw considerable action and he advanced quickly in rank. By 1777, then twenty-one, he was a lieutenant colonel and the commander of a regiment. He suffered through the 1777-78 winter at Valley Forge. Citing ill health as the reason, Burr resigned from the army in 1779, finished his legal education and built a successful law practice, eventually becoming a partner with Alexander Hamilton (with whom he later repeatedly clashed).

Burr married Theodosia Prevost in 1782; they had one daughter, Theodosia, who died at sea in 1783. His wife died in 1794. He married in 1833 a rich widow, Eliza Jamel, but the marriage ended after four months because of arguments over his money management practices.

Burr's first venture into public life came when Governor George Clinton made him attorney general of New York (1789–91). Then he went on to the U.S. Senate (1791–97). Far from being a shy violet, he advanced from that to presidential runs in 1796 and 1800.[17] He almost won the prize in 1800 when he and Jefferson both carried seventy-three electoral votes. The final selection was referred to the House of Representatives, which preferred Jefferson by a wide margin. Burr automatically became vice president. From that point on, the career curve of Burr was downward. And considering the character flaws he later exhibited, the nation was better off for it. He could have been the president.

Burr increasingly blamed Alexander Hamilton for his misfortunes. Enmity between them grew to such a pitch that in 1804 they met in a duel. Hamilton was killed. That ended Burr in high political circles for good.

Now an adventurer in search of wealth and prestige, Burr headed west to Texas and commenced a series of land deals and organizational moves that were self-serving and regarded by the United States as treasonable. He was charged and acquitted in 1807 and moved to England, hoping to gain support for a revolution in Mexico. He failed and was dismissed from the country. He met the same fate after journeys to Sweden, Denmark, Germany and France. He was a man determined to reach the position of greatness that he had almost achieved in the election of 1800. He failed.

Back in New York, broke and disillusioned, he resumed his law practice. He made one more attempt to gain recognition when in 1833 he married the rich widow mentioned above, but the marriage ended. He died three years later — the man who could have been, but never was.

Election Tone

No election takes place in a vacuum, each one being flavored with the events of the most recent years.

In the election of 1796, Supreme Court decisions were not a significant issue. Three men served as chief justice of the Supreme Court in the period from 1789 to 1796: John Jay, John Rutledge and Oliver Ellsworth. They were supported by seven associate justices. Important legal decisions were rendered but they were not politically controversial.[18] Most of the tension during the 1796 presidential election existed because, by instinct and position, Adams supported Washington's policies and Jefferson didn't.

Two opposing views of governance clearly emerged during the state ratification process of the new Constitution, which was not a quick and noncontroversial procedure. On the contrary, it was a slow and laborious process (September 1787 to May 1790) full of arguments and protests and one that was not fully accomplished until Rhode Island, the last holdout, finally signed on.[19] Nine states were required for ratification. The actual ratification date was September 17, 1787.

Massachusetts was the key to ratification.[20] It insisted on amending the Constitution before signing. Federalists insisted on an up or down vote on the original document. The compromise that broke the deadlock was this: Congress agreed to consider amendments after ratification. It is that compromise that led to the adoption of the Bill of Rights, the first ten amendments to the Constitution that resolved many differences between the parties—but not all. And those lingering differences loomed large during the 1796 election campaign, which, among other things, demonstrated that even the Founding Fathers, directly or through surrogates, were quite as capable of throwing rhetorical rocks at each other as are modern politicians.

The glow of victory and the shared pleasure of being separated from Britain and being free had worn thin as an adhesive by the time Washington ended his second term, and there was little between the newborn states that was shared with enthusiasm. Into that vacuum flowed simmering differences between leaders that evolved into passionate positions which demanded unified expression. Motivated anti–Federalists, led by Jefferson,[21] formalized positions in opposition to some of Washington's policies, and they gave themselves a name — Democratic-Republicans.

The day Washington hoped would never arrive was at hand: Two political parties (not yet recognized as such) with opposing ideologies competing for national power came into being, sometimes, as they evolved, placing party objectives above national interests, exactly the outcome he had predicted and feared most.*

*"Let me ... warn you in the most solemn manner against the baneful effects of the Spirit of Party."— George Washington, Sept. 19, 1796

Federalists— mostly wealthy landowners and businessmen — valued order as the necessary precondition for liberty. They promoted a strong central government that also perpetuated the hierarchal society that, at that time, actually existed in America — a natural hierarchy resulting from accomplishment and wealth. They were, in effect, the necessary party for the time, a group of elites who, under the leadership of the peerless Washington, pulled disparate forces together and created in fact the nation that the Constitution described in theory.[22]

Necessary though they were for the times, Federalists had within them the seeds of their own destruction. There was a monarchial tone about their approach that was out of step with the appetite for freedom that had motivated the revolt from Britain, and still motivated its citizens who wanted more than an elected government controlled by a small band of elitists (no matter how talented). They wanted a government in which they, through their representatives, actively participated. The Democratic-Republicans challenged centrist tendencies of Federalists and their international policies, epitomized by the successful projects of John Jay. Also, and importantly, the financial polices of Alexander Hamilton especially roused their ire.

The John Jay treaty with Britain was a political gift to Democratic-Republicans. Opposition to it drew men together because the fond memory of France as an ally was still alive — they favored France over Britain. It embarrassed Adams that his vice president differed so sharply over foreign policy toward two European powers, Britain and France. Needless to say, he had little meaningful contact with Jefferson during his four-year term, a fact that did little to sweeten the tone of the next election.[23]

Alexander Hamilton was another gift to Democratic-Republicans because of his well-known and highly influential views and practices. A favorite of Washington's, he was hyperactive as the first secretary of Treasury. His policies (nationalization of state debt, creation of a tax system, a currency, a national bank, etc.), a boon to the nation, were fiercely opposed by Democratic-Republicans.

Ironically, Adams' alliance with Hamilton, who was one of the most effective and influential of the Founders, was also a political liability because of Hamilton's advocacy for a standing army. That idea was unpopular with Jeffersonians, who wanted to make abundantly clear their desire to be rid of the British model of a centralized government that threatened liberty, which they claimed Adams preferred and which a standing army would make more possible.*

Federalists preached unity and strength, qualities that could not be provided, they argued, by a confederation of states turned loose in an avaricious

---

*Hamilton's persistent pressure to form a standing army was not entirely an impersonal, professional position. He visualized himself as its leader.

world like thirteen stray puppies. Democratic-Republicans responded Patrick Henry-like: "Give me liberty or give me death." Federalists offered assurances that a new form of monarchy was not their aim; skeptical Democratic-Republicans pointed to, among other things, Adams' writings on government in which he commented favorably on the British monarchy. Both sides dug in. Each side featured national icons: Federalists, for example, had Adams himself plus such esteemed personages as Hamilton and Jay; Democratic-Republicans featured Jefferson and James Madison and a new face on the scene, Aaron Burr.

Vice presidents, by the nature of the position, are not responsible for policy decisions, so hard information was lacking about Adams' political performance for opponents to use as the basis for an attack on his candidacy in 1796. Accordingly, Washington's more controversial decisions were attributed to Adams and personal attacks were mounted against him.

Opposing views about the candidates were expressed harshly, and personally, mostly through the media, including substantive assaults on their worthiness. With Adams, a barrage of editorial criticism appeared dealing with his aristocratic reputation, which by imputation questioned his loyalty to the Constitution, and there were charges that he used his influence to enrich relatives:

> John Adams is one of those men who never ... comprehended anything of first principles. If he had, he might have seen that the right to establish ... hereditary government ... never can exist in any generation: That it is of the nature of treason.— *Massachusetts Spy*, Worcester, MA, November 2, 1796, Volume XXV, Boston Public Library.

> [D]uring the sessions of Congress [over which vice president Adams presided] three lucrative offices have been given, two to his son and one to his son-in-law.— *City Gazette*, Charleston, SC, November 9, 1796, Volume XIV, Issue 2896, p. 2, Boston Public Library.

With Jefferson, questions were raised about his courage and steadfastness in times of danger, his fondness for the French, his antipathy toward the British and his inclination to pose as a populist:

> I consider firmness of mind in the President of the United States one of the most essential qualifications. ... [his] measures, brought forward in the House of Representatives [were] stopped, which measures would have inevitably brought us into the war [on the side of the French]; in this qualification [bias], I find Mr. Jefferson deficient.... It must be known to many that Mr. Jefferson discharged his duties [as Governor of Virginia] until the invasion of the state in 1781 when, on the approach of the enemy ... [he adjourned] to Charlottesville.... [H]e (Mr. Jefferson) showed a want of firmness that would seem to show he was not altogether fit for the executive office.—*Boston Gazette*, October 31, 1796, Issue 2194, p. 2, Boston Public Library.

> It is now become a common trick ... for every ambitious demagogue [referring to Jefferson] ... to vociferate in the language of liberty that every ... intelligent citizen immediately suspects them of some mischievous design.... Patriotism announces itself by deeds, not by words.—*Columbian Herald*, November 12, 1796, Issue 1858, p 2, Boston Public Library.

Then came personal insults aimed at appearance, motivation and character. In David McCullough's book, *John Adams*, it is noted that Adams was referred to in the press and elsewhere as "His Rotundity," unfit to lead the country, the "champion of kings, ranks and titles." Under him, it was said, hereditary succession would be imposed, making way for his son, John Quincy Adams.[24] Washington didn't fare any better: "incapable of friendship; a hypocrite." "If ever a nation was debauched by a man, the American nation has been debauched by Washington," Benjamin Franklin's grandson wrote in 1796.[25] Worst of all, according to Democratic-Republican campaign literature, Adams was a monarchist who did not support the Constitution.[26] Jefferson got his share too. He was a Jacobin (meaning he held extreme revolutionary views), a coward, and an atheist who would attack organized religion.[27]

During the campaign season, Adams, true to his belief that the office should come to the man, remained in his home in Massachusetts until electors voted. He assumed that the presidency would be bestowed upon him as past service — before, during and after the war — made him the logical and just successor to Washington. The appearance of Jefferson as the primary obstacle to the resolution of Adams' expectations and ambitions no doubt added to the list of behaviors that were redefining what once had been a close friendship.

Jefferson retired to his home in Virginia, feigning disinterest in the contest. But, ever the quiet, backroom dealer, he operated through surrogates and made no attempt to remove his name from the list of presidential candidates. His silence was a signal to his followers that he agreed to compete with Adams for the presidency.

And so the battle was joined between the two patriots, comrades during the formation of the Union. They now had diametrically opposite views on how to govern what they, as much as any other two men, had created.

Election Results

George Washington had no competitors. Other candidates in his time were, in effect, in search of the vice presidency. But when the leader-accepted-by-all withdrew, the contest was wide open. And Vice President Adams, whatever the value of his pre–Revolution deeds, did not carry with him the mystique with which his predecessor was blessed, nor was his personal sense of entitlement shared by the opposition, which by this time had assumed the more coherent form of the Democratic-Republican group.

The result of Washington's withdrawal, and the inability of any successor to offer equivalent prestige, was the first contested presidential election in American history and, indirectly, it was also the first formal step toward the formation of the two major political parties that are with us today.

The race was close. Adams and the things he stood for, or was associated with, were the stuff of the campaign: the Jay Treaty and the hard-line (as Jeffersonians saw it) attitude toward France, the various immigration and speech issues approved by Adams, the standing army, etc., all issues opposed by Jefferson and his men.

Election Results 1796

Candidates	Electoral Vote	%
Adams-F	71	31.1
Pinckney-F	59	25.9
Jefferson-DR	68	29.8
Burr-DR	30	13.2
Total	228	100.0

Source: *N.Y. Times Almanac 2009*, p. 125

Adams won with seventy-one electoral votes. It is said[28] that Jefferson was unsurprised by the results, which to him were appropriate and expected. Those results made it clear that tension between North and South, rooted in slavery and the economy that flowed therefrom, still existed. Adams took the New England states plus New York, New Jersey and (the closest things to southern states) Delaware and Maryland. Jefferson won the south, plus Pennsylvania.[29]

A notable consequence of the election is that it produced a president from one group and a vice president from the other. All recognized this weakness in the election system. Later it was corrected by adding Amendment Twelve to the Constitution in 1804, before the election of that year took place.

Adams and Jefferson, by this time, were political enemies. Their previous personal friendship also ended. Adams commented on Jefferson: "a self-serving, ambitious intriguer."[30] Jefferson's opinion of Adams was that he was "an oddly self-destructive man, too honest for his own good and too admiring of the British political system."[31]

The Adams Cabinet

By modern standards, the Adams cabinet was ridiculous, peopled as it was with political adversaries in high positions. But political parties did not exist, and the conventions of the time brought strange results. His cabinet was a mixture of men he had to have, those he wanted and some he chose in an attempt to make peace with the opposition, as follows[32]: **Vice President,** Thomas Jefferson, Virginia; **Secretary of State,** Timothy Pickering, Massachusetts, 1797–1800 (discharged by Adams); John Marshall, Virginia; **Secretary of Treasury,** Oliver Wolcott, Jr., Connecticut (1797–1800); Samuel Dexter, Massachusetts; **Secretary of War,** James McHenry, Maryland (1797–1800), Samuel Dexter, Massachusetts; **Attorney General,** Charles Lee, Virginia; **Secretary of Navy,** Benjamin Stoddert, Maryland.

Adams studiously tried to maintain neutrality during the war between the two great European powers, France and Britain. It was this balancing act that led to disputes and turnover in key cabinet positions; John Marshall was made the chief justice of the Supreme Court while serving as secretary of state.

The Adams Congress

The First Congress in 1789 was organized as follows[33]:

State	Senior Senator	Junior Senator	House of Reps.
Connecticut	Oliver Ellsworth	William S. Johnson	5
Delaware	Richard Bassett	George Read	1
Georgia	William Few	James Gunn	3
Maryland	John Henry	Charles Carroll	6
Massachusetts	Tristram Dalton	Caleb Strong	8
N. Hampshire	James Langdon	Paine Wingate	3
N. Jersey	Jonathan Elmer	William Patterson (resigned), Philemon Dickinson	4
N. York	Rufus King	Philip J. Schuler	6
N. Carolina	Benjamin Hawkins	Samuel Johnston	5
Pennsylvania	William Maclay	Robert Morris	8
Rhode Island	Theodore Foster	Joseph Stanton	1
S. Carolina	Pierce Butler	Ralph Izard	5
Virginia	William Grayson (died), John Walker (temporary), James Monroe	Richard H. Lee	10
Total			65
Speaker of the House Total	Frederick A. Muhlenberg		

Note: The position of Senate leader was not created until the 1920s.

The sixty-five representatives from the original thirteen states were led by House Speaker Frederick A.C. Muhlenberg. He was succeeded in 1791 by Jonathan Trumbull (1791–93); Trumbull resumed office as speaker of the 3rd Congress (1793–95). Jonathan Dayton assumed that role in the 4th and 5th congresses (1795–99) and he was in charge when Adams took office in 1797. Their service follows:

> Muhlenberg[34] (PA) Federalist and a delegate to the 1779 Continental Congress was elected to the House and to the role of speaker in 1789; he served as such in the 1st and 3rd congresses. His support of the unpopular Jay Treaty ended his public career. Trumbull[35] (CT) Federalist, Harvard, became Speaker of the House in the 2nd Congress; he served in the U.S. Senate in 1795 and 1796, after which he resigned and returned home to become governor of Connecticut for eleven consecutive terms.
>
> Dayton[36] (NJ), Federalist, Princeton (College of New Jersey), was a veteran

who had been a prisoner of war. He became the Speaker of the House in 1791 and served until 1799. Then he moved to the Senate (1799–1805). Dayton was a supporter of Aaron Burr and he became involved with the charges brought against Burr. He was not prosecuted, but the affair ended his federal career.

Contrary to popular opinion, Washington was not unthinkingly followed by all politicians of his day. His followers (Federalists) in the 1st Congress held a 57 percent majority in the House and 69 percent in the Senate. In the 4th Congress, his last, Federalists were the minority party in the House, but held their own in the Senate with 66 percent.[37] John Adams, on the other hand, not generally regarded as personable, rebuilt the Federalist majority in the House and strengthened even more its position in the Senate.[38] As a political leader, Adams was more effective than Washington.

There was nothing in the elections that formed the 5th and the 6th congresses to indicate that Adams' reelection bid would be successfully opposed. At the end of his term, the Federalist position in the House and Senate was 57 percent and 69 percent, respectively — an impressive showing.

The Adams Supreme Court

John Jay[39] was the first chief justice of the U.S. Supreme Court (1789–95). His successor, John Rutledge,[40] served four months while his confirmation was being considered in the Senate. In the end, largely because of his outspoken resistance to the Jay Treaty, Rutledge was rejected and Oliver Ellsworth was appointed in his place.*

Ellsworth (CT), served as chief justice during the 1796–1800 period.[41] He was a Federalist who, during the Constitutional Convention, coined the word "United States" in preference to "national" in official documents. He participated in preparing the first draft of the Constitution; he opposed the abolition of the foreign slave trade. He served in the U.S. Senate and as commissioner to France while serving on the Court.

Those who served on the Court during Adams' presidency are shown in table at top of next page. Ellsworth swore Adams in. Adams, before he left office, appointed the next chief justice, John Marshall, one of the greatest who ever served.

As a general rule, cases are selected for analysis when they contain elements that attract the interest of the voters in a given election cycle. There were important decisions in this period of interest to attorneys and students of law, but none with any particular political punch that would qualify them for analysis in a book of this type.

The nation in 1796 was young, innocent, vibrant and proud of itself. There

---

Rutledge suffered from bouts of deep depression. There were rumors that he was going insane; he made two failed suicide attempts.

Supreme Court Justices, 1797–1800

Judge	Began	Appointed by	Ended
Oliver Ellsworth (CT)	1796	Washington	1800
John Marshall (VA)	1800	Adams	1835
William Cushing (MA)	1790	Washington	1810
James Wilson (PA)	1789	Washington	1798
James Iredell (NC)	1790	Washington	1799
William Patterson (NJ)	1793	Washington	1806
Samuel Chase (MD)	1796	Washington	1811
Bushrod Washington (VA)	1799	Adams	1829
Alfred Moore (NC)	1800	Adams	1804

Source: Oyez, http://www.oyez.org/; Members of the Supreme Court,[42] http://www.supremecourtus.gov/about/members.pdf

Men in Black, Mark Levin, 2005, Preface

Note: James Wilson, a land speculator, fell into serious debt and was sent to debtor's prison. His son paid the creditors of the associate justice to keep him out of jail. He left town to avoid his creditors and lived a life on the run; he died a pauper and was buried in an unmarked grave.[43]

was no talk in those days of activist judges. The words of the Constitution were not tortured to find hidden meanings. When there was doubt about original intent, those who wrote it were available for consultation, a luxury that disappeared long ago.

Domestic Affairs Relative to Current Political Issues

The formal war with England was over, but the United States was still a vulnerable and appetizing baby to the great nations of Europe, who looked with envious eyes as the riches of the new nation were revealed.

Survival was the largest issue for the early presidents to confront, and it would continue to be until it became plain to outsiders that America could be a dangerous enemy and a valuable friend. And for the United States to survive during the Adams' presidency meant that relations with France and England had to be managed with great care. How best to do this was the issue that more than most separated the political leaders of the day.

Domestic Events

As a reflection of the times, as well as the depth of his background as a diplomat, Adams concentrated on foreign affairs and left most domestic issues for Congress to resolve.[44] But it isn't surprising that his predilection for dealing with international issues became as well the basis for congressional and judicial action.

Because of certain foreign policy problems (see "Foreign Affairs" below), the Federalist Congress levied new taxes that resulted in riots among Pennsylvania's farmers that were later called Fries' Rebellion (1799–1800). They and others believed that the taxes were actually put in place to support a large standing army and navy, which many people opposed. Some leaders of the movement were arrested and sentenced to death for treason. However, on the eve of the election of 1800, Adams pardoned them.

The Alien and Seditions Acts (see "Legislative Events," below) caused a political furor in the United States and much domestic turmoil. Potential war with France was the justification offered for them, but Adams' adversaries weren't persuaded. To them, the provisions of the law dealing with speech were a clear violation of the First Amendment. There were fifteen indictments and ten convictions under the Seditions Act during the final year and a half of Adams' administration. No aliens were deported or arrested, but hundreds fled the country in 1798 and 1799. One of those indicted was Benjamin Franklin Bache, editor of the *Aurora* and a frequent critic of Washington and Adams, who claimed that Adams was actually seeking war with France. Adams' wife, Abigail, said of him, "If that fellow ... is not suppressed, we shall come to a civil war."[45] When Jefferson became president in 1800, all prisoners were released.

It was Alexander Hamilton's ambition to become the commanding general of a large standing army of the United States. While there was support in the nation for an expanded navy as the first line of defense against European powers, many freedom loving Americans, with their deep-seated fear of a strong central government, opposed the idea of a standing army, preferring to think in terms of state militias as basic ground forces and a federal army raised only upon necessity.

By supporting Hamilton's view of things (Adams asked Congress for authority to federalize 80,000 militiamen), Adams carried a political burden that made more difficult his plans to build the navy and to strengthen coastal fortifications. To some people, such actions made him a warmonger. To others, he was trying to live up to his presidential oath: "preserve, protect and defend."

ECONOMIC GROWTH

Every administrator hopes to leave the nation in better financial condition than he found it. Adams accomplished this:

Gross Domestic Product, 1796–1800

Year	GDP (bil)	Real Growth	Debt (000)
1796	.41		80
1797	.41	0.0	84
1798	.41	0.0	82
1799	.44	7.3	79
1800	.48	9.1	78

Historical Statistics Colonial Times to 1957, p. 721; U.S. governmentrevenue.com; http://www.usgovernment revenue.com

The economy, stagnant when Adams assumed office, remained so for two years. Thereafter, growth resumed at an impressive pace that should have served Adams well in the upcoming election.

Public debt was $80 million when Adams took office; it was about the same in 1800. His administration balanced spending needs with available revenues. The nation was in better financial condition in 1800 than it was when he assumed office. His economic problems were mostly related to the expensive and destructive sea war with France, which disrupted foreign trade and caused losses to local merchants and seamen.* To maintain a balanced budget during normal times is commendable. To do such during a period of undeclared war (with France) while military forces are by necessity expanding, as Adams did, is outstanding.

LEGISLATIVE EVENTS

The Adams administration was not known for its active legislative agenda, but the laws that have been memorably attached to the Adams name were probably as responsible as anything else for his defeat in the election of 1800, especially those dealing with aliens.[46]

Legislative activity of the day indicated the importance of international events to a new nation that on the one hand was trying to organize and grow and on the other to protect itself against the most recent tenacious hand from Europe. Adams, always sensitive to the vulnerability of the new state, was, to many, overly vigorous in his zeal to protect it.

Some actions taken during his administration that helped to define the political climate of the times are explained below:

- 1798: The Alien and Seditions Acts, passed in June and July, three of which dealt with aliens and the fourth with political speech, allowed the president to arrest and deport aliens who might endanger the nation's security. The residency time needed to become a citizen was increased from five to fourteen years. And the act also prohibited "false, scandalous and malicious" writing or speaking against the U.S. government, the president or the Congress. Those in violation of the law could be fined or sent to jail for two years. The aspect of the law that dealt with political speech was regarded by Adams' adversaries as unconstitutional. Why did Adams do it? The nation was on the brink of war with France in the summer of 1798, hence the sternness of the acts—unwise, but under-

---

*The early years of the presidency are important indicators of how the most informed chief executives interpreted the Constitution relative to, among other matters, budget affairs. Obviously, Washington and Adams believed government spending on internal affairs should be governed by need, not by the availability of funds, and they shared the view that expensive wartime debt should be reduced as fast as possible. The absolute amount of debt dropped slightly under Adams, despite European pressures and the military buildup that was required to meet them.

standable. The jailing of Ben Franklin's grandson under the Seditions Act led to the general unpopularity of these laws and contributed to Adams' defeat in 1800. Signing the act was a blotch on Adams' sterling reputation as a principled statesman and patriot.

- 1798: A bill passed in the Senate authorized a standing army of 20,000 men. The debate on the issue continued through the rest of Adams' presidency.[47] Alexander Hamilton, who envisioned himself as its leader, and his supporters, were the prime movers of the idea and Adams was involved by association. The idea lost power in 1800 when the peace treaty with France was signed. But, since the news of the treaty was not known before the election, Adams, as a Federalist, carried the burden of Hamilton's policy to the voters and got zero benefit for his own successful policies with France.

- 1801: The Judiciary Act was passed by the lame-duck Federalist-controlled Congress, its purpose to perpetuate Federalist control of the judiciary. Adams filled many newly created judgeships with men of his persuasion, in less than three weeks, who became known as "midnight judges." Allegedly, Adams was authorizing their appointments in the midnight prior to Jefferson's assumption of power.[48] For a so-called nonpolitical man, this was a highly political action. Authorizing the midnight judges inflamed the political atmosphere and ultimately failed in its purpose. The new Congress repealed the act in March 1802. The Judiciary Act was another blow to Adams' image of integrity. For one who originally hated the notion of political parties, he soon mastered the tricks of hardball politics.

Taken together, these issues seemed to some people to support the accusation of Adams' critics that he was at heart a monarchist. This assessment became the foundation theme of his opponent's campaign. It clung to him for the rest of his life and it was eventually attached to his son, John Quincy Adams, as well.

It is unfortunate that the man so identified with the nation's fight for freedom should have this blotch on his reputation — not enough, certainly, to rub out any significant value from his overwhelming contribution to the cause, but enough to remind all of us that even great men have flaws, sometimes significant ones, with which they, too, do battle.

Foreign Affairs Relative to Political Issues

Since the threat to national security from European forces was a daily concern of the early presidents, foreign affairs were always at the top of their agendas. It was the same with Adams, by necessity and by choice. Relations with

France and England were the most difficult rapids to negotiate on the river that led to safety.[49]

The John Jay treaty, an accomplishment of the Washington administration, was regarded by Jay's adversaries as a sellout to the British. As vice president, Adams was associated with that arrangement. That, plus his failure to end the undeclared sea war with France, added substance to the charge that his foreign policy favored Britain and was leading the nation into war with France.

THE "XYZ" AFFAIR

Few international issues inflamed Federalist and Democratic-Republican relations more than the "XYZ" affair and its complicated history.[50]

Washington in 1796 sent Charles C. Pinckney to France on a conciliation mission. Foreign Minister Talleyrand refused to accept him. President Adams sent Pinckney back in 1797 accompanied by John Marshall and Elbridge Gerry on the same peacekeeping mission, only to be met by the same snub. This time, however, Talleyrand let it be known through channels that a bribe payment of $250,000 (to assist France, he said, to support its military) could change his mind.

Thusly was born the XYZ affair, so named to hide the names of three people who would organize the cash transfer to Talleyrand — a Frenchwoman and two bankers, one Swiss and one American. This ploy led to a remark attributed to Pinckney: "Millions for defense, sir; but not one cent for tribute."

FRANCE

The undeclared war on the high seas continued until, to the disgust of Hamilton and other Federalists (supporters all of a standing army and waiting to fight), Adams sent another peace mission of three men to France: William Murray, Oliver Ellsworth and William Davie. To the surprise of many, they returned with the Treaty of Mortefontaine, a commercial deal between the two nations that put an end to the undeclared sea war.[51]

Adams was called a warmonger by his adversaries because his request for troops led them to believe that he supported Hamilton's goal to establish a large standing army. Actually, he did not share Hamilton's long-term enthusiasms; but perception overcame reality, and charges against him lived on and he bore the political burden of the man's ambition. Actually, Adams' requests for troops, a larger navy, and improved East Coast fortifications were designed to discourage future invasions, not to attack anyone.

GENERAL

Despite criticisms they received, the Jay treaty with Britain and the Adams treaty with France were major foreign policy achievements of the first two presidents that helped to keep the European wolf away from the American door. Future peace wasn't assured, but valuable time was bought. And America grew stronger by the minute. It also helped that Napoleon's eyes never seriously turned west because he was busy building his European empire, a fact that also relieved the anxieties of the next president.

The election results of 1796 foretold the trouble that the new president could have in developing support for a unified foreign policy. The sectional split in the electoral vote announced the existence of two power centers with different interests and attitudes toward such things as international trade, associated tariffs, and, more broadly, a policy tilted toward France, Britain or neither.

Conclusion

Why was the election of 1796 so close when the heir apparent was so well qualified, and had served so well for so long?

Under Washington, fear of monarchism was stoked by the very demeanor of the matchless one. But it couldn't be expressed until a more vulnerable target appeared: John Adams. Then the competition began. Adams never shook his aristocratic, monarchist image. And the John Jay Treaty was heatedly resented by the political opposition, which regarded it as a love pact with Britain and an insult to France. Such things, together with the attractiveness of the populist message coming from those who represented one as formidable as Jefferson, were bound to attract a following that nearly destroyed Adams and his ambitions.

2

1800: John Adams
vs. Thomas Jefferson

(Electoral Votes, 138; Majority, 70)

Introduction

The Adams first term ended on a sour note. Men were in prison because they criticized administration policy; peace with France had been negotiated, but nobody knew about it before the election. So, from the outset, Jefferson's chances looked good; Adams' good points were hidden behind bad law (e.g., Alien and Seditions Acts) and the slow communication system of the day.

Electoral Process, Caucuses

The same electoral system was in place as before. The candidate with the most electoral votes became president; the man with the second-highest vote count became vice president. If two men shared a majority vote (as was the case in 1800, as Burr had the same vote count as Jefferson), the House chose the president from the top five candidates; the vice president would be the one in the remaining group who had the most electoral votes. If, in such a case, there was still a tie vote, the Senate would break the tie.

The 1800 election had unique characteristics. It was, for example, the first contest between two relatively formal political parties. The same names had been used before to describe the two opposing groups but now the separation went beyond nomenclature and became one of organization — the groups met and planned separately.

Federalists, once just a group with a particular political philosophy, had become a political party with specific ideas on how to govern, domestically and internationally, which they were prepared to defend. Democratic-Republicans were no longer just anti–Federalists. They too had become a separate political party with ideas for governance different from those that had prevailed under Washington and Adams. And they were in attack mode.

Adams was titular head of the Federalists; Hamilton lurked in the immediate background pulling many of the political strings that defined the party. President Adams, as expected, was chosen as the candidate during the Federalist caucus of 1800, which was held in Washington. Charles C. Pinckney, South Carolina, became his running mate.[1]

But the ticket was not as innocent as it appeared. Hamilton, no friend to Adams, lobbied to get Pinckney on the ticket because he hoped that support from the south would make Pinckney and not Adams the surprise winner of the election. Such a result would bring an added bonus to Hamilton. Adams, under Hamilton's scheme, with presumably the second-highest vote, would be consigned to at least four more years as a powerless vice president, out of Hamilton's way as a formidable political opponent.[2]

Jefferson led Democratic-Republicans by acclamation, with the trusty James Madison never far from his side. He was chosen, with Aaron Burr as his running mate, during the first Democratic-Republican caucus on May 11, 1800, in Philadelphia.[3]

Thumbnail Sketches of Top Candidates

This was a rematch of two former friends who were now bitter political enemies. The Adams star was descending because this champion of liberty:

- Had been reasonably charged with unconstitutionally muffling free speech, and with jailing innocent patriots who disagreed with him;
- Had been persuasively labeled a warmonger by his adversaries because of his inability to negotiate peace with France, and because of his expansion of the armed forces;
- Had given credence to the charge that he was a monarchist at heart because of his writings, his belief in a strong central government and his aloof mannerisms.

Jefferson, who was among those who levied these charges, was a man on the rise. His esteem as a Founder was equal to that of Adams and his image was untarnished. Things looked good for him on Election Day.

JOHN ADAMS, FEDERALIST, SITTING PRESIDENT

John Adams was seeking his second term. His first one had featured harsh conflict between Federalists, who had ruled from the time Washington became the nation's first president, and the newly formed Democratic-Republican Party led by Thomas Jefferson. Biographical material for Adams appears in chapter one of this book and will not be elaborated here except to say that his reputation was better in 1796 than in was in 1800.

CHARLES C. PINCKNEY, FEDERALIST

Born: 1746, South Carolina (brother of Thomas); **Education:** Oxford, military academy in France; **Wives:** Sarah Middleton (1773), Mary Stead (1786); **Children:** Three; **Died:** 1825.[4]

The Pinckneys were a prominent family in South Carolina and Charles carried the family banner high. His law career began in 1769; but when hostilities with Britain began, he put down his briefcase and picked up his musket. He had intensive active duty in South Carolina, Pennsylvania and Florida battles, which in 1780 led to his capture. He was released in 1782 and was discharged a brevet brigadier general, a true war hero. Pinckney resumed his law practice after the war and was active in politics locally and nationally (Constitutional Convention (1787), minister to France (1796)). He ran for the vice presidency or the presidency in 1800, 1804, and 1808.

An independent man, Pinckney turned down offers to become commander of the U.S. Army, a Supreme Court justice, and secretary of war or state. But in 1796 and 1797 he did agree to serve as minister to France, and thusly began his foray into an international intrigue that was born in France and became known as the XYZ affair,[5] a sordid escapade previously explained from which he emerged with honor. Upon his return from Europe, Pinckney signed on as a major general and continued in that capacity until, in 1800, an agreement was signed with France. Hostilities between the two nations ceased.

He lived for another twenty-five years practicing law and contributing to the society around him.

THOMAS JEFFERSON, DEMOCRATIC-REPUBLICAN

Born: 1743, Virginia; **Education:** Tutored, William & Mary College (he was fluent in five languages and read two others); **Wife:** Martha Wayles Skelton (from 1772 to 1782); **Children:** Six (he buried all but one); **Died:** 1826.[6]

Thomas Jefferson's parents, middle-class people, were determined to provide a high level education for their son, an attitude that placed the young student in Scotland at the age of nine. He lived with a clergyman who taught him French, Greek and Latin along with his regular studies. He completed his education in Virginia, studied law and at twenty-six was a member of that state's house of burgesses.

Jefferson's patriotic fervor was invigorated by his friendship with such activists as Patrick Henry and Richard Henry Lee, which made him comfortable with his election to join the Second Continental Congress in 1775, from which emerged the Declaration of Independence, the historical document that has been fundamentally traced to his talented pen.*

*Writing, not speaking, was the special talent of the young Virginian.

Fierce though he was in his search for independence, Jefferson didn't fight for it during the war, a political decision that during the heat of later political campaigns gave opponents the chance to label him a coward. Instead of fighting, Jefferson returned to Virginia and busied himself as a lawmaker, concentrating especially on revising property laws and diminishing the power of the Anglican Church, which in his view was not practicing religious tolerance.

Jefferson served two one-year terms as governor of Virginia during the war (1779–80). Then, after his wife died (1782), he retired from public life to his estate. The sedentary, contemplative life was not to be for Jefferson. The loss of his wife and his inquisitive mind and special talents demanded more of him. In 1783 he was back in the Continental Congress long enough to persuade its members to adopt the decimal system, which led to the creation of the dollar and the separation from the English pound.

Wherever he worked, Jefferson left footprints behind. As chairman of the committee that dealt with westward expansion, he presented foundation ideas that made possible the gradual assimilation of western territories into the union, and he established the notion that slavery should not expand westward. Although a slave owner himself, Jefferson believed slavery was an evil that should not spread beyond its existing confines: "Nothing is more certainly written ... than that these people are to be born free."[7]

Diplomacy called in 1783 and Jefferson was on his way to France. He succeeded Benjamin Franklin as minister and remained overseas until late 1789, following from afar the political developments in his homeland. He was one of those who thought the rights of individuals were not adequately addressed in the new Constitution, and he worried about the absence of a clause that would make endless presidencies impossible. Both of his concerns were later remedied with constitutional amendments.

Jefferson did not seek the position of secretary of state under Washington, but he accepted it (1789–94). This brought him into close proximity with Alexander Hamilton, secretary of treasury and the political leader of the Federalists. There was little about Hamilton that Jefferson trusted or agreed with. Hamilton's financial proposals, his nationalization of state debt, and the establishment of a national bank (which eventually led to the Federal Reserve System, currently in place) were regarded by Jefferson as unwise and unconstitutional. Also, he believed Hamilton's goal was to establish monarchist institutions so deeply entrenched that the new nation would inevitably adopt the British form of government. Disagreements so broad and so deep within the administration could not continue for long. And since Hamilton had Washington's ear, it was Jefferson who in 1795 resigned. His resignation was the first step toward the creation of an opposition group — Democratic-Republicans — led by him, which competed with Adams in the next two elections.

Much to the dismay of Washington and Adams, the dream of gentlemanly succession to the presidency disappeared with the resignation of Jefferson. In its place was that which they wanted to avoid, two opposing parties vying for power and separated by irreconcilable ideologies. They regarded this development as a dangerous threat to the highest value of the time: Unity! Although Jefferson's resignation signaled the development of an opposition party, there was no formal acknowledgement of such a development, and those who resisted Washington's policies were content to be known as anti–Federalists. And Jefferson busied himself with estate matters, content to pen criticisms of federal policies from afar.

Always pro–French, Jefferson despised the John Jay Treaty as a sellout to Britain, and during the Whiskey Rebellion (1794) his sympathies were with the farmers. The rebellion was essentially a resistance by westerners to new excise taxes recommended by Hamilton and approved by Congress. Refusal to pay amounted to a defiance of federal authority that Washington wouldn't tolerate. Hamilton sent 13,000 militiamen to quell the rebellion. The use of federal force in this way gave Democratic-Republicans an incident to use in support of their opposition to a standing army.[8]

Jefferson did not actively seek the office himself and he became Adams' vice president in 1796 only because the election system made it so. Working with Adams, who didn't share his policy visions, wasn't pleasant for Jefferson. And Adams, for obvious reasons, largely ignored Jefferson during his four-year presidency. Their old friendship burned away in the hot flames of partisan politics.

Jefferson's nomination in 1800 as a presidential candidate of the Democratic-Republican Party surprised nobody, but the appearance of Aaron Burr as an opponent of substance did. The consequence was an election that had dramatic elements in place to a degree that would have pleased a novelist or playwright: Federalist versus Democratic-Republican morphed into two Democratic-Republicans locked in a tie vote.

It was poor form to campaign for office during the early years of the nation and Jefferson abided by that unwritten rule, although he was much more active through surrogates than was Adams, who was relatively pure to the end. Once personal and political comrades and now enemies by any measure, these two titans of the intellect squared off in the election of 1800, which was destined to result in a controversial verdict. Both were prepared; both were willing. The people would decide.

AARON BURR, DEMOCRATIC-REPUBLICAN

Burr's biographic material is presented more fully in chapter one of this book and will not be elaborated here.

Aaron Burr, ex–attorney general and legislator, organized the Democratic Party in New York City and used that platform to launch his bids for the presidency.[9] His electoral vote increased with each appearance, until in 1800 he tied with Jefferson with seventy-three votes. Jefferson was chosen by the House; Burr served as vice president.

Burr, a talented man who demanded success of himself, failed to live up to his self-imposed standards and thereafter lived a destructive life.

Election Tone

"The presidential election of 1800 was an angry, dirty, crisis-ridden contest that seemed to threaten the nation's very survival."[10] Such a description of the presidential contest is appropriate conditioning for those who examine it. To understand the need for such a powerful introduction to the subject, one must keep in mind the still-perilous times during which the election took place and the jumpiness of an electorate that viewed every extraordinary incident, national or international, as the one that would topple the Union and bring chaos.

The Constitution was only eleven years old in 1800, and numerous incidents during those years kept people on edge. Powerful and respected leaders claimed that secretary of treasury Hamilton would ruin the Union with his policies of centralization; the fury of partisanship, as reflected in newspapers, caused President Washington to say that they would "tare [*sic*] the [federal] Machine asunder"; it took federal troops to put an end to the Whiskey Rebellion; the John Jay Treaty resulted in fierce political reaction; George Washington's retirement removed a security blanket that could not be replaced by any other man; Adams' Alien and Sedition Acts and the way they were received by other leaders was troubling. Taken together, such an unbroken, seemingly unending series of incidents, plus the continued antagonism of European powers, made people both powerful and ordinary fearful about the future.[11] Within such a context, two of the most prominent Founders competed for the presidency. And they disagreed on almost every important issue, which, by itself, was destined to add to the insecurity of the times. Who was right? What was the danger of being wrong?

Is it any wonder that candidates worried about Unity, and that each in his way would fight fiercely for the protection of it? And is it any wonder that supporters of each man — politician, newsman, citizen — were passionate and at times brutal agents of their principal?

This election, unlike the previous one, had the political record of a sitting president to evaluate and attack, a record that could serve as the primary subject matter of the campaign, with Federalists defending and Democratic-Republicans attacking. It was possible to be specific, rather than general:

- In 1796 the Democratic-Republicans called Adams a warmonger with designs against the French; but in 1800 they had the larger navy and the

Federalist drive for a standing army to point to as evidence of their charge.*

• In 1796 Democratic-Republicans pointed to Adams' imperious demeanor and scholarly writings when they accused him of monarchial designs; but in 1800 they had as evidence the legislation that pressed down on immigration and attacked First Amendment rights on free speech.

And in 1800 Democratic-Republicans could point proudly to their man Jefferson as the first vice president to oppose his own president's bid for a second term. That alone indicated the existence of a high state of rebellion, one that would make the upcoming election more than just interesting.

Campaign language quickly verified that assumption, some of it coming from an unexpected direction. The following comments, for example, came from a pamphlet written by Alexander Hamilton about John Adams that was published months before the election[12]:

> He does not posses the talents adapted to the administration of government, and that there are great and intrinsic defects in his character, which unfit him for the office of chief magistrate....
>
> [H]e was far less able in the practice than in the theory of politics....
>
> [H]e is a man of an imagination sublimated and eccentric; propitious neither to the regular display of sound judgment, nor to steady perseverance in a systematic plan of conduct.... [T]o this defect are added the unfortunate foibles of vanity without bound, and jealousy capable of discolouring every object....
>
> [I]f chance should decide in favour of Mr. Pinckney, it probably would not be a misfortune....
>
> [T]he disgusting egotism, the distempered jealousy, and the ungovernable indiscretion of Mr. Adams' temper, [are] joined with ... doubts about the correctness of his maxims of administration.
>
> [H]e is capable of being alienated from a system to which he has been attached, because it is upheld by men whom he hates.
>
> [H]is ill humours and jealousies [have] already divided and distracted the supporters of the Government; he has furnished deadly weapons to its enemies by unfounded accusations.

Perhaps worst of all, Hamilton wrote the following: "[H]e has made great progress in undermining the ground which was gained for the government by his predecessor, and there is real cause to apprehend ... it might totter, if not fall, under his future auspices." With that final insult Hamilton, a Founding Father, a friend to Washington, the super-effective first secretary of state who had worked shoulder to shoulder with Adams under Washington for eight years and currently was the most politically powerful Federalist, ripped apart the reputation of the president of the United States, who would most likely be the nominee of the party in the 1800 election. Truly it can be said: With friends like these, who needs enemies?

---

*News of the peace treaty negotiated by Adams' team did not arrive until after the election, which may have cost him the presidency. With the treaty in place the drive for a standing army lost steam, and the issue ceased to be important.

Adams had other enemies who freely aired their grievances against him in the newspapers of the day. The writings of James Callender (an ally of Jefferson's at the time) were typical. To Callender, Adams was a repulsive pedant, a hypocrite and a liar who behaved neither like a man nor a woman but instead exuded an ugly hermaphroditical aura.[13]

What stimulated such rancor between such civilized men and their minions? Certainly issues like the Judiciary Act of 1801[14] that packed the courts with Federalist judges had many Jeffersonians climbing the walls; Adams' handling of the Fries Rebellion[15] was disturbing to others; he still carried the pro–British label that had sprung from the John Jay Treaty; his administration was associated with the sordid XYZ affair.[16] And perhaps most of all, the Sedition Acts of 1798[17] represented to Democratic-Republicans the monarchial strain in Adams' approach to government that had disturbed them from the beginning.

But is that enough to explain the viciousness of the personal attacks that were commonplace during the campaign? Political issues like the above certainly explain why the two-party system came into being; they explain disagreements and debates. But what was the explanation for the passion?

Here one enters into the arena of speculation mixed with facts. Reference to the opening comments in this section seems appropriate — fear was afoot in the land. The Union was unstable; slavery hovered as a controlling background issue; the nation's most esteemed leaders were squabbling. Each side in the argument sold their case in survival terms. Nothing breeds passion more than a fight for survival. So, behind specific and obvious issues, most of which were based on Adams' most recent political decisions, the overriding issue was arguably the question that had not been satisfactorily answered during the first two presidencies: How should the new government be managed? Which ideology should dominate? And in this particular case, which type of leader would keep the nation safe?*

Washington's had been an administration of personality. The man himself hovered above issues; to the people he was the strong guardian who would sensibly, ethically and safely guide them through the early days of formation. He was unassailable. Those who opposed him, or worried about his courtly ways, held their fire and waited for an opponent more vulnerable — one not so dominant or prestigious. They waited for John Adams, the abrupt, never-personable leader who in appearance and demeanor was the very opposite of George Washington.

The first sign of political turmoil appeared in the 1796 election. While Washington had been unopposed in previous elections (his way was the country's way, the Federalist way was the right way), it wasn't the same with Adams. When he stepped forth to claim the succession he and others felt was his due, opposition candidates jumped from the political closet, all eager to take the

*Agreement has never been reached on these questions.

country in a different direction. Washington and Federalism were invulnerable; Adams and Federalism were vulnerable. It was the same doctrine but with a different leader.

The opposition failed in their first quest to defeat Adams. And then they boiled for four years awaiting another election — waiting to take another swing at the old patriot who had built an army and a navy and was, many charged, leading the United States into international wars and, by the way, was also protecting himself at home by making free speech illegal under a law that was still in force during the campaign, a law that had already jailed outspoken writers who dared to question its authority.

All of this venom spilled out in the written word. James Callender, Jefferson's surrogate, described the president as a wretch, impolite, unskillful and cowardly. That Jefferson tolerated such remarks is demonstrated by his comment: "Such papers [referring to Callender's work] cannot help but produce the best effects."[18] Callender, incidentally, was arrested under the Sedition Act, spent nine months in jail and paid a $200 fine.[19] *Aurora*, a leading newspaper of the time, and an unrelenting critic of Washington, continued — after a brief hiatus — its harangue against John Adams, who was "the advocate of a kingly government and of a titled nobility to form an upper house, and to keep down the swinish multitude.... [He] would deprive you of a voice in chusing your president and senate, and make both hereditary."[20] The editor of the paper, Benjamin Franklin Bache, a nephew of Benjamin Franklin, was arrested (later pardoned) under the Sedition Act.

These verbal brickbats were bad enough for Adams to contend with, but his own party members were after him as well. Alexander Hamilton's damaging comments were gleefully quoted by the opposition. But there was more for Democratic-Republicans to feast upon, to offer as evidence in support of Hamilton's scurrilous description of the president. For example, Timothy Pickering, secretary of state, was removed from office in 1800 because of his deep-seated disagreements over foreign policy with Adams. He was the implacable enemy of Adams until his death.[21]

James McHenry, secretary of war, was fired by Adams as incompetent. Their disputes over the future of the Federalists finally led to an abrupt separation.[22] Needless to say, discharged and bitter cabinet members are seldom helpful in a presidential campaign, and the fact that tensions existed in Adams' political family gave his opposition one more powerful bullet to fire at him.

Adams was aware of what Hamilton and others were up to, which was made evident in the following letter written almost a decade after the election to a friend, Joseph Lyman:

> The Leaders to whom the Federal Party has now blindly abandoned itself were never my Friends.... When France attempted to degrade us I exerted all my Industry to arouse inspire and animate my Fellow Citizens to Resistance, and with so much success that the then French government was compelled to retreat.

If, for this service I had no thanks from the Republicans, I had nothing but Inso-
lence and Scurrility from the Federalists. Look back and read the Federal Newspapers in Boston, New York and Philadelphia, of that Period. You will there see
how I was treated. If your Namesake of Springfield, who was then a Representative in Congress, one of the most amiable of Men, were now alive he could
inform you as he did me, with the kindest expressions of attachment to me, and
Indignation against the treachery of my pretended federal Friends. He assured
me that the Federalists in New York with Hamilton at their head had in Secret
Caucus agreed to sacrifice Adams. I had other Information from other Quarters,
that at the Meeting of the Cincinati at New York when they chose Hamilton
their President General it was agreed ... to sacrifice Adams and bring in Pinckney.
The Intrigues they practised to accomplish this were very extensive and very
Jesuitical. But to develop them would lead me too far. I will only add that the
Boston, and the Pensilvania, if not the South Carolina Federal Leaders were in
the same Plott.— They were assisted too by the Publications in England particularly the Anti-Jacobin then under the direction of Mr. Canning. I know that
French Influence drove me into banishment: but it would not have had the
Power if it had not been essentially assisted by the Pharisaical Jesuitical Machi-
avellian Intrigues and Influence of the leading Federalists.[23]

In terms of volume, Adams got more than his share of insulting coverage
by the press ("fool," "hypocrite," "tyrant"),[24] but Jefferson was not forgotten
by Adams' loyalists. For starters, in 1800 Federalists claimed Jefferson was dead.[25]
And things went downhill from there. One newspaper, for example, warned,
"Murder, robbery, rape, adultery, and incest will be openly taught and practiced,
the air will be rent with the cries of the distressed, the soil will be soaked with
blood, and the nation black with crimes." Others attacked Jefferson's deist beliefs
and said that he failed to exhibit the slightest respect "for the faith and worship
of Christians."[26]

As if the turbulence caused by the clash of two titans like Adams and Jefferson weren't enough, the machinations of Alexander Hamilton, the lurid prose
of writers like Callender and the emergence of Aaron Burr (opposed by Hamilton) added to the upsetting mix and, together, resulted in one of the bitterest
political confrontations in American history, during which candidates were
besmirched beyond recognition.

"Politics ain't bean-ball," is a modern saying that could be accurately
applied to the earliest days of American politics. When power is the prize,
human dignity often comes under attack.

Election Results, 1800

The election of 1796 resulted in an embarrassing end: A president from
one group (Adams) and a vice president from the opposition group (Jefferson).
The nomination process was modified in 1800 to correct that problem. But the
results of the 1800 election demonstrated that the system still had intrinsic flaws
that needed quick attention.

Handicappers, had they existed at the time, would have considered the race as a contest between Adams, the president, and Jefferson, the leading figure of the opposition. It didn't turn out that way. Sixty-five electoral votes were cast for Federalists, led by Adams; seventy-three were cast for Democratic-Republicans, shared by Jefferson and Burr.

Election Results 1800

Candidates	Electoral Vote	%
Jefferson-DR	73	52.9
Burr-DR		
Adams-F	65	47.1
Pinckney-F		
Total	138	100.0

Source: NY Times Almanac 2009, p. 125

Note: Burr had the same number of votes as Jefferson, which moved the election to the House and eliminated Adams and Federalists from consideration; Pinckney pulled 64 electoral votes.

So, Adams was out. Federalists lost; Democratic-Republicans won. But which Democratic-Republican? Under the rules then in place the House of Representatives would choose between Jefferson and Burr. On February 1801, after the thirty-sixth ballot (and with the help of Hamilton, who considered Jefferson the lesser of two evils), Jefferson was chosen. The seventy-three votes cast to the Democratic-Republican Party went to Jefferson.[27]

Sectional voting continued to reflect the impasse between north and south, a direct reflection of the overhanging slavery issue. Jefferson won the election essentially because Burr, a New Yorker, was on the ticket and won that state for his party. Jefferson also showed strength in Maryland and Pennsylvania, which he split with Adams. But his primary power base was the south, which he swept.[28] Adams took the New England states plus Delaware, New Jersey and a share of Maryland, Pennsylvania and North Carolina.[29] Ironically, the man who almost stole the presidency from under Jefferson's nose was also the man who was most responsible for his election — Aaron Burr.

Deep differences continued to separate north from south. True, Jefferson picked up tenuous support in New York. But unity had not been reached and, if Federalists did well in congressional elections (they did not) Jefferson would have stiff resistance during his first term.

The Jefferson Cabinet

Fortunately for Adams he was saved the indignity of having to return to his old post as vice president (an assignment that would have been insufferable for him or Jefferson) by the fact that Burr pulled more votes.

Overall, the cabinet was peppered with the names of the famous men of the times[30]: **Vice President:** Aaron Burr, New York; **Secretary of State:** James Madison, Virginia; **Secretary of Treasury:** Samuel Dexter, Massachusetts (1801); Albert Gallatin, Pennsylvania; **Secretary of War:** Henry Dearborn, Maine; **Attorney General:** Levi Lincoln, Massachusetts; **Secretary of the Navy:** Robert Smith, Maryland.

The Jefferson Congress

The 7th Congress of the United States had not yet created the position of Leader in the Senate. The House Speaker in 1800 was Theodore Sedgwick (F-MA); he was succeeded in 1801 by Nathaniel Macon (DR-NC). Jefferson's coattails were strong in the 1800 election, bringing him control of both Houses, which he added to in the midterm elections.

Pro-Administration Congressional Power

Congress	Year	House %	Senate %
6	1799	57	69
7	1801	64	50
8	1803	73	74

Appendix 1.1, 1.2

So strong was the Democratic-Republican position in the Congress that analysts of the time had reason to believe that Jefferson had brought the nation together, forging a unity that would overcome the remaining differences between the north and the south. Time would prove them wrong.

The Jefferson Supreme Court

John Marshall, a Federalist, was appointed by Adams in January 1801. Over the next four years he labored with six other associate justices, as follows[31]:

Supreme Court Justices, 1801–04

Judge	Began	Appointed by	Ended
John Marshall (VA)	1801	Adams	1835
William Cushing (MA)	1790	Washington	1810
William Paterson (NJ)	1793	Washington	1806
Samuel Chase (MD)	1796	Washington	1811
Bushrod Washington (VA)	1799	Adams	1829
Alfred Moore (NC)	1800	Adams	1804
William Johnson (SC)	1804	Jefferson	1834

Source: Source: Oyez, http://www.oyez.org/

Men in Black, Mark Levin, Preface

Justices of the Supreme Court, http://www.supremecourtus.gov/about/members.pdf

> *Note: Samuel Chase[32] in 1804 was impeached by the House. The charges went to the Senate for trial. The eight charges claimed he had exceeded judicial powers in various ways. He was acquitted on five of the charges, which was sufficient to clear him. It is said that John Randolph (VA) incited the charges out of political animosity.*

Given this mix of jurists, one would expect opinions[33] that reflected the world-view of Washington and Adams, which at the time was not pleasing to Jefferson and his followers. One case, *Marbury v. Madison,* is rated by legal scholars as one of the most important in the history of the court[34]:

MARBURY V. MADISON, 1803

The Facts: William Marbury was one of President Adams' infamous midnight appointments that were authorized during the last minutes of his administration. When Jeffersonians did not recognize his appointment, Marbury sued James Madison (the secretary of state, in those days, had national as well as international duties).

The Issue: Is the law that supported Marbury's appointment constitutional?

The Ruling: Chief Justice Marshall ruled that the law that governed Marbury's appointment was unconstitutional. In so doing, he established the doctrine of judicial review under which courts can declare statutes unconstitutional.

STUART V. LAIRD, 1803

The Facts: Laird asked the Court to uphold the ruling of a circuit court judge whose job had been eliminated. Stuart argued that only the court that issued the ruling could decide the question, that the Supreme Court did not have jurisdiction.

The Issues: Did Congress have the authority to abolish the circuit court in question? Can Congress require justices of the Supreme Court to sit as circuit judges (to replace the judge whose job was eliminated)?

The Ruling: Five justices led by William Paterson (Chief Justice Marshall did not participate), ruled affirmatively on both issues, and in so doing made clear the power that Congress has over the Supreme Court.

Domestic Affairs Relative to Political Issues

Thomas Jefferson typically gets high grades from historians and scholars who grade presidential performance.[35] Events during his first term provide the primary justification for this degree of admiration.

DOMESTIC EVENTS

Jefferson's political campaign had one central theme: He would not be another John Adams, the monarchist. This meant he would dismantle much of what Adams had created.[36]

Jefferson demonstrated his antimilitary streak when he sold much of the navy and cut the size of the army, despite the benefits to him — during the Tripolitan War — of the strong defense establishment Adams had built. This policy did not harm his presidency, which was at peace with major powers, but it wasn't helpful to future presidents who weren't so fortunate.

Jefferson pardoned those who were jailed under the sedition laws for speaking out against the government. The Lewis and Clark expedition began in 1803, an eight-thousand mile trek that extended west to the Pacific. Information gained during the adventure proved useful to many who later followed in their footsteps. Jefferson inherited sixteen states, and he welcomed Ohio during his first term. But his purchase of the Louisiana Territory was a promise of more states to come.[37]

The peace treaty with France, negotiated under Adams, and admirable budget control made it possible for Jefferson to jump at the chance to exploit in 1803 the need of Napoleon for cash and to buy over 800,000 acres of land for fifteen million dollars.[38] The Louisiana Purchase was a monumental achievement that changed history and established the foundation for the westward surge of colonists, which was to finally result in the coast to coast nation known as the United States of America. It was more than a purchase of land; it also marked the end of one more European claim (that of France) to American soil and the preparation for war against France that most certainly would otherwise have been fought to acquire it.

Finally, Alexander Hamilton, one of Jefferson's foremost political enemies, was killed in 1804 by Aaron Burr in a duel.[39]

Economic Growth and National Debt

Jefferson had a mixed economic history throughout most of his first term.

Gross Domestic Product, Public Debt

Year	GDP (bil)	% Growth	Public Debt (mil)
1800	.48	9.1	83
1801	.54	12.5	83
1802	.45	-16.7	80
1803	.48	6.7	77
1804	.54	12.5	86

Source: http://www.usgovernmentspending.com/federal _debt_chart.html; *Historical Statistics of the United States, Colonial Times to 1957,* p. 721

The economy was basically flat under Jefferson. But the aura of the "real estate deal of all deals" made all other numbers fade into insignificance. There was some question about the constitutionality of Jefferson's fast action, but the deal was such a good one that legal arguments fell on deaf ears. The acquisition made possible the expansion west that followed, a task that would have been a quarrelsome one (and a much more expensive one) had France stood in the way. Considering the fact that the Louisiana Territory was purchased, the small increase in national debt was justifiable.*

LEGISLATIVE EVENTS

The first term of Jefferson was not legislatively memorable.[40] The Judiciary Act (1802) basically reversed the Adams act of 1801. The Enabling Act (1802) authorized settlers in the eastern portion of the Northwest Territory to form the state of Ohio and established the procedures for the creation of future states from the West. Amendment Twelve (1804) provided for separate electoral ballots for president and vice president. This eliminated the possibility of another fiasco like that of Jefferson vs. Burr that had complicated the 1800 election. The difference in the appetite for lawmaking in 1800 compared with the modern legislative environment is striking.

IMMIGRATION

The Adams administration increased the residency requirement for naturalization from five to fourteen years.[41] The Jefferson administration restored the five years residency standard.[42]

Foreign Affairs Relative to Political Issues

Jefferson faced one unanswered charge made against him during the campaign: Was he tough enough to defend America? The other central foreign policy issue, a large standing army, disappeared when news of the peace treaty with France reached America's shores after the election.

JEFFERSON AS A DEFENDER

Washington and Adams worked diligently to keep America out of European wars or alliances that could lead to war, their policies sometimes ridiculed and insulted by Jefferson and his supporters and, at times, by other Federalists. But the hated Jay treaty quieted Britain for a time and the treaty with France,

*Fortunately for America, Napoleon was too busy fighting Europeans to worry about his American interests.

during Adams' last days as president, did the same. Jefferson, as was the case with his predecessors, had trouble on the high seas with foreign powers that interfered with trade. But for Jefferson, Britain and France were not the culprits. The pirates of the Barbary Coast were the main problem.

The United States and other nations had been paying bribes to the rulers of Morocco, Algiers, Tripoli and Tunisia (the so-called Barbary States) in return for safe passage to and from the Mediterranean Sea.[43] Then, in 1801, Algiers raised the price of safety to a level that energized the usually pacifistic Jefferson. He ordered a blockade and intensified diplomacy in search of an equitable understanding. Those tactics failed. So in 1804, he authorized an invasion force led by Lieutenant Stephen Decatur to attack Tripoli.* Hostilities continued until the treaty of 1805. Did Jefferson thereby erase all charges against him dealing with his courage and steadfastness in a time of war? Not really. Critics point to his destruction of America's military deterrent strength and note that, as wars go, Tripoli was a skirmish and it took Jefferson three years to authorize action.

Otherwise, Jefferson enjoyed four years of relative peace in a period that featured a working relationship with France (thanks to Adams) that was good enough to result in the Louisiana Purchase, the first major step toward westward expansion.

Conclusion

Why was the election of 1800 so close? With the smoke cleared it can be said that it was close because it was a test between a remote centrist, Adams, whose time had gone by, and an articulate populist, Jefferson, who was more in tune with the changing times and more comfortable with the political process. The election was nevertheless close because Adams was still a highly respected figure in the nation, with a powerful northern base.

The Federalist Party fell into total disrepair after Adams' defeat. Jefferson won the 1804 election with 87 percent of the electoral vote, and his party was not seriously challenged until 1836 when the Whig candidate (a successor to the Federalists) William Henry Harrison drew 37 percent of the electoral vote.

---

*Heroics of the Tripolitan War were given wide coverage in the press, which in turn triggered the familiar lyrics in the Marine hymn: "From the halls of Montezuma to the shores of Tripoli...."

3

1824: John Quincy Adams vs. Andrew Jackson

(Electoral Votes, 261; Majority, 131)

Introduction

Much had transpired since the last close election between the father of John Quincy Adams and Thomas Jefferson. And three Democratic presidencies, virtually unchallenged, had ruled the nation during the years that led to the subject election: Thomas Jefferson, James Madison and James Monroe.

- Thomas Jefferson (1805–08): Jefferson's second term was not as impressive as his first, and in some ways was deficient. His basic problem was his failure to deal decisively with British pressure on the high seas, a foreign policy thorn that had consequential domestic ramifications. France and England were at war, and both were harassing American ships. Jefferson adopted a neutral stance and hoped to profit from trading with both. It didn't work out that way. England especially got nasty. American ships were seized and fired upon; sailors were pressed into service. Jefferson's limp reply was the 1807 Embargo Act that, in effect, banned foreign trade. The law hurt American business so much that it was repealed in 1809. He handed the problem over to his successor, James Madison. One noteworthy accomplishment during Jefferson's second term that had continuing political ramifications was the passage of the Prohibition of the Slave Trade Act (1807), which forbade the importation of new slaves. The law embittered the South and pleased the North. The economy under Jefferson was relatively stagnant until 1808, when GDP jumped by 10 percent.[1] National debt dropped by 24 percent in his second term,[2] a commendable accomplishment aided by the fact that he sharply reduced the size and the cost of the military.[3]
- James Madison (1809–16): Madison tried to maintain peace but, unlike Jefferson, he prepared for war. He increased the size of the military[4] and, when England went too far, declared war in 1812. Almost 7,000 men

were killed or wounded in the two-year conflict[5] but, at the end of it, Britain's appetite to regain its American colonies has been crushed for good. The economy under Madison erratically grew until 1815, and was in a postwar slump when he left office in 1817.[6] War is expensive; national debt approximately doubled in eight years.[7]

• James Monroe (1817–24): Monroe inherited peace and a slumping economy. For five years he suffered a dropping GDP,[8] punctuated by the Panic of 1819[9] (massive foreclosures due to tighter lending terms). The economy bounced back in 1821 and 1822, but was stagnant when he left office. National debt was relatively stable during his last six years in office. Despite the hard times, Monroe maintained a strong military.[10] Legislatively, Monroe will be remembered for the Missouri Compromise (1820),[11] an attempt to create a system of new-state admittance that would maintain the same free-state, slave-state balance. Slavery remained a burning issue that influenced almost everything else and kept a strain on the unity of the nation. Monroe had sound foreign policy achievements, thanks to his clever secretary of state, John Quincy Adams. A deal with Britain (Rush-Bagot Treaty)[12] fixed the border between Canada and the United States and established joint occupation of Oregon for a decade; America bought Florida from Spain and persuaded it to abandon its territorial claims in the Louisiana Territory and Oregon.[13]

At the end of the Jefferson, Madison and Monroe era, the Union was made up of twenty-four states.[14] Western movement of the population indicated that more were to come. It also indicated that Indian problems would continue.

Relative to the 1824 election, Democrats could brag about the Louisiana Purchase under Jefferson, the winning of the second war of liberation under Madison and the further acquisition of territory under Monroe. Since all candidates were from the same political party, the only one who directly benefited from this history was John Quincy Adams, who, as Monroe's secretary of state, helped to create some of it.

Electoral Process, Caucuses

The elections of 1796 and 1800 revealed weaknesses in the election process that produced an incompatible president/vice president combination (Adams and Jefferson) and two men from the same party competing with one another (Jefferson and Burr). Both problems were solved when political parties were formed and with the ratification of Amendment Twelve of the Constitution. Candidates in the 1824 contest weren't faced with such issues.

Federalists put up a good fight in the 1800 election, and they could have won and prospered if the news of the treaty with the French ending the long undeclared sea war had reached America before the election. But fate ruled otherwise. Adams went down in defeat, and Jefferson opened the Democratic-Republican dynasty that was to control the White House for the next six decades, most of them unopposed. The election of 1824 was more of the same, all candidates from the same party. Monroe was out of the picture and the question was: Who will succeed him? There was no shortage of volunteers, but those who survived to do battle were John Quincy Adams, Andrew Jackson, William H. Crawford and Henry Clay.[15]

The usefulness of the usual party caucus, at which platforms could be set for the guidance of candidates and voters, fell into disrepute in 1824 because there was no competitor against which Democratic-Republicans could campaign as a group — there was no competing ideology. Candidates, therefore, resorted to sectional popularity to become official candidates.

John Quincy Adams, as Monroe's highly acclaimed secretary of state, should have been the heir apparent and probably would have been if the discarded caucus system had been utilized. But the demise of the Federalist Party, the common enemy of all Democratic-Republicans, had curiously damaged the unity of the remaining party and its capacity to control candidates and platforms. Sectional interests and sectional candidates came into vogue. Adams was just one more candidate with enough local support to compete, but not enough to gain an exclusive party nomination. So the four politicians approached the voters, each with a story to tell and positions to express. With no central theme to present to voters, it is not surprising that personality became a dominant issue, that popularity became more important than competence and that exchanges between competitors became bitter and insulting.

Thumbnail Sketches of Top Candidates

The Federalist Party was dead. Competition for the presidency was restricted to ambitious men from within the party, each of whom had a following. As Monroe's secretary of state, Adams was the heir apparent, and the favorite.

JOHN QUINCY ADAMS, DEMOCRATIC-REPUBLICAN

Born: 1767, Braintree, Massachusetts; **Education:** University of Leyden, Netherlands; Harvard College, law; **Wife:** Louisa Catherine Johnson; **Children:** Four (he buried three); **Died:** 1848.[16]

Growing up under the eyes and the supervision of his famous father, the great patriot and second president of the United States, was an academic lesson in itself that made possible the European education of the young John Quincy. After returning to Massachusetts and graduating from Harvard (1787), John practiced law in the Boston area until he began his career in the Foreign Service as minister to Netherlands (1794), Portugal (1796) and Prussia (1797).

Adams returned home in 1802 and served briefly in the Massachusetts State Senate. Next, it was the U.S. Senate (1803–08) for young Adams, who was on a fast track to someplace.

Adams, probably because of his early saturation with European culture, was what today would be called an internationalist, in the sense that he was not a markedly partisan politician, especially with respect to foreign affairs. Because of this, he found it philosophically consistent in 1807 to support President Jefferson's controversial embargo. Jefferson, of course, was a member of the Democratic-Republican Party that had unseated Adams' father as president, and John Q. Adams had been sent to the Senate as a Federalist from Massachusetts. His support for Jefferson enraged Massachusetts backers, cost him his seat in the Senate and ultimately sent him across the aisle to join the party of his father's worst political enemy, Jefferson.

Never one to remain idle for long, Adams, after splitting with Federalists and leaving the Senate, next appeared as minister to Russia (1809–14), then as minister to England (1815–17). Nobody in federal government was better versed in foreign affairs than John Quincy Adams, and it came as no surprise that he was chosen to serve in the cabinet of President James Monroe, a Democratic-Republican, as his secretary of state (1817–25).

Adams proved himself to be a diplomat of considerable skill. For example, the Convention of 1818 that fixed the present United States-Canadian border was his work, as were the Adams-Otis Treaty, which transferred Florida from Spain to the United States, and the treaty of 1824, which removed Russia as a threat to the Oregon Territory. And he had a heavy hand in the formulation of the Monroe Doctrine that for so many years has kept foreign influences away from Central and South America. Additionally, critics of the day gave Adams high marks as an administrator who ran a patronage-free State Department. He accomplished all of this despite a remote demeanor that seemed to make him ill fit for the role in which he excelled.

As the time for the 1824 election drew near, it was apparent that the field was wide open. James Monroe, a two-term president, could not run again. Vice President Daniel D. Tompkins was not on speaking terms with his president and did not represent a political hurdle of consequence. The Federalist Party wasn't a coherent organization capable of presenting a well-supported candidate and the other candidates from the Democratic-Republican Party did not intimidate John Q. Adams.

His father had his time; now it was the son's turn. He threw his hat in the ring.

ANDREW JACKSON, DEMOCRATIC-REPUBLICAN

Born: 1767, North or South Carolina (disputed); **Education:** Self-educated; **Wife:** Rachel Donelson; **Children:** One; **Died:** 1845.[17]

Jackson was the third child and the third son of Andrew and Elizabeth Jackson. Father Andrew was dead when Jackson was born, a victim of a logging accident. His mother moved to the home of her sister in South Carolina, where she raised her three sons.

Andrew was nine when the Declaration of Independence was signed, and four years later he was serving as a courier in the Continental Army, still a boy, out on his own. Hugh and Robert, Jackson's older brothers, were also in the service, and the price to the family of their patriotism was a heavy one.

The oldest brother, Hugh, died in battle in 1779; brother Robert died in 1781, the victim of smallpox, which he and Andrew contracted during a two-week period of imprisonment by the British. During that same period, Andrew's wrist was cut to the bone by the swinging sword of the British officer whose boots young Andrew refused to shine. Throughout the balance of his life Jackson's attitude toward the British reflected a resentment that was born during his two weeks in one of their prison camps. The loss of two brothers to the war was not the end of the blows he suffered. His mother was also involved in the war effort as a nurse. In the performance of her duties she fell ill with a fever and died.

As a boy of fifteen, Jackson was an orphan with no siblings to comfort or stabilize him. He spent the next two years living with relatives and for six months he served as an apprentice to a saddle maker. Although he had received no formal education, Jackson, through his mother, his friends in the army and his reading, had become sufficiently literate to operate for a time after the war as a schoolteacher. He didn't like teaching and in 1784, at seventeen, he set his sights on becoming a lawyer. Three years later he was admitted to the North Carolina bar, and in 1788 he became the prosecuting officer for the superior court of Nashville, Tennessee.

Tennessee, admitted to the Union as the sixteenth state in 1796, made Jackson its first congressman. The next year he was elected to the U.S. Senate but resigned after one session and returned to Tennessee to serve for six years on its supreme court.

Jackson was thirty-three when the century turned, with a full career already behind him as a lawyer, a congressman, a senator and a judge. But along the way, he maintained contact with the military. So it isn't surprising that in 1802 he was made major general of the Tennessee militia. After serving in several campaigns against the Creek Indians, Jackson was promoted in 1814 to major general of the U.S. Army. At forty-seven his judicial robes were far behind him. Jackson was active in the War of 1812 and emerged from it as the hero of the Battle of New Orleans, during which the British were decisively defeated.*

Such was his reputation after the war that Jackson, following a congres-

---

*During those years the nickname "Old Hickory" was attached to him, a tribute to his discipline and toughness.

sional resolution, received the thanks of the nation in the form of a gold medal. But his fighting wasn't done. In 1817 he led the expedition that captured Florida, did battle with the Seminole Indians and, in 1821, served as military governor of that state. That ended Jackson's military career — he was once more elected to the U.S. Senate in 1822 by his Tennessee supporters, and there he sat when the time came to prepare for the 1824 election.

Jackson surveyed the same scene that Adams appraised. Monroe was out of the picture; the vice president was no threat; the Federalist Party was dead. And he reached the same conclusion that Adams did: Why not me?

WILLIAM H. CRAWFORD, DEMOCRATIC-REPUBLICAN

Born: 1772, Virginia; **Education:** Private school, Carmel Academy, Richmond Academy, law, all in Georgia; **Wife:** Susanna Gerardin; **Children:** Nine; **Died:** 1834.[18]

Crawford's family moved to South Carolina in 1779, then to Georgia in 1783. As a young man, Crawford taught school for several years before he completed his formal education; he studied law and became a member of the Georgia bar. He was twenty when he opened his law practice in Lexington, Georgia. In 1804 he purchased his estate (Woodlawn) in Lexington and married Susanna Gerardin.

Successful from the beginning, Crawford kept adding to his holdings and by 1834 his estate had grown to thirteen hundred acres that were worked by forty-five slaves. He was content to live the life of lawyer-businessman-plantation owner. Ironically, his decision to write a digest of Georgia laws upset his bucolic existence. His work was published in 1801; it drew attention to him; two years later he was a state senator.

As such, Crawford became identified with one side of a bitter partisan battle that had been provoked by a scandalous land speculation deal. Crawford, a burly, straight-talking man, was in the middle of it. Duels broke out. He killed a political opponent in 1802; four years later, he was wounded in a second duel. His reputation as a dualist did not help his presidential aspirations.

Senator Abraham Baldwin died in 1807 and Crawford was chosen to succeed him. At 35, with an eventful life already behind him, his national political career began. He was reelected in 1811 and served until 1813, at which time (after refusing President Madison's offer to become secretary of war) he left the Senate to become minister to France, a position he occupied for two years.

Crawford was forty-three when he returned from France. He yearned to return to his plantation, but duty called again. This time he accepted President Madison's offer to serve as secretary of war, a post he filled for a short period before shifting to become secretary of treasury. From that position, Crawford made his first bid for the presidency, but the Democratic-Republican caucus preferred James Monroe. After the election, he continued on as secretary of treasury under his former rival. He was given high marks for his actions in that role.

With that background behind him, this highly qualified bureaucrat surveyed the field of competition for the presidential race of 1824, and he saw the same thing that they did. Opportunity! But Crawford was unsuccessful in his quest for the highest office in the land. He refused Adams' offer to continue as secretary of treasury and returned to private life. Back in Georgia he served as a supreme court judge until, in 1834, he died on the job.

HENRY CLAY, DEMOCRATIC-REPUBLICAN

Born: 1777, Virginia; **Education:** Public schools, law in Richmond; **Wife:** Lucretia Hart; **Children:** Eleven; **Died:** 1852.[19]

Henry Clay was the seventh son of nine children brought into the world by the Rev. John and Elizabeth Clay. His father died when he was four, leaving him, his mother, Elizabeth, and his brother a 464-acre farm and twenty slaves.[20] Elizabeth later married Henry Watkins, who became a loyal husband and an understanding stepfather to the boys.

Clay felt the boot of the British troops early in life when, under the leadership of Sir Banastre Tarleton (an officer who served under Sir Henry Clinton with a fighting unit called Tarleton's Raiders), they chased American troops into Virginia and slaughtered them. In the process of doing so, the home of three-year-old Henry Clay was ransacked.

Clay, educated in public schools, first went to work as a clerk in a drugstore. From that lowly beginning, he next studied law, and by the time he was twenty he was on his way to rapidly expanding Kentucky (too much competition in Virginia for a fledgling lawyer to prosper) to open his practice. Within a decade he was a highly successful trial lawyer, active in the social and political life of his state.

Clay's marriage to Lucretia Hart was successful and, together, they established a large plantation in Ashland, Kentucky, at that time a major agricultural center in the state. Farming and breeding livestock were added to his legal activities. Clay, a slave owner, did not favor the institution. Clay was twenty-six when he took his first step into politics by winning in 1803 a seat in the Kentucky general assembly. A Jeffersonian by training and inclination, he immediately clashed with Federalists in the assembly, a sign of things to come at the national level. Aaron Burr, in the midst of his troubled years in 1806, retained Clay as his lawyer, an assignment Clay dropped upon his election to the U.S. Senate in the same year.

Clay, one of those rare politicians who moved back and forth between the Senate and the House, became House Speaker in 1808; in 1810, he was back in the Senate. Then he was back to the House, to lead the Twelfth though the Sixteenth congresses. And it was from that position that he ran for president in

1824. Clay won the fewest electoral votes of the four contenders, but he put his considerable influence behind Adams, which resulted in the Adams presidency, much to the chagrin of Clay's major political enemy, Andrew Jackson. Another result of that alliance was Clay's appointment as Adams' secretary of state (1825–29).

Jackson and Adams went at it again in 1828 with Clay on the sidelines. When Adams was defeated, Clay returned to the Senate. From that seat he ran against Jackson in 1832 and lost.

He left the Senate in 1842 and, as a Whig, ran again for the presidency in 1844 against James Polk, which ended his presidential ambitions and returned him to Kentucky until, in 1849, the old warhorse returned to the Senate, until he died three years later.

Clay, remembered for many things, looms large in the pantheon of political giants of American history. The Missouri Compromise (1820), for example, is identified with him. His long career as a political leader silently testifies to his abilities, and his multiple presidential runs dramatize the fierce ambition that drove him — and frustrated him.

Election Tone

Election tone is determined by many things, including the reactions of the candidates and the public to recent history and to the immediate political environment. Two decades had passed since the last hold-your-breath election and, with time, the political landscape had changed as well — remarkably so.

The Supreme Court under Jefferson, Madison and Monroe was led throughout by long-serving Chief Justice John Marshall, who had been appointed by John Adams. Marshall was assisted by ten associate justices, including Brockholst Livingston,[21] a dualist, and Samuel Chase,[22] who was impeached by Jeffersonians but was found not guilty in a Senate trial.

The decisions reached by the Court had little political impact except for *McCulloch v. Maryland* (1819), which found that Congress has the constitutional authority to establish a national bank, a decision that infuriated Jeffersonians who had resented the idea of a central bank from the time Alexander Hamilton had first proposed it.

The presidency of Monroe was not unusually eventful, but it did deliver to the new president a nation at peace and emerging from a recession. Hope was in the air and political peace theoretically reigned because there was no opposition political party. But peace ended with the election campaign of 1824, and political warfare resumed — different to be sure, but just as tough as ever. Why? Because Monroe's vice president, Daniel Tompkins,[23] ordinarily the heir apparent was not acceptable to his president or to his party as a candidate, and because the party could not agree on a single nominee, an organizational weakness that stimulated powerful ambitions among powerful men. The consequence was an internecine campaign filled with personal smears and other irrelevancies. Instead of matters of substance those of personality, reputation, resumes and credibility became the battleground. Candidates competed against each other as men. And the language at times got rough.

Adams represented the interest of the northeast and favored high protective tariffs. An unexciting man on the stump, his main credential was his long and effective career in public service. He was portrayed by opponents as a Federalist in disguise. Political infighting conducted against him in the newspapers was rugged. Adams was the "aristocratic candidate"[24] who would destroy the power of the people and vest it in the presidency.[25]

Jackson, a senator from Tennessee and a war hero of Grant-like dimensions, was an attractive, personable campaigner. But his political views were unknown, and there were concerns about his temper and his reputation as a duelist. He had killed men in duels and had been wounded in various confrontations. Jackson's detractors said he kept a list of people he would hang after he was elected,[26] a wild exaggeration that drew attention to his temper. He drew votes away from Clay.

Crawford's experience as a politician compared well with that of Adams. Monroe's effective secretary of treasury was a strong candidate until a stroke in 1823 partially paralyzed him. Despite this and concerns over his honesty and dueling background, he continued to be a formidable competitor to the end,[27] with his power base was in Virginia.

Clay, the hard-drinking westerner,[28] was a dominating political figure of the day. He brought deep legislative experience to the campaign and was identified with the Missouri Compromise, which temporarily shelved slavery as a hot political issue. Clay, a Kentuckian, recognized Jackson as an enemy of his political ambitions. He too got his share of media bombs, but the major bombardments against him appeared not in this election but in 1832 when he went head to head with Jackson.

The race became stereotype versus stereotype: Adams, the closet Federalist; Jackson, the unschooled soldier; Clay, the drinker; and Crawford, the killer.* And so the campaign began. But there was another difference that turned the underdog candidate, Jackson, into a formidable challenger. For the first time, popular vote was important. States formerly appointed electors, but in 1824 sixteen of them chose electors in a popular election.[29] And Jackson, above all the others, was a popular man and a war hero.

Election Results, 1824

The Electors shall meet in their respective states and vote by ballot for President.... The person having the greatest number of votes ... shall be president,

---

*"We hope it will be borne in mind by the electors on Monday next, that William H. Crawford has been engaged in five duels and that in one of them he murdered the unfortunate Van Allen."

if such a number be a majority of the whole number of Electors appointed.—
U.S. Constitution, Amendment Twelve.

A single word, "majority," in Amendment Twelve launched the presidential
career of John Q. Adams and, at the same time, postponed the same for the
obvious choice of the people, no matter how measured: that choice was Andrew
Jackson.

Election Results 1824

Candidates	EV	%	Pop. (000)	Pop. %	Pop. %
Adams, JQ	84	32.2	113	30.9	42.8
Jackson, A	99	37.9	151	41.3	57.2
Clay, H	37	14.2	48	13.1	
Crawford, W	41	15.7	41	11.2	
Other			13	3.5	
Total	261	100.0	366	100.0	100.0

EV = Electoral Vote; Pop. = popular vote

Source: N.Y. Times Almanac 2009, p. 126

Jackson won eleven states: Alabama, Indiana, Illinois, Louisiana, Maryland,
Mississippi, New Jersey, North Carolina, Pennsylvania, South Carolina, Tennes-
see. Adams won seven: Connecticut, Maine, Massachusetts, New Hampshire,
New York, Rhode Island, Vermont; Crawford. Clay took Virginia, Delaware,
Georgia, Kentucky, Missouri, Ohio.[30] Absent Crawford and Clay, Jackson would
have been a big winner.

The nation was physically united but intellectually and emotionally split.
Adams won the antislavery vote; Jackson won most frontier states and split the
pro-slavery vote with Crawford and Clay. No matter who won, it was already
apparent that governing would be a difficult task.

Jackson, obviously the preferred candidate, did not win a majority of the
electors, in which case the next clause of Amendment Twelve dictated the next
step:

> [I]f no person have such a majority, than from the persons having the highest
> number not exceeding three on the list of those voted for as president, the House
> of Representatives shall choose immediately, by ballot, the President.—*Amend-
> ment Twelve, U.S. Constitution*

The system excluded Henry Clay for further consideration and the names of
the top three candidates, Jackson, Adams and Crawford, went to the House.
That put Clay, who was speaker of the House, in the position of kingmaker.
The president would be the one he wanted most, the one who would do the
most to adorn Clay's future.

Clay was approached for support by the three candidates. For Jackson, it
was wasted effort. The war hero had reason to believe the House would confirm
the will of the people, but like many outsiders to the political system, he got
whipsawed by insiders, led by Clay, who—with an eye on the future—would

not allow Jackson, a competitor in the west, to grow in political stature. It was the same with Crawford. He, like Clay, competed for southern support. Also, he and Clay were not on the same political wavelength. On both counts, he would not get Clay's support.

Through the process of elimination, this left the comparatively aloof Adams, a man for whom Clay had little personal regard but one nevertheless who shared many of his political views. Adams became Clay's tool, the man who on the one hand could provide him with some return on his presidential campaign investment and at the same time knock out of the political ring the man he considered to be his long-term rival for power, Andrew Jackson. So Clay, the 800-pound political gorilla in this case, swung his considerable congressional influence to Adams and carried him on his political back to the presidency. Adams was elected on the first ballot, by a margin of one vote.[31]

Thereafter, Adams made Clay secretary of state, an appointment later referred to by political opponents as the "corrupt bargain."[32]

Jackson was livid; he went public with his grievances. Clay had offered him the same bargain, he said, in exchange for support, but he had refused. Then Clay took the same deal to Adams, who accepted his support. In exchange, Clay became secretary of state.[33]

Clay of course denied the charge. Jackson resigned his Senate seat and vowed to return in 1828 to beat Adams.

The Adams Cabinet

Members of the Adams cabinet[34] were as follows: **Secretary of State** — Henry Clay, Kentucky; **Secretary of Treasury** — Richard Rush, Pennsylvania; **Secretary of War** — James Barbour, Virginia, (1825–28); Peter B. Porter, Connecticut; **Attorney General** — William Wirt, Maryland; **Secretary of Navy** — Samuel L. Southard, New Jersey.

This was an experienced, formidable group of men with no apparent weaknesses at any position.

The Adams Congress

The House Speakers under Adams were John W. Taylor (NY) (1825–27) and Andrew Stevenson (VA) (1827–29):

- John W. Taylor[35]: A lawyer; House of Representatives (1813–33); House Speaker (1820–21; 1825–27)[36]; lost his seat in the 1832 election and returned to private life; died 1854.
- Andrew Stevenson[37]: House of Representatives, with allegiance to William Crawford and Andrew Jackson (1821–34); House Speaker (1827–34)

under Adams and Jackson; minister to Great Britain under President Martin Van Buren (1836–41); returned to private life; died 1857.

Pro-Administration Congressional Power

Congress	Year	House %	Senate %
17	1823	83	92
18	1825	34	35
19	1827	51	46

Appendix 1.1, 1.2

The above graphic demonstrates that the party was badly split in 1824 and Adams began with powerful opposition in both houses of Congress. He improved his position in the midterm elections, but still lacked the power to command the political agenda. At the end, the party was still in power but severely split. A unifier was badly needed or else a new party would emerge to challenge the rule of Democratic-Republicans.

The Adams Supreme Court

To the extent that worldview influences judicial decisions, the mix of the court during the Adams administration was decidedly influenced by Jeffersonians.

Supreme Court Justices, 1825–29

Judge	Began	Appointed by	Ended
John Marshall	1801	Adams	1835
Bushrod Washington	1799	Adams	1829
William Johnson	1804	Jefferson	1834
Thomas Todd	1807	Jefferson	1826
Gabriel Duvall	1811	Madison	1835
Joseph Story	1812	Madison	1845
Smith Thompson	1823	Monroe	1843
Robert Trimble	1826	Adams J.Q.	1828

Source: Oyez, http://www.oyez.org/— Members of the Supreme Court,[38] http://www.supremecourtus.gov/about/members.pdf

President J.Q. Adams appointed one man to the Supreme Court, Robert Trimble.

A few cases,[39] like *Gibbons v. Ogden*, 1824 (steamboat law), *Osborn v. Bank of the United States*, 1824 (state versus federal law), and *Ogden v. Saunders*, 1824 (bankruptcy law), were of legal interest to insiders but, for the most part, vote-influencing issues were not prominent during these years. Most cases dealt with issues between people and states as the still-young nation learned how to balance individual and states' rights with an overarching federal government.

Domestic Affairs Relative to Political Issues

Adams entered office with the same charge that had haunted his father: He was an aristocrat, opponents said, posing as a Democratic-Republican who, given the chance, would impress once again the Federalist mold on the federal government. And, on top of that, because of the way he was elected he was charged with being an unethical, shady politician.

Neither charge was true, but Adams did have his own dream of how America should operate.[40] He visualized a northern economy in need of goods from the south and west to support its manufacturing. Its output in turn could be shipped to its suppliers to satisfy their various needs. Adams visualized a broad program to improve roads, bridges and waterways over which commerce would pass.

DOMESTIC EVENTS

Adams was never in control of the Senate. His congressional power improved in the election of 1826, but his congressional support for four years was never strong enough for him to control the political agenda.[41] Despite persistent opposition, Adams made surprising progress.[42] He extended, for example, the Cumberland Road to St. Louis and he began the construction of the Ohio and Chesapeake, the Delaware and Chesapeake and the Portland and Louisville canals and other projects that improved communication between states.

It was his vision that, with balanced agrarian and industrial development and with proper lines of transportation and communication, the United States could become self-sufficient, with each section of the nation feeding off the outputs of the other sections. The "Tariff of Abominations" that was passed in 1828[43] levied high taxes against incoming British goods. This pleased northerners, enraged southerners and hurt Adams politically. Adams maintained a steady hand on the size of the military — about 11,000 troops.[44] On July 4, 1826, John Adams and Thomas Jefferson died. In November of the same year the United States and Britain agreed on a settlement for damages suffered during the War of 1812.

ECONOMIC GROWTH

The Tariff of Abominations (see below) was made law in April 1828, and its impact on the U.S. economy was obvious. High taxes on imports were a serious bone of contention between the north and the south for years thereafter.[45] Except for his final year, Adams brought an impressive economic record to the 1828 campaign, but that was an important exception. Trading markets had been upset by the new tariffs with which he was identified. Adams continued the practice of presidents who preceded him — reduce debt during times of peace and good times. He and the Congress were responsible money managers.

Gross Domestic Product, Public Debt

Year	GDP (bil)	% Growth	Public Debt (mil)
1824	.75	0.0	90
1825	.81	8.0	84
1826	.86	6.2	82
1827	.91	5.8	74
1828	.89	-2.2	67

Source: http://www.usgovernmentspending.com/federal_debt_chart.html; *Historical Statistics Colonial Times to 1957*, p. 721

Missouri became a state in 1821 and left behind a twenty-four state union.[46] The Pacific was beckoning, and an ineluctable flow of settlers kept moving the nation toward what one day would be called its Manifest Destiny.[47]

LEGISLATIVE EVENTS

Adams did move some construction projects through Congress, but unfortunately he is most likely remembered legislatively as the president who signed into law the 1828 Tariff of Abominations, a tax designed to protect northern manufacturers.[48]

That law had major political consequences. The South resented it enough to bring about a constitutional crisis in the form of a document drafted by Vice President John C. Calhoun, which stated that tariffs were unconstitutional and could be nullified by states. Calhoun resigned in 1832, the first vice president to do so, to become a U.S. Senator from South Carolina. He was a lifelong powerful advocate for states' rights.[49] The South resented the tariff; markets were destabilized because of it. Whatever Adams' chances for a second term, they were sharply reduced because of it.

IMMIGRATION

Population in the United States in 1824 was slightly less than 10 million.[50] About 15,000 immigrants per year were coming into the country,[51] mostly from Western Europe.

Foreign Affairs Relative to Political Issues

Adams, prior to his presidency settled most important and outstanding international issues.[52] Ironically, this deprived him of the opportunity during his presidency of adding to his reputation. Also, opponents in Congress had their eyes on the 1828 election, and they weren't about to help him in any image-building enterprises.[53] Relatively marginal issues that remained were handled by secretary of state Henry Clay.

An example of Adams' inability to get funding from Congress relates to a meeting in Panama of the new Latin-American Republics to which he wanted to send two delegates. The subject matter of the meeting was to promote cooperation in the Western Hemisphere and it was appropriate — almost mandatory — for the United States to attend. But to make political points,* Congress refused to support the venture.[54]

And so it was that one of America's most experienced and successful diplomats had little to brag about as a foreign policy president. The major remaining issues with European powers had been resolved during the Monroe administration with Adams' help and there was little demand for his contacts and skills during his own presidency.

Conclusion

Why was the election of 1824 so close? The disintegration of the Federalist Party as a competitor would be a good place to start for those interested in an answer to that question. Not having a common enemy to attack, ambitious Democratic-Republicans attacked each other; and the presidential campaign became a test of personal charisma and the ability to marshal resources in the most effective way.

Jackson did that. He won the race. But disunity within his party produced too many candidates, which denied him the required margin of victory. This technicality threw the election into the land of political intrigue — the House — from which Adams emerged the winner. He won because, on this particular field of battle, he knew the maneuvers better than Jackson did.

*This short-sighted position, which harmed the reputation of the United States with its neighbors, demonstrates that partisan politics was at times just as nasty and just as crippling as it is today.

4

1876: Rutherford B. Hayes vs. Samuel J. Tilden

(Electoral Votes 369; Majority 185)

Introduction

The last close election took place in 1824 between John Q. Adams and Andrew Jackson. Adams won, but actually it marked the beginning of the Jacksonian era of politics that lasted at least until 1840.

Twelve presidents followed Adams and they governed during some of the most turbulent years in American history that featured some of America's best and worst leaders: Andrew Jackson, Martin Van Buren, William Henry Harrison, John Tyler, James K. Polk, Zachary Taylor, Millard Fillmore (vice presidential succession), Franklin Pierce, James Buchanan, Abraham Lincoln, Andrew Johnson (vice presidential succession), and Ulysses S. Grant.[1]

All presidencies have some importance, but not all had impact on the election of 1876. Two of them did: Abraham Lincoln and Ulysses S. Grant. The others served as historical backdrop for both political conventions and will be briefly highlighted as follows[2]:

- Andrew Jackson (1829–36)[3]: The first Democrat (the end of the Democratic-Republican Party); a war hero and the dominant political figure for almost two decades; one of the first presidents to directly seek public support; reduced national debt to zero. His Tariff Act (1812) and his opposition to a central bank caused political and financial turmoil that continued into the Van Buren presidency. His policies gave life to a new political party, the Whigs, that evolved into the Republican Party in 1856 (John Frémont was the Republican Party's first candidate).[4] His Indian policies were shameful and he did nothing to improve the slavery question.
- Martin Van Buren (1837–40)[5]: Jackson's banking policies matured under Van Buren in the form of the Panic of 1837.[6] He settled boundary line

issues concerning Maine, New York and Canada with Britain. His steady hand on that situation was not appreciated by all northern voters and cost him political support. He won the nomination of his party in 1840 but lost the election to William Harrison, the first Whig president and the symbol of the end of Democratic domination.

- William Henry Harrison (1841–44)[7]: The first Whig (1836) and the first presidential candidate to crack the Democratic monopoly of the presidency (1840) that began in 1800.[8] He served only a month as president (before dying of pneumonia).
- John Tyler (1841–44)[9]: Succeeded William Harrison. Rivals called him "his accidency." Spent most of his time fighting with rivals who questioned his authority. Despite this, he had accomplishments: the annexation of Texas, taking Florida into the Union.
- James K. Polk (1845–48)[10]: One of the presidents who expanded the land holdings of the United States, he defeated Mexico (1846–48) and acquired California, Nevada, New Mexico, Arizona, Utah, Colorado and Wyoming. He refused to run for a second term.
- Zachary Taylor (1849–50)[11]: A southerner who argued (ineffectively) against slavery. He served only sixteen months as president before cholera killed him. He was succeeded by Millard Fillmore.
- Millard Fillmore (1850–52)[12]: The Compromise of 1850[13] was designed to settle the slavery question and avert secession by southern states. It settled nothing but postponed secession for a few more years. He opened trade negotiations with Japan.
- Franklin Pierce (1853–56)[14]: He lost the support of his own party because he did not veto the Kansas-Nebraska Act,[15] a law that brought guerrilla warfare to Kansas and other parts of the south over the question of free state or slave state, an issue that gained new steam every time a new territory became eligible for statehood. This issue dominated the Pierce presidency, but it is worth noting that his efforts to govern were not entirely wasted: A trade agreement with Japan was signed; more land was purchased from Mexico that completed what is now known as New Mexico and Arizona; and a reciprocal trade agreement with Canada was signed.
- James Buchanan (1857–60)[16]: He failed to prevent the Civil War.
- Andrew Johnson (1864–68)[17]: There were two attempts to impeach him mounted by northerners who resented his "soft" treatment of southerners after the Civil War. A southerner, he refused to take harsh measures against the South and also vetoed civil rights legislation. By the end of his term, Republicans disowned him.

Except for Johnson, the deeds of these men represented the end of the pre– Civil War era, after which a new chapter in American history began. It is therefore no slight to say that these administrations had little relevance to the politics of 1876. By that time, slavery was over and the Union was thirty-eight states large and stretched from New York to California. A new time had begun, one that promised long-awaited peace over racial questions and soothing relations between regions of the nation. That's why, in the context of the 1876 election, Lincoln and Grant were the presidencies that most influenced the electors who gathered for their presidential conventions.

- Abraham Lincoln (1860–65)[18]: He led the nation into unity by confronting Southern secession and defeating it; he led the blacks out of slavery. He was a symbol of what America could become. Republicans held his image high with pride, gathering to themselves as much of his reflected glory as possible. The value of this image to a politician running for election was incalculable, made even more so by Lincoln's tragic end. National debt under Lincoln became a concern because of the costs of war. It never again became the non-issue it once was because the taxes needed to support war became a lure to politicians with the urge to do more with tax income than support government and saw opportunity to expand the role of government into the field of citizen services. So taxes were not reduced proportionately as the wartime need for them diminished.
- Ulysses S. Grant (1869–76)[19]: With his war record behind him, the image of Lincoln floating above him, and the South — mostly Democratic — in disarray, it is little wonder that Grant cruised to victory in 1868 and 1872. And it appeared that he too would be lifted to iconic status before he was through, despite the fact that he ruled during troubled economic times.[20] Then the scandals hit. Corruption was discovered in five departments: Navy, Justice, War, Treasury and Interior. People close to him were involved (he wasn't). The end result was a black smirch on the Republican brand that was turned into a rallying cry by Democrats. "Clean up Washington" was the theme of several campaigns thereafter. The stench of the scandals almost took Democrats to victory in 1880 and finally did so in 1884.

What happened under Grant became the red meat of the 1876 election, strong enough to minimize the inheritance of Lincoln.

Conventions

Political conventions came into being in 1832 in Baltimore when delegates thereto nominated Andrew Jackson as their presidential candidate for a second term.[21] Republicans, because their party had been in disarray for years, didn't have their first convention until 1856, appropriately enough[22] in Philadelphia. They nominated James Buchanan.

REPUBLICAN CONVENTION

The 1876 Republican convention[23] was held in Cincinnati (June 14–16). Twenty-four blacks attended. There was little from the recent past to inspire Republicans except the memory of Abraham Lincoln. But that was a major and proud exception, and these men were delighted to be known as the party of Lincoln, the man who saved the Union. On the other hand, General Grant, still popular, was kept in the background because of the scandals associated with his administration.

Ordinarily, a two-term president's vice president would be at least a major contender for the nomination. But in this case, it wasn't possible. Vice President Henry Wilson (MA) had died in 1875 in the Capitol Building in Washington, D.C.[24] That unfortunate event moved James G. Blaine (ME), former Speaker of the House with a reputation as a skilled debater, to the head of the list. But he failed to win the nomination over six ballots largely because of the political tone of the time and his part in setting it.[25]

Scandals during the Grant administration were a blotch on the Republican brand from which party members wanted to distance themselves. To do so, they needed a simon-pure candidate. And Blaine didn't meet the test. A member of the Senate during Grant's second term, his name was associated with a railroad scandal although no charges were levied against him.[26]

Rutherford B. Hayes, originally a dark horse prospect, became increasingly attractive to Republicans as it became apparent that Blaine could not muster the necessary support. Hayes was a war hero, a congressional veteran and a three-term governor of Ohio with an inoffensive manner and a clean reputation.[27] He fit the political profile Republicans wanted to present to the public. The nomination went to him; William A. Wheeler, a veteran congressman, was chosen as his running mate.[28]

Abolitionist Frederick Douglass, a black man, was the featured speaker at the convention. During his remarks, he chided Republicans for the manner in which they had freed the slaves and failed to realize that the blacks needed more: they needed financial and educational support in order to exercise and enjoy their freedom. He was right. It took time for blacks to prepare themselves for freedom, without much help from government, especially in the South, where black freedom was resented. The right of blacks to vote, despite Amendment Fifteen, continued to be denied by controlling whites (until the civil rights movement of the 1960s finally made it possible).

In addition to voicing typical complaints about the opposition, Republicans adopted a platform that emphasized civil rights for all citizens and the fulfillment of pledges made to veterans. Also, they supported tariffs for revenue and the distribution of land to homesteaders.[29]

DEMOCRATIC CONVENTION

The Democratic Convention[30] was held June 27–29 in St. Louis, Missouri, the first one to be held west of the Mississippi.

If banners were in fashion in those days, certainly the image of Jackson, the man who dominated American politics for two decades, would be flying high, as would that of Polk, the expansionist who won the west for the nation. Democrats didn't have a Lincoln to brag about, but these two icons were not, as the saying goes, Swiss cheese. But they didn't have the impact of the gift that Republicans gave to them — the Grant scandals.

Dominant themes featured the resentments of the ages, for example, the aftermath of Reconstruction and sectional animosities. But the big enchilada was the soft underbelly of the Republicans, its corrupt innards as they were revealed during the Grant scandals.

Two governors contended for the nomination: Samuel Tilden (NY) and Thomas Hendricks (IN). As with Republicans, Democrats were aware of the impact on the public of the Grant scandals. They sought a candidate who would symbolize their disapproval of such behavior, one who could believably lead a program of reform. Tilden was their man. He had battled Boss Tweed and other corrupt forces in New York, and he was well known as a reformer. Hendricks accepted the vice presidential nomination.

Democratic platform issues included a promise to repeal the Specie Resumption Act of 1875,[31] civil service reform (in reaction to the Grant scandals), restrictions on Chinese immigration (in response to concerns of increasingly powerful labor unions) and improved controls over the distribution of land that favored homesteaders instead of railroads (another indirect reference to the Grant scandals).[32]

There was no doubt about it; Democrats thought they had Republicans on the ropes because of corruption revealed under Grant. Expectations must have been high for an easy win.

Two pristine candidates were turned loose on each other, civilized men who would soon learn how close an election can be.

THUMBNAIL SKETCHES OF TOP CANDIDATES

Clean, clean, clean. With the Grant scandals still fresh in the voters' minds, both parties wanted a squeaky clean candidate. That's why James G. Blaine, the early favorite, didn't get the nomination — he had Grant-related baggage. Rutherford Hayes, on the other hand, fit the required profile. He was clean, experienced and a war hero — a very useful candidate. And on the other side, who could dispute the credentials of the man who had brought New York's political tyrant, Boss Tweed, to his knees— Samuel J. Tilden?

RUTHERFORD B. HAYES, REPUBLICAN

Born: 1822, Ohio; **Education:** Kenyon College (Ohio), Harvard Law (1845); **Wife:** Lucy W. Webb; **Children:** Eight; **Died:** 1893.[33]

Hayes' father, a successful farmer and businessman, died before Rutherford was born. His attentive mother, Lucy, guided him through his college years and a wealthy uncle sent him to Harvard. The education paid off for all: Hayes became a successful criminal defense lawyer in Cincinnati. Privately, he was influenced by his religious wife, who advocated temperance and the abolition of slavery, the latter issue being one that he fervently embraced.

Hayes was intensely patriotic, a characteristic demonstrated when, at thirty-nine, with three children and another on the way, he was one of the first to join the Union Army during the Civil War. The intelligence shown throughout his life to that point was quickly recognized by the military. As a major, Hayes' conduct on the battlefield earned him the respect of all, high and low. He was wounded five times, and at war's end had risen to the rank of major general. He was a legitimate Civil War hero.

Hayes was still in the service when nominated by his party in 1864 for the U.S. House of Representatives. He accepted the nomination with the understanding that he would not campaign. In a statement typical of him he said, "An officer fit for duty who at this crisis would abandon his post to electioneer for a seat in Congress ought to be scalped." The public loved it. He won, and the war ended in time for him to serve his term (1865–67). Then he returned to Ohio to take up his career there as governor (1868–72; 1876–77).

It is no surprise that Republicans saw presidential possibilities in the brilliant Ohioan, with his outstanding legal, military and executive record. But he was not the favorite going into the convention. That enviable strategic position was occupied by James G. Blaine. Blaine, Speaker of the House for six years during the Grant administration and in 1876 a member of the U.S. Senate, had the political credentials, but his reputation had been marred due to his relationship with certain railways that, his opponents charged, were corrupt. Most Republicans thought he had cleared himself, but others worried that any association with the Grant scandals would become a liability during the upcoming campaign.

Other candidates, more prominent than Hayes at the time, were secretary of treasury Benjamin Bristow (KY), Sen. Roscoe Conkling (NY), Gov. John Hartranft (PA), postmaster general Marshall Jewell (CT) and Sen. Oliver Morton (IN). Blaine's forces came within twenty-eight votes of pushing their candidate over the top. Then deadlock set in: he wasn't capable of attracting a majority, nor was any other candidate.

Out of the wings, after several ballots, came squeaky-clean Rutherford B. Hayes. And then he became the Republican candidate in one of the closest presidential elections in history.

SAMUEL J. TILDEN

Born: 1814, New York; **Education:** Sporadic (ill health), Yale, University of New York City, law; **Wife:** Single; **Children:** None; **Died:** 1886.[34]

Tilden became a practicing attorney in New York specializing in railroad law. He invested wisely in real estate and at an early age became wealthy. While northern millionaires moved to the Republican Party, Tilden was a contrarian. He, for example, supported Democrat Martin Van Buren, was critical of Republican Lincoln and opposed the radical Reconstruction that took place after the war.

Tilden assumed a leadership role in postwar New York politics, leading the effort as a reformer to cleanse the party of the influence of Boss Tweed and of gangsters who profited from dishonest maintenance schemes associated with the state's canals. Given the dark reputation associated with the Grant administration, this simon-pure crusader from New York was made to order for Democrats. Witness the enthusiasm reported by the *New York Times*[35]: THE CAMPAIGN OF 1876; DEMOCRATIC STATE CONVENTION; ... TILDEN ... A "MAN OF DESTINY."

Tilden lost this election in a manner (later detailed) that could have resulted in postelection furor. But to his credit, he advised supporters to cool off, and the potential crisis passed. He died a decade later.

Election Tone

Candidates themselves—their personalities and backgrounds—have an impact on the tone of an election campaign. Issues they choose to emphasize and words they utter have a direct impact on the hotness or coolness of the ongoing debate. But it's usually history that creates substantive issues. What the party in power did or what it failed to do becomes the stuff of meaningful discussion. Each candidate carries with him the history of his forebears. In 1876 there was much history since the last hair-raising election to consider, especially the deeds of the most recent Republican leaders of consequence, Lincoln and Grant. Lincoln's image hovered over the land and served as a subliminal asset for Hayes. But, by far, the presidential history that counted most in this election was Grant's.

The scandals that rocked the Grant administration didn't come out of nowhere. They were part of the corruption that grew out of the helter-skelter growth of the nation from east to west, accompanied by a ton of money that was won and lost every hour of every day. But whatever their sources, Hayes had to deal with them, which made it enormously difficult for him to recapture the confidence of the American voter. The Panic of 1873 had the same source. The surge of people and businesses to the west, all seeking their fortune in honest and dishonest ways, was a perfect seed ground for the graft and wild speculation that followed, all of it attacking a still immature banking system. Over 5,000 businesses failed in the early eighteen seventies; more than twice that amount in a seven-year period.[36] And that too was a record that Hayes had to deal with.

The Supreme Court, under presidencies from Jackson through Grant, had been led by four chief justices: John Marshall (1801–35); Roger B. Taney (1836–64), Salmon P. Chase (1864–73) and Morrison R. Waite.[37] Twenty-five associate justices also served, including some interesting characters[38]:

- Henry Baldwin (1830–44) was once hospitalized for incurable lunacy.
- Robert Grier (1846–70) suffered paralysis and mental decline in 1867 and served for three more years.
- Nathan Clifford (1858–81) was described by associate justice Miller as a "babbling idiot."
- Stephen Field (1863–97), toward the end of his service, didn't understand the cases before him.

Many cases were heard by these men, but *Prigg v. Pennsylvania* (1842) and *Dred Scott v. Sanford* (1857) had powerful political impact. The former case questioned the right of states to make laws that contradicted the Fugitive Slave Law. The case was important because northerners, constantly trying to help escaped slaves, wanted to avoid the draconian penalties of the federal law for doing so. The Court affirmed the federal law and ruled that attempts to avoid it were unconstitutional. The latter case featured one of the Court's most infamous decisions, to wit: No person descended from an American slave can ever be an American citizen. In making such decisions, the Supreme Court influenced the tone of this election and of all subsequent elections for so long as the decisions remained the law of the land.

So the election took place and, when seen in the context of the times, the results were no less dramatic than one would have expected in such an age.

Election Results, 1876

The popular vote, a reflection of pure democracy, is of no practical significance in a representative democracy. The Founders were quite deliberate in their desire to escape autocracy in the form of a king, as in Britain, or an undisciplined mob, as in the French Revolution, the latter being the special fear of John Adams, one often misunderstood, or cynically exploited, as a preference for monarchy.

An elected president chosen by electors (who in turn are chosen by the people) disciplined by the watchful eye of the Supreme Court is the American system. Under it, it's the electoral vote that counts. And Hayes won it — by a hair.

Election Results 1876

Candidates	EV	%	Pop. (000)	Pop. %	Pop. %
Hayes (R)	185	50.1	4,034	48.0	48.5
Tilden (D)	184	49.9	4,289	51.0	51.5
Other	0		90	1.0	
Total	369	100.0	8,413	100.0	100.0

EV = Electoral Vote; Pop. = popular vote

Source: NY Times Almanac 2009, p. 128

This was truly a tight contest between two candidates who had broad appeal across the nation. Hayes, for example, captured New England, but Tilden countered on the East Coast with Maryland, New Jersey and New York. Hayes took Pennsylvania and South Carolina, but Tilden parried with Virginia, West Virginia and North Carolina. And so it went across the nation.[39]

As voters registered their choices it became increasingly apparent that Tilden would win unless Hayes carried three states: Florida, South Carolina and Louisiana. In those days, black voters favored Republicans for obvious reasons and they, Republicans charged, were kept from the polls by intimidating Democratic workers. Corruption was charged. (This situation has a familiar tone to those who agonized over the results of the 2000 election.) Tilden was the popular favorite and he held the electoral lead, but Republicans challenged the vote count in South Carolina, Florida, Louisiana and Oregon, which left the results in dispute.

Ballots were sent to Washington to be counted. This caused disputes over what to count, what to reject and who to count. A compromise was reached by the creation of an electoral commission made up of sixteen men, five each from the House, Senate and Supreme Court, plus Justice David Davis, who was regarded as an independent.[40]

There was additional political jockeying during the procedure, but the ending was clear — Hayes won all contested states and the presidency by one electoral vote.

Contested States[41]

State	Hayes (mil:%)	Tilden (mil:%)
Florida	23.8: 51.0	22.9: 49.0
Louisiana	75.3: 51.6	70.5: 48.4
Oregon	15.2: 50.9	14.2: 47.4
South Carolina	91.8: 50.2	90.9: 49.8

Testimony heard during the vote-counting period revealed corrupt practices on both sides. Votes were traced to dead people; multiple voting was common;

officials manipulated documents; people were paid to vote, etc. Obviously, behind the squeaky-clean candidates, the not-so-clean subordinates tried to fix the election.[42]

The final decision was reached and accepted two days before Hayes was sworn in. The closeness of the election, and the process that decided it, left his political opponents—not all of them Democrats—in a mood more sour than usual. To them, Hayes should have lost the election, and the desire to correct that mishap in the near future was running high. To his credit, Samuel Tilden did not contest the final vote that cost him the presidency. Instead he persuaded enraged followers to accept the verdict and move on, a noble action that saved what could have been a national nightmare of uncertainty.[43]

The Hayes Cabinet

The Hayes cabinet did not contain the names of men of unusual prominence, but he seems to have chosen competent professionals, as follows[44]: **Vice President:** William A. Wheeler, New York; **Secretary of State:** William M. Evarts, New York; **Secretary of Treasury:** John Sherman, Ohio; **Secretary of War:** George W. McGrary, Pennsylvania (1877–89), Alexander Ramsey, Minnesota; **Attorney General:** Charles Devens, Massachusetts; **Secretary of Navy:** Richard W. Thompson, Indiana, (1877–80), Nathan Goff, Jr., Virginia; **Postmaster General:** David M. Key, Tennessee (1877–80), Horace Maynard, Tennessee; **Secretary of Interior:** Carl Schurz, Missouri. A few notes on Hayes' selections are appropriate:

- Appointing Key, a Democrat, to the cabinet caused unrest among Republicans.[45] This was not the first or the last time that an incoming president, as a gesture of unity, invited a political opponent into his cabinet. History labels this a naïve gesture that usually pays negative dividends. "Hire your own people" is an old maxim with eternal validity.
- Sen. Roscoe Conkling, leader of the New York Republican political machine, considered Evarts to be a competitor and resisted his appointment.[46]
- Carl Schurz was disliked by some Republican leaders because in 1872 he left the party to compete for the presidency, a failed attempt but, nevertheless, one that created political enemies.[47]

Except for the appointment of David Key as Postmaster General, Hayes' choices were orthodox—a group of talented, experienced men. But, as noted above, some were controversial, and they weakened support for Hayes within his own party—something he didn't need considering the power his avowed political enemies held in both houses of Congress.

The Hayes Congress

The days of the long-term speaker of the House and Senate leader had not yet arrived — those men who seemed to be in, or just behind, the seat of leadership forever. Since the presidency of John Q. Adams, the office of speaker of the house had changed hands eighteen times before Samuel Randall took charge of the 44th Congress.[48] Randall, a Democrat from Pennsylvania and a highly regarded career politician, remained in that position until Republicans became the majority party in the 47th Congress. The position of senate leader was not created until the 1920s.

Several presidents during the previous five decades had veto-proof power, but the right combination of power and opportunity had not yet arrived. Someday a man with an idea, the money and the power would appear as president and the American system would be put to the test. But there was no sign afoot that Hayes was going to be that man. He had a 52 percent position in the Senate and 46 percent in the House, and his opponent had won more popular votes than he. This meant only one thing — tough sledding, Mr. President.

The Hayes Supreme Court

Chief Justice Morrison R. Waite led the Court assisted by ten associate justices.

Supreme Court Justices, 1877–80

Judge	Began	Appointed by	Ended
Morrison Waite	1874	Grant (R)	1888
Nathan Clifford	1858	Buchanan (D)	1881
Noah Swayne	1862	Lincoln (R)	1881
Samuel Miller	1862	"	1890
David Davis	1862	"	1877
Stephen Field	1863	"	1897
William Strong	1870	Grant	1880
Joseph Bradley	1870	"	1892
Ward Hunt	1873	"	1882
John Harlan	1877	Hayes	1911
William Woods	1881	"	1887

Note: The Constitution does not stipulate the exact size of the Supreme Court. Initially, six was the size. It varied over the years (as high as ten) until the Judiciary Act of 1869 set it at nine, where it has since remained.[49]

Source: Oyez, http://www.oyez.org/

Justices of the Supreme Court, http://www.supremecourtus. gov/about/members.pdf

Men in Black, Mark Levin, 2005, Preface

Note: Nathan Clifford suffered a stroke in 1880 and was incompetent thereafter; Stephen Field was lame, ill and incompetent for at least his last year on the bench.

Chief Justice Waite, a Whig turned Republican, was not President Grant's first choice for the job. Essentially a nonpolitical figure, he was a surprise nominee, one made possible because Grant's first preference turned him down and the next three could not develop support in the U.S. Senate. Waite's views on judicial review served as guideposts for decades. He died in 1888.

It is never safe to assume that judges, once appointed for life, will rule on cases as their sponsors might have ruled. With that caveat, it is safe to say that one would expect few 5–4 rulings from this Court. Presumably, but not certainly, the Republican view of the Constitution would apparently serve as the foundation for most rulings.

A few voter sensitive cases[50] decided in the 1877–80 period are useful to review because in so doing the mood of the passing times becomes clearer:

MUNN V. ILLINOIS, 1877

The facts: The plaintiff owned and operated a grain warehouse and an elevator. Under state law, maximum prices were established for such elevators. The owner claimed that his rights under the Fourteenth Amendment to operate his own property were being violated.

The issue: Does a state have a right to impose maximum prices on a business that has an impact on public interests?

The ruling: The Court ruled that the state had such power when "such regulation becomes necessary for the public good." This important cornerstone ruling, which dealt with conflicting rights, has troubling overtones. Hence, it has been frequently tested.

MUGLER V. KANSAS, 1877

The facts: Kansas law prohibited the manufacture and sale of liquor. Mugler did both, and claimed Fourteenth Amendment protection.

The issue: Does the state have the right to prohibit a citizen from making and selling liquor on his own property?

The ruling: The Court supported state law. The state has the right to exercise its police powers over activities that could affect its citizens; Mugler's rights are conditioned on their impact on others. Cases regarding conflict between the power of the state and the rights of an individual are always important to freedom-loving Americans.

UNITED STATES V. REYNOLDS, 1878[51]:

The facts: The accused, a Mormon, married for a second time because it was his religious duty.

The issue: Does civil law or Mormon law prevail on the issue of marriage?

The ruling: Civil law prevails. The law is not waived because of ignorance of it, or because of the absence of illegal intent, or because of religious belief. The defendant broke the law and should be punished. He was fined $500 and served two years in jail. Some individual Mormons continue to practice polygamy, but the formal religion accepted the above ruling and renounced the practice as a requirement or privilege. The same issue is reappearing in the early twenty-first century, triggered by the growth of the Muslim population (and its adherence to Sharia law) and the growing conflict between Christian belief and U.S. law.

WILKERSON V. UTAH, 1878[52]:

The facts: A legislative act of Utah provided that convicted murderers be shot, hanged or beheaded. The defendant, a convicted murderer, was sentenced to be shot.

The issue: Is the state law constitutional? Is the sentence excessive?

The ruling: The court decision was proper under the circumstances. This was, in effect, an early case that provided a platform for those opposed to capital punishment. Legal protests against execution as a penalty have continued through the decades and are still with us today.

STRAUDER V. W. VIRGINIA, 1880:

The facts: A West Virginia law declared that only whites could serve on a jury.

The issue: Is the state law in violation of the Equal Protection Clause of Amendment XIV?

The ruling: Yes. Associate Justice William Strong (CT), appointed by President Grant, wrote this opinion. To decide otherwise, he said, would be "to put a brand on them affixed by law ... a stimulant to ... racial prejudice" and a barrier to the "equal justice that the law aims to secure." This decision, written after the Civil War, reflected well on the Court that would have to face many future civil rights cases involving blacks.

Civil rights, presidential power, capital punishment and church versus state issues were among those that busied jurists of the time. So what's new?

Domestic Affairs Relative to Political Issues

President Rutherford B. Hayes had four major domestic problems:

• To reestablish the dignity of the Republican brand by running a clean ship and by reforming civil service as possible.

- To maintain good relations with southerners who sought to regain dignity and power in the United States Congress.
- To soothe the ruffled feathers of dissatisfied Republicans who were disappointed in his cabinet choices, chief among whom was Sen. Roscoe Conkling (R-NY).
- To get the dormant economy going.

He made progress with some and failed in others.[53]

THE REPUBLICAN BRAND

A major achievement of Hayes came from his attack on the civil service system, which had been politicized beyond belief and was a source of continuing corruption. His determination to reform the system brought him into direct conflict with his long-time political enemy and the king of New York Republican politics, Sen. Roscoe Conkling.[54]

Chester Arthur (the future president), the chief executive of the New York Customhouse was loyal to Conkling.[55] The customhouse was the largest federal office in the land and collected 70 percent of the nation's revenue. Hayes attacked. Arthur was fired. Theodore Roosevelt, Sr. was in. Conkling responded. He rallied senators to block Roosevelt's appointment. Hayes didn't back off and, during the congressional recess, he appointed Edwin Merritt to replace Arthur. Congress reconvened. Conkling tried to sabotage Merritt during the confirmation process; he failed thanks to support for Hayes from Democrats, who were delighted to help Republicans destroy themselves with internecine warfare.[56]

The restoration of dignity to the Republican brand was directly related to reform of the civil service system. Short-sighted Republicans, like Conkling, resisted this because it disrupted their private fiefdoms. Hayes persisted and prevailed; the political result was good for the party but bad for Hayes.

SOUTHERNERS

Reconstruction was over except for continuing difficulties in South Carolina and Louisiana. Hayes had federal troops there and used them as a bargaining chip: he removed them in return for a promise from Democratic leaders in those states to enforce evenly the civil rights laws. The promise was given; troops were removed. Then the promise was broken. Blacks were kept from the polls, and southern states grouped once more as a solid block within the Democratic Party.[57]

Hayes' even-handed stance on racial matters made him more acceptable to moderates and to southerners. But his support for black rights was more rhetorical than active. His implementation of the Fourteenth and Fifteenth amendments was disappointing. Just as the issue of slavery had not been faced by the Founders and their successors until the Civil War forced a solution (Amendment Thirteen), so also did the next flow of presidents fail to enforce the provisions of Amendments Fourteen and Fifteen until riots in the 1950s and 1960s forced federal action.

One of Hayes' most important accomplishments is overlooked because it can't be measured. Powerful northern forces favored tough policy against the South. By opposing them, Hayes made enemies but, at the same time, he lowered the volume of discontent in the nation.

DISSATISFIED REPUBLICANS

The appointments of Key and Schurz to the cabinet disturbed some Republicans. And most of the major things that Hayes did thereafter disturbed others. Reforming civil service should have been appreciated by all Republicans, but it wasn't. And things went downhill from there. Hayes' southern policy, critics said, was too soft, his leadership on contemporary issues was disappointing. The truth is, Hayes had no political base in 1880.

ECONOMIC GROWTH

The business cycle has no presidential preferences. It comes and goes, indifferent to whoever is in charge. President Grant was in its grip in 1873. Immeasurably assisted by secondary costs of war, it destroyed his position in the House and for two years it also crippled the political fortunes of President Hayes. In 1879, it finally let go.[58]

Gross Domestic Product

Year	GDP (bil)	Change	Debt	Debt/GDP
1876	8.31	1.8	2.13	25.6
1877	8.52	2.5	2.11	24.8
1878	8.38	-1.6	2.16	25.8
1879	9.36	11.7	2.30	24.6
1880	10.40	11.1	2.09	20.1

Source: http://www.usgovernmentspending.com/federal_debt_chart.html

Historical Statistics Colonial Times to 1957, p. 721

The economy was relatively flat until 1879. Debt reduction was modest during the period.

Labor unrest, common around the country, featured the Great Railroad Strike of 1877.[59] Violence ensued in Baltimore, Pittsburgh and Philadelphia. Militias were called out; the Pennsylvania National Guard was deployed; locomotives, railroad cars and buildings were destroyed. Hayes didn't intervene with federal troops. In Pennsylvania, ten activists were hanged; in Chicago, thirty workers were killed.[60] Gradually, settlements were reached and by 1880 things were back to normal. Hayes didn't gain points for leadership during this period.

Long-term bonds were issued to finance the awesome costs of the Civil War, and "greenbacks" were floated (promises to pay without the backing of gold or silver) when that strategy failed to raise enough money. After the war, confidence in the ability of the government to redeem greenbacks at face value waned and their value plunged.[61] Hayes viewed the problem as an issue between honest and dishonest money, and by January 1879 greenbacks had been redeemed with gold coins.

No new states were admitted under Hayes. The total remained at thirty-eight.

IMMIGRATION

Almost 300,000 immigrants a year poured into the United States[62] in search of the freedom promised by the new, growing nation, with most of them coming from Western Europe and Canada. A new group of people had been created in America under the government formed by the Founders—men and women with the blood of many races coursing through their veins united by a common culture grounded in freedom.

Foreign Affairs Relative to Political Issues

Hayes had no serious problems with foreign powers.[63] Those he did have, with Mexico and China, were, in terms of impact, less international than national.

Groups of Mexican outlaws crossed the border. Hayes permitted U.S. troops to chase them back to Mexico, which disturbed Mexican leaders. This tension was reduced when chasing the renegades became a joint project. The irritant continued until the border was, in 1880, once more secure.[64]

Trouble with China essentially was a problem of immigration policy. When expansion demanded laborers to lay track and fill other low-paid jobs, the United States had an open-door policy. But when recession hit, American workers found themselves competing with Chinese workers for a day's pay, and they didn't like it. Pressure intensified to curb immigration (Chinese immigration was suspended for ten years in 1882).[65] (The Chinese problem during this era is remarkably similar to the Mexican labor problem in the early part of the twenty-first century, which is increasingly combustible.) Hayes didn't stop immigration of Chinese, but he did see the need to defuse the situation. The result was a new deal with China—a revision to the Burlingham Treaty,[66] which made regulation more possible.

The first attempt to link the Atlantic and Pacific oceans was mounted by a French diplomat, Ferdinand de Lesseps (builder of the Suez Canal), who proposed an ocean-level route through Panama. It was a private venture — he claimed — that didn't involve the French government and, hence, didn't fall under the Monroe Doctrine as unacceptable behavior by a foreign government.

Hayes opposed the idea and spoke out about it. But he didn't stop de Lesseps from seeking financial backers (at which de Lesseps failed) in the United States, nor did he stop his engineers from starting the project, backed by French money. Fortunately for the United States, the project failed. American engineers had predicted failure from the beginning. Perhaps confidence in the opinion of local experts explains Hayes' relatively weak posture on this issue. Otherwise, as in South Carolina and in the railroad strike, his leadership was not decisive; the absence of a French canal has more to do with de Lesseps' faulty engineering scheme than it does with Hayes' stance on the issue.

Conclusion

Why was the election of 1876 so close? The Grant scandals and the economic woes of the Grant administration were tough burdens for Hayes to carry during the campaign and undoubtedly cost him votes. On the other hand, the pains of Reconstruction besieged southerners and made it difficult for Democratic candidate Samuel Tilden to hold his southern constituency. And a phrase from the Democratic platform[67] deenergized some of his natural supporters: "[W]e do here reaffirm our faith ... in the equality of all citizens before just laws [and] ... in the liberty of individual conduct." To the ears of those who had been steadfastly resisting the implementation of Amendments Fourteen and Fifteen (which protected black rights), these were fighting words that cost Tilden southern votes.

Hayes had negatives to overcome; Tilden, a New Yorker, had to woo a suspicious southern constituency. Both were highly qualified. Out of such a formulation close elections can emerge, and that's what happened in 1876. This was a North versus South presidential election. When Hayes won the contested states in the South the victory was his.

After the close election of 1876, Hayes said he would not seek a second term. He didn't try for one, but there is also ample evidence that his party did not urge him to run.[68] His attacks on the patronage systems cost him too much support, and he slid into the pages of ancient history with friends in the North and some in the South — but not enough together to support a political career.

5

1880: James A. Garfield vs. Winfield S. Hancock

(Electoral Votes 369; Majority 185)

Introduction

The 1880 nomination process was wide open, even on the Republican side. The presumed frontrunner was sitting president Rutherford Hayes, but because he had alienated his natural allies by tampering with their patronage systems he wasn't even considered. He had pledged not to run for a second term, but his wishes were irrelevant. The insiders wanted nothing to do with him — he didn't play ball.

On the Democratic side, Tilden competed well against Hayes in 1876. His electoral vote count missed by a hair, and he actually pulled more popular votes. He should have been a shoo-in for a second shot at the job. The party was willing, but he was not. He was through with presidential politics.

In short, during this period when nobody, it seems, could make up their mind about where the country should go, the two major parties were once again starting from scratch, looking for the leader who would take them somewhere — a dangerous state of affairs.

Conventions

Both parties held conventions at which presidential and vice presidential nominees were chosen, Democrats in Missouri[1] and Republicans in Chicago.

REPUBLICAN CONVENTION

Ordinarily, the sitting president would be the favorite at the Republican convention, but President Hayes was ruled out for reasons previously mentioned.[2] Retired general and former president Grant was the favorite in Chicago, followed by Sen. James Blaine (ME) and secretary of treasury John Sherman. Grant's lead, consistent and formidable for thirty-six ballots, wasn't enough to overcome the unease many felt about breaking with the tradition of two terms per man established by George Washington. Presumably, they were also reluctant to bet the family fortune on the mixed values Grant represented — his personal popularity versus the history of his administration's scandals revisited.

Sen. Conkling and his allies, supporters of Grant, attempted to break the deadlock with a technical maneuver. They failed and the impasse continued. Finally, Blaine and Sherman, to avoid eternal deadlock, threw their support to John Garfield, which vaulted the relatively obscure congressman to a position of national prominence.[3]

Chester Arthur, ousted from his post at the New York Customhouse by Hayes as part of his cleanup of the Civil Service, became the nominee for vice president.[4] The selection of Arthur, a favorite of the New York political machine, was an indication that cronyism was still alive and well in the Republican Party despite Hayes' efforts to diminish its influence. Choosing him was a cruel insult to Hayes and everything he had worked for.

DEMOCRATIC CONVENTION

Democrats felt they should have won the 1876 election and were confident again as they approached the 1880 campaign, for understandable reasons. Hayes had been a relatively weak president because, primarily, he never had congressional support. The Republican Party was quarreling with itself because of disagreements with Hayes and his followers over southern issues, the currency and patronage. It seemed the time for change had arrived, and Democrats would be the beneficiaries of a new national mood.

There was no shortage of candidates at the Democratic Convention,[5] especially because their formidable 1876 candidate, Samuel J. Tilden, was out of the running. Major General Winfield S. Hancock (PA), Sen. Thomas F. Bayard, Sr. (DE), Rep. Henry B. Payne (OH) and Rep. Samuel J. Randall (PA) competed.[6] The field was deep, but the quality of the competition was not dangerous to the winner on the second ballot, Winfield S. Hancock. William H. English (IN) became his running mate.

Republicans campaigned for high protective tariffs—which appealed to the manufacturing sector — moderate Chinese immigration reform, protection of rights for blacks, a strong central government and a continuation of the reform work of civil service by President Hayes (hypocrisy on its face, considering the selection of Arthur as the running mate).[7]

As the "out" party, Democrats reviewed again the "stolen" election of 1876 and the scandals that preceded it. Given Hayes' effective reforms, however, there wasn't much productive gold in just slamming Republicans. So, other issues got more attention in their party platform: tariffs for revenue only, an end to Chinese immigration, the protection of states' rights, sound money backed by gold and silver and continuing civil service reform.[8]

The approach to tariffs was the only major issue where the parties substantially disagreed.

Thumbnail Sketches of Top Candidates

This was a race between a relatively unknown congressman and a military hero. That being the case, the record of past president Rutherford Hayes figured to be the central issue of the campaign, decorated by the personalities of the candidates.

JAMES A. GARFIELD, REPUBLICAN

Born: 1831, Ohio; **Education:** Williams College; **Wife:** Lucretia Randolph; **Children:** Seven (he buried two): **Died:** 1881.[9]

James Abram Garfield was the third child of Eliza and Abram. His father, a physical man who excelled at wrestling, died when he was an infant. Garfield spent his early years helping his mother scratch out a living on the family farm in Ohio. Like his father, he was known as a capable fighter.

Garfield was an outdoorsman who disliked farming. At sixteen he ran away to work on canal boats that operated between Cleveland and Pittsburgh, but sickness ended that adventure and sent him home to recuperate. His brief experience as a canal worker apparently made school more attractive to him than before. He was a late starter, but he prospered intellectually in Ohio institutions and graduated, at twenty-five, from Williams College. Garfield turned to teaching after graduation and soon advanced to become president of one of his earlier schools in Ohio. There he met, courted and wed Lucretia Rudolph. He also studied law on his own and passed the Ohio bar.

Politics captured Garfield's attention while he was still a college student. In 1856, he campaigned for presidential candidate John. C. Frémont, who won 33 percent of the vote running against James Buchanan.[10] Three years later he was in the Ohio legislature. Garfield identified with antislavery Republicans and, in 1860, he was active in Lincoln's successful campaign. He fully supported Lincoln throughout the war and welcomed the opportunity it presented to eliminate slavery once and for all. His fervor in this regard was troubling to some southerners. For example, he once said, "[T]he sin of slavery is one of which it may be said that without the shedding of blood there is no remission."[11]

Garfield was no armchair warrior. True to the genes of his father, he served gallantly during the Civil War, rising to the level of major general. His record as a soldier earned him the support of General Grant during the 1880 Republican convention. Garfield resigned from the Army in 1863 and, without campaigning, won a seat in the House of Representatives. In so doing, he followed the career path of Rutherford B. Hayes.

The next step for Garfield surprised him and everyone else. Grant's decision to seek a third term did not have enough support to bring success, but it was enough to render the opposition ineffective and to create the deadlock at the convention out of which, with the support of the minority candidates, Garfield emerged as the nominee.

WINFIELD S. HANCOCK, DEMOCRAT

Born: 1824, Pennsylvania; **Education:** U.S. Military Academy; **Wife:** Almira Russell; **Children:** Two (he buried both); **Died:** 1886.[12]

Winfield and his twin brother, Hilary, were raised by Benjamin and Elizabeth Hancock in a small town near Philadelphia. He attended local schools until, in 1840, the support of a congressman sent him to West Point. He was an average student.[13]

Hancock, after graduation, was assigned to the infantry as a brevet lieutenant. Originally sent to Indian Territory, he eventually ended up as part of the army led by General Winfield Scott during the Mexican War. His military career was advanced during that conflict, and he became first lieutenant as a reward for meritorious behavior during his various battlefield assignments. He remained in Mexico until the peace treaty of 1848 was signed.[14]

Back in the states, Hancock had various assignments, during the course of which he met and married Almira Russell. Now a captain, he went, with his family, to Fort Myers, Florida, after which he had a variety of assignments of no great consequence until the Civil War.[15] Brigadier General Winfield Hancock served in many battles with great distinction during the Civil War, including Fredericksburg, Chancellorsville and Gettysburg (where he was severely wounded), after which he was honored by Congress for "his gallant, meritorious and conspicuous share in the great and decisive victory." He remained active until war's end, then he returned to the West and Indian affairs. When General Meade died in 1872, Hancock was the army's senior major general, a fact that earned him a transfer to the East, where President Grant gave him the command of the Department of the Atlantic.[16]

Hancock's political ambition was never far from the surface despite his busy military career. While still in uniform, he made an unsuccessful bid for the presidency in 1876 and, stimulated by the success of other military men in politics (Grant and Hayes), he made his second attempt in 1880. This time he made it and would run against another soldier for the big prize.

Given his valiant service during the Civil War, it must have pained Hancock to hear his fellow soldier and former commander, General Grant, refer to him as a puppet of the Democratic leadership with an unquenchable appetite for center stage.[17]

Election Tone

The 1880 election campaign was not one in which a number of issues obviously and passionately separated the political parties. The "stolen" election of 1876 made for good rhetoric on the stump, it kept alive the sense of unresolved justice that invigorated loyal Democrats and there was a real difference on how, what and how much to tax, which actually boiled down into the old fashioned North versus South arguments.

The Supreme Court also stirred the pot in ways that affected the national mood. A review of the cases during the previous administration revealed that prohibitionists were gaining ground; civil law trumps religious law on the issue of marriage (aimed at Mormons, but could go further); the death penalty is constitutional; exclusion from jury duty because of race is unconstitutional. Each one of these issues affected someone's vote, somewhere.

The Grant scandals were ancient history, and the associated issue of civil service reform was, for all practical purposes, neutered by the performance of President Hayes—who had led the charge against the establishment — and by the fact that both parties listed this problem as important to them. Voters of the day could be excused for doubting the sincerity of Republican promises in this respect because most resistance to Hayes' efforts to cleanse the system was led by leaders within his own party, especially the highly influential Sen. Roscoe Conkling (NY).

Other issues helped to fill speeches and justified finger-pointing, but didn't show a wide gap in thinking between political parties. Chinese immigration, hard currency and care of veterans, for example, were matters of mutual concern that were approached and explained differently, but not in a divisive way.

So, although the election would prove to be especially close, it wasn't because of deeply held beliefs over the issues, or because the candidates ripped each other apart, but rather that the country, after Reconstruction, was still separated by bitter memories and frustrated ambitions. The South resented and resisted Amendments Fourteen and Fifteen; the North pushed for compliance and the Hayes administration had not enforced them, so slavery in a different form was still a hot issue. Politicians from the South were eager to protect their power base in the Congress, and those from the North did what they could to diminish it. Tariff wars were examples of this tug-of-war: high protective tariffs favored northern interests, tariffs for income favored only the South.

The candidates themselves were almost irrelevant to the results. Both were presentable; neither was unusually divisive. Garfield hardly campaigned at all, leaving the hard work to men like Roscoe Conkling and Chester Arthur. This strategy was not accidental. Garfield had a skeleton in his closet* that, fortunately for him, did not emerge and destroy him.

*The Credit Mobilier Scandal that tarnished the Grant administration was, among other things, a series of transactions between the company (Credit Mobilier) and certain congressmen that involved

Absent the efforts of Conkling and Arthur, vote-rich New York — and the election — could have gone Democratic. And it also helped that retired general Grant actively campaigned for Garfield and against his former subordinate, General Hancock. The mere fact that he did it took some of the luster away from Hancock's heroic image.

Hancock, for his part, was known for his lenient attitude toward the South, which accommodated his southern strategy (his base). That reputation, plus his stance against protective tariffs, was a problem for him in the North. To win, he had to penetrate it to a degree that seriously weakened Garfield. Who won New York, for example, was a critical question in this election.

Another side issue that affected the tone of the 1880 campaign was the presence of the Greenback-Labor Party's[18] nominee — another war hero— General James B. Weaver. Its concerns, some of them far-reaching, enlivened the debate.

THE WEAVER FACTOR

James B. Weaver headed the Greenback Party.[19] He practiced law in Ohio until the outbreak of the war, at which time he enlisted in 1861 as a private. He rose quickly through the ranks: first lieutenant 1861, major and colonel 1862, brigadier general 1864. After the war, Weaver served in various legal and political posts until, in 1878, he was elected as a Greenback to the U.S. House (1879– 81). He did not run for a second term, preferring instead to make his bid for the presidency. He was nominated by the Greenback-Labor Party.

The National Greenback Party was initially (1876) inspired by the desire to resist hard money and keep "greenbacks" in circulation, an action that would have brought inflation and, with it, the ability to reduce debt with cheap money. As time went on, and hard money took hold, the name of the movement changed to Greenback-Labor Party; its issues broadened to include a progressive income tax, women's suffrage and federal regulation of interstate commerce. It had followers and it was a political force to contend with. After the 1878 election, for example, it held fourteen seats in the House.

This was the beginning of a populist movement that evolved into the progressive movement, the transformative ideology that moved America away from the foundations established by the Founders.

Election Results, 1880

The election between two former soldiers on the heels of a relatively calm presidency was closely contested across the nation. The result in terms of electoral votes, which is all that counts, was decisive: Garfield, 58 percent. But in

the exchange of influence for value (graft). Garfield was one of those allegedly involved. He escaped charges at the time, and the issue did not destroy his career. But acting on the advice of President Hayes and others, he kept a low profile during the campaign.

terms of the popular vote, an indicator of national mood, the difference between the candidates, no matter how measured, was hair-splittingly thin.

Election Results 1880

Candidates	EV	%	(000) Pop.	Pop. %	Pop. %
Garfield	214	58	4,454	48.4	50.1
Hancock	155	42	4,445	48.3	49.9
Weaver			309	3.3	
Total	369	100.0	9,208	100.0	100.0

EV=electoral vote; Pop. = popular vote
Source: NY Times Almanac 2009, p. 128

Garfield won twenty states, chief among them being New York with thirty-five electoral votes and Pennsylvania with twenty-nine. He won New York by two percentage points, Pennsylvania by four points.[20] The win in New York, which essentially made Garfield president, was credited by many to the campaigning on his behalf by Sen. Roscoe Conkling and the vice presidential candidate, Chester A. Arthur, both opponents of civil service reform. Hancock won nineteen states, none of which had more than fifteen electoral votes.[21]

The election of 1880 made a clear statement: The war and Reconstruction were over and slaves were free, but the nation was still culturally and regionally divided.

Garfield (except for New Jersey, which he lost by a fraction) was president of the North. The South solidly backed Hancock. The West was in float. Hancock won California in a tight race; Garfield did the same in Oregon; Nevada was an easy win for Hancock.

This would not be an easy nation to govern.

The Death of Garfield and the Chester A. Arthur Succession

Charles J. Guiteau, thirty-nine, an emotionally disturbed man, was angry at President Garfield because he wasn't appointed to a consulship overseas. He stalked the president for weeks until the perfect opportunity arrived. When the president was exposed during a walk with secretary of state Blaine in the train station in Washington, Guiteau shot him in the back and was immediately apprehended.

Doctors couldn't remove the bullet and blood poisoning followed. Garfield died on September 18, 1881. Vice President Chester A. Arthur succeeded him. Guiteau wrote to Arthur: "Never think of Garfield's removal as murder. It was an act of God." Guiteau was hung on June 30, 1882.

THUMBNAIL SKETCH OF CHESTER A. ARTHUR

Born: 1829, Vermont; **Education:** Union College, law; **Wife:** Ellen Lewis Herndon (she died in 1880); **Children:** Three (he buried one); **Died:** 1886.[22]

Chester Alan Arthur was the fifth of eight siblings born to the Rev. William and Malvina Arthur. His father, a Baptist preacher, was a fervent abolitionist. The family moved to New York, where Arthur attended local schools. He worked his way through Union College in Schenectady as a part-time teacher and graduated in 1843 in the top third of his class.

After college Arthur taught, studied law, passed the bar and in 1854 joined a prominent law firm in New York. At twenty-five, his career was underway. He prospered in his legal career, during the course of which he appeared before the state's superior court and rubbed elbows with many political powerhouses of the day. He also met and married Ellen Herndon. He was thirty, she twenty-two.

Military duty called during the Civil War. Arthur joined the state militia and rose to the rank of brigadier general. As a quartermaster, he was responsible for the care and feeding of hundreds of thousands of soldiers, in the course of which he earned a high reputation as a reliable and capable administrator.

At war's end Arthur returned to his law practice, soon to become a wealthy man dabbling in local politics—a supporter of the New York Republican kingpin, Roscoe Conkling. Soon he became one of Conkling's closest associates, a relationship that paid off when the patronage king eased Arthur's way into the highly paid position of chief counsel to the New York City Tax Commission.

President Grant in 1871 (no doubt with a nudge from Conkling) made Arthur collector of the Port of New York, a position that involved the supervision of more than one thousand agents who collected about three-quarters of the nation's import duties. In that role he tolerated some of the most corrupt practices in the American political system, although he was never charged personally with illegal behavior.

President Hayes, committed to a reform of civil service, directly attacked Conkling's New York political machine, of which Arthur was a premium member. A commission formed by the president found Arthur's organization scandalously overstaffed. With difficulty, because of Conklings's influence, Hayes fired Arthur. Conkling and Arthur were eager to regain control of the port, and with that in mind and Hayes out of the way they supported Grant's bid for a third term. Now, with Garfield dead and Arthur in office, they had more than they had ever dreamed of.

The Garfield/Arthur Cabinet

Members of the Garfield/Arthur cabinet were as follows[23]: **Secretary of State:** James G. Blaine, Pennsylvania/Maine (1881), Frederick T. Frelinghuysen, New Jersey; **Secretary of War:** Robert T. Lincoln, Illinois; **Secretary of Treasury:** William Windom, Ohio/Minnesota (1881), Charles J. Folger, Massachusetts/

New York (1881–84), Walter Q. Gresham, (1884, see "Postmaster General," below), Hugh McCulloch, Maine/Indiana; **Secretary of Interior:** Samuel J. Kirkwood, Ohio/Iowa (1881–82), Henry M. Teller, New York/Illinois/Colorado; **Secretary of Navy:** William H. Hunt, South Carolina/Connecticut/Louisiana (1881–82), William E. Chandler, New Hampshire; **Attorney General:** Isaac W. MacVeagh, Pennsylvania (1881), Benjamin H. Brewster, Pennsylvania; **Postmaster General:** Thomas L. James, New York (1881), Timothy O. Howe, Maine/Wisconsin (1881–83), Walter Q. Gresham, Indiana (1883–84), Frank Hatton, Ohio/Iowa (1884–85). The overall impression one gets from this isolated review is confusion. There was some of that. But mostly the head count was large because Garfield was killed and Arthur wanted his own team, an understandable and sensible decision.

The Garfield/Arthur Congress

The 1880 election for the presidency was as tight as it gets, but Garfield had surprisingly strong coattails. Republicans in the House moved into marginal control; in the Senate, their minority position improved. Midterm elections changed the momentary return to respectability in the Congress for the Grand Old Party (GOP) in the House, but the party marginally increased its position in the Senate to a level far from veto proof but sufficient to control the agenda

Pro-Administration Congressional Power

Congress	Year	President	House %	Senate %
46	1879	Hayes (R)	45	43
47	1881	Garfield/Arthur (R)	52	49
48	1883	Arthur (R)	36	50

Source: Appendices 1.1, 1.2

J. Warren Keifer (R-OH)[24] led the House for the first two years of the Garfield/Arthur presidency. He was a lawyer and Civil War veteran (he resigned as a brigadier general) who was first elected to the House in 1877 and quickly rose to a position of prominence. He, among others, got caught up in the popularity reversal of 1884 and lost his seat. He finished his life in prominent positions in and out of Washington before he died (1932), including another tour of duty in the House (1905–11).

John G. Carlisle (D-KY)[25] began his six-year run as speaker of the House when the midterm election turned power back to Democrats. A lawyer with a busy background in state politics, Carlisle began a long career on the national scene in 1876 that included service in the House (1877–90), Senate (1890–93) and as secretary of the treasury under Grover Cleveland (1893–97). He died in 1910.

The Garfield/Arthur Supreme Court

Morrison Waite, chief justice of the U.S. Supreme Court when Garfield took office in 1881, was still ruling in 1884. Associate justices who served with him appear in the chart below:

Supreme Court Justices, 1881–84

Judge	Began	Appointed by	Ended
Morrison Waite (CT)	1874	Grant (R)	1888
Nathan Clifford (NH)	1858	Buchanan (D)	1881
Noah Swayne (OH)	1862	Lincoln (R)	1881
Samuel Miller (KY)	1862	"	1890
Stephen Field (CT)	1863	"	1897
William Strong (PA)	1870	Grant	1880
Joseph Bradley (NY)	1870	"	1892
Ward Hunt (NY)	1873	"	1882
John Harlan (KY)	1877	Hayes	1911
William Woods (OH)	1881	"	1887
Stanley Matthews (OH)	1881	Garfield	1889
Horace Gray (MA)	1882	Arthur	1902
Samuel Blatchford (NY)	1882	Arthur	1893

Source: Oyez, http://www.oyez.org/

Justices of the Supreme Court, http://www.supremecourtus.gov/about/members.pdf

Men in Black, Mark Levin, 2005, Regnery, D.C., pp. 3–4

Note: Nathan Clifford suffered a stroke in 1880 and was incompetent thereafter; Stephen Field was lame, ill and incompetent for at least his last year on the bench.

Garfield and Arthur appointed three new associates, replacing in the process the only remaining Democratic appointee, Nathan Clifford, an unusual number for a four-year presidency. When Arthur left office, the Court was solidly Republican.

A review of a few cases reveals the concerns and the mindset of the day.[26]

THE CIVIL RIGHTS CASES, 1883

The facts: The Civil Rights Act of 1875 provided, among other things, that hotel accommodations were to be made equally available to all persons. In five cases, black people were denied equal accommodations in privately owned facilities—a violation of the act.

The issue: Facts were not denied. Defense argued that the act had no jurisdiction over private affairs; it was an unconstitutional interference with individual rights.

The ruling: The Court agreed. The Constitution (Amendment XIV) limits Congress to deal with state, not personal, issues. The national government cannot correct private acts of discrimination. It is decisions like this that kept

blacks subdued after the Civil War, a perfect example of how legislative decisions and the culture cannot be separated; one influences the other. Five judges
(a majority) acting in concert can and do change the face of America.

UNITED STATES V. HARRIS, 1883

The facts: Harris and a lynch mob he led attacked a jail and released four
black prisoners. One prisoner died in the scuffle. The U.S. government brought
criminal charges against Harris under the Force Act of 1871, which provided
that it was a crime for two or more persons to conspire for the purpose of
depriving another of equal rights.

The issue: Is the act constitutional? Can it serve as the legal basis for
charges against the defendant?

The ruling: No. The national government has no jurisdiction over private
acts of discrimination. The Force Act is unconstitutional.

(Since it was the law of the land that discrimination against blacks must
stop, rulings like this indicated that either the Court was racially biased or it
was intellectually honest and bound by civil rights laws too vague to be effective,
laws that Congress was too divided to strengthen. Given that choice, one tends
to side with the judges. All were from the North or the West, areas where anti-
slavery/pro-freedom attitudes flourished. Congress, on the other hand, still had
a strong Democratic presence, a sure sign in those days that anti-black attitudes
were still alive and well. Just as Court decisions and personal behavior are
linked, a decision like this demonstrates how Court decisions can be linked to
congressional action or inaction and civilian unrest.)

HURTADO V. CALIFORNIA, 1884

The facts: Hurtado, never indicted for anything, went straight to trial,
based on written information, and was convicted of murder.

The issue: Were Hurtado's rights under Amendment XIV violated because
the state skipped the indictment procedure before a grand jury?

The ruling: No. Any legal process, including this one, which protects liberty and justice satisfies the demands of the subject amendment.

The civil rights cases were an early indication of how litigation by blacks
lifted the general awareness of the public to the importance of the issue and
helped to create the maelstrom of cases that progressively descended on the
Court during the next century. The Civil War ended in 1865. But more than
twenty years later the freedom of blacks, especially in the South, was still being
suppressed. And just as the existence of slavery inevitably led to the Civil War,
so also did the denial of rights earned and granted to blacks predict the civil
rights struggle that grew to momentous size in the next century. Justice denied
eventually brings huge penalties, a lesson America's politicians and judges were
to learn the hard way.

Domestic Affairs Relative to Political Issues

Civil service reform, tariffs, sound money and immigration policy were four immediate problems on President Garfield's agenda[27]; but since he died in September 1881, it was President Arthur who tackled hem. And political insiders had a dual reaction to his unexpected promotion. Would Arthur operate independently? Would he operate as Sen. Conkling's old friend?

CIVIL SERVICE REFORM

Conkling and his followers, who were never positive about how President Garfield would handle civil service reform and were somewhat disturbed by his comments on the subject during his inauguration speech, relaxed when Chester Arthur was sworn in. One of their own was in charge.

But would Arthur act as Conkling's man and protect the old-boy patronage system that bred corruption, or would he act as his own man and continue the good work of President Hayes? Would he make them proud Republicans, or apologetic ones? Questions about Arthur's integrity were realistic because of his past history as a loyal and leading member of Conkling's New York political machine. Would he defer to it, or would he be his own man?

Arthur danced to an in-between position. He signed the Pendleton Civil Service Reform Act of 1883,[28] which established examinations as the basis for promotion or appointment. On the other hand, the reform system he approved applied only to new employees; incumbents were protected. Pro-reformists, pleased about the establishment of examinations, were somewhat displeased because the program was prospective rather than retrospective. Antireform-ists—Conkling's supporters—were displeased because examinations would take the place of political influence (patronage), but they were somewhat mollified by the fact that their friends in existing positions would not be disturbed.

The immediate impact of the act was minimal, but over the long term the system was gradually cleansed of dead wood. This ended the first reform movement of President Hayes, the maverick who began it at the expense of personal popularity within the party. Since he lived until 1893, he shared in the celebration of those who had struggled with him to cleanse the corrupt system.

The Pendleton Act is the legislative memorial to Arthur's efforts. The administrative effect of it — over time — was to kill the spoils system[29]; the polit-ical effect was to make for Arthur implacable enemies in his own party. He and Hayes learned a hard lesson: Compassion and political durability do not always live peacefully together.

TARIFFS

Arthur, as a show of concern for southern issues, appointed a commission to examine the status of tariffs. This is the time-honored way for presidents to get progress on touchy issues. Arthur sought justification for lowering tariffs in a form that wouldn't devastate him politically. He could take credit if recommendations worked, or deny blame if they didn't.

The commission suggested cuts of more than 20 percent. Arthur couldn't sell those cuts to Congress, which finally passed legislation in 1883 that dropped tariffs on selected products by less than 2 percent. Congress then, as today, was reluctant to lower revenues.

Sound Money

Arthur continued to support the sound money policies of President Hayes. But the protection of the dollar involves more than that. For a president it means budget and debt control.

The federal surplus, despite a flagging domestic economy, continued and Arthur rebelled against the congressional solution for it — pork barrel spending. A prime example of this was the Rivers and Harbors Act of 1882. Arthur personally spoke out against this bill in a letter to the House of Representatives.[30] He vetoed it, but his veto was overridden and the bill passed. This was a vivid example of Arthur's weakness in the Senate.

Economic Growth

Hayes left a healthy economy behind and it continued to thrive for the first year of the Garfield/Arthur administration. Then it leveled off for three years before the business cycle struck again in the 1884 election year, normally bad news for the party in power.

Gross Domestic Product

Year	GDP (bil)	Change	Debt	Debt/GDP
1880	10.4	11.1	2.0	19.2
1881	11.6	11.5	2.0	17.2
1882	12.2	5.2	1.9	15.6
1883	12.3	.1	1.7	13.8
1884	11.8	-4.1	1.6	13.6

Source: http://www.usgovernmentspending.com/federal_ debt_chart.html

Historical Statistics Colonial Times to 1957, p. 721

The Civil War had brought with it a new air of relevancy to national debt. Prior to Lincoln, it was not normally a major concern. But during the war it rose rapidly and remained at relatively high levels thereafter. Chief executives as always had the problem of controlling and minimizing it, but the scale of responsibility was higher.

Garfield and Arthur governed during a period of a relatively stagnant economy, but related problems were not severe enough to cause federal deficits. As a consequence, debt resumed the downward course that began after the Civil War. The United States was in excellent debt position in 1884, which would make it possible for the next president to marshal the full borrowing power of the federal government to meet the next emergency, which, like rainfall, never fails to arrive.

The object lesson that earlier presidents (those closest to the Constitution) left behind relative to budget management was this: Borrow only for emergencies and repay loans when normal times reappear and protect borrowing power for future presidents to use. This rule of thumb was generally observed until the mid–twentieth century.

It is important to remember how early presidents protected the borrowing power of the nation. National emergencies often require borrowing. It is for that reason that debt levels were carefully monitored by these men — one never knew when the need for borrowing would appear. By implication, early presidents considered it to be responsive to the oath of office when they protected in this way one of the nation's most priceless assets: its credit reputation and, by indirection, the value of its currency.

Considering the uneven economic weather during his administration, Arthur did well as a money manager. The economy compared to 1880 had improved, but, on the other hand, a slow growing or sluggish GDP is not good news for any president.

Many voters blame the man in charge for bad times, and applaud him when things go well, deserved or not; it is inexcusable for well-informed media to do the same. Economic and international events, good and bad, come and go with the tides and answerable to no man. The consequences of them should never be simplistically reduced to who is in charge. Instead, the issue should be: Did the president address the crisis in a timely, aggressive and effective manner? If the president is innocent of cause and if he acted effectively to handle the situation, he should be held blameless if the results are negative; beyond that, he should be applauded for his cool-headed management ability. The same logic applies to positive results— no rewards unless his actions can be traced to effects.

The media owes this reasoning process to the public; and it seldom gets it because they are often as biased as politicians. In Arthur's case, the economy was still feeling the aftereffects of the Civil War and would not show vibrancy until the slave-free southern states once again learned how to be prosperous.

IMMIGRATION POLICY

Arthur had better luck with immigration than he did with tariffs. He protested when the Chinese Exclusion Act was proposed, arguing on behalf of the Chinese. The proposed twenty-year immigration ban was lowered to ten years, and he approved it. The pace of immigration increased during the 1880s as it had in previous decades. In 1890, total population was about 63 million,[31] 15 percent foreign born, mostly from Europe.[32]

FATHER OF THE STEEL NAVY

Rebuilding the U.S. Navy was not a campaign issue, but it was one that Arthur took up with gusto. The modernization of the navy was a primary project for him to such an extent that he is remembered as the "Father of the Steel Navy." He energetically sought steam-powered steel cruisers and other steel protected naval vessels. He also established the Naval War College and the Office of Naval Intelligence. John Adams would have approved.

Arthur obviously belonged to the school of presidents who believed that peace through strength is the sensible course. He modernized the most crucial element of national defense in those days, the navy, at a time when no war threatened the United States, a decision destined to benefit a future president.

NEW STATES, 1881–84

No new states joined the Union under Garfield or Arthur. The administration began and ended with thirty-eight states.[33] But the West was burgeoning with activity. The Wild West, with its shoot-'em-up cowboys and Indians, was morphing into settled communities and peace-loving ranchers who would soon make their bid for statehood.

Foreign Affairs Relative to Political Issues

Every president has his international problems, including the expected and the unexpected. Garfield and Arthur had their share.[34]

WAR AND PEACE

The United States was generally at peace with the world, and Arthur had no opportunities to prove himself as an international leader. His foreign policy reputation is mostly related to treaties made during his administration.

ATLANTIC TO PACIFIC CANAL

Arthur, like presidents before him, was interested in constructing a waterway that would link the Atlantic and the Pacific, the existence of which would obviate the need for the long ocean journey from East Coast to West Coast. With this in mind, a treaty was negotiated with Nicaragua that ceded to the United States a crucial stretch of territory.[35] Congress refused to ratify it, fearing that to do so would reawaken the slumbering acquisitive instincts of Britain, with whom the United States had a treaty that forbade a cross-country canal exclusively controlled by either nation.

Arthur had better luck with reciprocal trade agreements with Mexico, Spain and Santo Domingo, but his success bought him political enemies who represented American business interests concerned about foreign competition, men who would stand against him if he made a serious bid for a second term.

Conclusion

Why was the election of 1880 so close? First, it is important to note that the election was not close in the most meaningful sense as the electoral vote margin was significant. The reason for the close popular vote is captured in a single word: Disunity!

The Civil War and Reconstruction left a scar on the South that had not yet healed. And the time for healing was pressed further into the future by the reluctance of postwar presidents to support with all necessary power Amendments Fourteen and Fifteen of the Constitution. As a consequence, southern states reassembled as a political group opposed to integration. And they pursued with vigor the political power that would enable them to protect what was left of their lifestyle. Sectionalism, not party, was in 1880 the dividing line. And those who sought to win a national election had to be sensitive to that. The nation was no more united at the end of Arthur's term than it was in the beginning. His years in office were an indicator of the difficulty that any new president would face when he tried to govern. That is the significance of the close popular vote.

Otherwise, the 1880 election was an easy win for Republicans despite the fact that the party was devouring itself with internal competition. The comfortable electoral vote margin is simply explained: Free America (Garfield) had more electoral votes than Slave America (Hancock). Garfield took the North, plus Oregon; Hancock took the South, California, Nevada, plus (the only surprise) New Jersey.

Garfield's popularity was sectional, not personal. Arguably, any respectable Republican candidate would have done as well; any respectable Democratic candidate would have drawn equivalent support. And this would continue to be the case until the slavery issue was, in fact, resolved.

6

1884: Grover Cleveland vs. James G. Blaine

(Electoral Votes 401; Majority 201)

Introduction

Political stability was in the air until the scandals of the Grant administration (1869–76) once again caused the American people to lose faith in the
federal government. This was reflected in close elections, one after the other,
as voters looked for the man in whom they could place their trust. And this
election didn't help them much. In terms of personal attacks, it was one of the
worst.

Conventions

Arthur, like Hayes, had protected Republicans from themselves, but at a
cost that rendered him obsolete in the political world. He was nominated in
the 1884 election but didn't campaign and he withdrew after the fourth ballot
to swing his support to James Blaine. (Arthur died in 1886 of Bright's disease.)
Presidential and vice presidential candidates in 1884 were chosen at the
now firmly established national conventions of both parties.

REPUBLICAN CONVENTION

Republicans, the party in power, met in Chicago during the first week in
June.[1] President Arthur, a courtesy nominee, had several strikes against him.[2]
First, he became ill in 1882 and was diagnosed with Bright's disease. The public
was unaware of this, but insiders knew it and were concerned about his physical
ability to handle the job. Second, he made little effort to get the nomination,
which discouraged supporters. And third, the still powerful Sen. Conkling (NY)
opposed him because he went too far with civil service reform. Arthur allowed
his name to be put into nomination, but his supporters soon left him in favor

of the only significant challenger, James G. Blaine, who had a deep political background in the House and Senate. Sen. John A. Logan (IL) was chosen as his running mate.

The party platform advocated control of railroads, an eight-hour workday, the creation of a bureau of labor, and three other issues that carried over from election to election: Chinese immigration control, civil service reform and the granddaddy of them all, tariffs. Republicans preferred high protective tariffs, arguing that they protected American industry and jobs.

The Republican platform did not address the faltering economy. This is quite understandable. Why draw attention to a weakness? The great recession of 1873–79[3] took place under two Republican presidents, Grant and Hayes, and the economy under the most recent Republican, President Arthur, was relatively stagnant. This was a wide open hole in the Republican profile and Republicans knew it.

But they felt good about their nominee. He was a popular, talented man and it was believed he had a positive reputation with immigrants and Catholics, which if true meant he could pull votes from constituencies that ordinarily were typical Democratic strongholds. On the downside, when the party left the convention there was a serious division within it. Mugwumps, a group of reform-minded Republicans,[4] were not satisfied that the source of scandals that smirched the party brand under Grant had been rooted out. And they had not yet accepted Blaine, who they continued to identify with the corruption of that period as the man needed to clean things up. Republicans hoped party loyalty and agreement on other issues would keep Mugwumps loyal.

Before leaving the topic of Republican convention, it is appropriate to elaborate on the career of a man whose name keeps popping up in these close elections, Sen. Roscoe Conkling. Conkling[5] was born in 1829 into a political family in Albany, New York—his father was a Whig. Men like John Quincy Adams and Martin Van Buren were frequent houseguests. An unusually bright man, Conkling studied law and was at twenty-one Albany's district attorney. His political career was underway.

The Republican Party in New York was founded in 1854 with Conkling's help. Four years later, at forty-one, he was mayor of Utica. Next for him was the House of Representatives (1859), where he was known as a Lincoln supporter. From the beginning, he was antislavery; he wanted to take land from slave owners and give it to slaves.

State legislatures elected U.S. Senators in those days, and Conkling was chosen in 1867. He immediately became a firm supporter of U.S. Grant, and with Grant's help became a political powerhouse in his own state where he dominated the patronage system. And he used both of those positions to establish opposition factions to Presidents Hayes, Garfield and Arthur. It can be reasonably said that he was the eternal bee in the bonnets of Presidents Hayes and Arthur.

He ran against Hayes for the nomination of 1876, refused to campaign for him when he lost and haunted him with opposition while Hayes was president. He supported Grant over Garfield in the 1880 convention, opposed President Arthur (Garfield's successor) as a turncoat who tried to ruin his patronage system, and stood against Arthur during the convention of 1884. Finally, Conkling may have been equally destructive to the career ambitions of James G. Blaine. He campaigned against him during the 1880 convention. And during the 1884 election, Blaine, the Republican nominee, lost New York (48.25 versus 48.15 percent). Blaine had other problems in that state but a tempting question remains: Had Conkling been a friend rather than an enemy, would the results have been the same?

So why did Conkling have so much power over presidents and nominations? Answer: Mathematics! New York represented thirty-six electoral votes. Only Pennsylvania came close in terms of election influence (thirty votes). And no enemy of Conkling's was likely to carry New York, which at that time was a battleground state. Conkling left the Senate in 1881 and was not thereafter as influential. He died in 1888.

DEMOCRATIC CONVENTION

Democrats also met in Chicago during the first week in July.[6] The field was wide open: Grover Cleveland (NY), Thomas F. Bayard (DE) and Allan G. Thurman (OH). Thomas A. Hendricks (OH) was the uncontested vice presidential candidate. The drama in this convention centered on a technicality: Would the unit rule prevail, under which all electoral votes of a state went to the candidate who got the biggest vote in the state?

Just as the Republican Party had its kingmaker, Roscoe Conkling, so also did the Democratic Party have Tammany Hall, a political action group that in 1798 had been organized into the political force that won New York for the 1800 Jefferson-Burr ticket. It continued to be a potent force in New York City, most famously under Boss Tweed, until he was sent to jail in 1873. But the organization was a powerhouse again in the 1880s, and it didn't want to see its reform-minded governor, Cleveland, as the nominee of the Democratic Party.*

With that end in view, Tammany Hall lobbied the convention against the unit rule, preferring that each vote of each delegate for each candidate be counted as such. Once the vote was cast against their proposal, the result was as anticlimactic as it was inevitable. Cleveland, the reformer, secured the nomination on the second ballot. Sen. Thomas A. Hendricks (IN) was chosen as his running mate.

The Democratic Party platform contained the usual charges against the party in power, and it emphasized the need for immigration control of Chinese

---

Samuel J. Tilden, Democratic nominee in 1876, was instrumental in bringing Boss Tweed down.

people and underlined its support for organized labor. But to the extent that issues divided the parties, tariff policy headed the list by a wide margin, as it had for some time. But this time there was a difference with Democrats. Perhaps influenced by Greenback Party campaigns of the past, Democrats were now thinking more progressively about taxes—they wanted to tax luxury goods, more than other goods, which applied tax policy to only some classifications of citizens.*

Democrats too felt comfortable with their squeaky-clean candidate, Governor Grover Cleveland. He had escaped his controversial actions during the Civil War[7] and was currently known as New York's reform mayor/governor who got things done. The mood of the party when they left Chicago was impatience. They had lost the two previous elections by a whisker, and they didn't intend to lose another.

Thumbnail Sketches of Top Candidates

JAMES G. BLAINE, REPUBLICAN

Born: 1830, Pennsylvania; **Education:** Washington College, PA, law; **Wife:** Harriet Stonewood; **Children:** Seven; **Died:** 1893.[8]

Blaine taught in Kentucky's Military Institute after graduation from college, and in the Institution for the Blind in Philadelphia. He also studied law and eventually settled down in Bangor, Maine. There he put his literary gifts to work and soon became editor of two prominent newspapers in that state.

For Blaine, journalism was a bypath to his real career, politics. He was elected to the state legislature, served as speaker for two years and, in 1859, assumed leadership of the state's Republican Party. The House of Representatives in 1862 was the next step for Blaine where, in 1869, he became Speaker for three terms before moving to the U.S. Senate, where he spent four more years (1877–81).

Potomac fever first claimed Blaine in 1876. He was the favorite of the party, but the nomination eventually went to Rutherford Hayes because Blaine's name was associated with one of President Grant's railroad scandals. He was charged with nothing, but the perception of his record was not pure enough for Republicans who were trying to disassociate themselves from the Grant scandals. Such was his popularity that Blaine, despite the allegations, missed the nomination by only twenty-eight votes.

Blaine was back in the presidential race in 1880, this time competing with

*The Constitution was written to serve as the legal basis for governing "we the People." No special rights for or against groups or classifications were provided.

the forces of General Grant, who was seeking a third term. Had Grant been more temperate in his ambitions, Blaine would have been an easy winner. But Grant was Grant, and the convention locked because his popularity, not powerful enough to bring him victory, was nevertheless strong enough to ruin the chances of the other candidates. Facing reality, Blaine joined others and, together, they nominated John Garfield. It was during these political skirmishes that Blaine made an enemy out of Sen. Roscoe Conkling, a Grant supporter.

Garfield made Blaine his secretary of state, but Garfield's early death and the succession of Chester Arthur cut short Blaine's service in the position. Arthur preferred his own man, Frederick Frelinghuysen. Blaine's ambitions were undiminished, and in 1884 he was back at the well. It was his time — he won the nomination on the fourth ballot, despite spirited opposition from Conkling.

The campaign, which he lost, was bitter, and at its end, Blaine's presidential ambitions had cooled. But he remained active and became secretary of state for the winner of that contest, Benjamin Harrison. The bug hit him again in 1892 and he competed with Harrison for the nomination, and lost.[9] Blaine found time to demonstrate his literary gifts in the form of a book, *Twenty Years of Congress*, a brilliant historical work in two volumes.*

STEPHEN GROVER CLEVELAND, DEMOCRAT

Born: 1837, New Jersey; **Education:** No college; passed the bar in 1858; **Wife:** Frances Folsom; **Children:** Five (he buried the oldest); **Died:** 1908.[10]

Cleveland's father, a poor preacher, died when Cleveland was sixteen, which put him to work and made a college education impossible. While working with an older brother in New York City, he studied law and, at twenty-two, became a lawyer. He avoided military service during the Civil War by hiring a man to substitute for him, while he served as an assistant district attorney for Erie County.

Cleveland was a man's man, and a big one. "Big Steve," as poker-playing friends called him, kept busy practicing law; he dabbled in local politics, but remained removed from partisan squabbles. It surprised him as much as anyone when Democrats chose him to run for mayor of Buffalo. A relative unknown, he won. As mayor, Cleveland earned the reputation of Mr. Clean. He attacked corruption, and set an example for all city workers of hard work and long hours. The payoff? Political leaders liked what they saw, and ran him as their candidate

---

*The Notable Names Database (*NNDB*) contains a final paragraph worth quoting exactly: "Of singularly alert faculties, with a remarkable knowledge of the men and history of his country, and an extraordinary memory, his masterful talent for politics and statecraft, together with his captivating manner and engaging personality, gave him, for nearly two decades, an unrivalled hold upon the fealty and affection of his party." One cannot escape the feeling that America was deprived of a great leader when this talented man failed to break through the political system to reach the highest position of all, president of the United States of America.*

in the next gubernatorial race. He won! And it was from that position of power that he became a candidate for the presidency in 1884.

This was a quick rise for Cleveland—from mayor to presidential candidate in a political heartbeat. And there was another difference. "Big Steve" had morphed into "Uncle Jumbo." His weight, almost 300 pounds, had grown with his reputation.

Election Tone

Tariffs and corruption in government were the principal issues of debate in the 1884 campaign. The lagging economy should have been but, for some reason, Democrats didn't forcefully press it. Ultimately, personal attacks, not issues, decided the campaign. He who withstood the insults and the revelations best would survive.

TARIFFS

Tariffs were in fact a metaphor for how government should work, an argument that goes back to Adams versus Jefferson and one that continues today under a different label.

The question of how a government will work—its style—is answered to a considerable degree by its tax policy, because that, plus regulations imposed, are indicators of the degree of respect a government has for the rights of states and individuals versus those of the federal government. How to tax (tariffs, income, property) and the purpose of a tax (raise revenue or control behavior) are emotional issues that properly stoked can flame brightly throughout a campaign. Republicans, in those days, were the party of big government; Democrats argued for more state and personal control. Today, the argument is the same, but the roles have been reversed.

So it was natural that high, protective tariffs, favored by Republicans, versus progressive ones, favored by Democrats, became debating topics of consequence. But technical issues of this sort demand a long attention span from voters, something as rare in those days as it is in modern America. There had to be more to sustain voter attention.

CORRUPTION

Corruption has always been a campaign issue and always will be. Washington, the center of American power, the controller of billions of taxpayer dollars, is bound to attract adventurers with an erratic moral compass. Such was the case during this time period.

Republicans, since Grant, had an estimable record of progress. So the corruption issue morphed into a different form. Instead of being a fight between opposing parties, it became a wrangle within the party. There was a group within the party known as Mugwump reformers who were not satisfied with the pace of reform under Republican presidents, and they considered Blaine to be a part of the problem.[11] Part of Blaine's campaign strategy was to impose party loyalty on the Mugwumps—he needed their vote. He failed and Mugwumps bolted and supported Cleveland.

Serious issues like tariffs and immigration policy separated the parties, but that isn't what the 1884 election was about. The primary subject matter was the candidates themselves. Who was fit for leadership? It was Blaine versus Cleveland. And the punches thrown in this contest were heavy indeed.

CLEVELAND CAMPAIGN

Democrats had not held the presidency since James Buchanan left office in 1861, so they carried none of the burden of scandals that took place under Grant. And if they presented to voters a simon-pure candidate, the corruption debate would be entirely in their favor. They thought they did this when they nominated Grover Cleveland. True, he was known as a man's man who was no stranger to a glass or to a hand of poker with his male friends. But these mild unorthodoxies won him as many friends as enemies and were considered controllable nonissues when compared with his record as a reform mayor and as the governor who had the stomach to attack Tammany Hall, the corrupt political power base in New York City. But Democrats were not prepared for the revelations about the dark side of Cleveland's private life, which ultimately became a huge campaign issue. Just exactly who was this man from New York? And could a man with his background be trusted with the presidency?

Criticism of Cleveland was immeasurably enhanced when the shady aspects of his private life were uncovered. One incident serves as a model that embraces the essence of most charges against him. The *Wheeling (WV) Register* issue of August 8, 1884, sums up the scandal comprehensively:

- Grover Cleveland had interludes with various women, but they were always out of view of the public, until his latest partner, Maria Halpin, sued him and made public their relationship.
- Ms. Halpin was a woman of experience — this was not a case of seduction and false promises.
- She became pregnant and named Cleveland the father. He made provisions for the mother and child.
- Ms. Halpin was a drinker and a neglectful mother. She ended up in an asylum for a short while; the child went to an orphanage.
- When Ms. Halpin was released, Cleveland established her in a business in Niagara. She visited the child and finally abducted him.

- Ms. Halpin sued Cleveland. The case was settled by agreement. She gave up the boy in return for cash; the boy was adopted by a fine family and he knew nothing of his parentage.
- Reliable witnesses debunked the charge that Cleveland was a drunk, claiming he enjoyed a drink but did not overindulge.

Other newspapers chimed in, some chiding him and some defending him: In the *Boston Globe* of August 12, 1884, this statement appeared: "The charge that he has recently taken part in a drunken and licentious debauch in Buffalo ... is entirely false." And the hardnosed humor followed. "Ma! Ma! Where's my Pa?" his tormentors chanted.[12]

To his credit, Cleveland admitted to the truth of the sexual charges against him, and he ordered his campaign staff to do the same. An admission of wrongdoing plus a contrite attitude, he hoped, would be the best answer to attacks against him.[13] As good as these charges of high living were for Republicans, their ability to smear Cleveland was immeasurably enhanced when those charges were married to his qualifications to serve as president.

The question of Cleveland's experience was a legitimate one. As his short biography demonstrates, he was a pound light and a dollar short in that department. Few candidates for the presidency have had less experience than Grover Cleveland: sheriff, Utica, New York, 1871–73; mayor of Buffalo, 1882; governor of New York, 1883–84. For good reason, the nation's newspapers commented on this:

- *New Hampshire Sentinel*, July 16, 1884: "Grover Cleveland, a man not qualified to be president, and himself an extreme Independent though a Democrat in name ... a man independent of party obligations."
- *Duluth Tribune*, July 18, 1884: "Grover Cleveland ... has no national stamp. He is devoid of experience or ability, utterly lacking in that rich store of knowledge gained only by long years of ... experience in national questions ... no more qualified for the high office of president than for the high throne of a god."

Republicans hoped by battering Cleveland, with his sins and his inexperience, the weaknesses in Blaine would be overlooked, and Blaine's strengths would attract voters who were repelled by Cleveland's alleged debaucheries or were turned off by his resume. They pounced on both of these aspects of his background in an effort to prove that Cleveland was not morally or professionally worthy of being the president of the United States.

JAMES G. BLAINE CAMPAIGN

Perhaps Cleveland's campaign staff obeyed him about being candid about his misdeeds, but the old-fashioned idea of getting even might have crossed their minds. For starters, they knew that Republicans had turned away Blaine's two previous bids for the presidency for reasons that could be used against him in 1884. The most important and effective counterattacks against Blaine covered three areas of his background: His years during the Grant presidency as Speaker of the House; his courage; his alleged anti–Catholicism.

Blaine was a member of the U.S. House from 1863 to 1876 and he was the Speaker during most of Grant's presidency. This, as such, made him vulnerable to charges of corruption — he was a major figure during a tainted administration. But there was more. Opponents charged him with personal corruption because of his alleged favoritism toward certain railroads.[14] Blaine cleared himself in the House and to the satisfaction of many, but not to all.

Normally, Democrats couldn't make a decisive case against the Republican Party on the reform issue because, after the Grant scandals, Presidents Hayes, Garfield and Arthur had a fair record in this respect. But Blaine himself was a political gift that never stopped giving. Through him, the Grant scandals could be relived and the threat of new ones under such a man could be presented to voters as a realistic and frightening possibility. Newspapers picked up on that theme:

- *New York Times*, October 4, 1884: "The election of James G. Blaine would be a direct appeal to every young man to adopt dishonesty and effrontery as the methods of success."
- *Wheeling (WV) Register*, July 16, 1884: "Blaine's personal corruption has principally brought the decided aversion of the German voters against him, and his identification with the prohibitionists and Knownothing-ism has given additional strength to this aversion."
- *Wheeling (WV) Register*, August 14, 1884: "This is the whole issue — whether the next presidency shall be a man charged with public corruption [Blaine] or a man of incorruptible character and proved fidelity to public trusts [Cleveland]."

Blaine's courage entered the news cycle because of the revelation that he once ran away from a challenge to duel. During an age when dueling was an accepted way to seek justice, such a retreat was considered cowardly: *Wheeling (WV) Register*, August 4, 1884: "James G. Blaine skipped from Kentucky, when a young man, when challenged to fight a duel by a friend of an aggrieved party. If Republicans continue to throw mud at Cleveland's private character they (the Democratic press) may bring out some facts very unpleasant to Mr. Blaine."

Another nasty hit against Blaine was the charge that his first child was born before he married the mother. The incident was colorfully portrayed in the press: *Baltimore Sun*, August 15, 1884: "Blaine wronged his present wife in Kentucky and he fled to Maine; the young woman and her father followed him; he married her at the point of a shotgun." Blaine labeled these charges false. But the images stuck and probably cost him votes.

Such problems were enough to dampen the spirits of any candidate, but they weren't the only obstacles between Blaine and the presidency. He also had Roscoe Conkling and the Catholics to deal with, both of whom were critically important to him if he were to win New York and the election.

Conkling — a long-time political adversary of Blaine's still powerful in New York — had opposed his presidential ambitions before and could critically affect his success in 1884. Blaine's relationship with him is perhaps best described by repeating a description he once made of his long-time political opponent: "the turkey gobbler member from New York."[15] Winning New York absent enthusiastic support from Conkling would be difficult for Blaine; winning the presidency without carrying New York would be a Herculean task. Conkling's base (Oneida County) went to Cleveland by sixty-nine votes. When Garfield ran in 1880, with Conkling's energetic support, he took Conkling's base by 1,946 votes. The numbers say Conkling didn't support Blaine, and the lack of it cost Blaine and the Republican Party the presidency.[16]

Other problems mounted for Blaine as the campaign continued. And some people believe the last one may have been the proverbial straw that broke his political back: his reputation with the critically important Catholic voters in New York. Blaine's reputation for being anti–Catholic was well deserved and stemmed from his 1875 proposal, made while he was House Speaker, to amend the Constitution, as follows: "no money raised by taxation in any state for the support of public schools, or derived from any public fund therefore, nor any public lands devoted thereto, shall be under the control of any religious sect; nor shall any money so raised or lands so devoted be divided between religious sects or denominations."[17]

Those people who operated Catholic schools, the largest and most numerous denominational schools in the nation, and most other Catholics weren't enthused by this proposal or overly fond of its author. The amendment passed overwhelmingly in the House, but failed in the Senate. But that wasn't the end of it. State-level versions of it spread across the nation. Today, many states have a version of it[18] that places restrictions on the ability of state governments to financially assist sectarian schools. And its reach finally extended as far as the Supreme Court[19] (*Mitchell v. Helms*, 2000; *Zelman v. Simmons-Harris*, 2002; *Locke v. Davey*, 2004), where issues raised by these amendments continue to trouble society and the judicial world. This situation, standing alone, didn't help Blaine in New York, which had a large Catholic population.

But there was even more. In an age when anti–Catholicism was common[20] the Know Nothing Party stood out as being especially virulent. Two principles motivated them: The identification of Catholics as enemies of the state and the exclusion of foreign-born citizens from all offices of trust ... in the government, whether federal, state or municipal. Blaine's name was associated with the Knownothings. He denied he had ever been a member or a supporter. But doubt lingered. Some found hard evidence that they believe proved a link.[21]

With such a background it's easy to see how the next incident could be called the nail in his political coffin. A New York Presbyterian minister, and a supporter of Blaine, said at a rally that Democrats were "the party whose antecedents are rum, Romanism and rebellion,"[22] a nice sounding rhetorical alliteration that was exactly what Blaine at that moment did not need. The comment, widely interpreted as an anti–Catholic smear, combined with Blaine's existing relationship with Catholics, would hurt him badly in New York if he did not quickly and powerfully disown it and the sentiments that provoked it. He did not do so. And one more barrier to his success in New York — and in the election — was erected.

Election Results, 1884

The election results could not have been closer. The margin of victory, especially the popular vote, was thin.

Election Results 1884

Candidates	EV	%	Pop. (000)	Pop. %	Pop. %
Cleveland	219	55	4,875	48.5	50.1
Blaine	182	45	4,855	48.3	49.9
Other	0		325	3.2	
Total	401	100	10,055	100.0	100.0

EV=electoral vote; Pop. = popular vote

Source: NY Times Almanac, p. 128

The results to Democrats must have been more satisfying than usual — payback, in spades. Their man won by the same whisker that beat them four years before.

Blaine was hit hard by three happenings, one of which was half-expected, the other a surprise:

- The Mugwumps abandoned him. This was a bad blow, but not totally surprising. Their loyalty to Blaine was from the beginning doubtful.
- Roscoe Conkling's New York base voted for Cleveland, a complete turnaround from what had happened in the Garfield election. Leaders had expected that party loyalty would allow Conkling to forget his animosity toward Blaine and permit him to support the candidate with vigor, at least in his own county. The results suggest he didn't. And votes lost in Conkling's backyard cost Blaine a victory in New York, and the presidency.
- From this distance it seems strange that the father of the Blaine amendments would be popular with Irish Catholics, but such was the belief of Republicans when they nominated him, presumably because of various stands he had taken against the British on immigration issues during

his career.[23] Perhaps it was true at the time of the nomination. But when a supporter of Blaine's, the Presbyterian minister, described Democrats as the party of "rum, Romanism and rebellion," his romance with Catholics ended. The remark, which became a campaign rant, was a directly aimed insult at the Irish that Blaine did not contradict.[24]

The result? Blaine lost New York (48.25 percent vs. 48.15 percent), its 36 electoral votes and the election.[25] Why did he lose a state he should have won? Mugwumps? Conkling? Catholics? All three? Who knows? What is certain is that Blaine lost the election; Cleveland did not win it.

The above is reasonable explanation of how Blaine lost the election — there is no question that New York was the critical state to win. But there was actually more to it than that. Blaine won eighteen states versus thirty-eight states for Cleveland. But Cleveland's margin of victory in many states was very thin:

Cleveland Margin, Selected States 1884

State	EV	Cleveland Margin %	State	EV	Cleveland Margin %
CT	6	.94	IN	15	1.32
NJ	9	1.67	NY	36	.10

EV=electoral vote

Source: http://uselectionatlas.org/RESULTS/index.html

The electoral vote count was 218 versus 182. Give Blaine Indiana and either Connecticut or New Jersey, and he's the winner. In other words, Cleveland was lucky and Blaine wasn't.

The electoral map told another sad story. Cleveland carried every southern state, Blaine none. The wounds of war continued to divide the nation. The West, as it developed, was becoming a Republican stronghold. Blaine's margins were impressive: for example, California 7 percent, Oregon, 4 percent; Nevada and Colorado 13 percent.[26]

Given such a close victory, the logical prediction would be that Cleveland would have a hard time governing a nation that was still essentially split between North and South. Ironically, the governor of New York became president of the South.

The Cleveland Cabinet

The members of the Cleveland cabinet were[27]: **Vice President:** Thomas A. Hendricks, Indiana (1884–85, died),[28] Adlai E. Stevenson; **Secretary of State:** Thomas F. Bayard, Delaware; **Secretary of Treasury:** Daniel Manning (1885–87), Charles F. Fairchild, New York; **Secretary of War:** William C. Endicott, Massachusetts; **Secretary of Interior:** Lucius Q.C. Lamar, Mississippi (1885–88), William F. Vilas (see Postmaster General); **Secretary of Navy:** William C. Whitney, Massachusetts; **Attorney General:** Augustus H. Garland, Arkansas;

Postmaster General: William F. Vilas, Wisconsin (1885–88), Donald M. Dickinson, Michigan.

The hand of an astute politician aware of splinter groups within the party and the nation can be seen in these appointments, but on the surface they did not speak well for a president who seemed to be more interested in picking a cabinet with broad political appeal than one well trained in the tasks assigned. Impressions aside, however, the cabinet worked scandal-free as a group.

The Cleveland Congress

The Grover Cleveland presidential campaign had long coattails in the House and none in the Senate. This suggested that, aside from Cleveland's preference for a managerial presidency rather than a legislative one, he could start action in the House but would face a huge obstacle in the Senate. His strengths were weaker after the midterm election.

Pro-Administration Congressional Power

Congress	Year	President	House %	Senate %
48	1883	Arthur (R)	36	50
49	1885	Cleveland (D)	56	45
50	1887	Cleveland (D)	51	49

Source: Appendices 1.1, 1.2

John G. Carlisle continued as House Speaker throughout Cleveland's term. His biographical sketch appears in the preceding chapter.

The Cleveland Supreme Court

Morrison Waite, chief justice of the Supreme Court, administered the presidential oath to the new president, Grover Cleveland, and continued to serve as such until his death in March 1888, after which the Court moved into the hands of Chief Justice Melville W. Fuller. Associate justices who served under these men appear in the chart at the top of the next page.

Cleveland had two chances to appoint a Supreme Court justice and again he showed the astute political hand — as he had with cabinet appointments — by appointing one northerner and one southerner. He didn't change the sectional mix of the court he inherited, a decision that didn't add much to his popularity or the lack of it. Lamar was superbly qualified; Fuller may be fairly regarded as a political appointment.

A review of two cases of the time highlights some of the concerns of the day[29]:

Supreme Court Justices, 1885–88

Judge	Began	Appointed by	Ended
Morrison Waite (CT)	1874	Grant (R)	1888
Melville W. Fuller (IL)	1888	Cleveland	1910
Samuel Miller (KY)	1862	Lincoln	1890
Stephen Field (CT)	1863	"	1897
Joseph Bradley (NY)	1870	"	1892
John Harlan (KY)	1877	Hayes	1911
William Woods (OH)	1880	"	1887
Stanley Matthews (OH)	1881	Garfield	1889
Horace Gray (MA)	1882	Arthur	1902
Samuel Blatchford (NY)	1882	Arthur	1893
Lucius Q.C. Lamar (GA)	1888	Cleveland	1893

Source: Oyez, http://www.oyez.org/

Justices of the Supreme Court, http://www.supremecourtus.gov/about/members.pdf

Men in Black, Mark Levin, 2005, Regnery, D.C. p. 3–4

Note: Stephen Field was lame, ill and incompetent for at least his last year on the bench.

KIDD V. PEARSON, 1887

The facts: A state did not want to have liquor manufactured within its borders. It passed a law to prevent it. A company manufactured liquor and claimed exemption from state law because it sold the product out of state. The activity was stopped by the state.

The issue: The defendant claimed that state law conflicted with the power of Congress to regulate interstate commerce.

The decision: State law is valid. It seeks only to forbid manufacturing. It does not deal with interstate commerce, so that line of defense is invalid.

MUGLER V. KANSAS, 1887

The facts: Kansas law forbade the manufacture or sale of liquor within its borders. Mugler made and sold beer.

The issue: The application of the Fourteenth Amendment to Mugler's situation, to wit: "No state shall make or enforce any law which shall abridge the privileges or immunities of citizens ... without due process of law."

The decision: The state law is valid. Mugler has the right to make beer for himself, but the state has the right to exercise its police powers that govern the making or the selling of the product.

Liquor is the superficial subject matter of both of these cases, which seem trivial; but underlying issues were the rights of individuals and government, state and local, which are not trivial matters. And for a government that was almost one hundred years old, these rights were still being sorted out, case by case. So it is with free men who will always test the laws that restrain their liberty.

The bulk of cases in this era dealt with real estate and mining claims and other matters relating to the continuing movement of railroads, businesses and people moving west. The United States was still a teenager bursting with hormones.

Domestic Affairs Relative to Political Issues

All presidents have issues thrust upon them by history, the ones they create and those that develop in real time. Several are appraised below.[30]

TARIFFS

Tariffs were a bone of contention throughout the nineteenth century. Since the nation perennially existed as a divided one, no president could come up with an answer to who, why, what and how much to tax was satisfactory to the North and to the South. And it wasn't likely that Cleveland would do so, nailed as he was to his southern supporters. Previous Republican administrations had maintained high protective tariffs on imports. He attempted to reduce them and failed.[31]

CURRENCY

The Silver Purchase Act of 1878, in Cleveland's view, cheapened the value of the dollar, which he believed should be backed by gold. He tried to repeal it and failed. In so doing, he paid a political price because his constituency felt otherwise.[32]

ECONOMIC GROWTH

The rate of economic growth was slow to begin during Cleveland's administration, but it closed strongly. The recession that began under Garfield and Arthur in 1882 continued into the spring of 1885[33] before economic vigor once more appeared.

Gross Domestic Product

Year	GDP (bil)	Change	Debt (bil)	Debt/GDP
1884	11.8	-4.1	1.6	13.6
1885	11.6	-1.7	1.6	13.8
1886	12.2	5.2	1.6	13.1
1887	13.1	7.4	1.5	11.5
1888	13.9	6.1	1.4	10.1

Source: http://www.usgovernmentspending.com/federal_debt_chart.html

Historical Statistics Colonial Times to 1957, p. 721

Cleveland, from a political standpoint, was fortunate that his bad economic year was his first one. Debt was well managed.

PROHIBITION

Prohibition as such was not a major issue during the campaign, but the subjects of who could make and sell or tax liquor had already reached the Supreme Court. "Old Devil Booze" was frowned upon by some states that saw it as a moral issue. Cleveland opposed prohibition.[34]

CIVIL RIGHTS

Cleveland, given his remarks in his inauguration address, can be charged with hypocrisy. He said, "The fact that they are citizens entitles them to all the rights due to that relation and charges them with all its duties, obligations, and responsibilities." His actions bore no relation to his words. He sympathized with the efforts of his southern friends to limit civil rights; he favored segregation. In the language of 2010, he was a bigot — and a hypocrite to boot.[35]

Cleveland sympathized with Indians; he wanted to help them and, so to speak, almost killed them with kindness. He supported the Dawes Act of 1887,[36] which changed the community style of living favored by Indians, and tried to replace it with a sense of individual ownership of land, the cultivation of it and eventually the assimilation of it and its owner into the great society. The program was a disaster. Land ended up in the hands of unscrupulous whites; Indians were worse off than ever.[37]

The march of women to acquire equal rights began early in the 1800s, when Emma Hart Willard founded the first endowed school for girls.[38] Cleveland, the president, with pressure all around him, was approached by both sides for support. He did what any sane man would do when confronted by a determined female — he ducked. In so doing he made neither friends nor enemies.

In sum, Cleveland as a civil rights president was a disaster.

REFORM

Cleveland's significant reform work was limited to additional controls over railroads, which he accomplished by establishing the Interstate Commerce Commission.

Generally speaking, his congressional supporters were too busy getting even with Republicans to get energized over the reform issue, and it died on the vine.[39]

IMMIGRATION

Cleveland did not believe Chinese people would assimilate into American culture; he favored tight immigration controls.[40] He had reason to be concerned.

Immigrants had increasingly become a matter for social and political concern, especially in the 1800s when its rate almost doubled.[41]

The United States represented to oppressed people a chance for freedom and opportunity; it was natural for immigration to continue at a robust pace. These same inherent attractions placed on Congress a responsibility to balance the dreams of immigrants with the internal well-being of the nation. Most immigrants in the 1880s came from Europe and Canada.[42]

LABOR

The labor movement was on the mind of every politician in 1884. One event is enough to demonstrate why Cleveland gave the movement careful attention. Thirty thousand workers marched in 1882 in the first Labor Day parade on the streets of New York City[43]; The Federation of Organized Trades and Labor Unions (later to become the American Federation of Labor) passed a resolution stating that eight hours was to be a legal day's work after May 1, 1886.[44] The eight-hour workday was an element of the Democratic platform.[45] Congress made Labor Day a national holiday in 1894.[46] The American Federation of Labor was founded by Samuel Gompers in 1886, the inevitable response to the fights, quarrels and strikes that crisscrossed the nation.[47]

Congress established a Department of Labor and in so doing forever identified the Democratic Party with the interests of that institution.[48] This action also resolved a campaign promise made by Democrats at their convention.

GENERAL

Cleveland was not a groundbreaking lawmaker. He didn't promote much legislation, but he tried to stop a lot of it — 304 vetoes in four years — not surprising considering his weak position in the Senate. Presidents without Senate power can and do register their protest with the veto.

Presidential vetoes among the first twenty-one presidents were rare — 116 for the group, and President Grant was responsible for almost half (45) of them.[49] Not so with Cleveland. When he didn't like something, he said so.

Cleveland's domestic record is mixed. Especially notable is the fact that he did nothing significant to bring America's black citizens into the mainstream.

NEW STATES, 1885–88

For the second straight presidential term, no new states were added. Cleveland began and ended with thirty-eight states.[50] Most of the West was still in its formative period and soon to become allied with the other states.

Foreign Affairs Relative to Political Issues

Some American political leaders believed the United States should compete with Britain, France and others in building a foreign empire. Cleveland was not one of them. His focus was essentially internal. Nevertheless, he had to face a few problems, which in some cases required him to show that, if needed, he would stretch America's military muscles.[51]

VENEZUELA

Gold was discovered in a disputed area between British Guiana and Venezuela.[52] Both countries claimed title to the land in question and, therefore, to the associated mineral rights. Venezuela tried to strike a deal with Britain. Britain refused and Venezuela appealed to the United States for support.

Cleveland invoked the Monroe Doctrine (no foreign influence in the Americas) and sided with Venezuela. Britain, at the time troubled in South Africa (the Boer Wars), chose not to get involved with another faraway squabble and agreed to the Venezuelan request for arbitration. Nationally and internationally Cleveland was praised for standing up to one of the great world powers.

HAWAII

At the end of the Harrison administration a treaty to annex Hawaii was before the Congress. Cleveland studied the matter and withdrew the treaty because American diplomats, he believed, had improperly involved themselves in the internal politics of Hawaii.[53]

ATLANTIC/PACIFIC CANAL

The need for a canal that connected the two great oceans was an issue that first came up under President Hayes and was still on the presidential plate when Cleveland took over.

The Frelinghuysen-Zavala Treaty was before Congress. Under its terms, the United States could construct a canal that would be co-owned with Nicaragua. Cleveland studied the matter and withdrew the treaty because he disagreed with the idea.[54]

CUBA

Cuba was a gnawing problem of interest to many American political leaders, especially southerners, because it represented one more potential slave state.[55] Cleveland refused to take the bait and would not take sides in the fighting on the island. Congress threatened to recognize Cuba as an independent state; Cleveland refused to cooperate. The issue remained undecided and the Cuba problem has lingered to haunt all succeeding presidents up to the current day.

WAR AND PEACE

Cleveland showed he would use military power when the nation's interests were challenged.[56] The Venezuelan incident, for example, worked out as it did because of the veiled suggestion that the United States would, if necessary, back Venezuela's position with power. Also, he sent troops to Panama and Rio de Janeiro in support of local governments. And he sent warships to Samoa (where the United States, by agreement, maintained a naval base) when Germany made a move to take over the local government. Germany backed away.

GENERAL

Overall, Cleveland remained true to his principles. He was delicate and restrained in foreign dealings; he did not seek expanded territory; he showed appropriate force when necessary; he took the role of the United States under the Monroe Doctrine seriously.

Conclusion

Why was the election of 1884 so close? The most direct answer is: Because Blaine didn't win New York, and he should have. Which leads to the second question: Why did he lose New York? He lost by an almost infinitesimal amount. Roger Conkling, a powerhouse in New York, didn't like Blaine and didn't campaign for him. Blaine lost because he didn't carry districts that, with Conkling's support, should have been his. Verdict! Blame Conkling for Blaine's defeat, another example of intra-party squabbling denying victory to a major party.

The Mugwumps, a reform wing of the Republican Party never comfortable with the candidacy of Blaine, finally deserted him and supported Cleveland. This, combined with the Conkling influence, almost certainly cost him a win in New York, and in the election. The slogan of Blaine's supporter ("rum, Romanism and rebellion"), which clung to the candidate to a degree that disturbed Catholics in New York and elsewhere, cost Blaine important votes in important places. And, finally, there's the question of pure luck. Given a break in two of the following states, which he lost by a whisker, he would have won without New York: Connecticut, New Jersey and Indiana.

Cleveland didn't win the election; Blaine lost it.

7

1888: Grover Cleveland vs. Benjamin Harrison

(Electoral Votes 401; Majority 201)

Introduction

Democrats confidently approached their convention. Cleveland had weathered a tough storm during the 1884 campaign and had emerged the winner. He figured to have an easier time of it this time around. Republicans, however, weren't about to run with Blaine again. They wanted a new face, one less vulnerable to attack. Benjamin Harrison seemed to fit the profile they had in mind.

Conventions

Both political parties approached the 1888 election knowing that winning would be hard, uphill work.

Cleveland, the sitting president and the presumed nominee of Democrats, had survived the 1884 campaign of vilification directed against him; there was little fear that a rehash of his old sexual meanderings would have much traction during the upcoming election. On the other hand, his first administration was not so outstanding that it rubbed out the possibility of a rerun of the 1884 election, which he won mostly because of defections within the Republican Party and a lucky late election incident that alienated some of New York's Irish vote.[1]

Republicans also had their concerns. Division in the ranks was at least one of the reasons for losing the 1884 election, and the source of it, the Mugwumps, still had to be dealt with. Also, the situation in the critical state of New York was, as always, uncertain. Roscoe Conkling, the maker and breaker of presidential candidates, was dead (April 1888) and the loss of his influence in the state (when he chose to exert it) could not be calculated.

Both parties approached the starting line tentatively.

DEMOCRATIC CONVENTION

The convention was held in St. Louis during the first week in June.[2] It was no contest. President Grover Cleveland was chosen by unanimous acclamation. Levi P. Morton (NY) became his running mate. This was the first time a nominee had been chosen by acclamation since 1840, when that honor was bestowed on Martin Van Buren, a Democratic-Republican, who, like Cleveland, was running for a second term. (The Democratic-Republican Party became the Democratic Party in 1840.)

The lack of internal competition for Cleveland projected an image of unity that did not reflect reality. The party was in fact seriously divided, a condition that can affect campaign energy and voter turnout. All agreed that tariffs and tax policy were important issues, but conservative Democrats wanted more emphasis placed on states' rights. Populists argued that the free coinage of silver should be a central issue.

In addition to these philosophical differences, Cleveland had developed personal enemies, mostly those who resented his unwillingness to fully use the patronage powers of his office. Tammany Hall, the political powerhouse that dominated New York politics, was especially disappointed in Cleveland, and its support during the election was critical if Cleveland were to win that battleground state. The convention adjourned in that split condition, differences unresolved.

REPUBLICAN CONVENTION

The convention opened to a madhouse of competition.[3] Twelve nominees, including one black delegate, Frederick Douglass, threw their hats in the ring. Seventeen black men attended the convention; the Republican Party in those days was the political home of black citizens.

James Blaine, who almost beat Cleveland in 1884, was the early front runner, but his supporters were more interested in him than he was interested in another run at the presidency,[4] and they finally turned their attention to other candidates. The field narrowed, after repeated ballots, to two men: Sen. John Herman (OH) and Benjamin Harrison (IN). Herman's support wavered; Harrison surged ahead and emerged as the nominee, with Levi P. Norton (NY) as his running mate.[5]

The division over civil service reform that troubled the 1884 convention and campaign disappeared when Blaine dropped out as a candidate, and the issue itself was not in 1888 a matter of great concern for either party. The convention adjourned in a much more unified condition than was the case four years earlier. Republicans, because of this, could justify feelings of cautious optimism.

Their platform featured continued support for high, protective tariffs, tax reform, currency supported by gold and silver, protection of veterans' pensions and the elimination of polygamy. The Democratic platform emphasized tax reform and reduction aimed at lowering the cost of the necessities of life. In language and form, the platform was beginning to reflect many progressive ideas of the Greenback Party, which first appeared in 1880 and never appeared again after 1884 after finding a resting place within the welcoming Democratic Party.[6]

Thumbnail Sketches of Top Candidates

STEPHEN GROVER CLEVELAND, DEMOCRAT

Cleveland, the sitting president, was running for a second term. His biographical material is reported in chapter 6 and will not be repeated here.

BENJAMIN HARRISON, REPUBLICAN

Born: 1833, Ohio; **Education:** Miami University, Ohio; **Wife:** Caroline Lavinia Scott (1853); Mary Scott Lord Dimmick (1896); **Children:** Three; **Died:** 1901.[7]

Benjamin Harrison was born into a prominent, politically active family. William H. Harrison, ninth president of the United States, was his grandfather. Biographers claim Harrison believed he was destined for greatness.

Tutored at home during his early years, Harrison read widely, and found books more comforting than people. He gradually developed a cold and aloof persona, which earned him the nickname "the human iceberg." After graduation from college (he was a brilliant student), Harrison studied law. Following his first marriage, he moved to Indiana, established his law practice and soon became active in the Republican Party. He supported the first Republican candidate, John C. Frémont, in 1856 and he worked for Abraham Lincoln during the 1860 political campaign. When the Civil War called, he joined the Indiana volunteers and rose to the rank of brigadier general.

Harrison returned to his Indiana law practice and to politics after the war. He ran for governor and lost in 1876, but in the process and thereafter he became an influential political force in his state. A loyal Republican, he supported the presidential campaigns of Rutherford Hayes and James Garfield. In 1880, Indiana sent him to the U.S. Senate.

Harrison, an active senator who left a footprint, supported such things as veterans' issues, high tariffs, a modernized navy and land conservation. He voted against the position of his party on Chinese immigration and opposed those who would end it.

This was a time when U.S. senators were selected by state legislatures, and when party power in the state slid to Democrats in the election of 1886, he lost his Senate seat. By this time he had caught Potomac fever and a year later he aimed for the presidential nomination.

Harrison, during his years as a supporter of presidential candidates and as a U.S. senator, had picked up many political IOUs, and it wasn't surprising to find he was everybody's second choice during the early stages of the cluttered field of competitors (Blaine was first choice). He won the prize on the eighth ballot. Now he had the chance to prove he would be the great man he felt he was destined to be.

Election Tone

The 1888 election was only four years away from one of the bitterest political campaigns in American history. But it was different, very different. And the Supreme Court helped it to be that way. It was not only different, but to blacks and their supporters, it was also angrier. The Court decided that the government in civil rights issues could rule only on state issues, not personal issues as they were state business. With such rulings, the Court stripped the central government of power to enforce Amendments Fourteen and Fifteen.

Cleveland himself had run a rather benign administration that didn't seriously ruffle the feelings of too many people. And both parties had learned during the 1884 campaign that the pursuit of hardball politics as a means for reaching objectives carries a price. The "Rum, Romanism and Rebellion" comment, for example, made by one of Blaine's supporters, sounded good on the stump and at the rallies, but it may have cost Blaine a victory in New York, and the presidency. Generally speaking, the appetite for power was undiminished, but the tendency to seek it with tactics that strained the conscience had been cooled by time and experience.

The Candidates

The competitive situation between candidates was also different. Cleveland was in 1884 a relatively inexperienced politician who had lived a controversial private life and was an easy target for hardball tactics. The same man in 1888, now an experienced president who had demonstrated he could handle the job, had a wife who provided him with a scandal-free, stable family life. On a personal basis, he could not be productively attacked as he had been before. And no gentleman would do so, absent hard, current evidence. On the Republican side, Benjamin Harrison, a respected veteran of the Civil War and an admired attorney and legislator with well-developed political skills, was in no way related to Washington scandals. Nobody could call him inexperienced and his personal life was without blemish.

A Different Campaign Style

Given these circumstances, the presidential campaign was destined to be a temperate one unless some maverick operative stimulated once again the dark angels of politics. But that didn't happen. There were few untoward actions to ruffle the placid political waters.

There was one Republican plot, however, that could cost Cleveland some critical votes. A Republican, posing as a British immigrant, persuaded a British minister to voice an opinion, in a letter, about the upcoming election. The minister expressed a preference for Cleveland. The *Los Angeles Times* printed the letter and some believe it harmed Cleveland's chances.[8] He lost California by 2.8 percent, or seven thousand votes.

The candidates did little campaigning, leaving the spade work for their parties to handle. But they gave speeches, Cleveland from the White House and Harrison from his front porch.[9]

CLEVELAND'S ORGANIZATIONAL MISTAKE

It was not yet the practice for candidates to vigorously and personally campaign. Roscoe Conkling, for example, until his untimely death in April of the election year, managed Harrison's campaign; Cleveland relied extensively on his vice president. Nevertheless, some degree of involvement beyond casual was expected. On this measure, Cleveland was found wanting. He disliked the give and take of political campaigns and overly delegated election responsibilities. Vice President Thurman went on exhausting national tours that were too much for the old scholar to handle (he was seventy-five and in ill health).[10]

The various splits in the party, revealed during the convention, argued against an aloof, impersonal campaign. A hands-on approach was indicated. The party needed leadership that would unify an effective effort in the field. Cleveland didn't provide it.

CLEVELAND'S TACTICAL MISTAKE

The most emotional issues during the campaign were those that harkened back to the Civil War and Reconstruction. Cleveland, for example, pledged to return captured flags of the Confederacy to the South, a blatant attempt to attract sectional loyalties.[11] This tactic was of questionable value to Cleveland. Southern supporters knew where he stood on issues of importance to them. On the other hand, he needed support from the North and appeals to sectionalism weren't likely to lure it.

ISSUES RULED

In a civilized election, issues should be the subject of presidential debates whether conducted by candidates or by surrogates. And that was mostly the case in 1888.

The hottest issue was tariffs. Cleveland, the president, thought they were too high and said so. He didn't have the congressional support to do much about it in his first term, but he was still pushing for change in his final speech to Congress in 1887,[12] and he continued to do so during the campaign.

The press was tuned into this. For example, the August 14, 1888, edition of the *New York Times* quoted William F. Villas, a former secretary of the Interior, and a confidante of the president, as saying that due to the debate on the issue stimulated by Cleveland, the public was more aware of the importance of tariffs, and he predicted that "Democrats can sweep the nation on that issue."

MONEY

There was also a money differential in the campaign that worked to the advantage of Republicans.[13] Roscoe Conking and others raised enormous amounts from Republican businessmen who wanted to keep in power an administration that was friendly to the high tariffs that benefited them.

Democrats could not raise a competitive amount and, since money has always been the mother's milk of politics, Republicans could afford to organize and operate more effectively as an organization. This money imbalance in 1888 was important but not as critical as it would become in the television age. Access to newspapers and a good ground organization were the most important factors in the 1880s, and both were more dependent on effort than on money.

GENERAL

Apart from tariffs, strategies and money, there remained the general issue that had made all postwar presidential elections so competitive.

Segregation! Racism! Sectionalism! Civil rights! Call it what you will, but it, not party and issues, was the deep-down issue that kept the nation divided and elections close. Just as in the days of slavery, the South was determined to continue a lifestyle that subdued blacks; the North was just as determined to change that lifestyle and to give to blacks the full freedoms that were bought with the Civil War. If in 1888 this was still the central issue of the times, the election would be close and North and South, when results became known, would be as divided as before.

Election Results, 1888

Republicans won two of the three most previous elections, but with a nip here and a tuck there, either party could have won all three.

The country was in deadlock mode, the product of a new-state acceptance system that for years had deliberately balanced admissions to the Union to the satisfaction of the North and the South relative to the slavery question — one for you and one for me, etc.

The Civil War ended that system, but only two states had been added since (Nebraska and Colorado), meaning that the Union was still essentially in the electoral grip of the old system.[14] And the 1888 election results showed it.

Election Results 1888

Candidates	EV	%	Pop. (000)	Pop. %	Pop. %
Harrison	233	58	5,444	47.8	49.6
Cleveland	168	42	5,534	48.6	50.4
Other			405	3.6	
Total	401	100	11,383	100.01	00.0

EV=electoral vote; Pop. = popular vote

Source: NY Times Almanac 2009, p. 129

The electoral vote count suggests an easy win for Harrison. But the closeness of the popular vote indicates a struggle much closer and more complex. Harrison carried nineteen states—most of the North plus the West. Cleveland took Connecticut, New Jersey, Delaware, Maryland and the entire South.[15] The old hard-core coalitions were still in place.

The difference makers were newer states that due to distance from North/South conflicts or by date of admission to the Union were not as frozen in time as the others—states like Kansas (1861, once a furious battleground between North and South on the slavery question), Colorado (1876), Nebraska (1867), California (1850), Oregon (1859) and Nevada (1864).[16] These states collectively represented thirty-one electoral votes—almost as many as the biggest prize of all, New York, with its thirty-six votes. And Harrison took all of them, plus New York, an unbeatable combination in 1888.

Cleveland was beaten by sixty-five electoral votes. Give him New York, and he's the winner 204–197. This vividly demonstrates how close the election actually was. The important thing is not how many states but which states are in the win column. In 1888, four states had more than nineteen electoral votes: New York (36), Pennsylvania (30), Ohio (23) and Illinois (22).[17] Harrison won them all.

Election Results 1888
States with 20+ Electoral Vote %

Candidates	NY	PA	IL	OH
Cleveland	48	45	47	47
Harrison	49	53	50	50
Total	97	98	97	97

Source: http://uselectionatlas.org/RESULTS/

The dissident vote in 1888 was made up of the Prohibition and the Union Labor parties, people who if integrated would most probably support Democrats. In New York, Illinois and Ohio they were a factor in the race, which is a demonstration of a political truism: Dissidents never win, but they can ruin the chances of others, often the candidate of their second choice.

The electoral map told a sad story to southerners who resisted integration. To sustain their position, they had to keep their base and gain support from the North and West. Their prospects, which were tied to the effectiveness of the Democratic Party, were not as hopeless as they appeared to be. For example, they had already penetrated New England with wins in Vermont (12) and Connecticut (6); New Hampshire (4) was within short-term striking distance — the loss margin was below 3 percent.[18] They won New Jersey (9) and almost won the big prize, New York (36); Maryland (8) was a possibility, as were Ohio (23), Illinois (22), Indiana (15) and California (8).[19] In short, 143 electoral votes outside of the South were in play. The big prize was still in view.

This had meaning for future elections, and for the ability of Congress to deal with the single issue that was mostly responsible for keeping the South unified, and the nation split — segregation.

The Harrison Cabinet

The members of the Harrison cabinet were[20]: **Vice President:** Levi P. Morton, New York; **Secretary of State:** James G. Blaine (1889–92), John W. Foster, Indiana; **Secretary of War:** Redfield Proctor, Vermont (1889–91), Stephen B. Elkins, Missouri; **Postmaster General:** John Wanamaker, Pennsylvania; **Secretary of Interior:** John W. Noble, Missouri; **Secretary of Treasury:** William Windom, Ohio (1889–91), Charles Foster, Ohio; **Attorney General:** William H. Miller, Ohio/Indiana; **Secretary of Navy:** Benjamin F. Tracy, New York; **Secretary of Agriculture:** Jeremiah M. Rusk, Wisconsin.

On the surface, Harrison's choices seemed noncontroversial, with the possible exception of James G. Blaine, who, along with Vice President Morton, had participated in intra-party political battles over the years. Harrison was fortunate that his cabinet did not sabotage him because his so-called choices were not his at all. The election was so close that his party's leaders were the actual powers in Washington and, to gain support and win the election, they had sold the cabinet positions to those who could and did help.[21]

The Harrison Congress

Harrison began his presidency in strong congressional position: Fifty-four percent in the House and fifty-eight percent in the Senate. But the tide turned after two years— he lost ground in the Senate, and his losses in the House were disastrous.

Pro-Administration Congressional Power

Congress	Year	President	House %	Senate %
50	1888	Cleveland (D)	51	49
51	1889	Harrison (R)	54	58
52	1891	Harrison (R)	26	53

Source: Appendices 1.1, 1.2

If Harrison could have read the future he would have known that he had a two-year window to make a difference in Washington. After that, his lack of congressional support would make progress difficult. Democrats, with good reason, looked forward to an election turnover in 1892.

The Harrison Supreme Court

Melville Fuller, appointed by Grover Cleveland in October 1888, administered the presidential oath to incoming president Benjamin Harrison. Fuller's court, to say the least, was an interesting one. No Court, experts say, took more abuse than his, except for the Warren Court. The essential criticism was, in both instances, that they legalized their own value preferences, not so much under Harrison, but increasingly so over the future years. Fuller and Lamar were the only appointees of a Democratic president.

Supreme Court Justices, 1889–92

Judge	Began	Appointed by	Ended
Melville W. Fuller (IL)	1888	Cleveland	1910
Samuel Miller (KY)	1862	Lincoln	1890
Stephen Field (CT)	1863	"	1897
Joseph Bradley (NY)	1870	"	1892
John Harlan (KY)	1877	Hayes	1911
Stanley Matthews (OH)	1881	Garfield	1889
Horace Gray (MA)	1882	Arthur	1902
Samuel Blatchford (NY)	1882	Arthur	1893
Lucius Q.C. Lamar (GA)	1888	Cleveland	1893
David J. Brewer (KS)	1890	Harrison	1910
Henry R. Brown (MI)	1891	Harrison	1906
George Shiras, Jr. (PA)	1892	Harrison	1903

Source: Oyez, http://www.oyez.org/

Justices of the Supreme Court, http://www.supremecourtus.gov/about/members.pdf

Men in Black, Mark Levin, 2005, Regnery, D.C. p. 3–4

Note: Stephen Field was lame, ill and incompetent for at least his last year on the bench.

Fuller, originally from Maine, moved to Chicago to practice law and dabble in politics. He opposed Lincoln in 1860 and managed the campaign of Stephen

Douglas. He served as an Illinois legislator while building a lucrative legal practice. Cleveland offered Fuller the position of solicitor general, which he refused, but he accepted the offer to head the Supreme Court. His confirmation hearings before the Senate Judiciary Committee were testy because of his ties with big business, and it took three months to get him confirmed.

A review of a few cases that these judges decided reveals some of the concerns of the day.[22]

STRAUDER V. W. VIRGINIA, 1880

The facts: West Virginia law prohibited blacks from serving on juries
The issue: Does the state law violate the Fourteenth Amendment?
The decision: Yes. To deny such participation in the legal process solely on racial grounds is an assertion under law of the inferiority of blacks and a stimulant to the race prejudice that the amendment seeks to eliminate.

LEE YICK V. HOPKINS, 1886

The facts: Most laundries in San Francisco operated out of wooden buildings, two-thirds of which were operated by Chinese workers (by law and custom, Chinese people were excluded from many kinds of work). The city passed an ordinance that laundries in wooden buildings could not operate without a special permit issued by the board of supervisors. Yick, a long-time resident of the city, had operated a laundry for many years in a wooden building and held a valid license issued by the board of fire wardens. He continued to operate. He was arrested, taken to trial, found guilty and fined $10,000. He refused to pay the fine and was jailed.
The issue: Is the city ordinance discrimination in disguise?
The decision: Yes. The ordinance is a blatant attempt to exclude Chinese people from the laundry trade and is a violation of the Fourteenth Amendment. All charges against the plaintiff were dismissed. This ruling was foundational; it has since been frequently used to support judicial opinion.[23]

IN RE NEAGLE, 1890

The facts: Neagle, a U.S. marshal, was assigned by a U.S. attorney general to protect Justice Stephen Field, whose life had been threatened but no national statute empowered the attorney general to provide judges with bodyguards. A man approached Field in a threatening way and Neagle shot and killed him. State officials arrested and jailed him. The attorney general sought to release him by a writ of habeas corpus (relief from unlawful detention).
The issue: Is the state obliged to obey the writ?
The decision: Yes. The attorney general acted appropriately. The assign-

ment assured that national laws would be faithfully executed. Also, U.S. marshals have the same powers that state sheriffs and deputies would have to protect a judge like Fields. Crime seemed to be the issue, but federal versus states' rights was the central argument.

Decisions on race issues reflected more than justice. They also reflected the makeup of the Court, which was dominated by Republicans from the North who reflected the antisegregation attitudes of their culture. The legislative and the executive branches of government were deadlocked on racial issues, but the judicial branch at this time was the best friend in government for black citizens.

Domestic Affairs Relative to Current Issues

Harrison left much to measure because his observations and attitudes made known during his inauguration address were numerous and extensive.

TARIFFS/TAXES

The always-present and always-controversial issue of tariffs was important to President Harrison as well, as demonstrated by his backing of the McKinley Tariff Act (1890), a mixture of increased tariffs and duties or, in a broader sense, an attempt by the federal government to control the flow of goods through the free market with a system of rewards and penalties.[24]

One impact of higher tariffs was to temporarily add to the budget surplus in Washington and invite lavish expenditures. Republicans dealt with the surplus by spending lavishly on pensions, and other pork barrel projects that benefited the states of powerful congressmen — roads, bridges, government buildings, etc. Worthwhile endeavors like the improvement of shore defenses and the building of battleships also contributed to the high spending reputation of the Congress. This didn't buy popularity for Republicans at the polls,[25] and it caused the resurgence to power in the election of 1890 of the Democratic Party.

Tariffs as a main source of income had not produced a stable economy. It isn't surprising to learn, therefore, that in 1894 Congress passed an income tax law. Its constitutionality was successfully challenged in the next year.[26]

CIVIL RIGHTS/ELECTION LAWS

Relative to his promises to blacks, Harrison vigorously supported two bills that did not pass.[27] The first was the Force Bill, which would have established federal supervision of congressional elections; the second was the Blair Education Bill, which proposed federal aid for the education of blacks. Both were a response to the de facto refusal in the South to permit blacks to exercise their constitutional voting rights.

Although unsuccessful in moving the ball of segregation farther down the political field, Harrison must be given credit for trying to do what he said he would do, in his inauguration speech, about blacks and their voting rights.

ENVIRONMENT

How to handle land was a recurring issue during the growth years of the United States. Harrison had one answer that was copied by future presidents: The Land Revision Act (1891).[28] Under its terms, the first forest reserve in Yellowstone, Wyoming, was created.

REFORM

This was the era of giant corporations, like Rockefeller's Standard Oil, which by legal and devious means crushed all competition. Animosity toward these giants in the marketplace was responsible for the rise of union power. In the government, reaction was stern — the Sherman Antitrust Act (1890). Large corporations were unregulated until this law was passed.[29] The original law, too weak and vague to have much impact, was nevertheless a useful beginning point that future presidents gradually strengthened until it became an effective deterrent to too much power in one place.

Handling land in the West, frequently the source of discontent and scandal, was addressed in the Homestead Act (1893),[30] under the terms of which any white adult male could claim 160 acres of land if he worked the property for five years and built at least one building on it.

Harrison's record on civil service reform was conveniently inconsistent. Postmaster General Wanamaker, who held his position because of money he raised and personally donated to the Harrison campaign, notified the new president that he could not build the party without patronage. Obligingly, Harrison suspended civil service laws that protected postal employees. Within a year, forty thousand Democrats lost their jobs to the same number of Republicans. When the dust settled, Harrison restored civil service laws.[31]

CURRENCY

There existed in Congress a group that wanted to lift silver to the status of gold and with Harrison's backing they had the power to pass the Sherman Silver Purchase Act (1890),[32] under the terms of which the government was required to purchase each year a significant amount of silver. Supporters of the law reasoned that several worthwhile objectives would be achieved through its implementation:

- The political alliance of Republicans with silver interests in the West (who had supported the McKinley Tariff Act) would be further strengthened because silver would go up in value.
- Political support with farmers would improve because farm prices would inflate.
- Political support with debtors would increase because they would be able to reduce debt with a cheaper dollar caused by the inflation that would ensue.

The strategy backfired. Passage of the bill resulted in a run on the gold supply; silver production increased and more supply depressed its value also. Democrats demolished Republicans in the 1890 election. The law was later repealed.

IMMIGRATION

The Bureau of Immigration was formed in 1891.[33] Establishing a department does not solve a problem, but at least a framework for improved future supervision of immigration was put in place. This was a timely move. Immigration had more than doubled in the 1880s,[34] which placed considerable strains on the culture. Assimilation, not an easy process at any time, was not as difficult in the subject period as it is in modern America. Most immigrants (over 90 percent) in the nineteenth century came from the same nations as those who had founded and built the United States.[35]

DEFENSE AND THE ATLANTIC/PACIFIC CANAL

President Harrison indicated his commitment to a powerful navy in his inauguration speech, and he acted on it. He persuaded Congress to build more battleships,[36] but he failed to sell the idea of an Atlantic/Pacific canal through Nicaragua, which he felt was essential to the development of a two-ocean navy. The size of the active duty military force remained constant at about 39,000.[37] Again, Harrison deserves credit for putting his money where his mouth was.

GDP/NATIONAL DEBT

The economy grew during Harrison's years in office, but growth was not robust. One recession ended in 1888; 1889 was a recovery year; the next year was healthy until the third quarter then another dip of ten months followed. Fortunately, for the party, growth was robust again in the 1892 election year. Tension between North and South, a perennial concern of any president, now had extended to the West. Apart from racism, tariffs were the separating issue: Northern Americans favored high protective tariffs; farming states favored low tariffs and free trade.

Gross Domestic Product, Public Debt

Year	GDP (bil)	% Growth	Public Debt (bil)	% PD/GDP
1888	13.9	6.1	1.3	9.4
1889	13.9	0.0	1.2	8.6
1890	15.1	8.6	1.1	7.3
1891	15.4	2.0	1.0	6.5
1892	16.4	6.5	1.0	6.1

Source: http://www.usgovernmentspending.com/federal_debt_chart.html
Historical Statistics Colonial Times to 1957, p. 721

The passage of the McKinley Tariff Act (1890) added wood to the hot political fire that was already burning. Farmers were unhappy. General tension increased. The formation of the Populist Party (a nuisance in the 1892 election) was a direct result of it.

Some decisions made under Harrison were controversial, but they did not interfere with a further reduction in national debt, in absolute and relative terms. Since presidential power can in part be measured by the ability to borrow during emergency situations, Harrison's legacy in that sense was valuable to the next president.

NEW STATES

Six new states were added to the Union, bringing the total to forty-four: North Dakota, South Dakota, Montana, Washington, Idaho and Wyoming.[38] Each time a new state was added in the West, historic quarrels between the North and the South became less decisive in presidential elections. The ability of the South to maintain its segregated culture was threatened.

GENERAL

For a president who enjoyed congressional support for only two years, Harrison was effective. Laws passed with his approval—controversial or not—were substantial ones that had meaningful impact on the nation during and after his years in power. Harrison's waffling on civil service reform did not inure to his credit, but in many ways he did his best to make good on promises.

Foreign Affairs Relative to Current Issues

Harrison's remarks during his inauguration speech provided no hints that an aggressive and effective president in the international arena was about to move into the spotlight.

WAR AND PEACE

The first Pan-American conference was held in 1889, the purpose of which was to promote friendly relations and avoid confrontations so that all nations could grow and prosper.[39]

Harrison was not slow to show that he would use military force to defend the nation's interests or to support America's sense of justice:

- He threatened military retaliation when American sailors were killed in Chile. Chile bowed to U.S. demands, apologized and made a considerable peace payment.[40]
- The U.S. purchased Alaska in 1867 and, with it, held exclusive rights to fur-seal hunting. Britain disagreed over America's claims. Harrison held his ground. The matter was successfully referred for settlement to arbitration.[41]
- The Samoan islands (midway between Hawaii and Australia) hosted naval bases for the U.S. and Germany. Tension developed; war was in the air. Harrison held firm. The situation was settled in an international meeting held in Berlin.

TRADE

The McKinley Tariff Act also expanded a president's power to negotiate, without congressional consultation and advice, reciprocal trade agreements that bartered over tariffs and duty/import fees. This in turn created a need for a new bureaucracy to administer such deals. The Department of Commerce became an organizational reality in 1903.[42]

The University of Virginia's Miller Center for Public Affairs describes President Harrison this way: "No president since Lincoln pursued a more active public agenda."

Conclusion

Why was the election of 1888 so close? The short answer to that question is this: Harrison took New York and Indiana by the thinnest of margins—fifty-one electoral votes that fate placed in the Republican column. A reversal in those two states would have made Cleveland president. Cleveland also made tactical errors that may have weakened his position in northern states. Also, Roscoe Conkling's death, along with lukewarm support from Tammany Hall, could have cost him a New York victory.

But the overall impact of the election was another demonstration that issues, political parties and candidates were not decisive. That distinction belonged to the continued enmity between the North and the South over segregation and tariffs—the manufacturer versus the farmer; the constitutionalist versus the segregationist. That was the real battleground, not as decisive as before, but still the burden the nation had carried since its beginning—lack of unity and the fear of what would happen if divisive issues were faced head on.

8

1948: Harry S Truman vs. Thomas E. Dewey

(Electoral Votes 531; Majority 266)

Introduction

The last close election had been between Harrison and Cleveland in 1888, and fourteen elections had taken place since then, featuring ten presidents[1]: Republicans McKinley, Theodore Roosevelt, Taft, Harding, Coolidge (vice presidential succession) and Hoover, and Democrats Cleveland, Wilson, Franklin Roosevelt and Truman (first term).

Each presidency had its interesting aspects but only Theodore Roosevelt, Hoover, Wilson, Franklin Roosevelt and Truman (first term) had an impact on the 1948 election. The others had faded into the obscurity of political history and are briefly reviewed below[2]:

- Cleveland (1893–1898)[3]: The only man to serve two nonconsecutive terms, he was a pragmatic manager who observed the limitations imposed on the federal government by the constitution.
- McKinley (1897–1901)[4]: One of the expansionist presidents. After a successful war with Spain, a clash that seemed inevitable because of conflicting interests, America owned the Philippines, Guam, Hawaii and Puerto Rico and also temporary control of Cuba. He was assassinated in his second term and succeeded by Theodore Roosevelt.
- Taft (1909–12)[5]: He proposed highly unpopular antitrust and tariff legislation that moved his sponsor, Theodore Roosevelt, to disown him and make another run for the presidency, a decision that ended up embarrassing him, Taft and the Republican Party.
- Harding (1921–22)[6]: He died after two years in office and left scandals behind.[7]
- Coolidge (1922–28)[8]: A caretaker president, who succeeded Harding, then won big in 1924. He managed the nation's affairs and remained relatively

remote from the private sector, a trait that some admired and others criticized.

With the possible exception of Harding, these were honorable men who were competent in office, but their contribution to history had little impact on modern political events. Not so, however, with the other presidents. Their records and deeds helped or hurt the candidates in 1948, and have been influences in all campaigns since then.

- Theodore Roosevelt[9]: (1901–08): As the Louisiana Purchase was identified with Thomas Jefferson, so was the Panama Canal identified with Theodore Roosevelt (TR), the linkage making both men famous. But there was more to both men than that. In TR's case, for example, his expansion of the national park system and his general attitude toward the environment lifted the relationship of man to nature to a level that has made it a campaign issue ever since. Less understood and acclaimed, he was the first man to give to the progressive movement a legitimate place in presidential politics. He governed according to its precepts and is one of the two men to introduce them into the mainstream of political thought (Wilson was the other). After TR, the Republican Party was never the same. His views were shared by Thomas Dewey, the Republican nominee in 1948.
- Wilson (1913–20)[10]: If TR was the first to embrace progressivism, Wilson was the first to make it an integral part of the principles of the Democratic Party. He was the first chief executive to openly criticize the U.S. Constitution, once comparing it to "political witchcraft." His scorn for the creation of the Founders was also expressed as follows: "[I]f you want to understand the real Declaration of Independence, do not repeat the preface." The preface is the section that asserts "that all men are created equal, that they are endowed by their Creator with certain unalienable Rights, that among these are life, Liberty and the Pursuit of Happiness." Given this thought process it isn't surprising to find that Wilson is regarded as the man who, above all others, created the notion that the Constitution is a "living document." It must be, he said, "Darwinian in structure and in practice." The Democratic Party in 1948 was, intellectually, the party of Wilson. These same ideas made their way into the legal process and are, arguably, more powerful in 2010 than ever. Some hail this as modernism at its best; others regard it as an attack on the foundation of the American government. After Wilson, the Democratic Party was never the same.
- Hoover (1929–32)[11]: Whatever his competence and whatever his intentions, Hoover was thereafter known as the president who led the nation into the Great Depression. Dewey heard about it in 1948, and every Repub-

lican candidate at some time or another has been forced to deal with that bitter memory.

- Franklin Roosevelt: (1933–45)[12]: FDR became a Democratic icon during and after World War II. He shared Wilson's attitude toward the Constitution ("these political [constitutional] rights proved inadequate to insure us equality in the pursuit of happiness"). And out of his discontent came his economic bill of rights[13]: a job; adequate earnings; profit to farmers; fair trade for every businessman; a decent home; a good education; adequate medical care; and protection from the fears of old age, sickness and bad luck. A constitutional amendment could have been proposed to add these rights to the original Bill of Rights, but FDR preferred to lay it out there for his colleagues and others to see. Ever since, many Democrats and Republicans have acted on this proposal as if it had been ratified. (The recent position in the 2010 debate on health care is an example of this: some Democrats repeatedly referred to health care as a "right.") FDR's role during the war and his Social Security and GI Bill legislation are the best-known memories attached to his name. But his economic bill of rights has been more influential, as it has worked its way deeply into national politics and has transformed the role of government in the United States. FDR was a worthy disciple of Wilson, and his action and ideas influenced the 1948 election and every election since.
- Truman (first term, 1945–48)[14]: On the international front, Truman handled his post–FDR chores with surprising skill and ended World War II with his decision to use the A-bomb. Domestically, he was a worthy successor to his mentor, FDR. Under Truman's supervision, the cost of Human Services in the federal budget (1944 vs. 1948) grew more than five times. The proactive federal government envisaged by Wilson and implemented by FDR was continuing in the hands of believers like Truman. This was not an unpopular political position. Truman promised more of the same during his campaign. And Dewey, a more moderate progressive, was in no position to attack the modern trend.

So the political convention tables were set by the leaders of the past, and Democrats had the best of it. There was nothing that Theodore Roosevelt did that could erase the memory of Hoover and his mishaps. History was not something Republicans wanted to talk about. Democrats, on the other hand, were delighted to discuss Hoover at length and never grew tired of bragging about FDR, the longest-serving president in history.

The subliminal impact of Wilson and progressivism on the Democratic Party had not yet been identified by the public, but his influence served as the bedrock upon which most of their actions and speeches dealing with social services rested. To a lesser degree, the same was true with Republicans. Theodore Roosevelt's progressive ideas had been adopted by them, especially in the northeast, and Republicans were not inclined to unduly challenge the steps Democrats were taking into the private sector, which was becoming less private as time moved on. Finally, Truman's first term was nothing to be ashamed of.

History was on the side of Democrats. They had good reason to feel confident as they entered the convention hall.

NEW STATES

The final four of the forty-eight contiguous states were admitted during this era: Utah, Oklahoma, New Mexico and Arizona.[15]

CONSTITUTIONAL AMENDMENTS

Several constitutional amendments were ratified during this era: 1913: Amendment Sixteen (income taxes); Amendment Seventeen (election of senators by popular vote); 1919: Amendment Eighteen (prohibition); 1920: Amendment Nineteen (the right of women to vote).

Prior to Amendment Sixteen, taxes were impersonal and were not levied to achieve social goals. Thereafter, as income taxes began to dominate the revenue mix, the use of taxes to mold behavior and to redistribute wealth became at least as important as the need of them to support government. This was a transformative event in American politics and a seminal victory for progressives.

Amendment Seventeen satisfied an objective of progressives. Senators had been appointed at the state level and their terms were therefore subject to the ups and downs of local elections. Because of the amendment, state powers were decreased; the term of the senator was more dependent on their personal popularity which, in turn, was more susceptible to political pressure than a state would be.

Amendment Nineteen was long overdue, regardless of who sponsored or supported it. Amendment Twenty, moving the presidential year-end to the twentieth day of January, was ratified in 1933, a well as Amendment Twenty-One repealing Prohibition.

About two decades went by before another amendment was passed. Instead of going through this elaborate, time-consuming process, activists have gradually implemented the "living document" theory of the Constitution and have regularly "discovered" new rights for the government that are not enumerated in that founding document. As a consequence the constitutionality of laws has become an increasingly active aspect of the caseload of the Court.

Conventions

Symbolism was a vibrant member of each convention, but Democrats won the battle of history easily. President Cleveland, efficient but colorless, didn't add much to the parade of memories, but many remembered Wilson fondly, and the aura of FDR still hung in the air. Republicans could brag about McKinley and Theodore Roosevelt as loudly as they wished and they could sweep under the rug the forgettable presidencies of Harding and Coolidge, but nothing they could do would erase the memory of Hoover and the Great Depression. The good old days were not something they wanted to talk about. They had to forget the past and present a salable package about the future.

Truman, by 1948, had responded to critics more by deeds than by words. He had exceeded all expectations. But he had not yet convinced party leaders that he could win a general election on his own. And that was the mood in the Democratic convention. Republicans, for the same reason, were elated, confident they could defeat in 1948 Truman or any other Democrat. After all, they had Thomas E. Dewey as their candidate, one of the most impressive political figures of the time. Dewey, by the way, was also a progressive.

The excitement over the 1948 election promised to be high because, for the first time, the conventions would be televised,[16] and the public could hear the proceedings described and analyzed by such journalistic icons as Edward R. Murrow and Douglas Edwards.[17] Also, presidential primaries played a key role in the 1948 election — especially with Republicans — which brought the process closer to the people.

The first significant primary election was held in 1904 in Florida; Wisconsin and Oregon did the same in 1908; and by 1912 a dozen states participated. Twenty states were involved in 1920; then participation leveled off to seventeen to twenty states, after which they grew again in popularity to the levels seen today.[18]

In the earlier years, primary votes were informative but not decisive. They could add luster to, or subtract from, campaign momentum but did not determine nominee identification. Wilson, Taft, Harding, Hoover, Eisenhower and Dewey, for example, did not win the majority of primaries, yet they became their party's nominee.[19]

Governor Earl Warren got most of the Republican primary votes in 1948, yet he was not a serious contender for the nomination at the convention. Instead the party turned to Thomas Dewey. Dewey, in turn, proved that primaries could be important. Had he lost the Oregon primary with Stassen, who had two victories behind him, his reputation would have been diminished considerably and Stassen — or somebody else — might have ended up with the nomination.[20]

DEMOCRATIC CONVENTION

Democrats met during the second week in July of the election year in Philadelphia.[21] The mood of the party was dark. The midterm election of 1946 seriously dimmed Truman's chances to win the 1948 nomination. Democrats had lost control of the House and Senate. Party leaders interpreted that as an anti–Truman vote and they were on the hunt for a new candidate. Presto! Dwight Eisenhower. What a catch he would be. But was he a Democrat? That question was left dangling until the eve of the convention, when Eisenhower said he had no interest in being the Democratic nominee.[22]

The most important drama of the 1948 election took place during the creation of the party platform upon which the party's nominee would run. Opposing forces of consequence were the African Americans, now an important part of the party's base, and southerners who had control of strategic chairmanships in the U.S. Senate. Civil rights, especially as they pertained to blacks, was the divisive issue.

Truman, with a record of fairness with respect to civil rights, recognized the sensitivity of the issue and, like Roosevelt, preferred a bland statement of support within a platform that would satisfy nobody and would kick the issue down the road for later attention. Despite this practical political judgment made at the convention, there is no reason to doubt Truman's support for blacks. Two weeks after the convention, he issued an executive order that eventually ended segregation in the armed forces. He had on various occasions made statements of support for desegregation: "We can not endorse a color line at home and still expect to influence the immense masses that make up the Asian and African people."[23]

The party's Northern leaders refused to accommodate Truman's preference for a bland party plank on civil rights. They believed the time had arrived to take a firm stand on them, especially in four areas[24]: abolition of state poll taxes in federal elections; support for antilynching laws; a permanent fair employment committee; and desegregation of the armed forces.

To sell the tough party platform, Democrats recruited the ebullient mayor of Minneapolis, Hubert Humphrey, who said, "Friends, delegates, I do not believe that there can be any compromise of the guarantees of civil rights.... In spite of my desire ... to see everybody here in unanimous agreement, there are some matters which I think must be stated clearly and without qualification.... There will be no hedging, and there will be no watering down, if you please, of the instruments and the principles of the civil rights programs. My friends, to those who say that we are rushing this issue of civil rights, I say we are 172 years too late!"[25] The platform was approved (652–583). Truman was committed to it; blacks were pleased. The Mississippi delegation and some Alabamans walked out of the convention

Truman did his best in 1947 and 1948 to build general support among the various constituencies that made up the Democratic Party. His veto of the Taft-Hartley Bill was popular with labor; progressives nodded approval at Truman's support for such things as national health insurance, a minimum wage and housing programs; Jews were pleased when in 1948 he recognized the new state of Israel. Finally, his leadership during the war and his anticommunism stance drew support from those with security concerns, and with certain immigrant populations from Europe.[26]

But once politicians stroll away from principle and start to buy allegiance through patronage, favorable legislation or other forms of power behavior, they soon learn that to please one group is sure to displease another. Truman's actions in 1947–48 may or may not have been politically motivated, but reactions to them were. Two of his moves almost cost him the presidency.[27] First, Truman's anticommunism stance irked Henry Wallace. A known socialist and once Truman's secretary of Commerce (1945–46), Wallace disagreed with the president's anti–Soviet policy, spoke out against it and announced in January 1948 that he would be a candidate for the presidency representing the Progressive Party. His candidacy was designed to lure to himself the party progressives who had become Democrats under President Wilson. Second, Truman's comments as president favoring desegregation, and his acceptance of the party platform, drove some southerners to form the States' Rights party, headed by Strom Thurmond. After listening to Humphrey's speech on the party platform, a Tennessee delegate said, "[Y]ou are witnessing here today the dissolution of the Democratic Party in the South." This movement threatened to seriously weaken Truman's base in the South.

Once the internal fights had resolved themselves, Truman easily won the nomination, with Sen. Alben B. Barkley (KY) as his running mate. Truman came out of the convention in the fighting mode that was to become his trademark. In a fiery acceptance speech, Truman promised victory: "I will win this election and make these Republicans like it — don't you forget that!"[28] And he revealed his fundamental campaign strategy: He would not run against Dewey as much as he would run against the do-nothing Congress that stood in the way of his progressive ideas.

REPUBLICAN CONVENTION

Republicans met in Philadelphia during the third week in June of the election year.[29] Eisenhower was courted by them, as he had been by Democrats, but he refused the opportunity to compete for the nomination. His political allegiance was still unknown at this point. He did not campaign for either candidate.

The mood in Philadelphia for Republicans was upbeat. The unconquerable FDR was history; Truman by comparison seemed weak and vulnerable — his national approval rating by the polls was weak; midterm elections had returned both houses of Congress to Republicans. Republicans also had several well known and capable candidates: Gov. Thomas Dewey (NY), who had lost to Roosevelt in 1944; Gov. Harold Stassen (MN), former "boy wonder" of Minnesota politics; Gen. Douglas MacArthur, still on active duty in Japan and unable to campaign; Gov. Earl Warren (CA); Sen. Robert Taft (OH); and Sen. Arthur Vandenberg (MI). A look at the candidates follows:

- Dewey, leader of the eastern bloc of the Republican Party, was regarded as the front-runner, although he was disliked by many as a cold, calculating man.
- Stassen, the surprise candidate, was the most liberal Republican. He shook insiders when he won primary elections in Wisconsin and Nebraska that for a time made him the leading candidate.
- MacArthur, still on active duty, was available as a candidate. Supporters made a major effort in his behalf during the early primaries, but they were neutralized by Stassen's victories.
- Warren and Vandenberg, popular in their own states, made no serious attempt to campaign in others. They pinned their hopes on a deadlocked convention that would eventually turn to one of them.
- Taft, a conservative regarded by many as too dull to win a national election, campaigned against the New Deal. He damaged Stassen's bid by beating him in the Ohio primary.

Dewey, troubled by Stassen's early victories, established Oregon as the battleground between them. He sent his well-supported and powerful political machine to that state to prepare the way, and he agreed to a one-on-one radio debate (the first ever) with Stassen. Oregon went for Dewey, which, combined with Stassen's loss in Ohio to Taft, ended Stassen's presidential effort.

The first two ballots found Dewey well ahead, but not by the amount needed to capture the nomination. His opponents, after the second ballot, requested a recess during which they attempted to devise a strategy that would stop Dewey. They failed. Taft pulled out and Dewey became the nominee on the third ballot; he selected popular Earl Warren as his running mate.

Compared to Democrats, the Republican Party was an afternoon tea. Major divisions destined to split the party did not exist; a unified campaign was predicted. The party platform was straightforward, competitive with Democrats in the area of civil rights and concerns for the working man. Otherwise, they predictably supported Mom and apple pie. The Republican approach was concentrated not so much on ends, as it was on means. They too wanted a safety net for the needy and unemployed, but a different one, less dependent on government. They too wanted to protect workers, but not by making unions even more powerful. And they wanted a tougher anticommunist defense policy. Most of all, however, they wanted to remove the incompetent man from Missouri from the White House and replace him with a highly efficient one capable of handling such momentous duties.

When the two parties emerged from their conventions, the pundits had already figured everything out — Dewey would win easily. And the polls backed them up. According to Gallup, only 36 percent of the people thought Truman was doing a good job as president.[30]

STATES' RIGHTS CONVENTION

The States' Rights Party, known as Dixiecrats, held their convention in Birmingham,[31] Alabama, during the second week of the election year. They were a group of disgruntled southerners who disagreed with Democrats on civil rights issues. Separate but equal was their motto on things related to race. They opposed integration.

Dixiecrats hoped their movement (with an assist from Wallace's Progressive Party) would be strong enough to deprive major candidates of victory and move the election into the House of Representatives. There, it was believed, they could exercise their considerable congressional power and swing political deals that would roadblock further civil rights legislation. Gov. J. Strom Thurmond (SC) was nominated to represent the party, with Gov. J. Fielding Wright (MS) as his running mate.

Dixiecrats believed the 1948 civil rights platform, to which Truman was bound, represented the most intolerable intrusion into the culture of the South since the dark days of Reconstruction. Preservation of its position on race was the justification for the party's existence, but it was shrouded with more high-sounding phrases like states' rights, state sovereignty and constitutionality. A few planks of the party platform demonstrate this[32]:

- We oppose all efforts to evade or destroy the rights guaranteed ... to every citizen of this republic.
- We stand for social and economic justice (and oppose) any invasion ... of the constitutional rights of the states.... We oppose ... the police nation called for by the platforms adopted at the Democratic and Republican conventions.
- We stand for the segregation of the races and the racial integrity of each race.
- We oppose social equality ... by Federal fiat.

More than a solitary few were part of this movement—four states were sympathetic. They made life difficult for Truman; his name wasn't even on the ballot in Alabama.

The mere existence of this party, and the difficult fights that took place over the party platform during the Democratic convention, made it clear that the albatross that hung around the neck of the American political system was still alive and well. Progress was being made but it was an inch by inch struggle that left behind a clear trail of African American blood.

PROGRESSIVE CONVENTION

Progressives met in Philadelphia during the third week of July of the election year.[33] The party had a lineage that went back to the mid–eighteenth century. Its contagious ideas gradually became part of the political lexicon. Because of this, it disappeared as a separated minority party and reappeared to differing degrees in the language of the major parties, Democratic and Republican.

Theodore Roosevelt, a Republican, became the first champion of progressives, but he soon lost that crown to Woodrow Wilson, who was adopted by most progressives as their best hope to bring social justice and economic reform, featuring a more activist central government. A segment of the progressive population within the Democratic Party was not pleased with Truman's foreign policy (too aggressive), and they found his passion to control big business too tepid. Finally, they found distasteful the anticommunism efforts of the House Committee on un–American Activities.

Who better to lead such a group of malcontents than Henry Wallace, former associate of Presidents Roosevelt and Truman? A known socialist, and charged by some to be a communist, Wallace had long before publicly disagreed with Truman on foreign policy. The party platform of progressives was as anti–Truman as it could get, especially on foreign policy[34]: friendly relations with the Soviet Union; an end to the Cold War; an end to segregation; full implementation of voting rights laws; and universal health insurance.

Progressives didn't have a chance to win the election but, unlike the States' Rights Party, they didn't admit it. They unrealistically shot for victory in a national campaign. A conglomeration of liberals, communists and populists, they were often ridiculed; but they added color and tension to the preelection atmosphere. Would they siphon away (with an assist from the States' Rights Party) enough votes to throw the election into the House of Representatives, where anything could happen?

As the convention season ended, the election season began. Four well-known candidates capable of attracting lots of votes were turned loose. The most surprising thing under these circumstances was that so many pundits were so sure of the result — Dewey in a breeze.

Top Candidates

This was a wild field of candidates. Everybody was well known. Truman was president, Dewey was the buttoned down crime fighter from New York, Thurmond was a well known senator and Wallace was a former vice president.

To begin with, Truman, compared to Dewey, was the underdog, and with these other ex–Democrats running against him, the odds of his winning seemed even longer than expected.

HARRY S TRUMAN, DEMOCRAT

Born: 1884, MO; **Education:** High School; **Wife:** Elizabeth V. Wallace; **Children:** One; **Died:** 1972.[35]

Harry S Truman was born in Independence, Missouri, the first son of John and Martha. His father was a farmer and speculator. Truman had two siblings, a brother, John Vivian, and a sister, Mary Jane.*

Truman attended local public schools but could not go further because of his family's circumstances. After graduation he held a variety of minor jobs for five years; then he was called back to the family farm, where he toiled for another decade.

Service and training with the National Guard (1905–11) broke up the routine of Truman's life, and when the United States entered World War I in 1917 he helped to organize the Missouri Field Artillery. His unit was sent to France as part of the 129th Field Artillery and Truman was made a captain in charge of Battery D. He served with distinction, and when he returned he joined the reserves, rising to the rank of colonel. Truman volunteered again when the United States entered World War II in 1941 (he was fifty-seven). The army chief of staff, George Marshall, declined the offer.

Truman was co-owner of a clothing store (1919–22) when he married his childhood sweetheart, Bess Wallace. His store, located in Kansas City, was a fatality of the postwar recession and went out of business. Soon after, using local connections, he was made a judge of Jackson County, Missouri. With one interruption, he remained in that job until 1934, at which time he was elected to the U.S. Senate. He was reelected in 1940, and gained a national reputation because of his work as chairman of a special committee that investigated details behind defense contracts. It was this tour of duty that brought him to the attention of party leaders.

Henry Wallace was the sitting vice president at the time of the 1944 convention. A known socialist and internationalist, Wallace had lost favor with many party leaders, who convinced Roosevelt he would hurt the ticket. Accordingly, ever the political pragmatist, Roosevelt transferred his support to Truman. The man from Missouri became his running mate,[36] which led to his presidency in 1945 when Roosevelt died.

Now, in 1948, it was his turn to stand before the electorate and run for president based on his own record and his own personality. Analysts didn't give him much of a chance.

THOMAS E. DEWEY, REPUBLICAN

Born: 1902, MI; **Education:** University of Michigan; Columbia Law School; **Wife:** Francis Huff[37]; **Children:** Two; **Died:** 1971.[38]

Thomas Edmund Dewey was the only child of George, a newspaper publisher, and Annie (Thomas) Dewey. The family lived above his grandfather's general store.

Truman's sister never married, and became in 1950 Grand Matron of Eastern Star in Missouri. Eastern Star was at the time the largest fraternal organization for men and women in the world. John Vivian Truman became district director of the Federal Housing Administration in Western Missouri.

After graduation from law school, Dewey entered private practice with two New York law firms. On the side he did work for New York Republicans, which led to the beginning of his public career—chief assistant to the U.S. attorney for the Southern District of New York. Dewey's reputation reached national prominence when he was serving as a special prosecutor against organized crime, which led to his election in 1937 as district attorney of New York City. During his career as a prosecutor, Dewey was credited with nailing several well-known mobsters, including Lucky Luciano.

Dewey lost his first attempt to become in 1938 governor of New York. But he succeeded in 1942 and was reelected in 1946 and 1950. In 1944 Dewey became the Republican Party's nominee. Now, still serving as governor, he was trying again, this time against the more vulnerable Harry Truman, bringing with him an enviable reputation as a straight-shooting executive who ran a tight fiscal ship.

Most experts figured he'd win in a walk. He didn't. Dewey finished his term as governor and returned to private practice. He was instrumental in helping Dwight Eisenhower become the 1952 nominee of the Republican Party.

STROM THURMOND, STATES' RIGHTS

Born: 1902, SC; **Education:** Clemson University; **Wife:** Jean Crouch (1926); Nancy Moore (1946); **Children:** Four; **Died:** 2003.[39]

James Strom Thurmond, son of John, a lawyer, and Eleanor attended local schools and Clemson University where he majored in horticulture. After graduation in 1923 he functioned as a farmer, teacher, coach and superintendent of schools for several years. He also studied law under his father, passing, in 1930, the South Carolina bar. The legal background launched his political career as a county district attorney (1930–38). And it was during his stint in that occupation that he was elected to the South Carolina senate and, eventually, to the bench as judge of the Eleventh Circuit Court.

World War II interrupted Thurmond's career. He served with distinction in Europe and the Pacific with the 82nd Airborne Division and returned with his ribbons to make a successful bid in 1946 for governor of his state (1947–51).

Thurmond, a delegate to the 1948 Democratic convention, opposed the renomination of Truman and the party platform, especially as it related to civil rights. He, with other southerners, left the convention and formed their own States' Rights Party, which Thurmond headed. His party won four southern states in the general election, not enough to upset Truman.

Thurmond later appeared on the national scene in 1954 as a replacement for the deceased Sen. Burnet Maybank. As senator, he continued his record as a segregationist, being the originator, for example, of the 1956 Southern Manifesto, which spoke in opposition to the 1954 desegregation ruling of the Supreme Court (*Brown v. Board of Education*).

The Republican Party beckoned to Thurmond in 1956, and he responded by crossing the aisle and supporting the candidacy of Barry Goldwater. His days as a segregationist were over. His support was instrumental in 1968 in the formation of the southern strategy that elected Richard Nixon (1968).

Thurmond was 100 years old when in 2003 he finished his senatorial career. He died soon after. Even in retirement, Thurmond was powerful. Senate leader Trent Lott, because he made complimentary remarks about Thurmond at a 2002 dinner, was accused of being a racist and had to step down as Senate leader because his comments allied him with a man who was once an avowed supporter of desegregation.

HENRY A. WALLACE, PROGRESSIVE

Born: 1888, IA; **Education:** Iowa State College; **Wife:** Llo Browne; **Children:** Three; **Died:** 1965.[40]

Henry Agard Wallace was the son of Henry Cantwell Wallace, a prominent farm journalist, and secretary of agriculture under President Coolidge. He began his career following in his father's footsteps as a farm journalist and gained a substantial reputation as an expert in the field. This led to the formation of his company, Pioneer Hi-Bred, which made him a wealthy man.

National politics entered Wallace's life in 1933 when President Roosevelt made him secretary of agriculture, a post his father had filled a decade earlier. Wallace, like his father, had been a Republican until his appointment, but thereafter switched parties and became an enthusiastic supporter of Roosevelt's New Deal. He remained in that position until 1940, when he was nominated to become FDR's running mate. He served as vice president for four years (1941–44).

Wallace was an active vice president. FDR named him chairman of the Board of Economic Welfare, and the Supply Priorities and Allocations Board, both of which were involved with the production, purchase, allocation and shipment of wartime supplies, which made him an important member of FDR's war cabinet. While handling his duties, Wallace came into conflict with conservatives from his own party, especially Jesse H. Jones, secretary of commerce.

Wallace added to his enemies list with a 1942 speech entitled "Century of the Common Man," which in the next year reappeared in book form. He and his book were well received by the public, but others, including party leaders, Winston Churchill and conservatives were disturbed by his views.

Wallace's goodwill tour in 1943 of Latin America also proved to be controversial. On the plus side, he persuaded twelve countries to declare war against Germany; on the minus side, Wallace insisted on union clauses in Latin America contracts that required fair wages and working conditions and obligated the United States to pay for half of the cost of such improvements. Such clauses were resisted by Jesse H. Jones, secretary of commerce.

As the end of his term neared, Wallace had become known as a socialist with an attitude toward communism that was overly sympathetic. Combined with his other altercations with party leaders, this proved too much of a burden for FDR to carry into his next election. He dropped Wallace as vice president and ran with Harry S Truman.

FDR didn't drop Wallace completely. Ironically, he made him secretary of commerce, succeeding his old rival, Jesse Jones, who was forced to resign. When Truman succeeded FDR, he could find no common ground with Wallace, who thought Truman's attitude toward the Soviets too harsh. Truman fired him.

Wallace returned to his career in journalism and became editor of the *New Republic* magazine. As such, he consistently attacked Truman's policies, especially the Truman Doctrine, which pledged financial and military support to Greece and Turkey to prevent their falling to Soviet control. Wallace wrote that such a belligerent attitude would result in a "century of fear."

Given his nature, his positions and Truman's alleged vulnerability, it came as no surprise to find Wallace as a presidential candidate under the banner of the Progressive Party. He did not win a single state in the general election. The presidential run marked the end of Wallace's political career, and he returned to farming interests and to writing. His political attitudes changed with age. He supported the Korean War. His book, *Where I Was Wrong*, was an apology for his previous positions on the Soviet Union. He, a Democrat, even supported the reelection in 1956 of Republican President Eisenhower.

He died of Lou Gehrig's disease in 1965 in Connecticut.

Election Tone

Each election is influenced by what happened before. This one was no exception. It has been established that trips down memory lane during this election were almost the exclusive territory of Democrats. Anything positive Republicans could say about McKinley or Theodore Roosevelt could be instantly parried by the mere mention of Hoover and the memories of the Great Depression that his name triggered.

So, it was FDR all the way, as far as nostalgia went. And Truman used it. He was willing to defend his own record since he had taken over from FDR, but he didn't hesitate to invoke the memory of his illustrious predecessor to great advantage whenever it suited him. History might reveal FDR's weaknesses, but in 1948 he was to most Americans the president with the vibrant personality who had seen them through World War II and the Great Depression. Truman could do no wrong riding on the great man's coattails whenever it suited him. Dewey had no such luxury. History was something for him to stay away from.

Because of the actions and the policies of preceding presidents, Truman and Dewey faced an electorate accustomed to vote buying on a large scale and the lure or the fear of tax changes that could, at the stroke of a pen, alter their lifestyle or their economic security. Government was deeply into their lives. This was no longer the government of the Founders; this was the government of Wilson and Roosevelt.*

Truman, as progressive as FDR, liked it that way.† Perhaps pundits overlooked it, but Truman and his party were keenly aware that the civilian work force of the United States government was about 1.5 million people larger than it was when in 1933 FDR took office.[41] Most of them owed their jobs to the governmental style of two Democratic presidents; they were unlikely to vote for a "smaller government" Republican.

Also, the state election machinery confronting Truman and Dewey was accustomed to the patronage that had flowed from Democrats to them over the past sixteen years. The public that candidates confronted were also accustomed to the social programs that were associated with Democrats and they were gradually internalizing them as rights, a feeling that Democrats, in the FDR tradition (his economic bill of rights) sold and catered to. These tangible and intangible factors were of inestimable value to Truman and, across the board, worked against any Republican candidate.

There was another factor that made the voters Truman and Dewey confronted different from those that, say, Harrison and Cleveland faced — Supreme Court decisions.[42] The Court was ruled in the 1893–1948 period by four chief justices: William H. Taft (1921–30), Charles E. Hughes (1930–41), Harlan F. Stone (1941–46) and Fred M. Vinson. And they were assisted by more than two dozen assistant justices, some of them being well known and well remembered: Oliver W. Holmes (1902–32), Louis D. Brandeis (1916–39), Hugo L. Black (1937–71), Felix Frankfurter (1939–62) and William O. Douglas (1939–75). Controversial decisions came out of this group that influenced voter behavior in 1948, for example[43]:

- Black voters would be disillusioned and angry. *Plessy v. Ferguson* (1895) legalized "separate but equal" as a method for dealing with them socially, educationally and professionally, thus condemning them to inferior status. Some light at the end of the tunnel was provided by three other rulings: *Gaines v. Canada* (1948), *Sipuel v. Oklahoma* (1948) and *Shelley v. Kraemer* (1948). But it wasn't enough. *Plessy* was still national law.
- Businessmen were forewarned: The Supreme Court was looking over the shoulders of businessmen at their practices, including the obligation to give workers a chance to join unions— they must confer and negotiate with them or face Supreme Court sanctions: *Holden v. Hardy* (1898);

*The federal income tax was by this time the major revenue raiser. Personal and corporate income taxes amounted to 70 percent of total revenue. The day of using the tax system to redistribute wealth had arrived.
   †President Truman sent a message to Congress recommending national health insurance (and did the same in 1945) and got nowhere.

Lochner v. New York (1905); *Muller v. Oregon* (1908); *Nebbia v. New* York
(1934); *NLRB v. John & Laughlin Steel Co.* (1937).

• Protestors were forewarned: A president has great power during war and
it was demonstrated by Wilson and FDR. Beware of crossing the line,
or face jail. Even the innocent are sometimes vulnerable: *Schenck v.
United States* (1919); *Whitney v. California* (1927); *Hirabayashi v. United
States* (1943).

• Other news: Price controls are constitutional; government can tax agriculture, but it can't control it — that's state business.

In addition to rulings of the Court, two constitutional amendments (sixteen
and seventeen) previously discussed added flavor to the mix.

It was the new era of electoral politics. The progressive agenda had made
the system of government established by the Founders a campaign issue, not
expressed as such, but taking the form of actions: Intrusions by the government
into the private sector in the form of controls; income redistribution (the tax
system); social activism (expanded relief programs) — activities foreign to most
presidents prior to Wilson. The trend was slowed under Harding and Coolidge,
but it picked up momentum again under Hoover and was brought to full flower
under FDR. It was lovingly protected by his successor, Truman, who promised
more of the same in his second term.

Dewey was the heavy favorite to win in 1948 but, except for the Republican
comeback in the 1946 congressional elections and the tendency of many to
underrate the man from Missouri, the undercurrents within the political system threw suspicion on that early confidence. Candidates campaigned only
indirectly against each other. Both expended most of their energies trying to
persuade the public to join their cause. One did so entertainingly and win-
ningly — Truman; the other did not — Dewey.

TRUMAN CAMPAIGN

During his acceptance speech, Truman said he would call Congress back
into session and dare it to pass all the liberal-sounding legislation endorsed in
the Republican platform. He said, "The battle lines of 1948 are the same as they
were in 1932 when the nation lay prostrate and helpless as a result of Republican
misrule and inaction." *New York Times* radio and television critic Jack Gould
judged it perhaps the best performance of Truman's presidency: "He was relaxed
and supremely confident, swaying on the balls of his feet with almost a method-
ical rhythm."[44]

True to his word, Truman, after the nomination, called Republicans into
a special session of Congress. There he presented it with a list of his desired
legislation, knowing his attempt would fail. The session lasted two weeks and,
as expected, Truman's program was not passed.[45] The trap was sprung. Thereafter, the thrust of his campaign was against the "do nothing" Republican-con-

trolled Congress that persistently voted against his progressive ideas. And he campaigned against Congress as vigorously as any man in history.

His campaign began in September.[46] As Truman's train pulled away from Washington, Vice President Barkley yelled, "Mow 'em down, Harry." To which Truman replied: "I'm going to give 'em hell." And thusly was his nickname born: "Give 'em hell, Harry."

Truman was not a good speaker; poor eyesight made him lean over to read prepared speeches. On the other hand, he was a voluble and interesting man in small groups when speaking naturally. Handlers studied this image problem and arrived at a solution that worked: Truman would speak from an outline and then wing it as ideas came to him or as circumstances changed. In this way he gave more than 130 speeches over the next two weeks.

His folksy ways were well accepted and entertaining. Reporters were fond of him; audiences responded as he lambasted the "good for nothin'" Republicans in Congress who, he warned, would repeal the New Deal — and they would replace the party that had saved the nation during the Great Depression and led it during the Second World War.[47] During primary and presidential seasons, Truman's entourage covered 21,000 miles; he visited 250 cities and gave more than 300 speeches.[48]

Mr. Republican, Sen. Robert Taft, ridiculed Truman for badmouthing Congress at "whistle stops" across the nation. In so doing, he did two favors for Democrats. He gave a catchy name to Truman's campaign (a whistlestop campaign), and he insulted small town America by implying that small cities (whistlestops) weren't worthy of a candidate's time. Votes are created by small mistakes like this.

Truman took advantage of everything that could help him, including voters' fears of losing benefits, and mistakes made by buttoned-down Dewey during his campaign (which were surprisingly frequent, if minor).[49] Even the lack of adequate funding was at times turned to an advantage. For example, Truman's fund-raiser allowed the networks to cut Truman off in the middle of a speech, which drew much publicity and useful contributions. Another time, when a station manager said he would cut the president off because of a lack of money to pay for time, reporters jumped on the story. Letters of indignation were written, and again campaign contributions went up.[50]

In his final campaign speech, Truman said, "The smart boys say we can't win. They tried to bluff us with a propaganda blitz, but we called their bluff; we told the people the truth. And the people are with us. The tide is rolling. All over the country I have seen it in the people's faces. The people are going to win this election."[51]

The campaign over, Truman returned to Independence, Missouri. On Election Day, he had a sandwich and a glass of buttermilk and went to bed at six-thirty. For some reason he awoke at midnight, in time to hear broadcaster H.V. Kaltenborn announce that Dewey would eventually win by a huge margin.[52]

Truman went back to bed until awakened by a secret service agent at four o'clock to listen to the radio. It was Kaltenborn again, this time announcing that Truman was well ahead on popular votes, but his failure to draw a sufficient number of electoral votes would move the election to the House of Representatives (which was the hope of the States' Rights Party). It was over at 10 o'clock. To the surprise of everyone but Truman, he had won the election.

DEWEY CAMPAIGN

Dewey also drew large crowds during a campaign that was low key, even bland, and he was inclined to make small mistakes. At one stop, for example, he said it was nice that the kids in the audience were given a day off from school — it was a Saturday.[53]

All campaigners make mistakes, but when Mr. Perfect makes them, media wolves pounce. Dewey's campaign was littered with small errors that were magnified by the press, jumped on by Truman supporters and turned into campaign slogans. His critical remarks, for example, about a train engineer who made an error that could have been dangerous was turned by Truman into a criticism of all engineers, who were not as dangerous as the great engineer, Herbert Hoover, who had steered the nation into the Great Depression.

Truman occupied himself by blasting Congress[54] and selling voters on the idea that only he, plus congressional control, could keep the New Deal intact. Dewey, for his part, dealt with large ideas and gave the impression that Truman was irrelevant to the discussion. Perhaps he was lulled into this approach by polls, which consistently had him ahead comfortably. (The final preelection poll by Gallup saw Dewey ahead by five points.)[55]

All agreed that Dewey appeared presidential, but at the same time (assisted by the little-man-on-the-wedding-cake image that had clung to him) he was regarded by many as somewhat of a prissy milquetoast, the direct opposite of down-to-earth, give-'em-hell Harry. He was a formal man. And unlike Truman's, Dewey's campaign, like the man himself, was tightly disciplined. He gave the same dull speech at every stop, one that contained high ideas and few specifics.

Reporters traveling with Truman enjoyed the man and the mission; they followed him wherever he went. Those traveling with Dewey enjoyed neither, and they were slow to leave the campaign train when he left it to speak elsewhere. In an attempt to describe the difference between the two campaigns, a White House staffer said, "On the Dewey train, newspapermen played bridge and drank martinis and manhattans; on the Truman train, they played poker and drank scotch and bourbon."[56] Instant portrait: Plutocrat versus Everyman.

Not everyone was pleased with the reserved tone of the Dewey campaign. His running mate, Gov. Earl Warren, for example, once exclaimed, "I wish just once that I could call somebody an S.O.B." Nor was it well received by some influential members of the press. Truman, by them, was referred to as feisty and personable, affectionate terms that, whatever his politics, embraced the man. Dewey, on the other hand, was "the only man who could strut sitting down" or who made his appearance "like a man who was mounted on casters and given a tremendous shove from behind." And it didn't help to foster a macho image to end sentences with "period," or to flavor his speeches with "Oh, Lord" and "Good Gracious."[57]

Nevertheless, the feeling of confidence within Dewey's entourage was persistent to the end. Sidney Shallett, in the *Saturday Evening Post*, wrote, "The Governor of New York talks not like a man who wants to be president, but like a man who already is president."[58]

THURMOND CAMPAIGN

The States' Rights Party had no delusions of winning.[59] Its hope was to derail the Truman campaign and throw the election into the House, or failing that to cause Truman's outright defeat. Either way, Democrats would be taught the importance of the South, and that awareness would weaken the civil rights movement.

The states' rights argument against desegregation was looked on suspiciously as a cover for racism. But the topic of states' rights with some southerners, including Thurmond, was a real concern of those who didn't like the idea of the federal government mandating any kind of behavior to states. For them, the issue wasn't race, it was federal power run amok. In a March 1948 poll, only a third of the people supported Truman's civil rights programs.[60]

As measured against other southerners, Thurmond was a racial moderate who placed states' rights as a central issue in the campaign, whether the specific topic was the integration of the races, or anything else that was, as he saw things, a state's business. His campaign, mostly through southern states, was as independent as the man. He enjoyed campaigning and the public adulation that came with it. Generally speaking, he ignored the campaign director and canned speeches, preferring to set his own agenda and use material prepared by his staff. While observing his candidate's rush from town to town, the belabored Dixiecrat campaign director was heard to decry Thurmond's attempt to appear at every little "pigtrail" in the South.

Thurmond's press reviews from the North were surprisingly positive. As an aspiring politician, he had not run racial campaigns. As governor of South Carolina, he had governed even-handedly and opposed the poll tax and acted energetically against mob violence. The *New York Times* described him as a man who embodied the "personality of the Old South and the New." H.L. Mencken, of the *Baltimore Sun*, wrote: "[Thurmond is] the best of all the presidential candidates, [but] all the worst morons in the South are for him."[61]

The Thurmond campaign was geographically limited but otherwise had all the trappings of a traditional campaign — offices throughout the South, stickers, banners, buttons and a roster of speakers.

Some people in the movement saw the beginnings of a third party; others, including Thurmond, disagreed. He campaigned hard, but after the election he separated himself from Dixiecrats and pursued his career as a U.S. senator, first as a Democrat and later as a Republican.

HENRY WALLACE CAMPAIGN

Truman had his whistle stop tour of the nation to enliven the campaign.[62] Wallace, because of his positions and the way he sold them, added color as well. The civil rights planks of the Progressive Party did not differ that much from the competition, but Wallace's demonstrations of sincerity were much more forceful. Black and white candidates of his party campaigned side by side, for instance, and Wallace would not appear before a segregated audience, nor would he patronize segregated hotels and restaurants. A barrage of eggs and tomatoes hurled at him and his black secretary was not an unusual occurrence on the Wallace tour.

Disclosure of the "Guru letters" at discrete intervals succeeded in embarrassing Wallace during the campaign, making him appear weird to some voters. Somewhat of a mystic in search of a comfortable religious faith that would lead him to "Eternal light and life," Wallace had cultivated a friendship with a Russian painter/mystic, Nicholas Roerich.[63]

In the correspondence they exchanged, Wallace referred to Roerich as "Dear Guru," and in the body of his letters he often referred to well known personalities by unusual names: Secretary of State Cordell Hull was "the sour one"; FDR was "the wavering one." And he included phrases like "Long have I been aware of the occasional fragrance from the other world, which is the real world." Correspondence of this type, when revealed, leads to wisecracks, and does not add to the stability of one's image.

Another nail in the coffin of Wallace's campaign was based on the charge that, at worst, he was a communist, or, at best, sympathetic to those who were. To add to this problem, the Communist Party endorsed him. Prominent journalists like Dorothy Thompson and H.L. Mencken jumped all over this, much to Wallace's discomfort. Wallace had no chance to win, but his participation sharpened some of the issues and made for great newspaper copy.

THE POLLS

Polling was in its infancy, but those who were active reported favorably on Dewey up to the last minute. Generally speaking, they gave him a five to fifteen point lead up to Election Day. Elmo Roper, a leading pollster, announced in September that he would poll no more because Dewey was a certain winner.[64]

That feeling was so pervasive that the head of the Secret Service was with Dewey in New York on election night.

Election Results, 1948

Truman versus Dewey: The accidental president versus the-man-born-for-the-job — or so the press and the pollsters believed.

Election Results 1948

Candidates	EV	%	Pop. (000)	Pop. %	Pop. %
Truman	303	57.0	24,106	49.5	52.0
Dewey	189	36.0	21,970	45.1	48.0
Thurmond	39	7.0	1,169	2.4	
Wallace	0		1,157	2.4	
Other	0		290	.6	
Total	531	100.0	46,692	100.0	100.0

Source: NY Times Almanac 2009, p.131

EV=electoral vote; Pop. = popular vote; Source: http://www.u-s-history.com/pages/h262.html

Truman won with a 114 electoral vote margin — 57 percent of all electoral votes. According to the self-imposed definition of a close election, this election didn't qualify for analysis; it looks like a walloping electoral victory and it exceeds the popular vote threshold. But like many things political, there was more to it than the statistical result, including the inability to reach a conclusive verdict until the morning after Election Day. So — author's privilege — it was included.

Truman's electoral enemy was Dewey plus fringe parties that, in effect, tried to pull him down. Republican popularity was a potential threat, but disunity within the Democratic Party made it more so. As a consequence, Truman's victory in the most important states was dangerously marginal. And the tallying of votes continued through the night until mid-morning of the next day, when the news that shocked the nation was released.

Truman had beat the so-called unbeatable. He had won the day against the smug, super-confident Republicans and the power play of the rebels and progressives within his own party.

Election Results 1948
States with 15+ Electoral Votes
Winning Percent

Candidates/ Votes	NY 47	PA 35	IL 28	CA 25	OH 25	TX 23	MI 19	MA 16	NJ 16	MO 15
Truman	45	47	50	48	50	66	58	55	46	58
Dewey	46	51	49	47	49	24	41	43	50	41
Total	91	98	99	95	99	90	99	98	96	99

Source: http://uselectionatlas.org/RESULTS/

David Liep's Atlas, http://www.uselectionatlas.org/

There are 249 electoral votes in these ten states, 47 percent of the total. Dewey should have been (and was) competitive in California; he figured to lose Texas and Missouri. The other states should have been his. Some were; some were not:

- New York: The state should have been the harbinger of things to come. It is Dewey's home state, the place where he made his reputation as a crime buster and governor. He won by a hair. Wallace was the minority opposition. Without his involvement, Truman would have won the state easily. This statistical victory for Dewey was actually an embarrassment to him politically.
- Pennsylvania: A close, but decisive win for Dewey.
- Illinois: A close win for Truman, but decisive. A major disappointment for Dewey, costing twenty-eight electoral votes.
- California: A close win for Truman, but more decisive than it appears. The Progressive vote was higher than the winning margin, a vote that mostly would have gone to Truman absent Wallace's race; a disappointment to Dewey, but not a complete surprise.
- Ohio: A close win for Truman but, again, more decisive than it appears because it was Wallace who kept the election so close. This result was a disappointment to Dewey at a cost of twenty-five electoral votes.
- Texas: A decisive Truman victory. No surprise here.
- Michigan: A huge Truman win and a disappointment to Dewey at a cost of nineteen electoral votes.
- Massachusetts: A huge Truman win and a disappointment to Dewey of sixteen electoral votes.
- New Jersey: Appeared to be an easy win for Dewey but, like New York, it was actually an embarrassment to him. Absent the fringe vote, the man from Missouri would have come close in this state and might have won it.
- Missouri: A big win for Truman in his home state despite competition from the States' Rights Party.

Losses in Illinois (28), Ohio (25), Michigan (19) and Massachusetts (16)[65] cost Dewey 88 electoral votes. Toss in California (25), and the total is 113 votes. He lost the election by 114 votes. Conclusion: He couldn't hold his natural constituency.

There is one more point: Wallace hurt Truman in Connecticut (8), Maryland (8), Michigan (19), New Jersey (16), New York (46); the States' Rights Party beat him in Alabama (11), Louisiana (10), Mississippi (9) and South Carolina (8).[66] A total of 135 electoral votes are involved in these states, each of which was lost to Truman as a result of a split in the Democratic Party. With that split, he beat Dewey handily; without it, he would have demolished him.

The 1948 election is traditionally listed as one of the close ones because Truman won it with less than 50 percent of the popular vote and because the announcement of the winner was dramatically late. Analysis reveals, however, that his head-to-head popular vote with Dewey was comfortable and his surprising national strength offset the impact of fringe parties, which pulled him to a convincing electoral win that would have been even larger with a unified party behind him.

The Truman Cabinet

The Truman cabinet[67] was made up of typical professionals, including some of the memorable men in American history (Dean Acheson; George C. Marshall) as follows:

Vice President: Alben W. Barkley, Kentucky; **Secretary of State:** Dean Acheson, Connecticut; **Secretary of Defense:** Louis Johnson, West Virginia (1949–50), George C. Marshall, Pennsylvania (1950–51), Robert Lovett, Texas; **Attorney General:** J. Howard McGrath, Rhode Island (1949–52), James P. McGranery, Pennsylvania; **Secretary of Agriculture:** Charles F. Brannan, Colorado; **Secretary of Labor:** Maurice J. Tobin, Massachusetts; **Secretary of Treasury:** John W. Snyder, Arkansas; **Postmaster General:** Jesse M. Donaldson, Illinois; **Secretary of Interior:** Oscar L. Chapman, Virginia/Colorado; **Secretary of Commerce:** Charles Sawyer, Ohio.

Truman's choices were not too controversial. Questions of cronyism were raised over the appointments of Louis John in defense and John Snyder in treasury. Conflict between cabinet members was not extraordinary except in the instance of Johnson versus Acheson over the most desirable shape of defense, a continuing and controversial subject because of rifts within the defense establishment. Johnson lost the argument and was fired.

The Truman Congress

The initial greeting of Truman by the voters had been powerfully negative and Democrats lost control of Congress for the first time in years. But his actual performance on the job won the loyalties of former supporters. They came flocking back to the fold in 1946 and made a clean sweep of the contest. During the midterm election, Truman lost some support, but maintained enough control to protect the fruits of the Roosevelt/Truman administrations.

Pro-Administration Congressional Power

Congress	Year	President	House %	Senate %
80	1947	Truman (D)	43	47
81	1949	Truman (D)	60	56
82	1951	Truman (D)	54	51

Appendix 1.1, 1.2

Bold type-minority position

The position of the Democratic Party in the 80th Congress explains in part Truman's underdog status when the election campaign began. And the power of his coattails to once more establish Democratic dominance in both houses of Congress was nothing short of outstanding. The weakness of the Dewey presidential campaign was shrouded in election statistics. But there was nothing obscure about congressional races. Here Democratic dominance was unmistakable.

In the House and the Senate, pro–Truman allies took over and gave to Truman another great chance to continue the work of his predecessor. During his final two years, however, control slipped and, based upon the ever-sensitive slippage in the House, the prospects for Republicans in 1952 looked good.

Sam Rayburn (D-TX) was Speaker of the House during Truman's presidency, except for two years under Joseph Martin (R-MA). The Senate for the first time appointed a Leader in 1920 (Charles Curtis (R-TX). During Truman's years, the position of Majority Leader was filled by three Democrats and one Republican: Alben Barkley (before he became vice president), Scott Lucas (IL), Ernest McFarland (father of the GI Bill)[68] and Wallace White (R-ME).

The Truman Supreme Court

Chief Justice Fred Vinson headed the Supreme Court during Truman's second term. He had a distinguished resume. After serving eight terms as a loyal Democrat in the House, he accepted an appointment to the U.S. Court of Appeals, Washington, D.C., where he served for five years. He resigned from that post to join the Roosevelt administration as head of the Office of Economic Stabilization and, later, the Office of War Mobilization. A New Dealer to the core, he presumably got a warm welcome from like-minded associates.

Supreme Court Justices, 1949–52

Judge	Began	Appointed by	Ended
Fred M. Vinson (KY)	1946	Truman	1953
Hugo L. Black (AL)	1937	Roosevelt	1971
Stanley Reed (KY)	1938	Roosevelt	1957
Felix Frankfurter (MA)	1939	Roosevelt	1962
William O. Douglas (MN)	1939	Roosevelt	1975
Frank Murphy (MI)	1940	Roosevelt	1949
Robert H. Jackson (PA)	1941	Roosevelt	1954
Wiley B. Rutledge (KY)	1943	Roosevelt	1949
Harold Burton (MA)	1945	Truman	1958
Tom C. Clark (TX)	1949	Truman	1967
Sherman Minton (IN)	1949	Truman	1956

Source: Oyez, http://www.oyez.org/ — Members of the Supreme Court, http://www.supremecourtus.gov/about/members.pdf

Men in Black, Mark Levin, Preface

Note: Hugo Black was a former Ku Klux Klan member. He suffered a stroke in 1969, which impaired his memory. By 1971, constant pain in his head made it difficult to concentrate, and his short-term memory was poor. Paranoia followed. In effect, he was unable to perform his duties for more than two years, yet he remained active. Felix Frankfurter was a character witness for the Soviet spy Alger Hiss. Legal ethicists were troubled by his behavior during Brown v. Board of Education (he leaked privileged information). William O. Douglas was a known womanizer. His frequent marriages and divorces with younger women did not add to the dignity of the Court, and they brought to him financial hardship, which led him to seek supplemental income from questionable sources. A stroke in 1974 impaired his faculties, but he would not retire and his colleagues refused to count his vote until he did.

A summary of a few cases that might have influenced voters of the day follows[69]:

SWEATT V. PAINTER, 1950

The facts: A Texas law school provides separate but equal facilities for black students.

The issue: Is separate but equal a constitutional response to the Equal Protection Clause?

The decision: No. In this state, the mere separation from the majority of law students harms students' abilities to compete in the legal arena — facilities are not equal.

(This was an apparent, but not a real, reversal of the "separate but equal" doctrine. The Court ruled this way because the facility for blacks was obviously less than equal. The ruling actually confirmed the hated doctrine. Apologists for the Court might hasten to point out that the majority of sitting justices were Southerners. It doesn't work. The decision was unanimous.)

McLAURIN V. OKLAHOMA, 1950

The facts: A black student was admitted to Oklahoma State University on a segregated basis; the student was given equal education opportunity.

The issue: Does the University program satisfy the requirements of the Equal Protection Clause?

The decision: No. "The Fourteenth Amendment precludes differences by the state based upon race."[70] Segregation is forbidden.

This decision marked the end of segregated graduate and professional education protected by *Plessy v. Ferguson,* a huge victory for blacks and their supporters.

DENNIS V. UNITED STATES, 1951

The facts: Communist Party operatives were convicted under the Smith Act for actively advocating anti–American ideas.

The issue: Does the conviction violate First Amendment rights?

The decision: No. There is a difference between philosophical discussion and advocacy.

ZORACH V. CLAUSEN, 1952

The facts: New York law allowed students to be dismissed from class to attend religious education programs at another location.

The issue: Does the law violate the provisions of the First Amendment?

The decision: No. There is "no constitutional requirement which makes it necessary for government to be hostile to religion."

It is painful to see that almost a hundred years after the Civil War the issue of segregation still gnawed away at the innards of America. But, more important, it was heartening to see decisions from the Court that were slowly, but persistently, allowing blacks the equal rights to which they were entitled.

Domestic Affairs Relative to Current Political Issues

Democrats, back in power in 1949, controlled both houses of Congress, not with a veto-proof majority but with sufficient clout to continue in the FDR mold. And Truman lost no time in making his most formidable move within the area of social welfare. In 1950 he expanded Social Security to cover ten million more workers; benefits were increased, as was the payroll tax.[71] Two years later the cost of the program was three times higher.[72] Thusly does a social program grow and then explode.

LEGISLATIVE EVENTS 1949–52

Postwar problems, internal security issues and the threat posed by Korea prevented Truman from the vigorous pursuit of his progressive tendencies, plus the fact that he lost his congressional wallop in the 1950 elections. Nevertheless, he left memorable legislative victories behind:

1949

- The Central Intelligence Agency Act[73] established the agency that has existed ever since.
- The Housing Act,[74] a response to urban decline, provided aid for slum clearance and urban redevelopment.
- The minimum wage was increased.[75]

The idea of a minimum wage imposed by the federal government has been a hot issue ever since the populist/progressive movements first appeared in the previous century. The humane argument for one is obvious. The argument against is no less valid but not as obvious: a high minimum wage hurts those it is designed to help by closing down low-wage job opportunities for beginners. Whichever argument prevails, there is no explicit constitutional authority to support the federal government's interference in such contractual decisions.

1950

- Social Security coverage and benefits were increased.[76]
- The Federal Civilian Defense Act[77] centralized internal security matters in a new agency, the Federal Civil Defense Agency. This act was provoked by fear of nuclear attack from the Soviet Union and it promoted such things as security cellars.

Another interesting development during this period was the work of the Sen. Kefauver (D-TN) Committee,[78] a Senate investigative unit that probed for the first time in depth the activities of the Mafia in the United States. The work of the committee was productive. Legalized gambling initiatives, in Massachusetts, Montana, Arizona and California, were defeated; seventy crime commissions were established in cities across the nation. Publicity associated with this work vaulted Kefauver into the national spotlight.

COMMUNISTS IN GOVERNMENT

The Truman administration was plagued by accusations that there were communist spies in the American government:

- The McCarran Security Act (1950)[79] empowered Congress (Senate Internal Security Subcommittee) to conduct hearings in a search for communists, a law that gave Sen. Joseph McCarthy a forum for his communist hunt, which was partly justifiable but sometimes brutally handled. The committee had a life of twenty-seven years. McCarthy ended up censured and disgraced for his tactics. Communists in government were found and convicted.
- House Un-American Activities Committee (1938–75)[80]: This investigative unit was on the hunt for active communists in the private sector. It is most famous for its investigation in 1947 of the motion picture industry and its identification of the "Hollywood Ten," people from various crafts employed by the industry who refused to answer questions. They were branded "reds" and blackballed. Their sympathizers are still enraged by the memory of these hearings.

ECONOMIC GROWTH

Postwar unemployment problems went surprisingly well for Truman, aided considerably by the GI Bill, which permitted veterans to go to college for four years. But the postwar inflation rate was a real problem. For example, the rate in 1946 was about 8 percent and conditions were rough for two more years until the economy corrected itself. Two years of calm followed before the inflation balloon went up again. During the election year it cooled again to 2 percent.

Misery Index, 1946–1952
Percentage

President	Year	Interest	Inflation	Unemployment	Total
Truman	1946	1.5	8.4	3.9	13.8
Truman	1947	1.6	14.7	3.9	20.2
Truman	1948	1.9	7.7	3.8	13.4
Truman	1949	2.0	-1.0	5.9	6.9
Truman	1950	2.1	1.1	5.3	8.5
Truman	1951	2.6	7.9	3.3	13.8
Truman	1952	3.0	2.3	3.0	8.3

Source, interest: http://www.nber.org/palmdata/erp/b73.html

Source, inflation: Inflationdata.com

Source, unemployment: http://stats.bls.gov/cps/cpsaat1.pdf

The United States benefited from war business. Then came the lull at the war's end. In 1951 growth resumed aided by the reconstruction business that came from Europe.

Gross Domestic Product, Public Debt

Year	GDP (bil)	% Growth	Public Debt (bil)	% PD/GDP
1948	256.0	9.8	216.3	84.5
1949	271.3	6.0	214.3	79.0
1950	273.2	.1	219.0	80.2
1951	320.3	17.2	214.3	66.9
1952	348.7	8.9	214.8	61.6

Source: Historical Tables 2010, 1.2, 7.1

Bold = war years

The economy was flat in 1950, but then the needs of war (Korea) and the rapid rebuilding of the military turned things around into boom times again. (After the big war, Truman eviscerated the military, dropping active forces from 12.1 million to 1.5 million in 1950,[81] all of this while the Soviets were blustering and North Korea was snarling. Then war broke out in Korea and the U.S. became the lead nation in an attempt by the United Nations to bring the conflict to a close. In 1951 and 1952 defense spending exploded.)[82] This was a different economic world. The GDP (unadjusted dollars) was more than thee times bigger than it had been under Hoover, and the nation would never again return to prewar size. As an international power and trader, America was destined to grow even larger.

One is inclined to view the Truman record on debt management in one of two ways: (1) He divided excess revenues rationally by lowering debt at a steady pace and spending the balance on progressive social programs; (2) Excess revenues should have been directed to debt until interest expense in the federal budget was less than, say, 5 percent of total nondefense spending. In other words, praise or criticism of his money management policies depends on how one views the role of government.

During the Roosevelt regime, British economist John Maynard Keynes became the guru-of-the-day, and the attitude toward government spending and debt was forever changed. Under Keynesian theory, balanced budgets as a federal objective are old-fashioned relics of no value to a modern government. Such an attitude is defended by respected economists who believe in a hyperactive central government. Keynes' theories remained dominant until the presidency of Ronald Reagan in the 1980s.

CONSTITUTIONAL AMENDMENTS, 1921–1952

Amendment Twenty-two in 1951 was added to the Constitution. It placed a two-term limitation on presidents, a belated response to the FDR phenomenon.

Foreign Affairs Relative to Current Political Issues

The world of 1948 that President Truman faced was not as complex as the one he faced in 1945, but it was a larger and more complex world than any president, other than FDR, ever had to deal with. The war was over, but consequences of it were not, and they were of importance to the United States. Europe was ravaged and on those terms needed assistance. But Europe was more than that. It was also a market for American goods; the American economy would not long remain robust if the rest of the world was in a shambles. Something had to be done to fix that by those who were still standing strong after the war. The United States was the world's best hope.

Military pressure also continued; it didn't end with the surrender of Germany and Japan (1945). Soviet troops moved into North Korea in the same year. The U.S. responded with troops in South Korea, and the Cold War officially began. Yesterday's ally had become today's enemy.

The United Nations was in operation and the reconstruction of Europe was underway, which was good news. But on the dark side, North Korea claimed jurisdiction over the South in 1948, and war was on once again. North Koreans did the shooting, but the Soviet Union was the enemy dressed in Korean clothing.

Such was the global background when Truman faced the world in 1948, a world he had helped to form during his years as vice president and president.

Legislation was passed during and after the war years that addressed the international problems of the day. Selected items follow:

- 1945: Two acts were passed. The Export/Import Bank Act[83] provided assistance to American companies that participated in European reconstruction. The Bretton Woods Act made the United States a member of the International Monetary Fund, and the International Bank for Reconstruction and Development. The U.N. Participation Act[84] was a part of the same package concentrated on international cooperation. Three years later, the American commitment to provide direct assistance to war ravaged nations, including Germany, was of inestimable value to the rebuilding of the Europe that exists today.
- 1948: Through the Economic Cooperation Act of 1948 (the Marshall Plan), the United States provided more than $13 billion in aid to Europe despite the attempt by the Soviets to disrupt the flow of goods. Although its full value wouldn't be known for years, the passage of this act was a feather in the cap of presidential candidate Truman in the 1948 campaign. The unforgettable Berlin Airlift (1948–49) kept product moving into Berlin despite Soviet resistance.[85]

America and the Soviets had widely different views on what the postwar world should look like. With the United States, the aim was reconstruction and cooperation; with the Soviets, it was expansion and power.

By 1946, Winston Churchill, alarmed at Soviet behavior, warned of an "Iron Curtain" being drawn around the Soviet area of influence. By 1947, the Soviets (thanks to American spies on the Soviet bankroll) were an atomic power and the resident authority in Czechoslovakia, Poland, Hungary, Yugoslavia, Bulgaria and Romania.[86] Given such tensions, a legislative response and other responses were expected and were delivered. For example:

- 1946: The Atomic Energy Act[87] banned the sharing of technology and established the Atomic Energy Commission to regulate and assist atomic facilities.
- 1947: The Truman Doctrine[88] pledged support to threatened allies.
- 1951: The Mutual Security Act[89] was the Marshall Plan in reorganized form. The Mutual Security Administration was formed to administer all foreign aid programs, including military and economic. Democracy versus communism was the clash that filled the minds of 1951 leaders.

Most of Truman's significant actions in the legislative area took place while he was powerful in both houses of Congress. Over his final two years, declining power in Congress plus growing international pressures essentially made him a foreign affairs president.

During the Korean War, Truman resumed his duties as commander-in-chief. Gen. Douglas MacArthur, at the time serving as, in effect, governor of

Japan, was recalled to duty as supreme commander of allied forces in Korea. The war was ongoing when Truman left office in 1952. His most memorable act during that conflict was his decision in 1951 to terminate Gen. MacArthur because of policy disagreements.

So ended the administration of Harry S Truman, a turbulent time in which to serve for the most experienced and most hardened and able of diplomats. For a humble senator from Missouri, with no foreign policy experience, it appeared to be an unfair, almost impossible assignment. But Truman assumed it, and he delivered the goods. Because of this, historians have treated him well in their presidential rankings and he rates seventh, a step above Ronald Reagan and a step below Andrew Jackson.[90]

Conclusion

Why was the election of 1948 so close? It wasn't, from an electoral vote standpoint. The popular vote was close, and that made the electoral vote in many states doubtful until the last votes were counted.

Truman's victory is regarded by many as the greatest comeback in political history. At election time, his popularity according to polls was in the mid-thirties. His party had lost badly in the 1946 election; Republicans had a young, attractive and competent team. But voters were ahead of pundits in this election. They championed a different Truman, a man who didn't need a comeback at all, a man who was rewarded for more than three years of stalwart service in the office of president.

The election was close in the sense that it was a nail-biter. That is a fact. But standing alone, it's misleading. It wasn't Dewey who almost defeated Truman; it was two men from his own party — Wallace and Thurmond — who almost accomplished what Dewey couldn't do. Disunity within the Democratic Party, not Dewey, made the election close. Absent the challenge of those two men, their supporters would have overwhelmingly supported Truman and the essential truth of the campaign would have been revealed. It was a resounding success for the Democratic Party.

9

1960: Richard M. Nixon vs. John F. Kennedy

(Electoral Votes, 537; Majority, 269)

Introduction

The last close presidential election had been between Harry Truman and Thomas Dewey, from which Truman emerged the surprise winner. His dramatic presidency saw the end of the Second World War and the beginning of the Cold War that featured the Korean War.

The latter two became Eisenhower's problems to deal with. Those two presidencies served as background for the subject election.

In terms of the 1960 election, Truman (1949–52)[1] left behind several things, some personal and others professional. On the personal side, the popularity of this very likable man soared during his first term (after he succeeded FDR); but toward the end of his presidential career, it had dropped to levels not experienced by any president before him and only by the disgraced Nixon after him.[2] Rumors about communists in government, the controversial firing of Gen. Douglas MacArthur and the Korean War, still ongoing when Truman retired, are cited as causes for this. In 1960, his inherent appeal to people had been somewhat repaired, but he was not as popular or as well regarded at that time as he eventually would be. On the professional side, Democrats could brag in 1960 about Truman's loyalty to the progressive tradition* established by Wilson and FDR (the cost of Social Security tripled[3] during his last term due to expansion of the program). Also worthy of continuing admiration was his performance during World War II and during the rebuilding of Europe (the Marshall Plan). Even as early as 1960, the fact that Truman's presidency was a substantial one was gaining recognition. On balance, his record was an asset to Democrats, but not to the extent it might have been had the Republican opponent been someone other than Richard Nixon, whose anticommunist cre-

---

Democrats were proud of their aggressive social agenda and, at the time, it was well received by the public.

dentials were impeccable and whose mere presence brought back memories of the communist scare during Truman's years over spies in high positions.[4]

The profile of the America that Eisenhower (Ike) (1953–60)[5] inherited was molded by FDR and Truman. Postwar America (1948) had a GDP four times larger than 1932[6]; debt was thirteen times larger,[7] the number of federal employees three and one-half times larger.[8] This was a new nation with new burdens, domestic and international, and a new political system to go with it. Overall, according to historians, Ike handled himself well.[9] He entered the presidency with one of the best reputations in the world and lost little of it during his eight-year presidency. In terms of the subject election, Ike was one of the most popular presidents. He was a constitutionalist with moderate progressive leanings—difficult to attack from the left. In 1960 he was remembered fondly for his personality and also as the man who ended the Korean War, and who, by his mere presence, served as a deterrent to another one. The fact that Richard Nixon served as vice president to such a man was a priceless asset to him during the election.

To the extent that the past colored the present in a positive way, Democrats still had images of the peerless FDR and a somewhat battered Truman to reflect upon and to dignify their brand name, but Republicans had the more current presence and image of Ike to use as a symbol of a dignified past and of hope for the future. Since Nixon was directly associated with the Republican icon and JFK stood removed from the giants of his party, history was more helpful to Nixon than it was to his opponent.

Conventions

This convention, like all others, was partly shaped by the ghosts in the convention hall, recent leaders who had brought credit or discredit to the political party. Both organizations could be proud in that respect. Nixon had a marginal advantage by looking backward; for John Kennedy (JFK), the forward vision would have to carry the day. Which man would America choose: The experienced Nixon or the personable JFK?

REPUBLICAN CONVENTION

The 1960 Republican convention[10] was held in Chicago in July of the election year. It didn't promise to be a controversial one. Vice President Richard Milhous Nixon was the heir apparent and no serious challenger was on the immediate horizon, although there were rumblings about the possibility of New York's governor, Nelson Rockefeller, entering the race. A highlight of the proceedings was a speech by Barry Goldwater in which he withdrew his name from consideration. Thereafter, Nixon did not have a nomination problem. A

competent, well-regarded vice president, he also had the support of an enormously popular president, Dwight Eisenhower.

Nixon's potential challenger, Rockefeller, didn't have much of a chance to
upset Nixon's bid,[11] but he did have the prestige and the political clout to upset
party unity and, perhaps, deal a blow to Nixon's election chances. What he
decided to do and how he went about doing it was the only suspenseful characteristic of the convention.

THE ROCKEFELLER FACTOR

Rockefeller wanted the presidency. And there were reasons to believe he
could be a competitive candidate. He came from one of America's most prestigious families and, as a consequence, his name recognition across the nation
was instantaneous; he had control of more electoral votes than any other governor and thereby had considerable influence throughout the eastern section
of the nation; his appearance and demeanor were more television friendly than
Nixon's. Also, the missile gap with the Soviets and other defense and foreign
policies of Ike's with which Nixon was identified represented inviting areas of
attack in a campaign that Rockefeller, as an outsider, wouldn't have to face.
Given these assets and issues, Rockefeller understandably entertained the notion
of competing with Nixon for the nomination. Rockefeller, however, also had
negative characteristics that had to be weighed: Most delegates, for example,
were moderates or conservatives, and Rockefeller was neither.

After measuring all factors, Rockefeller decided his chance to win the
nomination was slim. He made it known late in 1959 that he would not be a
candidate.[12] Nixon and his supporters breathed a sigh of relief when this
announcement was made, thinking this was the end of the Rockefeller threat
and believing party unity was thereby assured.

Then came the game changer: The U-2 incident.[13] It reawakened Rockefeller's interest in becoming a player in the formation of the party platform. A
clear and new vulnerability in Eisenhower's policies had arisen, and it gave
Rockefeller additional leverage to influence the party platform that, at the last
hour, was a matter of hot dispute between conservative and liberal factions
within the party.[14]

Desperate to achieve unity, Nixon called Rockefeller and a deal was formed
between them known as the "Pact of Fifth Avenue." It contained fourteen mod-
ifications to the platform that dealt with domestic and foreign policy that met
with Rockefeller's approval. In return, Nixon received Rockefeller's assurance
of support.[15] Rockefeller announced the agreement to the press just before the
convention opened and party leaders were livid. Goldwater, for example, who
opposed Rockefeller's liberal ideas, referred to the deal between Nixon and
Rockefeller as "the Munich of the Republican Party."[16] To cool things down,
Nixon made a quick trip to the convention.[17]

It was over. The threat of a split party was averted; the platform was written and accepted. Nixon was nominated on the first ballot — 1321 votes out of 1331 cast. Sen. Henry Cabot Lodge was nominated as his running mate and the selection of Lodge was understood to be a bow toward the eastern establishment of the Republican Party.[18]

The major elements in the Republican platform are discussed at length below.

DEMOCRATIC CONVENTION

Democrats held their convention in mid–July of the election year.[19] They arrived with a deep field of candidates eager to reclaim the throne of power held so long by FDR and Truman that had been taken from them —for eight years— by the greatest celebrity of World War II, Gen. Dwight D. Eisenhower.

The first Democratic challenger[*] of Eisenhower's popularity was Adlai Stevenson, who twice lost to Ike and who, almost as a courtesy, made himself available in 1960 in case none of the others captured the convention. Then came Hubert Humphrey (MN), Stewart Symington (MS), Lyndon Johnson (TX) and John Kennedy (MA):

- Hubert Humphrey: U.S. Senate 1948–64.[20]
- Stewart Symington: U.S. Senate 1952–76.[21]
- Lyndon Johnson: U.S. Senate 1948–60.[22] (Johnson did not announce his candidacy for the nomination until just before the convention.)
- John Kennedy: U.S. Senate 1952–60.[23]

With four senators competing for the big prize, Potomac fever had grown large.

Prior to this election year, primary contests were interesting but inconsequential. The first one was held in 1901 in Florida. By 1912, a dozen states were holding them,[24] and in 1960 there were sixteen contests.[25] Each candidate had the option to compete in them or to campaign for their cause as they saw fit. Regardless of which choice they made, they entered the convention as equals in pursuit of delegates, but those who competed with success rightfully felt more secure than the others about the support of a given number of delegates.

Humphrey and JFK competed in primaries; Johnson and Symington ignored them, preferring to work through party leaders. In head-to-head contests in West Virginia)[†] and Wisconsin (Humphrey territory) JFK defeated Humphrey[26] and brought the competition down to three men — himself plus Symington and Johnson. JFK arrived at the convention flush with delegates,

---

Theoretically, Estes Kefauver should have been the leading candidate. But he had tried twice before (1952 and 1956) and was unwilling to do so again. He made it known in 1959 that he was not a candidate.

†*The win in West Virginia was of special importance to Kennedy and to the Democratic Party because it temporarily put to rest the argument that a Catholic candidate could not win a national election.*

the living example of why presidential candidates of the future would embrace primaries as the most certain road to convention victory.[27]

Symington had little support. Johnson made a final attempt to slow down the Kennedy machine (headed by brother Robert) by challenging the front runner to a televised debate before Texas and Massachusetts delegations. JFK performed well, and that was the end of Johnson — victory was JFK's by a comfortable margin on the first ballot.

The surprise of the convention was JFK's choice as a running mate, Lyndon Johnson, which some, including brother Robert, regarded as an attempt to mix oil and water. JFK, on the other hand, thought it was a wise political move that would strengthen his hand in the South.

The apparent ease with which Kennedy won the nomination is a tribute to the organization behind him, not to the lack of opposition. Harry Truman, for example, a Johnson supporter, worried about JFK's youth, inexperience and competence, as opposed to Johnson's proven leadership. And Eleanor Roosevelt, a Stevenson supporter and hostile to the possibility of a Kennedy nomination, added the mystique of her name to the subtle campaign of Stevenson to become a compromise candidate by announcing to the press his availability and by punctuating her support for him by attending the convention in an unplanned appearance.[28]

Republican and Democratic Platforms

Political platforms are no longer relatively short statements of principle. Since Roosevelt and the advent of the "welfare state," how to get a slice of the federal budget has become a routine game with activists who represent various causes, ranging from cultural to business to education and economics.

Lobbyists in search of pledges surged to Washington,[29] all ears persistently tuned to party platforms and speeches, each candidate measured against the modern political yardstick of "What's in it for me?"* Additionally, the United States became a world power after World War II, which added complexity to the job of governing and words to inauguration speeches.

Party platforms went on and on after World War II, each part of them of interest to someone, but all parts too much for most.

And so it was in 1960. Both platforms were extensive, but only certain parts of them transcended time and events, the ones that usually swing votes one way or another in issue-driven elections— war and peace, the economy (the

*It is a treasured American right to lobby for a special cause. But when lobbying goes too far, it turns into pressure and it invites corruption. Once it became the general practice of Washington to reward individuals, groups, states and businesses with special assistance, hordes of lobbyists poured into the city in pursuit of the latest prize, or to protect the last one. The effect of this has subtracted from the efficiency of government and represents the seed bed of the scandals that routinely smirch the reputations of both political parties.

misery index), tax policy, budget/debt, civil rights, social programs, and foreign policy and leadership, hereinafter referred to as the primal issues.

Because of their fundamental importance in close elections, the differences between the parties on these issues as stated in their party platforms[30] will be comparatively presented in this and the remaining chapters of the modern presidency:

WAR AND PEACE

Policies relative to Taiwan and Cuba were different and became hot issues during debates. Otherwise, the positions of the two parties were remarkably similar. Give Nixon an advantage, but not to the degree expected.

THE ECONOMY

Nixon could not hide from the record of recessions. This gave JFK an advantage, but not to the degree expected. Most Americans were happy.

TAX POLICY

Neither side was outspoken on this issue, leaving the impression that both were somewhat embarrassed by the high tax rates. Nixon had a small advantage here because of the relative reputations of the parties on this issue.

BUDGET/DEBT

The Eisenhower record was not unusually vulnerable on this front. Deficits had been relatively modest, caused in his first term by the costs of war and in his second by the surging costs of social programs initiated by Democratic presidents. JFK was wise not to talk too much about budget, or the modest increase in debt. Given the circumstances under which Ike operated, his fiscal legacy was a small plus for Nixon.

CIVIL RIGHTS

Eisenhower had a good civil rights record. He was a progressive on social issues and his record was not unusually vulnerable here. Nixon, by association, shared Ike's reputation. Democrats had a built-in advantage here because of their connections with FDR and the labor movement.

SOCIAL PROGRAMS

Eisenhower and Nixon had a good record with respect to social services, but Nixon's bag of goodies was not as full as Kennedy's. One specific issue that clearly separated the men was of major importance: Medical care for the aged — how to do it, how to finance it.* But the fundamental difference between them and the parties— one that served as the root of all arguments over the expansion of government into the private sector — was the acceptance or rejection of Roosevelt's Economic Bill of Rights[31] and what those rights meant in terms of government action.

Democrats, in general, accepted them as if they had the status of the first ten amendments to the Constitution (the Bill of Rights). Republicans in general accepted them as idealistic meanderings that did not have the force of law. The bill was as follows: The right to a useful and remunerative job; the right to earn enough to provide adequate food and clothing and recreation; the right of every farmer to raise and sell his products at a return which will give him and his family a decent living; the right of every businessman, large and small, to trade in an atmosphere of freedom from unfair competition; the right of every family to a decent home; the right to adequate medical care and the opportunity to achieve and enjoy good health; the right to adequate protection from the economic fears of old age, sickness, accident, and unemployment; the right to a good education.

The question here is not the validity of these aspirations. Spoken from the pulpit, or from a leader who makes clear they are expressing a personal conviction, they can be accepted in good spirit and reflected upon. But when spoken by the leader of the nation in an official voice, and in the context of constitutional criticism, the implication is there that these are constitutional rights that government has the obligation to bring into being. Therein lies the logic that supports the entry of government into private affairs, that lifts the need for social programs from the realm of "good ideas" to that of dogma.

The Constitution makes no mention of such specific rights; nowhere does it suggest that even if they did exist, it would become the responsibility of the federal government to resolve them. It concentrates instead on specifying the few specific rights of the central government and leaves all other matters to the states and the people. This is not an accidental characteristic of the Constitution. The framers of it had protested against centralized power and had finally fought it to gain liberty. Their interest was in creating a government with limited powers that could not do to Americans what England had done to them.

Progressives accepted these new "rights" with the soberness of constitutional scholars. Laws dealing with such matters, they felt, were no longer governed by the pre–Roosevelt Constitution, which, according to the followers of Republican Theodore Roosevelt and Democrats Woodrow Wilson and FDR, was obsolete, a belief never openly expressed (because it treads on sacred ground), but believed de facto by those politicians and judges who routinely

---

Democrats favored the payroll tax system as the method of financing medical care for the aged. This eventually became the case and proved to be an inherent weakness of the system as, over time, the worker/retiree ratio diminished.

ignored the stated limitations on federal authority imposed on the government by Article 1 and Amendments Nine and Ten.* Progressives accept the Rooseveltian amendments as reasonable adaptations to the times (the Constitution, they claim, is a living document that must be adjusted to the needs of the day). Conservatives reject this as political heresy (the Constitution means what it says, or what the Founders meant it to say).†

It was difficult to handicap this issue at election time. But the national tilt was to the left on such issues in 1960, and JFK gets the nod.

FOREIGN POLICY

There was agreement of the identification of the nation's primary enemies and on the need for a stalwart military, so foreign policy positions were similar, differing more in style than in substance. Nixon's was more muscular, JFK's more diplomatic and more idealistic. Nixon had the edge here, but not to the degree expected. The U-2 incident and the space race reduced, but did not eliminate, Nixon's advantage on this issue.

LEADERSHIP

JFK desperately needed something to boost his leadership credentials. In a negative way, the Soviet lead in the space race and the embarrassment of the U-2 incident chipped away at the lofty Eisenhower/Nixon foreign policy profile, but that wasn't enough. Television debates proved to be the answer. JFK stood toe to toe with one of the most informed men in the world and emerged unscathed. This didn't nullify Nixon's acceptance as being the leader in this respect, but it considerably reduced the distance between them. JFK, given his background, came out of the campaign stronger than expected on the issues. Next came personal qualities—appearance, style, vision. And here he had a decisive lead.

And so the conventions ended, with both parties reasonably united and ready to compete with two attractive candidates, the Republican Nixon because of his training and obvious competence and the Democrat Kennedy with his youth and charisma, in many ways a clash of the old versus the new. Confidence was high on both sides.

---

*Words are important. The Founders believed that human rights come from God and cannot be given by or removed by any state (Declaration of Independence). Mixing state power with the powerful word "rights" is dangerous. That which is given by the state can be taken away by the state. Where confusion exists about this, tyranny can follow. If freedom comes from the state, it can be taken away without due process-hence, Hitler, Stalin, etc.

†As a preface to his bill of rights, FDR expressed his belief that the Constitution was a document of the past that, in many ways, no longer applied to modern circumstances. It would be useful for conservatives to recognize that those on the other side are more than big spenders; many are sincere missionaries fighting the good fight as they see it. To them, conservatives are political pagans. Laws and judicial decisions since 1960 have increasingly reflected the progressive point of view.

Thumbnail Sketches of Top Candidates

Richard Nixon was the heir apparent in the Republican Party and although Nelson Rockefeller presented some hurdles to negotiate, it was no surprise that this veteran forty-seven-year-old politician would win the nomination. The consensus was that he had been a useful and effective vice president.

The selection of JFK had not been so obvious. He had plenty of competition at his convention and needed the full resources of his family's fortune and political clout to reach his goal. He was four years younger than Nixon, but his political experience in terms of time or quality didn't compare favorably with Nixon's, a difference with which he struggled throughout the campaign.

RICHARD M. NIXON, REPUBLICAN

Born: 1913, CA; **Education:** Whittier College, Duke Law School; **Wife:** Thelma Patricia Ryan; **Children:** Two; **Died** 1974.[32]

Richard Milhous Nixon was born on a lemon ranch, the son of Francis and Hannah and the second of five brothers. Theirs was a life of limited income and hardship, made more difficult by the death of two brothers and the failure in 1922 of the farm. The family moved to Whittier, California, and Francis eked out a living as a manager/owner of a combination grocery store and gasoline station, in which all the family members worked.

Nixon, a superior student, attended nearby Whittier College and continued to work in the family store. His grades qualified him for a scholarship to Duke University Law School, where he excelled. He was president of the student bar association and a member of the law review. He returned to Whittier after graduation in 1937 to practice law with a local firm. For fun and relaxation he participated in community plays, in which pursuit he met schoolteacher "Pat" Nixon. They married in 1940. Two years later they moved to the center of American politics, Washington, D.C., where, for a few months, Nixon worked for the Office of Price Administration. This experiment with bureaucracy ended with his enlistment in the same year in the navy. He served with distinction in the South Pacific.

Politics entered Nixon's life after the war. He accepted in 1946 the offer of local political leaders to run against Rep. Jerry Voorhis (D-CA),[33] and he succeeded. Thereafter, the Nixon family became quasi-fixtures in Washington; his experiences as a congressman prepared him for heavier duties he would one day pursue. One of Nixon's assignments in particular made him a national figure. In 1948, as a member of the House Un-American Activities Committee, he led the investigation that uncovered the Soviet spy Alger Hiss.*

*The deep animosity toward Nixon began with the Hiss case. It was not until the end of the Cold War that Hiss' supporters would accept his guilt. During the interim years, Nixon was stigmatized by many in the elite media as a persecutor of innocent people.

Nixon, easily reelected in 1948, added to his reputation in 1950 when he ran against Helen Gahagan Douglas for a seat in the U.S. Senate. By this time he was known as a fierce anticommunist and, as such, he was critical of Douglas' alleged political leanings and those of her Hollywood friends (she was the wife of actor Melvin Douglas). Although Nixon's comments earned him the enmity of another powerful public relations institution, the movie industry, he won the election by more than a half-million votes. It was a rough campaign that featured Nixon's attacks against the alleged beliefs of Douglas and her supporters—"She is pink right down to her underwear." Douglas responded by coining a nickname for Nixon that was picked up by the press, one that followed him for a political lifetime — "Tricky Dick."

At age thirty-seven, Nixon, a rising political star, immediately added to his anticommunist credentials by being consistently critical of President Truman's policies. It was a sign of the times that fear of the Soviets was high. Rumors of spies within the government and the War in Korea, for example, were real-time events that fueled worries about a possible nuclear confrontation. For that reason, Nixon's reputation as an anticommunist and as a Cold War warrior served him well politically and brought him to the attention of the 1952 Republican nominee for president, Dwight D. Eisenhower.

Nixon's youth, his popularity in vote-rich California and his national reputation for being on the right side of the Red scare drew Ike's interest and he selected him as his running mate on a ticket that, for two terms, devastated the opposition and transformed Nixon into one of the best trained political servants in American history.

Nixon confronted a scandal during the 1952 campaign that threatened his rising star. The *New York Post* claimed he was being unduly influenced by donors who were contributing to a secret fund used by Nixon for personal reasons. Armed with the report of an auditor, Nixon appeared before the largest television audience in history (up to that time) and successfully defended himself to the nation, to Ike and to the Republican Party. The net effect of the scandal was to make him more popular than ever.

Now it was time for the undefeated Nixon to test his strength and win the highest prize of all — president of the United States.

JOHN F. KENNEDY, DEMOCRAT

Born: 1917, MA; **Education:** Harvard; **Wife:** Jacqueline Bouvier; **Children:** Three (one died); **Died:** 1963.[34]

John Fitzgerald Kennedy (JFK) was one of the nine children of Joseph and Rose Kennedy. Joseph, a well-known financier, ambassador and government executive, played a large role in the careers of all of his children, especially the boys, Joseph Jr., John, Robert and Theodore (Ted).

JFK attended local private schools until 1937, when he joined his older brother Joe at Harvard. Never a healthy man, it was during these years that he ruptured a disk in his spine and developed a back condition that was to plague him for the rest of his life. He wasn't as ambitious as his brother, who, with his father's urging, had political goals; JFK's grades were average.

The family, with the exception of Harvard students Joe and Jack, moved to England in 1937 when Joseph Kennedy was made ambassador to England by FDR. His father's job increased JFK's interest in world history, which was stimulated further by trips, during summer vacation, to England and other European countries. During these years, Hitler and Mussolini ruled Germany and Italy, each with obvious appetites for more territory and power, and in 1939 war began. During his senior year at Harvard, JFK chose as the subject for his thesis why Great Britain was unprepared for war with Germany. It was published in 1940 as *Why England Slept*.

Joe and JFK enlisted in the navy, Joe as a pilot and Jack as commander of a patrol torpedo boat. Both served with distinction. JFK survived his legendary exploits with PT-109 and its crew. Joe did not survive but died in 1944 when his plane blew up during a mission over Europe. Joseph Kennedy was devastated by his oldest son's death. He had eagerly supported the young man's political ambitions. But when he lost him to the war, he transferred his attention to JFK, who, to that point, was not similarly driven but was considering a postwar career as a writer or a teacher. But his father persuaded him to fill the role that had been planned for brother Joe. Perhaps JFK began his political career as an act of loyalty or obedience to his father. Thereafter, however, there is no evidence that he did not share his father's ambition, or fail to appreciate his guidance and support.

JFK ran for a seat in the House in 1946 and, with the help of the organization assembled by his father, he won. He was twenty-nine, and his political career was underway. After three terms in the House, JFK turned his eyes in 1952 to the senatorial contest. The incumbent, Henry Cabot Lodge, a Massachusetts baron, was a major figure in the Republican Party. To defeat such a man would be humiliating for Republicans in the state and the nation and a prestigious victory for the young congressman. Again, with father Joseph and his organization at his side, JFK won and, in so doing, he announced to the political world that a new star was rising.

But this wasn't enough. From the beginning, first with Joe and now with JFK, the goal of the father of the clan had been to win the presidency. And this determination in 1956 was shown again. After only four years in the Senate, JFK made his bid for the vice presidential nomination on the Stevenson ticket. He lost (for the first time) to Sen. Estes Kefauver, who had gained fame as chairman of the Special Committee on Organized Crime.

It is doubtful that JFK and his father were interested in the vice presidency. It is more reasonable to assume that JFK, guided by the wily eye of his father, assumed Eisenhower would win, and that as the vice presidential candidate on the most recent Democratic ticket, he would emerge in 1960 as a frontrunner. Undeterred by his defeat, JFK, recognizing the preferred position Kefauver was in, immediately went into campaign mode after the 1956 election of Ike to a second term. He launched a four-year effort to win the nomination of his party in 1960. He was forty-three and eager to assume the duties of the most powerful office in the world — president of the United States.

Election Tone

Nixon and JFK were two politically precocious men. Both were young in age, but, curiously, this similarity was lost during the heat of the campaign, as Nixon became identified with Ike, the protector of the old, and JFK became the flag carrier of the next generation, the representative of the New Frontier (a campaign slogan).

Bragging rights about history were more even in 1960, as the memory of Hoover and the Great Depression faded and the huge reputation of Dwight Eisenhower was added. Democrats still had FDR to brag about (it was too early to evaluate Truman); Republicans had Ike and his international reputation as a more current icon. Both sides had sweet memories to elicit, which is another way of saying that nostalgia wasn't unduly decisive for either but probably worked better for Nixon because he was closely identified with Ike.

In 2010, it is easy to say that Supreme Court rulings that favor civil rights will result in credit to the Democratic Party because, since the 1960s, it has become known through its social programs and its legislative initiatives as the party for the blacks. Prior to 1960, this was not the case. During pre–Civil War days, Democrats were largely responsible for keeping slaves in bondage. Lincoln, a Republican, freed them; Grant was arguably the most black-friendly president prior to World War I — the key Amendments Fourteen and Fifteen were ratified during his administration. Democrat Wilson was a racist who did nothing for blacks.[35] The Democratic Party had split over the issue of race in 1948. Truman prior to the 1960s had the only positive civil rights record that Democrats could brag about, and even he argued against a strong civil rights plank in the 1948 platform. Given this background, it is difficult to gauge the impact of Supreme Court rulings between 1949 and 1960 on party popularity, probably because of Truman they benefited both parties but Republicans more so because of their deeper pro-black attitudes, which included Ike and his use of troops to implement integration law.[36]

Chief justices during those years were Fred M. Vinson (1946–53) and Earl Warren. They were assisted by fourteen assistant justices,[37] including Hugo Black, an ex–Ku Klux Klan member; Felix Frankfurter, who served as a character witness for the Soviet spy Alger Hiss; William Douglas, whose adventures with females led to financial troubles and questionable dealings; and Charles Whittaker, who had to retire after five years of service because of a nervous break-down.[38] These men rendered rulings that had substantial voter impact[39]:

- The wall of separation between blacks and whites began to crumble in 1950 (*Sweatt v. Painter*; *McLaurin v. Oklahoma*) and 1953 (*Hernandez v. Texas*) and then turned to dust in 1954 when *Brown v. Board of Education* overturned the separate but equal doctrine of *Plessy v. Ferguson* (1896) that had kept Americans apart for a half-century. This was a day of national celebration. To which political party did blacks say "thank you" in 1960? Nobody at that time was sure of the answer to that question.
- Despite the Brown ruling, southerners continued to resist integration, which in turn brought *Cooper v. Aaron* (1958) to the Court. This case dealt with the responsibilities of states to conform to federal law, the law handed down in *Brown*. The decision was clear and firm. States must integrate as specified in *Brown*. Another celebration was also appropriate at that time for blacks, and for all those who believed in the dignity of the individual.
- The religious issue, relative to First Amendment protection, raised its head in 1952 (*Zorach v. Clauson*) when a state law was unsuccessfully challenged that allowed students to be dismissed from class to take religious courses elsewhere.

Similar cases would begin to pour into the Court over the subsequent years.

Nixon, although about the same age as JFK, seemed older and he carried the vulnerable slices of Ike's record. JFK had no baggage to defend and his serious personal vulnerabilities (sex life, health, indifferent political career, religion) were not made into campaign issues by Nixon, who restricted most of his criticism to JFK's youth and inexperience. JFK's Catholic faith was a problem he personally and successfully dealt with in appearances before non–Catholic clergy and in speeches on the stump. Nixon left it alone. He concentrated on the great domestic and international issues of the day. His demeanor and his experience demanded respect. JFK, no intellectual lightweight, engaged in the debate in an effective way and, additionally, did it with a style that stirred hope, especially in the young.

Both were good speakers, but audience reaction was different. Nixon's audiences were instructed, JFK's inspired. Nixon himself was admired, JFK was loved. Nixon spoke of what had to be done, JFK of what man can do. Nixon was poor show business, JFK a star. And since television was coming into its own, especially in a political sense, it was an ideal time for a star to be born.

Nixon could have been a candidate in any presidential age. He had earned his dues the hard way; he had been effective in Congress and influential as a vice president. No man had ever been better trained to assume the office of the presidency. He was a man from the past who would not have fared well in contemporary politics; he was the last sovereign-like candidate, remote and competent. People supported Nixon, like him or not, because they expected him to do a good job.

JFK was a candidate in 1960 because it was a time when background and training were no more important in an election than appearance, personality and rhetoric. In an earlier day, a presidential campaign would likely have been beyond his reach because his administrative potential was untested. Although Truman broke the ice with his folksy "whistle stop" 1948 campaign, JFK was the first truly modern presidential candidate, intimate and friendly. People supported him because they liked him; he made them feel good and hopeful, and they hoped he'd do a good job.

Why were these things so? Television! FDR had his fireside chats. Truman and Ike had access to television, but neither was disposed to use it unduly or capable of exploiting it efficiently. Nixon too would have preferred a political world without it. But it was here to stay and unavoidable. JFK was born for it. He embraced it and, many say, his ability and willingness to use it may have won him the election.

Television Debates

The power of television to influence voters was never better exemplified than it was in the four 1960 debates between Nixon and JFK. Both, in the prime of their lives, bore the confident demeanor of one who had never been defeated in a popular election; both were gifted speakers; both appeared to be in robust health (although JFK's vibrant appearance concealed serious physical problems, and Nixon in the first debate did not make a positive physical impression). Nixon was more experienced, JFK more charismatic.

Critics gave the edge to Nixon as a debater when the events were scheduled; the same critics applauded JFK's performance during and after the debates. Nixon handled himself according to expectations; JFK surprised most observers because of his familiarity with a wide range of issues.

The sponsors of the four debates[40] were the three television networks, ABC, CBS and NBC. The debates were held in Chicago, Washington, D.C., Los Angeles and New York City, in that order. Moderators were Howard K. Smith, CBS; Frank McGee, NBC; Bill Shadel and Quincy Howe, ABC. Three or four panelists posed the questions to candidates. Responses were usually limited to two and a half minutes; rebuttal time ranged from a half minute to three times that amount. Opening and closing statements in the first and last debates took eleven minutes; they were not allowed in the second and third debates.

The first debate[41] dealt with domestic affairs and established one thing in the first ten minutes: JFK could stand toe to toe with Nixon as a debater, an important accomplishment because it helped to minimize the experience differential between them. Nixon, better trained, didn't appear to be so in the debate. And in front of a camera, it is appearance that counts, at least as much as reality.

JFK unapologetically presented himself as a progressive in the tradition of Wilson and Roosevelt who believed in an active role for government in the private sector. Nixon, with equal boldness, championed limited government and economic growth in the private sector as the goal of a Nixon administration. Voters had a clear choice between two forms of government, which can be simplistically summarized as one that concentrates on the needs of the nation (Nixon) and one that concentrates on the needs of its citizens (JFK).

Nixon represented the pre–Roosevelt chief executive officer who busied himself with the huge affairs of the nation, nationally and internationally, and delegated other concerns to the states and the people. JFK represented the intimate, fireside chat-type president who brought to work every day a clergy-like concern for the comfort and well-being of Americans. Nixon was boss; JFK was daddy.

But when all the talking was done, the thing that turned the debate to the advantage of JFK was not his warmth and comparative coolness or the comparative quality of his answers. Visual impact was his weapon of choice.[42] He looked young, handsome and tan. Nixon, worn down by an extensive campaign and illness, looked thin, vulnerable and unshaven in the first debate, made worse by the fact that he rejected makeup.*

The experience issue worked to Nixon's advantage. But JFK[43] minimized his vulnerability by adroitly deflecting awkward subject matter into his vision for the future — he was the forward looking candidate. Nixon, JFK said, represented the party that would undo the progressive legacy of Wilson and Roosevelt, while he, on the other hand, would continue that great tradition.

The media assisted JFK in minimizing Nixon's alleged advantage by quoting Ike, who, when questioned about Nixon's contribution to his administration, quipped that, if given a week, he'd come up with an answer. Ike's remark was made unthinkingly and Nixon's response to it during the first debate was reasoned; but the words, endlessly repeated, remained as a blow to his image as a seasoned, involved executive.

The second debate[44] was open to questions on any issue, a severe test for JFK, especially in the area of foreign affairs. Among the questions raised were those dealing with freedom in Cuba and the U-2 incident, which resulted in the cancellation of a meeting between Eisenhower and Khrushchev. Both candidates handled questions with confidence and skill. But there was a difference: Nixon was expected to, there was doubt about Kennedy. In short, for JFK to emerge from such a debate as strong, or stronger than before, he had to compete well; for Nixon to do the same, he had to win.

---

*Nixon, hospitalized for two weeks for a knee injury, was twenty pounds underweight when he appeared on the first debate; he lost forever the power of first impression. Thereafter he paid more attention to the theatrical aspects of the debate and physically competed on more even terms.

The third debate,[45] designed to deal with questions on any subject, essentially focused on the danger of communism, specifically as it related to the islands of Taiwan, Quemoy and Matsu. The underlying issue, however, was Nixon's implied position that he would resist communism anywhere to a more reliable extent than JFK. Both were aggressive; both appeared competent.

The fourth debate[46] was devoted to foreign policy. Cuba and how best to fight communism were central issues. JFK cleverly managed a flimflam position on Cuba, first saying he would not interfere with its internal affairs then later contradicting himself; but he did so with such aplomb that he suffered little political damage. Nixon emphasized the importance of resisting the attempts of communism to expand. His approach was more focused and event driven. JFK's was more internationalist — he would Wilson-like vigorously sell freedom throughout the world as a way of blocking Soviet expansion.[47] Nixon's stance toward the Soviet Union, China and Cuba was narrower in scope and more muscular in nature. JFK's plans, broader in scope and more diplomatic in form, were powerful enough in impact to narrow the lead that Nixon originally had on such issues.

From a pragmatic standpoint, it can be said that JFK won the debates. Experts differ, however, and consensus says JFK won the first, Nixon the middle two and the fourth was a draw. If true, as noted before, JFK was indeed the winner because he competed better than expected. This commonsense observation cannot be demonstrated. Actually polls, before and after the debate, did not show significant change,[48] which leads to the apparently illogical conclusion that they had little impact.

Whatever their actual influence, the debates changed the face of electoral politics. Qualifications, in the formal sense, would no longer be the ultimate test for a candidate. Henceforth, appearance, communication skills and rhetorical ability to reach the inner core of voters would be of equal or, sometimes dangerously so, more importance than background. As a consequence, demagoguery loomed as an increasing political danger of the future to a far greater extent than ever before. A sweet-talking, false-bottomed rogue who would not advance to high position in the society of the Founders could in future years, with the help of the tube, become president of the United States of America.

And so the campaigns of the candidates began, Nixon the early favorite because of experience and because of his association with Eisenhower. His downside was the fact that Republicans had steadily lost congressional power under Ike, and the suspicion was alive that Ike's policies (and Nixon's chances) were not as popular as the man himself. Democrats, acutely aware of their ascending power in Congress, read that to mean that America was ready for change, the kind of change that JFK — young, handsome and apparently vigorous— symbolized and articulated.

The two candidates, remarkably similar in their broad goals, both young men in the prime years of their lives, spoke of change and the need to contain communism. The arguments centered on how to do it and who would do it best.

NIXON CAMPAIGN

Nixon's central campaign theme — continuity and experience — was his basic defense for attacks against Ike's foreign policy. JFK's youthful appearance assisted Nixon in making the case that he was the candidate with the experience to handle the job, that JFK was too green for the task.[49] On disputed international issues, Nixon's positions were clear and firm. He linked the Soviet Union with most international disturbances; he pledged to resist communist expansion wherever it threatened. The portrait he painted was this: I am the experienced Cold War warrior; JFK is an inexperienced upstart. Concerning domestic issues,* Nixon had a mixed case to sell, especially because the misery index was high.[50] But he had many arguments to defend the spotty economic record of Ike's administration; he defended the anti-inflation policies of the Federal Reserve, and he argued forcefully for its continued independence.[51]

From Nixon's standpoint, Ike's record of partial accommodation to progressive ideas was useful. While assuring his political base of his conservative credentials, he could also woo independent voters as a middle of the road politician. He couldn't and didn't offer a full, Democratic style plateful of government-directed benefits, but he could righteously claim he was not indifferent to such things. This didn't swing the advantage on such matters to him, but it did take the edge away from some of JFK's seductions. This was a difficult balancing act for Nixon. Barry Goldwater and others were suspicious of his conservative outlook, especially after his accommodation agreement with Gov. Rockefeller concerning party platform issues. As things turned out, Goldwater was right — Nixon was not a reliable conservative.

Tactically, Nixon set a challenging goal for himself. He announced after the convention his intention to campaign in all fifty states,[52] a gesture made to underline his pledge to be president to all Americans. This dramatic pledge, which he kept, robbed Nixon of the time needed to modify his schedule to accommodate his needs in vote-rich states. And this undertaking was made even more difficult when he developed a knee problem that hospitalized him for two weeks (which accounted for his wan appearance at the first debate).

Despite health problems, Nixon kept his promise, but as a tactic, the whole enterprise was inefficient. He wasted precious time visiting states he had little chance to win, like the New England states, and spent too little time in battleground states, like Illinois, Minnesota and Missouri. An egregious example of this is the way Nixon spent the final weekend before the election — he was in Alaska (three electoral votes), while JFK was giving speeches in vote-rich states

---

*Kennedy saw government action as the cure for the recession; Nixon saw tax reform, a free Federal Reserve Bank and a free market as the answer.

like New Jersey, Ohio, Michigan and Pennsylvania.[53] For a candidate with the political savvy of Nixon, this was inexcusably inefficient strategy.

Nixon wanted campaign assistance from Eisenhower but didn't ask for much for two basic reasons: (1) He was eager to prove he was his own man; (2) Mamie Eisenhower, in an emotional phone call, asked Pat Nixon to persuade her husband not to ask for much activity from Ike. She was concerned about his health.[54] Ike did provide some support for his vice president during the latter days of the campaign[55] on a limited basis. The reaction, from a political point of view, was mixed. On the positive side, the fact that he participated took much of the sting away from the derogatory remark he had earlier made about Nixon that had been so broadly quoted. On the other hand, some people interpreted his late entry as a sign of panic in the Nixon camp.[56] The Nixon entourage at the end of the campaign was confident, but not cocky. The general sentiment among pundits seemed to project a close election. Few Nixon supporters disagreed.

Kennedy Campaign

JFK didn't need to be told that his religion and his inexperience were two huge obstacles he had to overcome in order to be found acceptable as a candidate by the majority of the electorate.[57] He had demonstrated his electability to his colleagues, before the convention, by his success in the primaries, especially against Hubert Humphrey in Wisconsin and West Virginia. Convincing the public at large, however, was a more challenging endeavor, especially when polls showed that the public would be slow to accept an untried young man as the leader of a nation engaged in a frightening Cold War with the Soviet Union and, to a lesser extent, Red China.

JFK directly confronted problems presented by his Catholic faith. No Catholic had ever been elected president, and the only one who got close to it was Al Smith, who got hammered in the national election of 1928 against Herbert Hoover.[58] The essence of the issue was simple: Non-Catholics (the majority of voters) feared the influence of Rome over a Catholic American president. It was JFK's task to persuade them that he could administer the affairs of state free from that influence and at the same time be privately obedient to its tenets.

He gave a series of speeches covering the religious issue, and he was especially effective when in September 1960[59] he gave a major address on the subject that included the following: "I believe in an America where the separation of church and state is absolute, where no Catholic prelate would tell the president (should he be Catholic) how to act, and no Protestant minister would tell his parishioners for whom to vote; where no church or church school is granted any public funds or political preference; and where no man is denied public office merely because his religion differs from the president who might appoint him or the people who might elect him."[60]

Thereafter, JFK exposed himself to questions posed by prominent Protestant clergymen about his views on matters that dealt with the relationship between church and state. His performance was broadly applauded. Clergymen gave him high marks and religion as a major issue disappeared from public view, although few doubted it would influence final votes in ways that were both good and bad for JFK, with the balance impossible to calculate.

The topic of foreign affairs was the area where JFK was most vulnerable. Here Nixon, vice president for the renowned and still popular Eisenhower, was clearly the more experienced man who engendered the feeling of security that had been attached to the fatherly figure of Ike. JFK used minimization as a way to reduce Nixon's image as the experienced successor of the venerated Ike. For example:

- Questions could be raised that dimmed some of the sheen associated with Ike's policies: The capture of the U-2 and the aftermath; the space advantage of the Soviets, whose commendable exploits had yet to be matched by the United States; tensions in Cuba. JFK pounded away on such questions, raising doubts about the quality of Nixon's experience.
- Specific problems plucked from eight years of accomplishment, plus the permission to criticize Ike without penalty, which Republican Rockefeller provided during his presidential bid, enabled JFK to refer to Nixon as "experienced in failure" and to invent such phrases as "space gap and missile gap" that, in a few words, hinted that Ike and Nixon were behind the times and that he — young, tanned, handsome and well-spoken — was the modern man who could lead America into the new technical age.
- "If you give me a week, I might think of one," Eisenhower quipped when asked about Nixon's contribution to his administration. This was a remark sent from heaven to the JFK campaign.[61] It never stopped giving. Unintended though it was as a characterization of Nixon's value to Ike, it nevertheless served as a potent buster of the Nixon image.

Using such tactics, JFK reduced the advantage Nixon had originally held on foreign affairs and allowed him to concentrate more forcefully on national issues, like the economy and the expansion of the progressive social system.

JFK focused economic remarks on the misery index, which was at its highest point since 1940.[62] High interest and unemployment rates were especially fruitful areas to explore. He turned the attempt by the Federal Reserve to combat inflation into an evil plan that boosted interest rates and thereby increased the cost to the buyer of all credit purchases and made business loans tough to get, thereby causing unemployment. And he insinuated that he would act to curb the Federal Reserve's independence.*

*Executive interference into the independent activities of the Federal Reserve was a frightening prospect for conservatives.

Nixon had logical responses to these charges, but elections turn on existing realities, not on logic. The condition of the economy, however caused, worked to the advantage of the Democratic ticket. Rather than concentrating on the comparatively limp social services offerings of Republicans, JFK made a direct appeal to all welfare groups by suggesting general increases, but especially to the aged. He advocated universal health care for them and in so doing he firmly established his credentials as a progressive.

He had no competition on such subjects except to leave hanging the question that would define the future of America: Did the voters prefer a cradle-to-grave system of security from a large and activist government, or did they prefer the risks of freedom that went with a small, removed central government? Having minimized Nixon's advantage on foreign policy and having made his points on the economy and having made his promises of security to the poor and the aged, JFK during the final days of his campaign was content to repeat his standard messages until, out of the blue, another event happened that he quickly turned to his advantage.

Martin Luther King, Jr., was arrested in October 1960 during a sit-in protest, charged with violating the trespassing law.[63] JFK telephoned him and came to his aid. Nixon, as vice president, could not interfere with an ongoing legal process, so the public relations opportunity was wide open for JFK and he drove through it. In the process, he gained the trust of many black voters.

Strategically, JFK ran a more self-serving campaign than Nixon. He visited states that counted, avoided those that didn't. On the last weekend before the election, for example, while Nixon was campaigning in Alaska (to complete his fifty-state promise), JFK gave speeches in vote-rich states he needed to win. JFK ran a good race using an organization that Hubert Humphrey once labeled "terrifying,"[64] because of its wealth and efficiency. At the end of the campaign, confidence was the mood, tempered by the realization that most of the political wise men predicted a close race.

Election Results, 1960

Election results, in terms of popular vote, couldn't have been closer; the electoral vote for JFK was more decisive. But the two results are linked closely because of vote tampering charges in critical states, especially in Texas (the home state of Lyndon Johnson, JFK's running mate, who had won his first election to the Senate in 1948 by eighty-seven votes on the basis of a scandalous vote count),[65] and Illinois (a state in which JFK's father had extensive holdings and influence).*

*(1) The results of Johnson's contested election in 1948 went all the way to the Supreme Court, to no avail. (2) Joseph P. Kennedy bought in 1945 the Merchandise Mart in Chicago-4.2 million square feet. It attracts more than three million visitors annually and is the world's largest commercial building.

Election Results 1960

Candidates	EV	%	Pop. (000)	Pop. %	Pop. %
Kennedy	301	56.3	34,221	49.7	50.1
Nixon	219	40.9	34,107	49.6	49.9
Byrd	15	2.8	337	.5	
Other			164	.2	
Total	535	100.0	68,829	100.0	100.0

EV=electoral vote; Pop. = popular vote;

Source: NY Times Almanac 2009, p. 132

Byrd was not a candidate, but received fifteen electoral votes from delegates who refused to support Kennedy: Mississippi (8), Alabama (6) and Oklahoma (1).

The fringe vote, from a numerical standpoint, could have made a difference in two states, Illinois and New Jersey. From a practical standpoint, however, they did not, because in each case the loser was Nixon. It is theoretically unlikely that fringe voters, mostly Democrats, if turned loose would have voted for Nixon.

Election Results 1960
States with 15+ Electoral Votes
Winning Percent

Candidates/ Votes	CA 32	IL 27	MA 16	MI 20	NJ 16	NY 45	OH 25	PA 32	TX 24
Kennedy	49.6	50.0	60.2	50.9	50.0	52.5	46.7	51.1	50.5
Nixon	50.1	49.8	39.6	48.8	49.2	47.3	53.3	48.7	48.5
Total	99.7	**99.8**	99.8	99.7	**99.2**	99.8	100.0	99.8	99.0

Bold type = fringe vote had theoretical impact in that state.

Source: http://www.uselectionatlas.org/

Charges of scandal levied against counting methods in Illinois and Texas made it reasonable for Nixon to question the count in those states and in Michigan, and New Jersey as well, because of the closeness of the vote — eighty-seven electoral votes. A swing of forty-three votes would result in victory for Nixon. Several combinations could have worked if a recount went his way, such as Illinois plus Texas; Michigan combined with either Illinois or Texas; New Jersey plus Illinois. The Republican National Committee mounted legal challenges, but Nixon stayed away from them and the results became a matter of record.

The electoral vote totally misleads the casual reader about the closeness of this race; the popular vote provides the proper setting. This was an extraordinarily close election in all respects. A win, either way, would have to be considered as lucky — the victor in ten states won by a margin of 2 percent or less. Nixon took twenty-seven states, JFK twenty-three.[66] Both men had pockets of strength in the other's backyard. Nixon, the loser, and JFK, the winner, drew more popular votes than any pre–1960 presidential candidate except for Ike. Together, they drew more total votes than any pre–1960 election.

Now it was over. Winning of the presidency, the dream of Joseph P. Kennedy, first for his son Joe (killed in World War II) then for his second son, Jack, had come true. Not accustomed to losing, and one with the power and means to reach grand objectives, Joseph Kennedy basked in the pleasure of seeing his son inaugurated and enjoyed his role as adviser until, in December 1961, a stroke rendered him speechless. He died in 1969.

The young president took over the Oval Office in January 1961 determined to continue the reinvention of America. His influence, and that of his successor and his followers, would change the face of America, to the delight of progressives (now increasingly called liberals) and to the chagrin of originalists, who, with their intense devotion to constitutional clauses that limit the role of the federal government, were once again on the outside looking in.

The Death of Kennedy and the Lyndon B. Johnson Succession

John F. Kennedy was shot on Friday, November 22, 1963, in Dallas at 12:30 P.M.[67] He was pronounced dead at 1:00 P.M.; Lee Harvey Oswald was arrested as a suspect at 1:55 P.M.; the casket was placed on Air Force One at 2:18 P.M.—Jacqueline Kennedy, the first lady, and Vice President Lyndon B. Johnson were aboard; Vice President Johnson was sworn in as president at 2:38 P.M.; Air Force One arrived in Washington at 5:00 P.M.; after questioning, Oswald was charged with the murder of Kennedy at 11:26 P.M. (Dallas time). Oswald was in the custody of Dallas police on Saturday, November 23, 1963; interrogation continued until 1:10 P.M.; Oswald was officially told of the charge against him at 1:35 P.M. Dallas police interrogated Oswald again on Sunday morning, November 24, 1963. Preparations were completed for the transfer of Oswald to the county jail at 11:10 A.M. During the transfer process at the Dallas police station, Jack Ruby shot and killed Oswald.

The Warren Commission was established to determine the facts of the case, on November 29, 1963. Its members were: Chief Justice Earl Warren, Senators Richard Russell (D-GA) and John Cooper (R-KY), Representatives Hale Boggs (D-LA) and Gerald Ford (R-MI), Allen Dulles, ex-director of the C.I.A. and John McCloy, ex-president of the World Bank. The commission had the services of a general counsel, fourteen assistant counsels and a staff of twelve.

Proceedings began on December 3, 1963. The final report was delivered to the president on September 24, 1964 — the conclusion: Lee Harvey Oswald, acting alone and without accomplices, killed John F. Kennedy. Also, no connection was found between Oswald and Ruby; conspiracy theories were dismissed.[68] The decision was not well received by all. Comprehensive criticisms abounded that focused on minute details. Conspiracy theories floated that blamed the assassination on formidable sources, including:

- The Soviets, because Oswald once lived there and retained Marxist connections.
- Cuba, because of alleged assassination projects against Castro.
- The Mafia, because of alleged connections between the Kennedys and the crime syndicate.
- Vietnam, because of the president's role in the assassination of Diem, president of South Vietnam.
- Lyndon Johnson, because he allegedly wanted to be president.
- CIA, because it allegedly disapproved of JFK's policies.

These theories persist because of public skepticism. According to Gallup polls, about half of the public in 1966 did not accept the findings of the Warren Commission. Ten years later, more than 80 percent felt that way, and that number has held steady ever since.[69]

Thumbnail Sketch of Lyndon B. Johnson

Born: 1908, TX; **Education:** Southwest Texas State Teachers College, Georgetown Law School (one year); **Wife:** Claudia Alta Taylor; **Children:** Two; **Died:** 1973.[70]

The Johnson family had deep Texas roots as cattlemen, farmers and soldiers for the Confederacy. Lyndon's father, Sam, was a gregarious farmer and businessman who found his way into politics in his late twenties as a state representative. He made poor personal and business decisions that cost him the family farm. Johnson's mother, Rebekah,[71] was a cultured woman who studied literature at Baylor University and the University of Texas and taught elocution.

Johnson graduated from high school in 1924 and spent a year in nondescript jobs until in 1925 he entered Southwest Texas State Teachers College. He worked his way through college and, time permitting, got involved with campus politics, debates and the school newspaper. He dropped out of school in 1927 but returned a year later and in 1930 graduated. Thereafter, he embarked on a teaching career.

Johnson's entry into politics was partly due to the influence of his father, who had served five terms in the state legislature during which he became close to Sam Rayburn, a rising political star. As a sideline to his teaching career, Johnson got into the thick of things in 1930 when he campaigned for a state senator, Welly Hopkins, who was making a successful run for a seat in the House of Representatives. This activity resulted in an appointment to the office of Rep. Richard Kleberg as his legislative secretary.

Johnson immediately displayed the skills that eventually earned him the reputation as the great arm twister. He became friendly with the aides of men like President Roosevelt and Vice President Garner, and he was practically adopted by Sam Rayburn. Johnson's rise was steady thereafter. He led a Texas youth association in 1935; two years later, he successfully ran for Congress.

In 1940,[72] Johnson was a lieutenant commander in the Naval Reserve; in 1941, he was on active duty; in 1942, he was back in the House of Representatives, where he served until 1949. He had unsuccessfully run for the Senate in the early 1940s and tried it again in 1948. This time he won, but the stench from the election process continues to the present day. Charges of fraud were plentiful but Johnson, assisted by legal ally Abe Fortas,[73] prevailed. And the tale of one of the most memorable political careers in history continued.*

Johnson's storied career as a U.S. senator continued until he became John Kennedy's running mate in 1960. He is regarded as one of the most influential Senate leaders in history, a loyal defender of the progressive policies and ideas of Presidents Wilson, Roosevelt and Truman.

The Kennedy/Johnson Cabinet

When Johnson took over in 1963, he essentially retained the Kennedy cabinet,[74] as follows: **Vice President:** Hubert Humphrey, Minnesota; **Secretary of State:** Dean Rusk, Georgia; **Secretary of Treasury:** C. Douglas Dillon, New York; **Secretary of Defense:** Robert S. McNamara, California; **Attorney General:** Robert F. Kennedy, Massachusetts; **Postmaster General:** J. Edward Day, Illinois (1961–63), John A. Gronouski, Wisconsin; **Secretary of Interior:** Stewart L. Udall, Arizona; **Secretary of Agriculture:** Orville S. Freeman, Minnesota; **Secretary of Commerce:** Luther H. Hodges, North Carolina; **Secretary of Labor:** Arthur J. Goldberg, Illinois (1929–42), W. Willard Wirtz, Illinois; **HEW:** Abraham A. Ribicoff, Connecticut (1961–62), Anthony J. Celebrezze, Ohio. The surprise choice was Dillon, a Republican. His qualifications were impeccable, but the choice must have irked highly partisan Democrats.

In general, this was a qualified group of leaders. Those who later left their posts did so to move on to higher positions. "His [Johnson's] success in ... attracting men of ability ... is now well known.... [S]ome of the administration's severest critics ... express unqualified admiration for the cabinet."[75]

The Kennedy/Johnson Congress

JFK had big ideas that would go nowhere without congressional backing. True, he needed popular support and had made his appeal for it in his inaugural

*Abe Fortas first met Johnson in 1945. Johnson appealed to him for help during the 1948 election. Fortas persuaded Supreme Court justice Hugo Black to overturn a ruling unfavorable to Johnson, a reversal that won the election for Johnson. Johnson remembered: As president, he made Fortas in 1965 an associate justice of the Supreme Court. When Chief Justice Warren resigned in 1968, Johnson nominated Fortas to succeed him but he was rejected. Fortas eventually found his way to the Court as an associate justice but resigned after a brief tenure because of fees he had received that allegedly represented a conflict of interest.

address. But Democratic congressmen and senators sitting every day in congressional chambers, voting every day for Democratic ideals, were the hardcore stuff out of which successful presidencies emerged, a lesson that Ike learned the hard way. As popular as he was, Ike enjoyed modest control only during the first two years of his presidency; thereafter his East Coast brand of middle-of-the-road conservatism, which lacked iron, lost favor and turned him into a president who became more famous for the activity of his veto pen than he was for legislation.

JFK had a good beginning as Election Day 1960 began. Democrats had control of Congress, but what would it be when the levers had been pulled in all fifty states? Would he be in a situation of power, or would he be a toothless tiger with no political clout? The former proved to be the case. He not only had control, he had veto-proof control. His liberal agenda had a clear road ahead.

Pro-Administration Congressional Power

Congress	Year	President	House %	Senate %
86	1959	Eisenhower	35	35
87	1961	Kennedy (D)	60	64
88	1963	Kennedy/Johnson	60	66
89	1965	Johnson	68	68

Appendix 1.1, 1.2

Bold type=minority position

Sam Rayburn (D-TX), who had become a Washington institution as the longest sitting speaker in history, was still in control of the House in 1961[76] and was followed in that position by John McCormack (D-MA),[77] a professional politician who shared many political allies in his home state with JFK and who was a personal friend of Rayburn, the retired speaker, and John Garner,[78] FDR's vice president. McCormack was a certified Washington insider.

JFK was greeted in the Senate by a politician who was to become as famous for his durability as Senate leader as Rayburn was as House speaker, Mike Mansfield.[79] During the years of FDR, Democrats ran the House and the Senate, usually with veto-proof majorities. With such majorities a president can change a nation. And FDR did. The Democratic express was still underway at the end of Ike's presidency, waiting for the next social engineer to move the Wilson/Roosevelt/Truman legacy ahead.

Enter, JFK, with absolute congressional control.

The Kennedy/Johnson Supreme Court

Ike's years were obviously fecund ones for the legal profession, with much of the activity centering on civil rights and communists in American society. In the Kennedy/Johnson era, still under Chief Justice Warren, the fear of internal communism faded, but civil rights activity increased.

Supreme Court Justices, 1961–64

Judge	Began	Appointed by	Ended
Earl Warren (CA)	1954	Eisenhower	1969
Hugo Black (AL)	1937	Roosevelt	1971
Felix Frankfurter (MA)	1939	Roosevelt	1962
William Douglas (MN)	1939	Roosevelt	1975
Tom Clark (TX)	1949	Truman	1967
John Harlan (NY)	1955	Eisenhower	1971
William Brennan	1956	Eisenhower	1990
Charles Whittaker	1957	Eisenhower	1962
Potter Stewart	1958	Eisenhower	1981
Byron White	1962	Kennedy	1993
Arthur Goldberg	1962	Kennedy	1965

Source: Oyez, http://www.oyez.org/ — Members of the Supreme Court,[80] http://www.supremecourtus.gov/about/members.pdf

Men in Black, Mark Levin, Preface

Notes: Hugo Black was a former Ku Klux Klan member. He suffered a stroke in 1969, which impaired his memory. By 1971, constant pain in his head made it difficult to concentrate, and his short-term memory was poor; paranoia followed. In effect, he was unable to perform his duties for more than two years, yet he remained active. Felix Frankfurter was character witness for the Soviet spy Alger Hiss. Legal ethicists were troubled by his behavior during *Brown v. Board of Education* (he leaked privileged information). William O. Douglas was a known womanizer. His frequent marriages and divorces with younger women did not add to the dignity of the Court, and they brought him financial hardship, which led him to seek supplemental income from questionable sources. A stroke in 1974 impaired his faculties, but he would not retire. His colleagues refused to count his vote until he did. Charles Whittaker had a nervous breakdown after five years of service, which led to his resignation.[81]

Warren and Brennan,* Ike's appointees, and activist judges, mated well with Roosevelt/Truman appointees. It's no surprise, therefore, that the Court established in political and legislative concrete many foundation civil rights laws that govern racial discrimination. On social matters, its rulings were in some cases controversial.

It is doubtful that any judicial appointee proved to be more of a surprise than Earl Warren. A lifelong Republican, he was involved in presidential politics in 1948 and 1952 at the highest level. For much of his tenure, he led a solid bloc of liberal justices who led the way to changes—for example, in constitutional criminal procedure — and he became in the process known as the activist leader of an activist Court, something nobody expected when he was appointed.

Some rulings that hint at the concerns of the time follow[82]:

Brennan is another of Ike's appointees who allegedly embarrassed him. If so (and that's not certain), it was his own fault. Again falling victim to the desire to be known as a middle-of-the-road politician, he appointed a Democrat, Brennan, to the vacant seat and got in return what most Democrat judges deliver-activism.

SCALES V. UNITED STATES (1961)

The facts: Scales belonged to an organization that advocated the forceful overthrow of the United States government. Scales claimed protection under the Internal Security Act that, he claimed, permitted membership per se.

The issue: Does the Internal Security Act protect Scales from the consequences of his actions, under the Smith Act?

The decision: No. Per se membership permitted under the Internal Security Act does not embrace destructive organizations.

MAPP V. OHIO (1961)

The facts: Police illegally searched a home of Mapp's and find obscene materials. The evidence was used to convict her. She claimed constitutional protection.

The issue: Is persuasive evidence obtained during an illegal search excluded in a court of law?

The decision: Yes, evidence is expunged. Mapp was freed. This cornerstone ruling continues to plague proceedings as litigants and judges try to figure out when the exclusionary rule applies.

ENGEL V. VITALE (1962)

The facts: New York authorized a voluntary, short, nonsectarian prayer to be said in all public schools. Engel protested as a violation of the First Amendment.

The issue: Is Engel's claim correct?

The decision: Yes. By providing the prayer, New York officially approved of religion. This 6–1 decision is the first in a series that eventually eliminated all religious activities in schools and in many public ceremonies, a dramatic attack on tradition.

ROBINSON V. CALIFORNIA (1962)

The facts: California law made it illegal to use drugs. The user was caught, convicted and sentenced to ninety days.

The issue: Did his sentence constitute cruel and unusual treatment under the Eighth Amendment?

The decision: Yes. Imprisoning a person afflicted with an illness is cruel and unusual.

Here the Court consecrated a self-developed habit as a disease. It was not asked to rule on the nature of drug addiction, a debate that continues today. Doing so was, to many, a harmful act of judicial activism.

There were other cases during this period of social turmoil, many dealing with different slants of the same fundamental questions: race, speech, obscenity and religion:

- Public school students cannot be required to read bible verses and recite the Lord's Prayer (*School District of Abington v. Schempp*, 1963).
- The same ban applies to public ceremonies (*Murray v. Curlett*, 1963).
- Employees have the right to refuse to work on the Sabbath-day of their church (*Sherbert v. Verner*, 1963).
- A state cannot criminalize the expression of unpopular views (*Edwards v. South Carolina* (1963).
- Obscenity is ultimately not obscenity until (in effect) the Supreme Court, applying the Roth test, says so (*Jacobellis v. Ohio*, 1964).
- Discrimination in restaurants is unconstitutional (*Katzenbach v. McClung*, 1964).

On and on it went in this extraordinarily active period. The plight of blacks in search of the pragmatic rights that had for so long been more theory than fact, and the steps they took to dramatize their case, energized other activists across the nation to seek their fair share of the legal benefits that flowed from protest and litigation. The total effect brought a crushing case load to Washington,* where riots and marches in the street, once reserved to Europeans, became equally commonplace in the U.S.

Domestic Affairs Relative to Current Political Issues

By no stretch could it be said that JFK entered the White House with a mandate to implement his liberal (formerly "progressive") agenda. But he acted as though he did. And the reason for that is simple: He had Congress by the throat. True, his victory over Nixon had been marginal, especially when measured by popular vote, or the geographical distribution of it. But it was a victory; he was president. And he did have veto-proof power in Congress. Given lots of plans, high ambitions and plenty of power, one would expect a deluge of legislation from the Kennedy whiz kids. But such wasn't the case.

DOMESTIC EVENTS

The Kennedy presidency, due to its untimely ending, was more symbolic than substantial. The major events took place after his death.[83]

ECONOMIC GROWTH

JFK inherited a healthy economy and his tax policy formed in 1963 helped to keep it that way.

In 1945, 1,460 cases were in the docket; 1960, 2,313–up fifty-eight percent.

Gross Domestic Product, Public Debt

Year	GDP (bil)	% Growth	Public Debt (bil)	% PD/GDP
1960	518.9	5.9	236.8	45.6
1961	529.9	2.1	238.4	45.0
1962	567.8	7.2	248.0	43.7
1963	599.2	5.5	254.0	42.4
1964	641.4	7.0	256.8	40.0

Source: Historical Tables 2010, 1.2, 7,1

Bold = war years

Under JFK overall tax rates were cut and the top rate was cut from 91 percent to 70 percent. The mere idea of a tax cut coming from a Democrat was by itself stimulating to the private sector; the fact of it helped to maintain a high level of growth. JFK proposed the tax cut, but it was Johnson who got it through Congress after JFK's death.

The increase in debt under Kennedy and Johnson of $20 billion was caused by some of the indirect costs related to the expanded role of the United States in Vietnam, by a surge of investment in space and by a 42 percent increase in the cost of social services.[84] Increased costs related to foreign policy and space can be defended. The rate of increase in social services cannot; it was unsustainable and should have served as a clarion call to all responsible politicians to restructure existing programs before they got out of hand. This was especially so during a time of war when history informs that once the trigger is pulled one never knows what next will happen, or for how long. This is an appropriate time to comment on two financial indicators that will be of continuing interest as time passes — the absolute size of public debt and the ratio of debt to GDP.

Some people take undue comfort in the ratio. It proves, they say, the soundness of the dollar. There is truth in that. But a positive trend in this ratio is entirely dependant upon continued economic growth at a rate that outpaces the ability of Congress to overspend and create deficits. Any disturbance in the economy, or any expensive external conflict or internal disaster, will cause the ratio to soar and the value of the dollar to weaken. The other side of the coin is this: Continuing high debt and deficits bring increased interest costs that are a deadly drag on the federal budget. By the beginning of the 21st century, for example, interest costs had become one of the largest line items in the national budget.

LEGISLATIVE EVENTS

Given the personality, vigor, ideas and power of Kennedy, his legislative record was not impressive. Some notable domestic achievements follow[85]:

- Housing Act, 1961[86]: Directed funds to chronically poor areas.
- Manpower Development and Retraining Acts, 1961–63[87]: Aimed at workers with skills in depressed industries in need of new skills.

- Mental Retardation Planning, Mental Retardation Facilities and Community Mental Health Centers Acts, 1963[88]: Designed to improve the quality of life for previously overlooked citizens.
- Equal Pay Act, 1963[89]: Prohibits pay discrimination based on gender.

These domestic successes fall into the paternalistic pattern of federal programs initiated by FDR. Problems JFK saw triggered the usual liberal response — a federal solution. No effective opposition resisted him on such popular and relatively noncontroversial issues.

On national issues requiring the kind of leadership that would attract the loyalties of disparate groups, the personal Kennedy magnetism that had charmed the general public during the election failed to have the same effect on those who knew him as a sitting representative and a senator. This was especially true with issues known as his big four: (1) A strong civil rights bill; (2) federal aid to elementary and secondary schools; (3) a major tax cut; and 4) Medicare for senior citizens.

Kennedy did not submit his civil rights initiative until 1963. It encountered stiff southern resistance and was still unresolved when he died. His attempt to provide direct aid to schools bumped into the Catholic issue he had encountered during the election and his personal opposition to federal support for Catholic schools wasn't enough to unite the party. His planned tax cut did not take place until after his death. Medicare was still being debated while he was alive.

Based on what he had talked about as a candidate, and what he proposed as president, it was obvious that a progressive, in the FDR mold, occupied the White House. Based upon legislation passed, it was equally obvious that major elements of his agenda still awaited a leader with the will and ability to unite the veto-proof power of the Democratic Party and make it the effective legislative tool that it could be.

CONSTITUTIONAL AMENDMENTS, 1961–64

Two amendments were added during the 1961–64 period, as follows: Amendment XXIII (1961) provides the District of Columbia with the same number of electors as the smallest state in the Union. This was a response to continuing efforts of some to make the District of Columbia a state. Amendment XXIV (1964) affirms the right of all citizens to vote irrespective of their record of paying poll taxes. This was a response to those who continued to obstruct black voters based upon technicalities.

Foreign Affairs Relative to Current Political Issues

Throughout his campaign, and in his inauguration speech, JFK made it plain that, while accepting the need for a staunch military, he preferred to shift the emphasis in foreign policy away from military preparedness to a global-wide policy of active diplomacy that emphasized nonmilitary supports. Some of his early legislative moves[90] underlined his intentions to make such a policy an immediate reality:

- The Peace Corps Act, 1961[91]: This was a follow-through of a promise made by JFK in his inauguration speech: "We pledge our best efforts to help them help themselves." The corps is still active and stands as a permanent legacy of the thirty-fifth president of the United States. Over 195,000 volunteers since 1961 have served in 139 countries.
- Arms Control and Disarmament Act, 1961[92]: (1) Arms control became a key component of national security policy. Goals were established for coordinating disarmament with other defense strategies; (2) the Arms Control and Disarmament Agency was created and standards were established for integrating all aspects of defense policy.
- Foreign Assistance Act, 1961[93]: Consolidated statutory authorities under a single regime to provide nonmilitary assistance to friendly countries to develop their resources and improve their living standards.

The burdens of actual leadership fell upon JFK with unusual suddenness. In April 1961 the Bay of Pigs fiasco took place, a two-day military attempt at unseating Castro that was a complete failure.[94] Blame for this failure is still hazy, but the consequences of it were clear — the United States and its new president were embarrassed. Fair or not, it appeared apparent that the absence of Ike — the most highly esteemed military man in the world — in the White House carried a penalty: a new, green leader supported by a new, green team in charge of national security.

Failure in Cuba was hardly the most desirable backdrop for JFK's summit meeting in July 1961, in Vienna, with Nikita Khrushchev. Consistent with his pledge to seek peace through diplomacy, JFK scheduled the meeting with the Soviet premier early in his presidency, a decision that to some was evidence of his determination to seek new ways to peace and to others was a reflection of how naive he was to expect profit from negotiations with global, valueless bullies. The meeting was a flop. Following it, Khruschev announced he would solve the Berlin problem unilaterally. JFK promised a military response to aggression. Two months later, the Berlin wall was a physical reminder of the depth of the enmity between the Soviet Union and the Allied forces.* Sensing weakness in Washington, the Soviets remained on the offensive, this time testing the resolve of the United States to live by the terms of the Monroe Doctrine.

Men and missiles were smuggled into Cuba, which was now recognized as a Soviet satellite. By the time U.S. intelligence caught up with the scheme,

*It is seldom mentioned, but the mere fact of Ike's presence in the White House, with his impeccable World War II reputation (which was as high in Moscow as it was in Washington), was a powerful deterrent against Soviet aggression. The boldness of the Soviets during the Kennedy years is traceable to the absence of an Eisenhower-like presence in the White House.

the Soviets had nuclear-armed missiles and over forty thousand troops in Cuba — less than one hundred miles from Florida. Much has been made, appropriately, over what happened after the missiles and the troops were identified. Little or nothing has been made over how such a buildup could have occurred unnoticed by the CIA. This was an enormous intelligence failure that could have resulted in World War III. Once the information became known, JFK acted promptly. The blockade of Cuba went into effect; Soviet ships were turned back on the high seas; the Soviets capitulated; men and missiles were removed. In return, the U.S. removed its missiles from Turkey.

The space race had become an international issue under Ike. JFK had made much of the space and missile gap during his campaign. Now it was time to do something about it. JFK was long on rhetoric in 1961 while the Soviets were even longer on performance. Gagarin was the first astronaut to orbit the earth. The U.S. responded with flights by Alan Shepard and Gus Grissom, which represented progress but not yet at the Soviet level. JFK set as a goal a man on the moon in a decade. From 1962 on, the American space program took charge. Names like Glenn, Carpenter and Cooper made headlines with their flights into space.[95] The American reputation for excellence was once more intact.

The Soviets had essentially a two pronged approach to the Cold War against the United States and its allies: (1) Aggression and intimidation in Europe to keep the Iron Curtain nations in line, in which they were highly successful. (2) Aggression through satellite nations on the global stage — for example, Korea, Cuba and Vietnam.

Vietnam was the last of these to take place in Kennedy's lifetime. It was a war that Ike didn't want to fight and he resisted pressure from his staff for a military buildup,[96] a lesson JFK ignored. At the time of JFK's death, over sixteen thousand troops were in Vietnam, some of them Special Forces taking casualties. Additionally, the U.S. was inextricably wound up in South Vietnam's political affairs and played a part in the assassination of its president Diem.

Negotiations between nuclear nations concerning testing regimes had been ongoing for almost a decade when, in August 1963, JFK signed the first agreement on such matters with the United Kingdom and the Soviet Union. The agreement prohibits testing underwater, in the atmosphere or in outer space but permits it underground. Signatories pledged to work toward an end to the armaments race and environmental pollution from radioactive substances.[97] Some regard this treaty as being JFK's supreme foreign policy achievement.[98]

JFK's presidency was not what he or others expected it to be. His legislative accomplishments were modest; his involvement in foreign affairs was more absorbing than planned and represented a series of major ups and major downs.

Because his tenure was so short, Lyndon Johnson carried the weight of the Vietnam War on his shoulders, but it was JFK who turned it into a war in the first place, a decision that in the long view of history is destined to chip away at the Camelot image that his supporters and friendly historians have thus far created. Vietnam changed America in ways that are still felt; JFK may one day be more closely associated with the pain attached to it.

Behind the clouds of war, while the nation's eyes from 1960 to 1964 were fastened on diving planes, brave soldiers, dead bodies and riots in the streets, the progressive agenda was attached to the federal budget to such a degree, and with such a firm foundation, that America was set on a path to massive debt and ultimate insolvency.

Conclusion

Why was the election of 1960 so close? It shouldn't have been; it should have been an easier Democratic win. The Eisenhower luster was gone; Nixon was good, but not that good; the misery index was high; the missile gap, overstated by JFK, nevertheless made the point that the space race was being led by the Soviets; a steady loss of Republican power in the Congress suggested voter sentiments favorable for Democrats. These things were all Republican negatives and Democratic positives. But it wasn't an easy win. One reason that seems to stand above all others is the perception of leadership capacity mated with the perilous times.

Bubbles of warfare existed, or threatened, around the globe, led by the daily realization that the Soviet Union had the capacity to deal a mortal blow to the United States. That a godless government had such power was, by itself, enough to make Americans nervous. So, the theory goes, the public appraises candidates first through the prism of national security. Perhaps many people wanted to vote for JFK for the reasons noted above but were restrained from doing so because of fear of the unknown. Nixon, the experienced man, drew more of the fear vote. His close relationship with Ike and, presumably, his ready access to him if needed at some future time was a reassuring factor in his favor. JFK, on the other hand, was a gamble in an uncertain time. His war record brought him respect, but not gravitas.

A Nixon win would have actually been a surprise given the circumstances that existed. But as things turned out, he lost a winnable election that had once appeared to be lost cause. Results might have been different if his campaign promise of visiting fifty states had never been made; he had paid more attention to his physical appearance during the first debate; and Ike had come forth early in the campaign with language that neutralized the impact of his widely publicized comment about Nixon's competence.

History may ultimately say that voter concerns about JFK's ability to handle foreign affairs and national security caused the close election and that they were well founded (Cuba, Vietnam). But only one thing is certain: John F. Kennedy won one of the nation's closest presidential elections. Sometimes the simplest reason is the best. Kennedy was the first television president. His smile and appearance were the most valuable political assets in the entire campaign.

10

1968: Hubert H. Humphrey vs. Richard M. Nixon

(Electoral Votes 538; Majority 270)

Introduction

The last close election in 1960 saw John Kennedy (JFK) defeat the incumbent vice president, Richard Nixon. Lyndon Johnson (LBJ) succeeded to the presidency in 1963 after the assassination of JFK. He then ran on his own and served for four more years after a resounding victory in the 1964 election in which he defeated the conservative icon Barry Goldwater with 61 percent of the popular vote — the highest in history — and an even more humiliating electoral vote of 486–52.

Woodrow Wilson persuaded the Democratic Party to establish progressive ideas as their motivators, and FDR demonstrated how America could be changed by implementing them despite constitutional clauses that seemed to obstruct them. But it was LBJ — who learned his lessons well — who added, to a staggering degree, a series of social benefits to the base established by FDR and changed forever the nature and purpose of the American government. By the time he left office, Food Stamps (1964), Medicaid (1965), Student Aid (1966) and Medicare (1967) were imbedded in the federal budget as additions to the family of social service costs known as Human Resources.[1] This began a spending trend that turned America into a twisted form never envisaged by the Founders.

Under Ike, the cost of all social services in the 1959 budget, including Social Security, was $25 billion. When Johnson left office (1968) the cost was $59 billion. And then it soared (1980, $313 billion; 1990, $619 billion, 2009, $2.2 trillion).[2] Under Ike, the cost of social services in 1959 was 51 percent of the cost of national defense; in 1971, it was, for the first time, more expensive than defense; in 2008, the cost of social services was three times more expensive than defense.[3] Under Ike, public debt in 1959 was $235 billion; in 2008, public debt was $5.8 trillion.[4] It is a political fact of life that to make such a radical change in governmental focus requires the congressional majorities with which LBJ was blessed; it is equally true that to undo or redirect or restructure social programs requires the same level of congressional power. That never came about. Republican presidents thereafter never had Johnsonian power and could not stop the growth of these costs.

All of the ramifications of LBJ's policies, and of the spending attitudes he popularized, were not known in 1968, but enough was known to sound the clarion call to all politicians that they were embarked on an unaffordable course of action. Under LBJ in his last term there was a deficit in every year, each year larger than the one before and none of them caused by the Vietnam War.[5] Public debt increased by 34 percent[6] at a moment in time when a united effort to restructure programs into affordable form should have been underway. Nothing was done, nor has anything substantial been done since, hence the debt and hence the modern concerns for the liquidity of the United States.

This was the fiscal heritage that Democrats had to dealt with in 1968. In terms of the immediate economic climate they had to explain a stifling misery index[7] that to some degree was troubling every voter. In terms of the underpinning of the policies left behind, they had to justify the decision of the government to expand social services during a time of war and they had to demonstrate they could afford the programs they were selling.

Unfortunately, arcane topics like budgets and debt seldom move the public until they severely hit the pocketbook. For that reason, most attention was directed at the war policy of the administration, which in 1968 was so unpopular that it practically nullified the importance of the commendable civil rights progress that took place while the riots in the streets turned America into a circus of protestors, the likes of which had never been seen before. This mix of the unknown related to the budget monster that had been unleashed and the riots in the streets became too much for LBJ. He got out of it, leaving to others the problem of justifying what he had done.

In the short term, the Vietnam problem dominated LBJ's record. It was a liability to Democrats; an asset to Republicans. In the long term, LBJ ultimately will either be known as the American president who set the nation on a humane course that became the envy of the world or he will be vilified as the one who destroyed the America of the Founders and led his new creation into the forgotten pages of history.

Conventions

Apart from his war record, most Democrats were proud of LBJ's accomplishments. He brought to the presidency a sterling reputation as one who could get things done. He was also a southerner who could be expected to get support for his agenda from that part of the nation. He did just that by applying available tools to their maximum effect: his personal skills, sympathy for the assassinated president and his southern roots. The result was a series of legislative accomplishments that would have made FDR proud and that changed America from the land of the Founders to a redesigned nation conceived by Wilson, FDR and Johnson.

But the war was the 800-pound gorilla in the room. It overpowered all other accomplishments of the LBJ administration and took from them the power they should have had politically. And the shining smile of JFK wasn't enough to rub out the stain on the Democratic brand with which the Democratic candidate in 1968 would have to deal. On top of this, the special cause movements were still in full bloom. The war and civil unrest were huge Democratic problems during the election year.

In March 1968, LBJ announced he would neither seek nor accept the nomination of his party.* With LBJ retired, the Democratic nomination was wide open, with Vice President Hubert Humphrey the leading contender.

DEMOCRATIC CONVENTION

Democrats held their convention in Chicago during the third week of August.[8] The title of Norman Mailer's book *Miami and the Siege of Chicago* captures the tone of the two conventions, especially the Democratic affair. Why was that convention so chaotic? It all began with the announcement by LBJ that he was unavailable as a candidate. This left the field to antiwar contenders such as Robert Kennedy, Eugene McCarthy and George McGovern, which tended to soothe the activists.

Then the other shoe dropped: Vice President Hubert Humphrey announced his interest in the nomination. His name in the race was, to activists, the same as LBJ's— it was the red flag that drew the attention of the bull in their gut. And so the chaos began. How could it not? LBJ's influence, via Humphrey, was still alive; George Wallace, another war supporter, was added to the mix. And then two more pre-convention bombs were dropped: Martin Luther King, Jr., and Robert Kennedy were both assassinated, the former while resting in Memphis from his civil rights demonstrations[9] and the latter while campaigning in Los Angeles.[10]

Sen. George McGovern, not yet a national figure, was soon eliminated as viable competition,[11] and, with Kennedy's death, McCarthy attracted the antiwar activists. Wallace's success during the primaries simply agitated activists even more, although he had no chance to win the nomination.

The divisive image of the Vietnam War hovered over the convention and, in effect, smothered all other issues into insignificance. The nation was in a state of turmoil over the continuation of that war; delegates looked at every

*"I'm tired. I'm tired of feeling rejected. I'm tired of waking up in the middle of the nights worrying about the war."-Lyndon Johnson

candidate through the prism of war and peace. And because Humphrey, a supporter of LBJ, was the only standing candidate of prominence, delegates were raucous; onlookers were violent.* Antiwar leaders coordinated the efforts of more than one hundred groups to form a march. Activists, like the leaders of the Youth International Party (YIPPIES), planned to bring 100,000 young adults to the convention to demonstrate (they couldn't get a permit, but came anyway).

The antiwar movement drew unsavory characters, Abbie Hoffman and Jerry Rubin, for example.[12] They were associated in 1968 with the Chicago Seven, which had a violent confrontation with the police. Hoffman was later charged with selling cocaine (1973) and served a year in prison. (What was seen in Chicago mirrored what could be found in other parts of the country. Riots, for example, followed the King assassination; student protestors had shut down Columbia University earlier in the year. America was bubbling with discontent.)

The climate in Chicago was such that Democratic leaders and television networks wanted to move the convention to Miami. But even more powerful forces, including LBJ, intervened to keep it in Chicago. Mayor Daley promised to keep the peace (the carrot) and threatened to pull away from Humphrey if the convention were moved (the stick). It stayed! But the peace wasn't kept. While delegates argued, the Battle of Michigan Avenue took place on national television. Thousands of protestors appeared in support of McCarthy. Mayor Daley deployed more than 10,000 police officers and 15,000 state and federal officers to handle the crowd. Violence ensued; demonstrators were beaten. It was a national embarrassment.[13]

Within the convention, conditions weren't as violent, but they weren't calm and deliberate either. Humphrey arrived with enough delegates to win, but uncertainty was in the air because so many delegates were uncomfortable with his stance on the war. Mayor Daley, for example, wanted Ted Kennedy as the candidate, but that idea didn't fly. There was also a credentials fight over who was qualified to sit and vote at the convention. If Humphrey's supporters lost it, antiwar delegates would vote against him in as many as fifteen states, which could throw the convention into turmoil. He won the fight, and that ended his worries.

The antiwar delegates were active to the end, marching around the hall when possible singing "We shall overcome." And some nomination speeches were lively. Sen. Abraham Ribicoff, for example, when nominating Sen. George McGovern, referred to the "Gestapo" tactics on the streets of Chicago. This enraged Mayor Daley and triggered the unsurprising array of signs the last day of the convention that read "We love you Daley." Humphrey won the nomina-

---

*LBJ's favorability rating was in the low thirties, his Vietnam policy in the low twenties. Many Democrats-the most active ones-wanted him and his war out of sight.

tion by more than one thousand votes and Sen. Edmund Muskie was chosen as his running mate.

The mood of the party was, at best, mixed when the convention closed. Could they pull together and keep the presidency? Could they maintain congressional power? Would they?

The major elements in the Democratic Platform appear below.

THE REPUBLICAN CONVENTION

Miami was chosen by Republicans as the site of their 1968 convention held during the first week in August. Unlike the circus held by Democrats a few weeks later, the event was orderly.[14]

There were almost a dozen candidates, but only five emerged with notable support during early stages of the first ballot: Richard Nixon (CA), Nelson Rockefeller (NY), Ronald Reagan (CA), James Rhodes (OH) and George Romney (MI). Rhodes and Romney soon dropped out; Rockefeller, the liberal, and Reagan, the conservative, tried to stop the Nixon express to a first ballot victory, but couldn't.[15] Opposition from the Rockefeller wing was a consideration, but the real danger to Nixon was Reagan's influence with conservative southern states. Nixon solved this problem by promising influential Sen. Strom Thurmond that he would choose a conservative for his running mate. With that problem behind him, Nixon moved on to an easy first ballot nomination. Conservative Gov. Spiro Agnew (MD) became his running mate.

The return of Nixon could have been the headline of the convention. After the 1960 election, few would have predicted his return to presidential politics, absent some interim duty in high public position. And after his 1962 defeat in a race for governor of California, most observers considered his political career to be dead. It seemed as though Nixon agreed with that analysis when he said to the press after that humiliating defeat, "You won't have Nixon to kick around anymore because, gentlemen, this is my last press conference."[16]

But he surprised everybody, perhaps even himself. Initially, he retired from politics to practice law and to build equity for himself and his family. But he was available to fellow Republicans for a speech or an appearance. He was chosen to give the speech that introduced the 1964 nominee, Barry Goldwater, to the delegates at the San Francisco convention, and he campaigned for him and other candidates, earning in the process the gratitude of the growing base of conservatives in the party.

Goldwater lost by a humiliating margin to Lyndon Johnson[17] and it looked like Nixon had allied himself with a loser and a losing movement, which would surely drive him back to political obscurity. But the movement wasn't dead, and it had found a new and more charismatic leader, Ronald Reagan. But Reagan had a problem in 1964 that stood in the way of his attaining stature in presidential politics—experience. He started to mend that weakness in his resume in 1966 with his successful bid for the governorship of California.

While Reagan was building his credentials, however, Nixon was on the move. During the 1966 election season, for example, he campaigned for conservative candidates and otherwise assisted conservative leaders. In so doing, he collected IOU's that were too much for the newly elected governor of California, Reagan, to overcome in 1968.[18]

The Republican campaign ended on a high note. The congressional barometer said Democrats still owned Congress, but the Democratic convention clearly showed a party in disarray. Facts on the ground suggested that current congressional power was destined to change as Nixon led the Republican Party to a significant victory.

The major elements in the Republican Platform appear below.

AMERICAN INDEPENDENT PARTY CONVENTION

Third parties usually disappear into the mists of time as unimportant fringe movements that affect little or nothing. But that is not always the case. The Progressive Party, for example (under various names), dates back to the 1880s as a fringe movement of minor consequence. But it was based upon real, unanswered concerns and, because of that, it evolved in the controlling ideology of the Democratic Party of 1916, and (except for the election of 1924, when Democrats were hopelessly divided and the Progressive Party reappeared) it has remained so ever since. The candidacy of Sen. Strom Thurmond in 1948 was also a matter of significance because it highlighted the continuing national struggle with desegregation. And so it was again in 1968, this time with desegregation plus law and order as triggering issues under the leadership of Gov. George C. Wallace (D-AL) and his American Independent Party.

From the beginning, there was no doubt who would be the nominee of the party — Gov. George C. Wallace.[19] There was a reason for this: Wallace in 1964 ran for the Democratic nomination and competed in three primaries: Wisconsin, Maryland and Indiana. He did surprisingly well, winning about one-third of the vote in each state.[20]

Wallace's first choice in 1968 for his running mate was Happy Chandler, a former governor (KY) and better known as the ex-commissioner of baseball. This drew mixed reactions.[21] An insider, for example, allegedly approved because Wallace already appealed to the "nuts in the country" and with someone like Chandler on the ticket he could also get "some decent people." On the other hand, many Wallace supporters would have nothing to do with Chandler because he supported the hiring of Jackie Robinson, a black man, by the Brooklyn Dodgers. (Robinson was the first black man to play in the major leagues. He started in 1947 and had a brilliant career that in 1962 took him to Baseball's Hall of Fame in Cooperstown, NY. The Dodgers retired his number (42) in 1972.[22]) The nays won the argument and Wallace settled for Gen. Curtis LeMay. LeMay, at the time the chairman of an electronics company and the former head of the strategic air command, was a supporter of the use of nuclear weapons, a reputation that did little to attract voters to the Wallace ticket.

Democratic and Republican Platforms

The two parties agreed that communist nations were the enemy, but that was about it. There was little agreement on anything else. Controlling Republicans believed they were forced by the times to accept a busier role for government in private affairs and under Eisenhower they had done so, but there were still clear differences between the parties that were reflected in their platforms.[23] Those who claimed that the vote no longer mattered because both parties were much the same were wrong. There was a clear distinction between them that overwhelmed similarities.

The primal issues from campaign to campaign remained the same: war and peace, the economy (the misery index), tax policy, budget/debt, civil rights, social programs, foreign policy and leadership. War and civil rights had a sharper edge in 1968 because of the riots in the streets associated with both. Also, the addition of Amendment Twenty-Four (1964) to the Constitution, a major step in civil rights legislation, removed the remaining excuses for denying the right to vote to blacks.

Party platforms covered all issues rather elaborately, but only the above will be discussed.

WAR AND PEACE

There were sharp differences on foreign policy issues on both sides of the Atlantic. Democrats were stuck with LBJ's policy of being opposed to a fast drawn-down in Vietnam. Republicans favored a transfer of responsibility to the South Vietnamese, a de-Americanization of the war and a vigorous pursuit of peace with honor. Both sides agreed the military should be expanded and that NATO should be strengthened.

THE ECONOMY

Democrats stood on their record — no recessions, sustained growth, and unemployment lower than the inherited rate. Unfortunately for them, voter memory is short and toleration for pain is weak. During the election year, the misery index was 13.9 — the highest since World War II — and inflation plus interest rates were destroying buying power.[24] Republicans had a strong position on the economy.

TAX POLICY

Republicans couldn't fault Democratic tax policy. It was aggressive and effective. But they objected to tax increases in 1966 and 1968 and argued that tax reform and simplification were imperative, especially aimed at the private sector in ways that stimulate job recovery and strengthen the U.S. competitive position. Democrats were proud of their record. Tax rates were lower than those inherited, but they continued to support progressive tax rates. They agreed that tax reform was needed. Historically, Republicans have the advantage on tax issues, but it wasn't as pronounced in this election.

BUDGET/DEBT

Republicans voiced concern over the endless expansion of social programs and climbing debt. They argued for spending cutbacks and lower taxes when the war ended. A balanced budget and lower debt was their stated goal. Democrats had little to say on this subject, but they agreed that a balanced budget was a goal. On this little understood, unglamorous subject, Republicans had the stronger position.

CIVIL RIGHTS

The Democratic Party had the bragging rights for the Civil Rights Act of 1964 and the Voting Rights Act of 1965, two landmark pieces of civil rights legislation. Nothing Republicans could say could minimize the importance of that record. Democrats had the clear advantage here and it was politically important. It guaranteed for them the black vote and the vote of many others who had supported over the years the black cause.

SOCIAL PROGRAMS

Democrats declared their position briefly and dramatically: They had declared a war on poverty. Republicans dodged constitutional issues related to such an intrusion into private affairs and contented themselves with nitpicking ideas on how to make the new welfare state work better. Their most effective arguments had to do with costs, which were zooming. Restructure, they argued, competing federal programs; revise welfare and security programs that stifle work motivation; states and communities should be organized to solve their own problems. Americans in 1968 were acutely aware of new benefits flowing from Washington and were only remotely aware of the dangers of an expanded government. The result: Advantage Democrats.

FOREIGN POLICY

There were important areas of agreement: Negotiate arms control agreements with the Soviets; protect Israel; support the 1965 Immigration Act, which featured the reunification of families. Apart from Vietnam, Republicans criticized Asian policy, notably the failure to negotiate arms control agreements with China and general policy toward the Soviets. Czechoslovakia had fallen and the Soviets were stronger and more threatening than before. Democrats were on the defensive on foreign policy matters; they lost standing because of the war. Advantage Nixon.

LEADERSHIP

Both candidates were experienced and whatever the claims of superiority of one camp over the other, they had little voter impact. Both had difficult personalities to measure. Some had difficulty taking the ebullient Humphrey seriously; others had trouble liking the dour-appearing Nixon. Overall, Vietnam scarred the Democratic brand as leaders and gave Nixon an automatic lift on this issue.

Riots in the streets to an unparalleled level drew more intensive attention in the party platforms to inner city problems and to law and order issues. The former was actually a part of the civil rights conversation in a different form. Those affected by them, mostly Democratic voters, were amenable to Democratic solutions (more federal aid); those disturbed by civil order questions raised were mostly Republicans. Overall, Democrats carried a good civil rights and social-program record into the election that attracted many voters. They didn't have much more going for them.

American Freedom Party Platform

From the beginning, it was Wallace's objective to appeal to southerners who were discontented over civil rights legislation, and to all Americans frightened and offended by violence on the streets.

The platform of the American Freedom Party (AFP)[25] presented more extensive interests and had conventional things to say about expected topics: war/peace, foreign policy, the economy, education, etc. But the meat and potatoes issues, civil rights and law and order, were the important ones.

The party's platform enumerated the rights reserved for the federal government (Article I, Section 8) under the Constitution plus the additional limitations on federal activism imposed by Amendments Nine and Ten. Then it went on to make its central points:

- The Federal Government ... has ... usurped many powers not delegated to it....
  [It] has forced the states to reapportion their legislatures, a prerogative of
  the states alone ... has attempted to take over and control the seniority and
  apprenticeship lists of the labor unions ... has adopted so-called "Civil
  Rights Acts," particularly the one adopted in 1964, which have set race
  against race and class against class, all of which we condemn.
- It shall be our purpose ... to ... restore to state governments those powers ...
  which have been illegally and unlawfully seized by the Federal Government,

in direct violation of Amendment Ten of the Bill of Rights. [States' rights issues had legal merit with respect to some actions of the federal government, but with respect to desegregation it was a stretch to define civil rights as a states' rights issue. Article I Section 8 of the Constitution states (in addition to specific rights enumerated) that "Congress shall have the Power To ... provide for ... the general welfare of the United States...." Few would objectively argue that the general welfare of the United States benefited from segregation, or that the elimination of it would not be beneficial, or that the abuse of that clause in other instances justifies its continued abuse in this one.]

• We advocate and seek a society and a government in which there is an attitude of respect for the law and for those who seek its enforcement and an insistence on the part of our citizens that the judiciary be ever mindful of their primary duty ... of punishing the guilty and protecting the innocent.... We urge full support for law enforcement agencies ... and a situation in which their actions will not be unreasonably fettered by arbitrary judicial decrees.

• Our forebears ... wisely provided and established, in the Constitution of the United States ... the Judicial, whose duty and responsibility it is to interpret and construe those laws, not to enact them. In the ... past three decades, we have seen the ... Supreme Court ... exceed its authority by enacting judicial legislation ... which would never have been enacted by the Congress.... It shall be our ... purpose ... to ... urge the adoption of an amendment to the ... Constitution whereby [each] member of the Federal judiciary at District level be required to face the electorate on his record at periodical intervals.... With respect to the Supreme Court and the Courts of Appeals [we] would propose that this amendment require re-confirmations of the office holder by the United States Senate at reasonable intervals. [Much of the language in the AFP platform may have been inspired by racism, a charge often applied to its standard bearer, George Wallace, but there were others who had been deeply offended by Supreme Court decisions that led to increased power for the federal government and less power to states and to individuals, which they regarded as unconstitutional. Such people, plus the racists, were the prime targets of the Wallace campaign.]

Concerning personalities, nobody could dislike Humphrey with his ready smile, but some wondered if he was reaching beyond his abilities. Nixon, on the other hand, had successfully shed the "tricky Dick" image and presented to voters the visage of a serious, competent and experienced leader who seemed right for the times. Finally, there was the cocky, tantalizing Wallace. Despite his reputation as a racist, he had a sizable following. Who would he help? Who would he hurt?

The race was on: Humphrey, Nixon and Wallace. The differences between them as men couldn't have been greater. Their political visions were equally disparate. The people had a clear choice.

Thumbnail Sketches of Top Candidates

There were no unknowns in this race. Both Humphrey and Nixon had auspicious congressional careers before serving as vice president, and Wallace had become well known as the rebellious governor of Alabama during the civil rights struggle. There was no personal enmity between the major candidates to juice up the contest, although the press could be depended on to deliver its customary anti–Nixon rhetoric.

HUBERT H. HUMPHREY, DEMOCRAT

Born: 1911, South Dakota; **Educated:** University of Minnesota, Capitol College of Pharmacy, Colorado; Louisiana State University; **Wife:** Muriel Fay Buck; **Children:** Four; **Died** 1978.[26]

Hubert Humphrey spent his early years in South Dakota, but received his college education in Minnesota and a pharmaceutical education in Colorado, after which he returned home to work in his father's drugstore. Not content with a career in pharmacy, Humphrey returned to college to earn his masters degree, which led to teaching and further study.

Politics entered his life when in the period 1940–43 he was employed by the Works Progress Administration (WPA) and other wartime agencies. This activity whetted his appetite for the political life and in 1943 he unsuccessfully ran for mayor of Minneapolis. Undeterred, he bided his time until the next election, keeping busy teaching and working as a news commentator and as manager of an apartment building.

Patience paid off and he became mayor of Minneapolis in 1945 and served until 1948, at which time he was elected to the U.S. Senate. Well known as a liberal, he served in that body until, in 1964, he became Lyndon Johnson's running mate.

After the presidential election, Humphrey returned to teaching in Minnesota until, in 1971, he was sent back to the U.S. Senate, where he continued to function until his death.

RICHARD M. NIXON, REPUBLICAN

See chapter 11 for more details.[27]

Nixon returned to California after his defeat in the 1960 election and wrote his book *Six Crises.* Then he took the political gamble of his life: He ran in 1962 for governor of California. If he won, he would have a huge platform from which to launch another presidential campaign (he was only forty-nine); if he lost, benefits related to his background as Dwight Eisenhower's vice president would be lost and his chance for a political career would be seriously weakened, if not demolished. He lost the election, and his exit at his last press conference was bitter: "You won't have Dick Nixon to kick around anymore."

A legal career followed in which he enriched and distinguished himself. He also kept in political touch, however, and campaigned for other Republicans, including Barry Goldwater, with great success; he built loyalties that led to his nomination, once again, as the Republican candidate for president of the U.S.

GEORGE C. WALLACE, AMERICAN FREEDOM PARTY

Born: 1919: **Educated:** University of Alabama; **Wife:** Lurleen (deceased), Cornelia (divorced) and Lisa (divorced); **Children:** None; **Died:** 1998.[28]

George Wallace, born in Clio, Alabama, was one of the four children of George and Mozell Wallace. His father, a farmer who did well during World War I, was a victim of the Great Depression. When he died in 1937, the family was broke and Mozell sold the farm to resolve family debts.

George attended local schools and became well known in high school as an accomplished boxer before he moved on to the University of Alabama law school and the beginnings of a professional career that was interrupted by World War II and the call to duty. Wallace, a staff sergeant in the Air Corps, served with distinction in numerous combat missions until his medical discharge, caused by the aftereffects of spinal meningitis, a disease that nearly took his life.

Always interested in politics, Wallace had assisted his grandfather's successful campaign for probate judge and, after the war, he reentered the political arena, this time as an appointed assistant attorney general of Alabama. A year later he won an election that placed him in the Alabama house of representatives. At that time, his views on racial matters were not extreme. An example of this was his behavior as a delegate to the 1948 Democratic convention — he did not support Harry Truman, but he refused to leave the convention, as many of his southern friends did.[29]

Wallace became a judge in 1953 in the Third Judicial Circuit Court. In 1958, in a race for governor, he was defeated by a candidate who was supported by the Ku Klux Klan, a racist organization Wallace had openly criticized. At this time, Wallace was the favorite candidate of the NAACP. That unsuccessful gubernatorial campaign and election taught Wallace a lesson. He would never be governor of his state if he continued to hold moderate views on race. At that moment, and for years thereafter, Wallace was as racist in his views as anyone in the South. His reward: In 1962 he became governor of Alabama in an easy victory, having run on a pro-states' rights, pro-segregation platform. In his inauguration speech, Wallace — the NAACP favorite four years earlier — said, "I say segregation now, segregation tomorrow and segregation forever." There are few better examples of how unrestrained political ambition can corrupt a human being.

Wallace attained national fame a year later when he stood before the doors of the University of Alabama and denied admission to two black students, a violation of federal law. Federal marshals stepped in; Wallace stepped aside and the South was never the same again. (Eisenhower applied the federal pressure that resulted in this confrontation. Seldom given credit for civil rights progress, Ike was actually the first to put serious teeth into the federal laws that governed desegregation.)

Armed with his new national reputation as a protector of states' rights, Wallace mounted his first presidential campaign as a Democrat in 1964, during which he did well enough to mount another in 1968, this time as leader of the AFP. His presence during that presidential race did not go unnoticed.

Election Tone

Vice President Hubert Humphrey was fifty-seven in 1968, Richard Nixon fifty-five. Both potentially had many more years of productive political life before them. But it was highly likely, especially with Nixon, that the candidate who lost would not appear again on the political landscape.

The passion in the campaign came not from any deep animosity the candidates had for each other but from events that had shaken the nation for good or for bad over the past four years—riots in the cities, antiwar peace marches, the war in Vietnam and its associated casualties, the loss of support from the elite media, etc. For example, Walter Cronkite in 1968 one of America's most revered media figures, after a visit to Vietnam, reported: "Who won and who lost the great Tet offensive against the cities? I'm not sure. The Vietcong did not win by a knockout, but neither did we. The referees of history may make it a draw." When LBJ heard of this analysis he said, "That's it. If I've lost Cronkite, I've lost middle America."[30] A month later, LBJ announced he was out of the 1968 presidential race.

The charismatic figure of John Kennedy was in 1968 no longer a potent political force. Instead, there was the image of the dour and defeated LBJ, which clung to Hubert Humphrey like a wet blanket on a hot day, an image Nixon could easily contend with. Nixon, on the other hand, could resurrect the image of Ike as he chose and without apology. Bragging rights in 1968 most certainly belonged to Republicans.

The Supreme Court, as is often the case, played a role in setting the tone of the subject election. Earl Warren, the sole chief justice during this period, was joined by twelve other associate justices, and some of the decisions they made[31] upset the legal landscape as much as Great Society programs upset the relationships among states, people and the federal government. A few examples follow.[32]

Miranda v. Arizona (1965). The interrogation of prisoners without notifying them of their right to counsel and their protection against self-incrimination is unconstitutional. Evidence so obtained may not be used in a court of law. This decision has reverberated through the decades and continues to be a tool used by defense attorneys and against law enforcement. The consequences:

Some innocent prisoners have been protected; some terrible criminals have escaped punishment. This was a 5–4 decision that energized the base of both parties.

Griswold v. Connecticut, 1965. The Constitution does not explicitly protect the right to privacy. Here the Court ruled in a 7–2 decision that one can infer its existence by studying the Bill of Rights, especially in the First, Third, Fourth and Ninth Amendments. A succession of abortion cases followed that cite Griswold as the ultimate authority; by 1990, the number of abortions tripled. Few if any Court rulings have had more impact on American society.

Loving v. Virginia (1967). Antimiscegenation laws, which ban interracial marriages, are unconstitutional. This was a 9–0 decision. To its credit, the Court was often unanimous in civil rights rulings. When this is not true in cases of great social import, legislative input is needed to clarify or change law. Most voters were pleased with any decision that clarified black rights or made clearer racial questions.

United States v. O'Brien (1968). Burning a draft card in a public place as a sign of opposition to war qualifies as protected speech under the Constitution. Laws against some forms of symbolic speech are constitutional when they further an important government interest, they are not aimed as such at minimizing free speech, and the restriction on speech is insignificant when compared to the government's interest. This was a 7–1 decision (Marshall absent). During a period when war protests were as common as mud, many voters were pleased or infuriated by this decision.

The genie was out of the bottle. The Supreme Court was on the move, deciding cases they would not have been heard a generation before. There seemed to be no end to the Court's reach, as if it had lost faith in the ability of local institutions and circuit courts to make rational decisions. Not only was it deciding the most important constitutional issues, the role the Founders expected it to play, it also assumed the role of Super Mom.

Such decisions were not a major part of campaign rhetoric as such, but each candidate knew that the voters they faced were different from the voters that had existed before some of these decisions were made, and that the voters would blame political parties as much as they blamed the Court for them. As a general rule, for example, antireligion rulings angered Republican voters. Candidates were called upon to defend or criticize such decisions.

Television debates did not appeal to Nixon (chastened by the Kennedy-Nixon debates of 1960) and he did not accept the invitation to debate Humphrey. Accordingly, he carried into the election the untouched image of himself that he had cultivated over the recent years. On the other hand, the ebullient Humphrey, who projected well on television, was denied the chance to add to his image as a leader by debating toe to toe the formidable Nixon.

More than usual, recent events colored the tone of the 1968 election. And seldom if ever had a president dealt with so many major issues as LBJ did in his last four years as president; how he handled them hung over the election campaigns like a dark cloud.

TELEVISION DEBATES

There were no television debates in 1968. Nixon wisely avoided them. He had nothing to win by giving the articulate and friendly Humphrey a chance to charm an audience that — Nixon had learned — was heavily influenced by such things.

Presidential Campaigns

HUMPHREY CAMPAIGN

Hubert Humphrey carried a heavy load during the campaign as the defender of LBJ's policies. He could brag about civil rights legislation, for example, but even that area of triumph contained the bitter as well as the sweet since many southerners, who ordinarily would vote Democratic, were not as enthused about this monumental victory as others were. After he signed the civil rights bill, LBJ said, "We have lost the South for a generation."[33]

Whatever Humphrey had to say about anything, the Vietnam War trumped it. It was ongoing, lives were being lost; it was unpopular and he supported the policies that began it and perpetuated it. He began his campaign by joining the Labor Day parade in New York.[34] But the smile on his face didn't fool anyone. He had a tough row to hoe, and he knew it. Like all candidates from an entrenched administration, whether a president seeking a second term or a vice president seeking to succeed his boss, Humphrey's default position was defensive. And his job wasn't made any easier by a press that kept insisting that LBJ was running his campaign.

Tom Wicker, for example, in his New York Times column of September 25, 1968, caught the tone of this perfectly: "[M]ost Democratic leaders ... want Mr. Humphrey to demonstrate his independence from President Johnson." Wicker went on to appraise Humphrey's campaign and the candidate himself. His evaluation was rather harsh: "The worst of these problems in California, as everywhere, is that Mr. Humphrey has no real standing of his own. He seems to be the weakling puppet of the White House, the tool of the labor bosses and southern Governors, a burnt out case who left his political manhood somewhere in the dark places of the Johnson Administration." Wicker concluded his withering piece by expressing the major concern of Democratic leaders: "What they are seeking is neither a policy nor a performance, but the truth about the man himself."

Obviously, Humphrey had as much of an image problem as Nixon did, but for a different reason. Nixon's critics found him to be too cold, too tough and too merciless; Humphrey's saw him as being too soft, too weak and too reliant upon LBJ. In a time of war and riots on the streets, Nixon's negatives were less harmful than Humphrey's.

Humphrey got a break in October. The bombing of North Vietnam stopped; the chance for peace talks in Paris loomed large. These events allowed Humphrey to get away from the past and add a message of hope to his speeches, which made him more attractive to supporters who had strayed away or were uncommitted.

The signs of changed times in the political world were evident. Humphrey was an old-fashioned campaigner; Nixon was modern. Humphrey was not as well organized at the beginning of his campaign; he didn't enter as many primaries, an arena that provides election teams with experience that becomes invaluable during the actual campaign. On the other hand, he — like Nixon — had managers to worry about and protect his image. And he too had fund-raising affairs that weren't even contemplated a decade before. But whatever he did, Nixon did more — and did it better.[35]

Humphrey had ninety-five fund-raising committees, which enabled wealthy supporters to spread their contributions within the law; at the end of televised speeches he'd ask for money. But his most reliable source of funds came from the historically reliable unions, who contributed 70 percent of all funds raised. In the other camp, Nixon raised even more money. He had 150,000 small contributors, and a good supply of wealthy ones to whom he could turn; he lifted the time-honored fund-raising dinner to a new level. In a series of $1,000 affairs televised in twenty-two locations, he raised millions with a single speech. Money was important in the 1960 election, but it arrived for good in 1968, with a roar. And politics hasn't been the same since.

Good war news was followed by good poll news. The difference between Humphrey and Nixon was closing during the final weeks. In November, the chance for a close election loomed as a distinct possibility. Hope surged in the Humphrey camp.

NIXON CAMPAIGN

Nixon and his handlers first had to overcome a basic problem — Nixon's alleged unpopularity.[36] Despite the fact that he won a huge popular vote in his 1960 loss to John Kennedy, the press characterized him as America's most disliked politician, an allegation no doubt influenced by two facts: He had lost his bid in 1962 to become governor of California (which marked him as a loser), and while a congressman his work on the House Un-American Activities Committee resulted in the identification of Alger Hiss as a Soviet spy. The committee's work was linked with "McCarthyism" and carried some of the same stench. Also, Hiss was a favorite of academics. Nixon's effective work earned him the eternal enmity of the major media. Was Nixon actually America's most disliked politician or was this a reputation the media was trying to sell? His 1960 vote said it was a lie; his loss in California said it was a maybe.

Either way, it was a gamble Republicans were slow to take because one thing was sure: In a television age, Nixon was not the warm and fuzzy type who would win votes with charm. Nixon was smart, tough and experienced. That was the package to sell to the voters. And he got help from an unexpected source, the *New York Times*. In a column of September 25, 1968, Tom Wicker favorably noted that Nixon had shown firmness in the past and that this year he "dealt firmly with his loser's image by taking on all comers in the state primaries."

The determination to package the real Nixon was not immediate, however. Initially, the attempt was made to make him the friendly, next-door neighbor type. But it didn't work. He could be your governor or mayor, but not your next door neighbor. Inevitably he morphed into what he was: a highly experienced, polished and professional politician. So the election image was altered: Candidate Nixon was re-presented as a man of grit, brains and determination in a televised series of "Man in the Arena" town hall meetings across the nation during which he took questions from citizens. The theory was: If he can't get their love, he can earn their respect — he is formidable; he endured hard times.

Nixon's themes during the campaign were based upon the discontents of the times.[37] The antiwar movement fueled Nixon's promise to end the draft, and there were hints in the media that he had a plan to end the war; riots in the streets became a law and order issue; the active stance of the Johnson/Humphrey administration on civil rights resulted in a strategy designed to lure discontented southern voters; radical rulings from the Supreme Court that were changing the American way became a promise to appoint originalist judges.

Nixon stayed above personality politics but he was tough on issues.[38] Americans were troubled, for example, by riots on their streets and in their neighborhoods, they feared the drug culture and they listened to Nixon's charge that Democrats were too soft to restore peace. Nixon's ambiguous posture on the war and the draft was, at the least, a change from the discredited policies of LBJ, which Humphrey defended. It was easy to criticize a Supreme Court for rulings that in another time would have been unimaginable.

The Nixon campaign demonstrated with complete clarity that the day of managed candidates had arrived, caused mostly by the proliferation of television. No longer was a candidate's appearance an extraordinary event; no longer was he a distant, Olympian-like figure to be viewed with awe. Television had reduced candidates to intimate, reachable, human form, and as such they were accepted or rejected for what they appeared to be as people, as well as for their known abilities as professionals. Because of this, packaging and packagers became part of the political culture. Being liked became as important as being qualified.

Nixon led in the polls from the beginning. But as election day drew near, the polls tightened.[39]

WALLACE CAMPAIGN

Third party candidates emerge when major parties are either too active or too passive in some area of public interest. Nothing important enough to support a significant third party movement had appeared since the 1948 election, which had triggered the candidacy of Sen. Strom Thurmond, who had the same hope as Wallace — deadlock the election and force it into the House of Representatives, there to negotiate power away from those who sought to desegregate the South.

LBJ's civil rights legislation once more raised the hot issue of desegregation in the South. It was accompanied by raucous behavior within the civil rights and antiwar movements, which raised law and order to an issue of new prominence. Wallace pounced on discontents raised by those events and made them his issues. And with his colorful rhetoric and his fearless, bulldog personality, he drew significant attention — enough to reel in 70 percent as much in campaign contributions as Humphrey.[40]

The uninhibited, free-wheeling Wallace added spice to the campaign[41]:

- Concerning demonstrators: "If any demonstrator ever lays down in front of my car, it'll be the last car he'll ever lay down in front of."
- Concerning the antiwar movement: "Doves in this country ... are the cause of ... Americans being killed...."
- Concerning military spending: "Why does the Air Force need expensive new bombers? Have the people we've been bombing ... been complaining?"
- Concerning hippies: "The only four letter words they didn't know are work and soap."
- Concerning the Democratic and Republican Parties: "There isn't a dime's worth of difference between them."

Wallace represented danger. He competed with Nixon for the law and order vote and he gave southern Democratic voters, who turned away from Humphrey because of his position on civil rights, a champion for their cause. He was more acceptable to them than Nixon.[42]

Election Results

The electoral vote showed Nixon winning by landslide proportions. But the popular vote clearly illustrates how close the election actually was. The reason for the confusion was the surprising national strength of Wallace, whose popularity had been regarded by many as, at best, regional.

Election Results 1968

Candidates	EV	%	Pop. (000)	Pop. %	Pop. %
Nixon	301	55.9	31,785	43.4	50.4
Humphrey	191	35.5	31,275	42.7	49.6
Wallace	46	8.6	9,901	13.5	
Other			243	.3	
Total	538	100.0	73,204	100.0	100.0

EV=electoral vote; Pop. = popular vote;

Source: NY Times Almanac 2009, p. 132

Wallace won five states, and he earned one electoral vote in another, as follows:

Election Results 1968
Wallace's Electoral Votes
Winning Percent

Candidates/ Votes	AL 10	AR 6	GA 12	LA 10	MS 7	NC 1*
Nixon	14	31	30	24	14	40
Humphrey	19	30	27	28	23	29
Wallace	66	39	43	48	63	31
Other	1					
Total	100	100	100	100	100	100

*Wallace took one vote of North Carolina's twelve votes.

Source: http://www.uselectionatlas.org/

Wallace was a candidate known most for his positions on racial segregation and law and order. In the above states, segregation was the hot issue. Based upon that certainty, it is probable that Humphrey benefited from Wallace's popularity in the Deep South, because Wallace's supporters, if forced to choose between the two leading candidates, would have either stayed home or gone to Nixon. They would not have voted for the man who represented the party platform that had driven them to their current status as Dixicrats.

Nixon won North Carolina's 12 electoral votes. Wallace took the others— 45 electoral votes that Nixon, not Humphrey, might have won. Wallace had influence in other sections of the country as well, where his positions on law and order resonated to the detriment of the other candidates, mostly of Nixon because Humphrey was closely associated with the violence in the streets that had occurred on his watch and that came close to destroying the convention that nominated him. Of the eight states with more than fifteen electoral votes, the Wallace vote was critical in all but New York.

Election Results 1968
States with 15+ Electoral Votes
Winning Percent

Candidates/	CA	IL	MI	NJ	NY	OH	PA	TX
Votes	40	26	21	17	43	26	29	25
Nixon	47.8	47.1	41.5	46.1	44.3	45.2	44.0	39.9
Humphrey	44.7	44.2	48.2	44.0	49.8	43.0	47.6	41.1
Wallace	6.7	8.5	10.0	9.1	5.3	11.8	8.0	19.0
Total	**99.2**	**99.8**	**99.7**	**99.2**	**99.4**	**100.0**	**99.6**	**100.0**

Bold type = fringe vote had theoretical impact in that state.

Source: http://uselectionatlas.org/RESULTS/

Nixon won California, Illinois, New Jersey and Ohio.[43] Absent the Wallace vote, it is almost certain that his victory in those states would have been even larger.

Humphrey won Michigan, New York, Pennsylvania and Texas. His margin of victory in each case except New York was less than the Wallace vote. With or without Wallace, Humphrey would have won New York. But in the other states, it is likely that Nixon would have been the winner of the additional 75 electoral votes that Wallace rook away from him.

To summarize, Wallace hurt Nixon in the South and elsewhere. With no Wallace to contend with, Nixon's margin of victory would have been even larger. The election was a firm rejection of Democratic policies by the general public with the exception of black voters—94 percent of blacks voted for Humphrey.[44] Absent their support, the election would have been a rout.

The Nixon Cabinet

Nixon chose competent men,[45] some of whom were to become unusually well known because of their skill (George P. Shultz), some because of their double-dealing (Spiro Agnew) and others because of the roles they played in the scandal that forced Nixon to resign (John Mitchell, Elliot L. Richardson). Nixon's choices were: **Vice President:** Spiro Agnew, Maryland; **Secretary of State:** William P. Rogers, New York; **Secretary of Defense:** Melvin R. Laird, Nebraska; **Secretary of Treasury:** David M. Kennedy, Utah (1969–71), John B. Connally, Texas, George P. Shultz, New York (1972–74), William Simon, New Jersey; **Attorney General:** John Mitchell, Michigan/New York; **Secretary of Agriculture:** Clifford M. Hardin, Indiana (1969–71), Earl Butz, Indiana; **Secretary of Commerce:** Maurice H. Stans, Minnesota; **Secretary of HEW:** Robert H. Finch, Arizona/California (1969–70), Elliot L. Richardson, Massachusetts (1970–73), Caspar Weinberger, San Francisco; **Secretary of HUD:** George Romney, Michigan (1969–73), James T. Lynn, Ohio; **Secretary of Interior:** Walter J. Hickel, Kansas/Alaska; **Secretary of Labor:** George P. Shultz (1969–70, see Secretary of Treasury), James D. Hodgson, Minnesota (1970–73), Peter J. Brennan, New

York; **Secretary of Transportation:** John A. Volpe, Massachusetts (1969–73), Claude S. Brinegar, California; **Postmaster General:** William M. Blount (1969–71, privatized in 1971), Alabama.

Vice President Agnew resigned in 1973 charged with bribery and tax evasion. Secretary of state Rogers was an old political ally of Nixon's. Attorney general Mitchell was involved in the Watergate scandal and served nineteen months in prison. Secretary of agriculture Butz had to resign because of a racist joke he told and was later jailed for tax evasion.

John Connally was the surprise figure in the Nixon administration, not because of questionable qualifications, but because of party affiliation. He was once a political intimate of Lyndon Johnson, who, to Republicans, was an ideological Satan.

The Nixon Congress

Nixon won the election handily, from an electoral vote standpoint, and the analysis of it shows that his margin of victory actually understated his superiority over Humphrey. However, one raw fact remains— only 43 percent voted for him. The plus side of that sobering fact is that 57 percent were opposed to the policies represented by Humphrey. The question: Would the same voters turn away from their congressmen and deliver to Nixon the legislative clout he would need to modify, change or reverse existing policies? The answer: No! Democrats after the election had a 56 percent majority in the House — down one point; in the Senate, fifty-seven percent — down 7 percent. Nixon was to become a president without legislative tools.

Pro-Administration Congressional Power

Congress	Year	President	House %	Senate %
90	1967	Johnson	57	64
91	1969	Nixon (R)	**44**	**43**
92	1971	Nixon	**41**	**44**

Appendix 1.1, 1.2

Bold type=minority position

Nixon had John McCormack (D-MA) and Carl Albert (D-OK) to deal with in the House and Mike Mansfield in the Senate. Both had helped LBJ in his plans to change America into a nation that valued social programs at a level at least equal to national defense and the protection of the dollar. If it was Nixon's natural bent to soften or reverse this movement, he had little chance to do so, given the realities of congressional power. (There is considerable doubt about Nixon's conservative credentials. Although he had spent a career defeating Rockefeller Republicans, his actions in office suggested he was closer to them ideologically than, say, he was to Goldwater.)

The message to Nixon from the election was this: Stop the war! Stop the riots! Leave everything else alone.

The Nixon Court

Earl Warren was chief justice when Nixon took office.[46] Appointed by President Eisenhower, it was expected he would exercise restraint over activist tendencies of a Court packed with Roosevelt and Truman appointees. The opposite was the case. Under his leadership, the Court continued to rule on matters that infringed upon the territory normally occupied by the legislative branches of government, state and federal.

Nixon had an early chance to provide the Court with new leadership when in 1969 Warren resigned. Warren Burger seemed a good choice.[47] Burger had come up the hard way. A leader from the start, intellectually and athletically, he ultimately prospered as a member of a prominent law firm, and he taught law on the side. An early supporter of Harold Stassen's presidential bid, he also assisted Eisenhower in the 1952 election. Ike made him an assistant attorney general after the election; later, he was a justice in the U.S. Court of Appeals for the District of Columbia (thirteen years). Through his rulings and his writings, Burger became known as a critic of Warren, and as a constitutional originalist. This, plus his background, appealed to Nixon and made the judge an obvious candidate for Warren's vacated position.

The Senate Judiciary Committee, not as partisan as it is today, followed the tradition of approving a president's qualified candidates. Burger was in; Warren was out, and he turned out to be as controversial as Warren. The Nixon court should have been an originalist court because it was made up of judges predominately chosen by himself and Eisenhower. Eisenhower and Nixon chose Warren, Burger, Harlan, Brennan, Stewart, Blackmun, Powell and Rehnquist. Black, Douglas, White and Marshall were chosen by other presidents.

The activist New Dealer Black was on this Court for three years; Douglas, a fellow traveler, endured for Nixon's first term and beyond. The more moderate White was a fixture. Otherwise, it should have been a conservative court wedded to the originalist interpretation of the Constitution. But it wasn't. Why? Because it is a myth that appointed "conservative" judges will remain conservative. Not so, however, with liberal appointees, who tend to remain true to the party that selected them.

A review of a few of the serious cases of the time dramatizes the issues that were troubling then, as they continue to be today.[49]

STANLEY V. GEORGIA (1969)

The facts: the police conducted a legal search of the defendant's home and discovered obscene materials. He was tried and convicted of violating a state law that forbids the possession of obscene materials.

Supreme Court Justices, 1969–72

Judge	Began	Appointed by	Ended
Earl Warren (CA)	1954	Eisenhower	1969
Warren Burger (MN)	1969	Nixon	1986
Hugo Black (AL)	1937	Roosevelt	1971
William Douglas (MN)	1939	Roosevelt	1975
John Harlan (NY)	1955	Eisenhower	1971
William Brennan (NJ)	1956	Eisenhower	1990
Potter Stewart (OH)	1958	Eisenhower	1981
Byron White (CO)	1962	Kennedy	1993
Thurgood Marshall (MD)	1967	Johnson	1991
Harry Blackmun (MN)	1970	Nixon	1994
Lewis Powell (VA)	1972	Nixon	1987
William Rehnquist (WI)	1972	Nixon	1986

Source: Oyez, http://www.oyez.org/ — Members of the Supreme Court,[48] http://www.supremecourtus.gov/about/members.pdf

Men in Black, Mark Levin, Preface

Notes: Hugo Black was a former Ku Klux Klan member. He suffered a stroke in 1969, which impaired his memory. By 1971, constant pain made it difficult for him to concentrate, and his short-term memory was poor and paranoia followed. In effect, he was unable to perform his duties for more than two years, yet he remained active. William O. Douglas was a known womanizer. His frequent marriages and divorces with younger women did not add to the dignity of the Court, and they brought to him financial hardship, which led him to seek supplemental income from questionable sources. A stroke in 1974 impaired his faculties, but he would not retire and his colleagues refused to count his vote until he did. Thurgood Marshall became indifferent to his duties in his later years; *People* magazine in 1982 called him a television addict. He kept his seat for as long as his likely replacement was a conservative. "If I die, prop me up and keep on voting," he told his clerks. Concerning the Constitution, he observed, "I [do not] find the wisdom, foresight or sense of justice exhibited by the framers particularly profound."

The issue: Is the state law constitutional?

The decision: No, 9–0. The First (speech) and Fourteenth (privileges and immunities of citizens) amendments prohibit criminalization of ownership of such materials; the Court distinguished between ownership and production or distribution, which, it said, could be regulated.

RED LION BROADCASTING CO. V. FCC (1969)

The facts: The FCC has a "fairness doctrine" that requires radio and television broadcasters to present a balanced presentation of public issues. The doctrine essentially confines itself to personal attacks and political editorializing. License renewal becomes an issue if compliance is challenged. The defendant challenged the constitutionality of the doctrine.

The issue: Does the fairness doctrine violate First Amendment protection of free speech?

The decision: No, 7–0. Broadcasting rights are different from the personal right to free speech. The fairness doctrine actually enhances free speech rights because it promotes balanced speech. The Court warned that if experience demonstrates that the doctrine chills free speech its constitutionality would be revisited. In *Miami Herald Publishing Co. v. Tomillo* (1974) Chief Justice Burger opined that government-controlled access (license control as a reward or punishment) "dampens the vigor and the variety of public debate." The doctrine in 1987 was abolished after President Reagan vetoed the attempt by the Democrat-controlled Congress to make it law.[50] This effort was an attempt by some to muzzle the commentary of outspoken conservative voices on radio and television.

ALEXANDER HOLMES V. COUNTY BOARD OF EDUCATION (1969)[51]

The facts: A black man challenged his conviction as a rapist. He was indicted by an all white grand jury under a selection system that discriminated against blacks and women. The conviction was affirmed by the Louisiana Supreme Court.

The issue: Was the defendant's constitutional right to a fair trial abused by the jury selection process?

The decision: Yes, 7–0. "It has been established that a criminal prosecution of a Negro cannot stand under the Equal Protection Clause of the Fourteenth Amendment if it is based on an indictment of a grand jury from which Negroes were excluded by reason of their race."

SWANN V. CHARLOTTE-MECKLENBURG BOARD OF EDUCATION (1971)

The facts: Little practical progress had been made since the *Brown v. Board of Education* case in 1954 made separate but equal schools unconstitutional. This issue was brought to a head in the subject case.

The issue: Are federal courts constitutionally authorized to oversee and create remedies for constitutionally mandated desegregation?

The decision: Yes, 9–0. Once a violation of previous mandates has been identified, federal courts have broad and flexible powers, including the forced busing of children to particular schools. Forced busing and the power of federal judges to achieve segregation became hot issues throughout the nation, including the North.

LEMON V. KURTZMAN (1971)

The facts: Pennsylvania state law permitted the funding of salaries and supplies in nonpublic schools (mostly Catholic) that were related to nonreligious education.

The issue: Did the state law violate the establishment clause of the First Amendment?

The decision: Yes, 5–3. To be constitutional, such funding must not violate any of the following three qualifications: (1) It must have a secular purpose; (2) it must neither inhibit nor advance religion; (3) it must not result in excessive entanglement of government and religion. Since funding went mostly to Catholic schools, the Court found that the state law did not pass the "entanglement" test and was, therefore, unconstitutional.

EISENSTADT V. BAIRD (1972)

The facts: Under Massachusetts law, contraceptives may be distributed only to married men and women. After giving a lecture at Boston University, Baird distributed them to an unmarried woman. He was charged with a felony.

The issue: Was the state law constitutional?

The decision: No, 6–1. The law's distinction between married and single people fails to pass the "rational basis" test. Withholding from single people a right that married people have under *Griswold v. Connecticut* (1965) requires rational argument that was not successfully made in this case. "If the right of privacy means anything, it is the right of the individual ... to be free from unwarranted government intrusion into matters so fundamentally affecting a person as the decision ... to bear or beget a child." This is one of many decisions of this type that followed *Griswold*.

FURMAN V. GEORGIA (1972)

The facts: The defendant was discovered burglarizing a home. While attempting to escape, he fell and his gun went off and killed a resident. He was convicted of murder and sentenced to death.

The issue: Did the murder sentence violate Amendments Eight (cruel and unusual punishment) and Fourteen (equal protection) of the Constitution?

The decision: Yes, 5–4. The punishment was deemed excessive. This decision caused all states to review their death penalty laws as a protection against Supreme Court difficulties.

So another turbulent judicial era ended. Civil rights issues were as hot as ever. *Griswold* had raised a privacy issue that will haunt courts until law and perceived morality are once more joined; the relationship between church and state, once easy and comfortable, had become testy and worrisome.

Independence, freedom and liberty are burdens as well as privileges. Skill and will are required — in the form of an educated and informed citizenry — to manage them. In 1972, the pages of history were beginning to test the American wisdom and will to do it well. In many ways, Supreme Court decisions form a useful scorecard of progress or deterioration in a society.

Domestic Affairs Relative to Current Political Issues

Nixon and Johnson did not have to deal with world wars, as did Wilson and Roosevelt, but they otherwise dealt with more major issues simultaneously than any other American presidents. War in the Pacific, a Cold War, riots in the streets, stress in the Middle East and other problems were served to them on a daily basis. If the two presidents sometimes appeared irrational, perhaps they had reason to be.

DOMESTIC EVENTS

This was a violent time, a period of social revolution. Civil rights and anti-war activists caused riots in the streets and kept the nation on edge. And they were assisted by the drug culture, which was glorified by news coverage of the Woodstock Festival in New York, a three-day orgy of sex and narcotics that in many respects symbolized the tattered condition of American culture. These, plus the bread and butter issues, were the primary domestic concerns of the ordinary American in 1968, and it is through this lens that the domestic affairs of the time will be appraised.

Nixon was a moderate progressive hiding in the political clothing of a conservative.[52] The size of government expanded on his watch. For example, the Occupational Safety and Health Administration (OSHA) and the Environmental Protection Agency (EPA) were created. And, beyond Supplementary Security Income (SSI), other additions to the "welfare state" took place on his watch: the expansion of the Food Stamp Program, large increases in Social Security, Medicare and Medicaid benefits, etc.

To the dismay of conservatives, Nixon was a "get along, go along" president on domestic matters, spending money that wasn't available and, in the process, dimming the distinction between the parties. As president, he became what he once allegedly opposed — a Rockefeller Republican.

ECONOMIC GROWTH

The Kennedy/Johnson years were almost free of economic problems.[53] But in 1968, the election year, federal receipts (despite higher tax rates) increased only 3 percent,[54] hardly enough to cover costs associated with the dream state Kennedy and Johnson had created. This reduction in federal revenue was a harbinger of the economic woes Nixon was to experience.

The first recession hit the Nixon administration in 1969. It was relatively light, caused in part by the effort of the Federal Reserve to curb inflation via higher interest rates and tighter credit.[55] A better idea of the growth in the economy is seen by scanning the flow of GDP adjusted for inflation (in 2000 dollars).

Gross Domestic Product, Public Debt

Year	GDP (bil)	% Growth	Public Debt (bil)	% PD/GDP
1968	868.5	7.2	289.5	33.3
1969	948.3	9.2	278.1	29.3
1970	1,012.9	6.8	283.2	28.0
1971	1,080.3	6.7	303.0	28.0
1972	1,176.9	8.9	322.4	27.4

Source: Historical Tables 2010, 1.2, 7,1

Bold = war years

Gross Domestic Product, Inflation Adjusted
1968–72

Year	GDP (bil)	Growth %	Year	GDP (bil)	Growth %
1968	3,543.5	-	1971	3,806.6	1.6
1969	3,700.0	4.4	1972	3,960.0	4.0
1970	3,747.3	1.3			

Source: Historical Tables 2010, 10.1

The charts above demonstrate that the apparent robust growth in GDP during these years was inflation caused.[56] Two flat years caused huge deficits that caused debt to grow by $32 billion.[57] Unemployment rose, federal revenues shrank and inflation persisted.[58] Deficits were heavy; budget daylight has been rarely seen since, primarily because social service costs grow faster than revenue.[59] Deficits and climbing debt thereafter became the normal expectation. Nixon's reaction to the recession and to the inflation that plagued him was to, among other things, establish price controls, the last thing one might have expected from a Republican president.[60]

The Misery Index[61] is a reliable rule of thumb indicator of economic health. LBJ left behind an index of 13.9, which characterized the size of the economic problem that Nixon inherited. Nixon's first term ended with an index of 13.7, but the mix of elements was different. The end result was, however, the same — misery in the marketplace.

Kennedy and Johnson began the new era. The belief in balanced budgets and controlled debt went out the window, not so much in political rhetoric as in actual practice. Since their era, no president has finished his presidency with less debt. Now it was Nixon's turn. Would he turn the clock back? Would he restore rationality to the federal budget? Who knows for sure what he might have done if congressional control had been his to the extent it was LBJ's. The fact is, he never had anything remotely equal to the congressional power of his predecessor, which means the FDR/LBJ model of government continued to grow — and so did national debt.

The size of national public debt is directly related to the federal budget. Given a deficit, it goes up. Given a surplus, it might come down, depending on who is in charge. The choices: Tax reduction, debt reduction or more spending.

During the LBJ and Nixon presidencies deficits were commonplace; debt grew. Politicians realize that constant increases in debt make the public uneasy because it leaves the impression that the nation's leaders are fiscally irresponsible. To offset this image, it became popular in the 1960s to feature another statistic: The size of the debt to the size of GDP, a ratio that makes leaders look better ("Oh yes, debt is higher, but as a measurement against GDP it's lower.") Hooray! Or, hooray(?).

It is pleasant to have a declining ratio of debt to GDP; and in Nixon's case, GDP grew at a faster pace than deficits, a condition that produced a favorable ratio. But in the meantime, interest expense in the federal budget went up more than $5 billion because the absolute amount of debt grew by more than 11 percent. Which would you rather take to the bank, the improved ratio or the $5 billion?

Turn the pages of history and see what uncontrolled spending does to a federal budget.[62] In 2008, "Interest" was the third largest category of expense in the budget, exceeded only by Human Resources and Defense. In 1960, "Interest" was 14 percent of the cost of national defense and in 2008 it was 41 percent. In 2014, it is predicted that it will be 71 percent of the cost of national defense. This is fiscal lunacy. By the time Nixon and Ford left office debt had become a national security problem because social programs were crowding out the ability of the nation to service its debt and to defend itself.

LEGISLATIVE EVENTS, 1969–72

Action is followed by reaction, which means in practical terms that concerns of the people under a progressive administration inevitably appear in Washington in the form of federal regulations or laws. Under LBJ, for example, literally a storm of legislation went through Congress because Democrats had veto-proof congressional control, because LBJ was a skilled and persuasive legislator and because he took full advantage of the national sympathy for Jack Kennedy and his unfulfilled plans.

Nixon, too, sensed the public pulse and some legislation that came into being during his first term reflected this. He dealt with things such as crime, worker safety and drugs, which are normal federal concerns, and others that tested constitutional limits of federal power[63]:

- The Organized Crime Control Act (1970) launched "a total war against organized crime."
- The Occupational Safety and Health Act (1970) established OSHA and through it a larger role for the government in the workplace.
- The Controlled Substances Act (1970) was an attempt to coordinate all laws and regulations dealing with illegal substances and the abuse thereof.
- Title IX, Education Amendments (1972), prohibits sex discrimination in

school programs (and opened the door for equal female participation in such things as law, medicine and sports).
- Supplemental Security Income (1972) assists those who are aged, disabled or blind and have very limited income and resources.[64] SSI appears to be a complete sell-out by Nixon to the left. Actually, it was a substitute for a collage of state laws that were aimed at the same needy group; it federalized inefficient state programs. Question: Was federalization (growth of the central government) the only remedy?

CONSTITUTIONAL AMENDMENTS

One more amendment was added to the Constitution under Nixon in 1971, Amendment XXVI, which permits eighteen-year-old citizens to vote.

Foreign Affairs Relative to Current Political Issues

President Nixon was more aware than anyone that his power over domestic affairs was severely limited because congressional power was not his. By necessity and inclination, therefore, he sought to leave his mark on foreign affairs.

Experienced politicians like Nixon are aware that many presidential ambitions disappear into the deep chasms of the bureaucracy, which is ruled by career employees who survive presidential changes. They are the faceless and unassailable who reside in the political house known as Washington. To avoid this fate, Nixon centralized foreign policy control in the White House. Secretary of state William Rogers and secretary of defense Melvin Laird handled their normal duties, but actual decision-making was often the exclusive business of Nixon and his right-hand man, Henry Kissinger.[65]

It was Nixon's hope to normalize relations with the Soviets and China and use them to force North Vietnam into a peace agreement. China and the Soviets were not friendly toward each other in 1969 and border clashes were common. Nixon saw opportunity in this tension between the communist nations. This plan did not work out as intended, but progress was made. After preliminary and secret visits to China by Henry Kissinger, Nixon and Mao Zedong in 1972 met in Beijing, a widely televised event that was hailed as a first important step toward rapprochement.

Apparently the Soviet Union feared a friendly relationship between China and the United States because soon after Nixon's journey to Bejiing he received an invitation to meet with Premier Leonid Brezhnev. This meeting was to mature into treaties that did much to reduce nuclear tensions: Strategic Arms Limitation and Antiballistic Missile treaties.

Nixon's strategy yielded little, however, with respect to Vietnam. The war continued. Peace talks failed; threats failed. And when Nixon ordered a temporary invasion of Cambodia to disrupt enemy supply lines, the domestic roof fell in; he had riots, street marches and demonstrators up to his hips. Despite the fact that he pulled troops out of Vietnam and had diligently pursued peace talks, the Vietnam War had become his war. JFK and LBJ were off the hook; Nixon took all the heat. Students during this period rioted at Kent State University (OH) and four were killed as the National Guard attempted to restore order. Two weeks later, two more students were killed by the police in a similar melee at Jackson State University (MS).[66]

A perfect example of how one president takes the heat for something he inherited was the My Lai massacre (1968), which matured scandalously on Nixon's watch.[67] My Lai was a village in the Son My District in South Vietnam. The district was heavily mined and well protected by the enemy. American troops under the command of Major William Calley had been killed and maimed there in recent weeks, and a search and destroy mission was organized to confront the enemy. There was no reported opposition as Calley's men approached the village of My Lai, yet Calley ordered his men to enter it firing their weapons. Pent up resentments and emotions apparently took over and when the firing stopped over three hundred men, women and children were dead.

News of the atrocity did not reach the American public until 1969, when the story of it — based upon an interview by an American reporter with a veteran who had been told of the incident by soldiers who had been there — was published. Calley (who said he was following orders) was tried and convicted of murder and sentenced to life in prison. The massacre was condemned by all, but there was sympathy for Calley and the situation in which he found himself. In the end, he was pardoned in 1974 by Nixon.[68]

Peace negotiations continued and at reelection time (1972) Kissinger announced a deal was in the making. Given the circumstances, one must give Nixon good marks in foreign affairs. Nothing was worse; much was better.

Conclusion

Why was the election of 1968 so close? Vietnam is the single-word answer. A more complex answer is this: The election appeared to be close for two reasons. Wallace made it harder for Nixon to win a popular vote as impressive as his electoral vote and the black vote switched powerfully to Democrats in 1968 (and thereafter). Black neighborhoods in the South, for example, gave Humphrey 95 percent of their votes.[69]

War, always a difficult issue in a campaign, was especially so in this one because discontent with it converged with civil rights protests and the negative impact of the social revolution, which rebelled against all forms of authority. National pandemonium was the result and its national bogeyman was the president of the United States. Nixon was the direct beneficiary of this discontent.

11

1976: Gerald F. Ford
vs. Jimmy Carter

(Electoral Votes 538; Majority 270)

Introduction

There was one intervening presidency between the subject of this chapter and the last close election, Richard Nixon's, whose term was finished by Vice President Gerald Ford. There have been many scandals under several presidents over the years, but if it's reasonable to measure the importance of them by the results of them the Nixon scandal was the worst. He resigned in 1974 in disgrace, the first president in American history to do so.

Nixon/Ford (1973–76): Nixon carried the same horrific load that had driven LBJ into retirement — the Vietnam War, racial conflict, protests and riots associated with both, the Cold War with the Soviets, general international instability and an antagonistic press. He won his first election in 1968 by a wide electoral vote margin; despite his problems with the war, he trounced George McGovern in 1976. But his personal characteristics plus unending pressure led him to make faulty decisions that, under the threat of impeachment, led to his resignation.

In terms of the 1976 election, his triumphs in foreign policy were lost in the wave of disgust that accompanied the Watergate scandal and his ultimate withdrawal, and he created for the Democratic nominee the winning issue in the presidential campaign — clean up Washington. Gerald Ford, a caretaker president, also approved two actions that did not help his election chances: A general pardon for Nixon and the embarrassing withdrawal of American troops from Vietnam. It can be said that his election contest with Jimmy Carter was close only because his essential decency shone through and because Democrats selected a weak candidate.

History was not something for Republicans to brag about in 1976.

Conventions

Who had bragging rights? Who could hold a recent president up high as their hero? Neither party could do this. Republicans had the ghost of Nixon, Democrats the ghost of LBJ. But there was a difference. There was no doubt in the public's mind that Nixon had been guilty of misdeeds that justified his resignation. It was different with Johnson. Some close observers could see the harm already being done to the financial structure of the nation because of unaffordable (and popular) commitments being made to the public in the form of entitlement programs, and they could extrapolate a dark future if trends didn't change. But to a substantial section of the public (aside from the Vietnam War), LBJ was a heroic figure, especially to blacks. He advanced civil rights and expanded the safety net to an unbelievable extent.

To the candidates, LBJ was a mixed blessing. The heroes that candidates could muster came from the deep recesses of history — comforting, interesting but not dynamic. Neither party bragged too much about the past in this election.

Anticipation was in the air as convention time approached. Would Ford succeed in his bid for a term of his own, or would he forever be defined as a loyal member of a failed presidency? Would Ronald Reagan, or some other Republican hopeful, wrest the crown of succession away from him? Of all the Democratic hopefuls who were lining up to challenge the Republican nominee, who would prevail?

REPUBLICAN CONVENTION

Kansas City was the site of the 1976 convention, which took place during the third week in August.[1] Given the disarray of the party due to Watergate, one would have expected several contenders for the nomination, in addition to the frontrunner, President Gerald Ford. But the field was surprisingly light. Comedian Pat Paulson and the perennial contender Harold Stassen (1948, 1952, 1964) muddied the water a bit, but only Gov. Ronald Reagan (CA) provided serious opposition. Running against an incumbent president who was popular with, and part of, the Washington establishment is no easy task. But Reagan proved to be a formidable opponent with a clear point of view that attracted many voters which, when added to an attractive, articulate and compelling personality, gave Ford all he could handle.

The candidates competed in twenty-eight primaries. Reagan won eleven, including vote rich California and Texas. Because of this, he entered the convention with enough support to block an automatic victory for Ford. He had a chance to work the room at the convention; his message was straightforward[2]:

• Foreign Policy: The Ford policy toward the Soviets (détente) was weak-kneed; Reagan opposed the Strategic Arms Limitation Treaty (SALT);

he wanted to cool relations with China and give more support to Taiwan; he believed that giving a pardon to Vietnam draft dodgers was a mistake.

• Domestic Policy: Reagan blamed Ford for not fixing the deficit problem; he wanted to downsize government and reduce the power of federal politicians to meddle in the private lives of citizens; he believed that such things as education, food stamps, welfare, Medicare and Medicaid should be handled by states; by transferring federal programs to states, he believed he could save $90 billion, balance the budget and reduce taxes; he referred to Ford as a poor leader.

Reagan ran against Washington, D.C., as a champion of the ordinary citizen who, he said, was being neglected by the system, a system he vowed to change. As usual, he phrased his beliefs well: "Our nation's capital has become the seat of a buddy system that functions for its own benefit, increasingly insensitive to the needs of the American worker who supports it with his taxes." In a nation torn by war, racial tension, high taxes and growing debt, this message resonated powerfully.

Watergate was not a negative for Ford during the primaries.[3] But he had other problems with the Republican base that weakened him, just as they strengthened his opponent, Reagan. Pardoning Vietnam draft dodgers was unpopular; his continuation of a policy of détente with the Soviets was questioned by many; part of the blame for the shameful exit from Vietnam was on his back; many chafed over the growth of regulation and the undue influence of the environmental lobby; conservatives deplored the growth of the welfare state and the deficits that went with it.

Ford's strengths were simple but effective. More than most politicians, he was a genuinely nice man with ordinary ways that made voters feel comfortable. Even his occasional clumsiness was endearing to many people. Ford's so-called clumsiness, an invention of the press, was based upon a few mishaps. Actually, Ford may have been the best athlete ever to hold the presidency.[4] On the aggressive side, Ford demonstrated he could give as strong a punch as he took. He portrayed Reagan as a dangerous right wing ideologue who would be easily defeated by Democrats while he (Ford), a calm, proven and presidential leader, could bring victory to the party.

According to the polls, Ford was the underdog in his primary race with Reagan (40 to 32 percent). But he did well enough to enter the convention in a strong position.[5] Since a sitting president with party support is extraordinarily powerful at a convention, a promise here and there was enough to gather the few remaining votes he needed to win — 1187–1070. One reason he won was his willingness to drop Vice President Rockefeller from the ticket and appoint a man more acceptable to conservatives, Sen. Robert Dole (KS).

Ronald Reagan, after the election, joined Ford on the stage sharing the cheers of a united party ready to do battle with its Democratic challenger. But the Republican stride as the convention ended was not a confident one. Ford trailed Carter by more than thirty points in the polls.[6]

Major elements of the Republican platform appear later in this chapter.

DEMOCRATIC CONVENTION

The Democratic convention was held in New York City during the second week in July.[7] With Watergate and the ignominious departure of the United States from Vietnam as the historical backdrop, it was expected that competition for the nomination would attract even more nominees in 1976 than usual from a party that had been out of power for eight years.

With twenty consecutive years of presidential power under Roosevelt and Truman and then eight more under Kennedy and Johnson as its recent history, Democrats had come to act as if the office of president belonged to them and that the administrations of Eisenhower and Nixon were temporary aberrations of nature that had to be fixed as soon as possible. Watergate made their point: Nixon never should have been president in the first place.

An assortment of prominent figures from the elite pool of talent in the party threw their hats into the ring[8]: Sen. Birch Bayh (IN), Sen. Robert Byrd (WV), Sen. Lloyd M. Bentsen (TX), Gov. Edmund G. Brown, Jr. (CA); Gov. Jimmy Carter (GA); Sen. Frank Church (ID), ex–Sen. Fred R. Harris (NM); Sen. Henry M. Jackson (WA); ex–Gov. Terry Sanford (NC); Gov. Milton Schapp (PA); Ambassador R. Sargent Shriver (PA); Rep. Morris K. Udall (AZ); Gov. George C. Wallace (AL).

Two former presidential candidates were briefly in the mix: (1) Hubert Humphrey considered another run when primaries appeared to be headed for deadlock, but he changed his mind; (2) Adlai Stevenson was unpersuaded by Mayor Daley of Chicago to mount a campaign. Except for Wallace and Jackson the remaining faces were new to presidential politics. And as the race began, Carter was the underdog, a stranger to most voters beyond the borders of his native state of Georgia.

Contests were held in every state and it soon became apparent that Bentsen, Harris, Sanford, Schapp and Shriver had no support. Humphrey, Stevenson and Byrd, momentary candidates at best, removed as targets the states of North Dakota and Minnesota (Humphrey), Illinois (Stevenson) and West Virginia (Byrd) and they remained loyal to their reluctant warriors. The race boiled down to Bayh, Brown, Carter, Church, Jackson, Udall and Wallace.

Whatever chance Wallace had (which ranged from slim to none) disappeared when Carter showed strength in the South. Wallace took only Mississippi, Alabama and South Carolina during the primaries; the rest of the South was Carter's. Jackson did no better. In addition to his home state of Washington, he took Alaska and impressively won in New York and — shockingly — in Massachusetts. But that was it for him, and the race became a contest for five men: Bayh, Brown, Carter, Church and Udall.

Bayh, an early favorite in the election sweepstakes, was active but unsuccessful. Finishing third in Iowa and New Hampshire and getting trounced in Massachusetts persuaded him to pack it in — one more down and four to go.

Brown expected to have strength in the West, and he did. He took his home state, California, and its neighbor, Nevada. But that was the end of it. He was out. Udall also turned out to be a regional candidate who could claim only his home state, Arizona, and one other, Wyoming. Frank Church and Carter were the only ones left.

Church, the destroyer or savior of the CIA — depending on your point of view — turned out to be the most formidable opposition for Carter. In addition to his own state, Idaho, he took four others in the Northwest. But it wasn't enough. Carter had no strength in the West; he owned most of the South and had pockets of strength everywhere else. He benefited from the large field, who knocked each other out of contention, a fate from which he was saved because he claimed to be, and was, a different candidate unsullied by the political atmosphere in Washington that, all agreed, was poisonous. In this case, being the odd ball paid off. He entered the convention with enough delegates to win. Walter Mondale became his running mate.

Carter's message to the convention, and to the nation, was a popular one: he would restore honesty and integrity to the government in Washington. With Nixon in mind, Carter's followers applauded enthusiastically.

Unlike previous conventions that featured divisions within the party, this one had a calming and unifying effect that began with the keynote address by Barbara Jordan, the impressive black representative from Texas, and ended with the image of Carter, Wallace and Coretta Scott King standing together on the podium. Confidence was high when the convention adjourned. The smell of a decisive victory was in the air,

Major elements of the Democratic platform appear below.

Democratic and Republican Platforms

As the federal government got bigger, so did party platforms.[9] In 1976, it took 20,000 words for Republicans to define themselves and 21,000 for Democrats. The increase was caused by the enormous growth of government. In 1940, for example, there were 1.1 million federal civilian employees; in 1975 there were 2.8 million, an increase of 155 percent.[10] This was primarily the result of two factors: (1) Larger world responsibilities since World War II; (2) larger social responsibilities that followed a more liberal interpretation of federal power under the Constitution.

Each election usually carries one or two issues that dominate all others.

In the 1930s, it was the depression, in the 1940s World War II in the 1950s Korea, in the 1960s Vietnam and in 1976 the Watergate scandal. The size of government and its expanded duties were also questions of mounting concern that divided the two major political parties. These two topics had to be added to the primary issues that kept all presidents occupied:

WATERGATE

Ford could mitigate Watergate's damage to the Republican brand by pointing to such things as the elimination of the draft and the pardoning of draft dodgers, but he couldn't completely erase the image of Nixon's departure from Washington on Air Force One, the shock that followed the pardon he gave to the fallen president or the televised pictures of the last Americans leaving Vietnam, fleeing for their lives. That does not mean all other issues were totally irrelevant. Ford had other strengths and weaknesses that Carter had to deal with to maintain his advantage. But Watergate and Vietnam dominated the election and gave to Carter an invitation to victory.

GOVERNMENT

Democrats made no specific reference to the growth of government in their platform, which by itself was a statement. They limited themselves to comments on how to increase efficiency in providing services. Republicans, consistent with their views on the value of freedom and states' rights, were appalled by the growth in government and, in many words, said so in their platform: "Citizens are demanding the end to the ... increase in the size of ... government. All steps must be taken to insure that unnecessary federal agencies and programs are eliminated...." The nation was still ambivalent about this issue, but on balance most Americans continued to favor freedom over security. As such, however, this was not an important campaign issue.

ENVIRONMENT

Protecting and nourishing the environment is an important issue for everybody. Maintaining a healthy economy is also important. These objectives sometimes clash; at that point they become political. Environmental lobbies, mostly married to Democrats, have increasingly influenced federal policy. Both parties express determination to maintain a healthy environment, but there was a clash between them that is dramatized in a sentence drawn from the Republican platform: "We also believe ... that the emphasis on environmental concerns must be brought into balance with the needs for industrial and economic growth...." The question is this: When environmental concerns and economic needs clash, who wins? Republicans said the needs of man are supreme; Democrats, judging by their actions, leaned toward parity or the environment, but with cautious language. This issue has become so politicized that rational decisions concerning it are rare. The needs of the belly outweighed the well-being of the sparrow with most people in 1968.

EDUCATION

The clash between the parties is made clear by reading two sentences drawn from the platforms of both parties: Republican — "Throughout our history, the education of our children has been a community responsibility. But now federal ... programs pressure local school districts into substituting Washington-dictated priorities for their own. Local school administrators and school boards are being turned into bookkeepers for the federal government." Democratic — "The Democratic Party pledges its concerted help through special consultation, matching funds, incentive grants and other mechanisms to communities...."

ENERGY

The Arab/Israeli War of 1973, followed by an embargo of oil from Arab states directed toward those like the United States who had supported Israel, had a powerful impact. Dependence on foreign, mostly unstable, governments for oil is obviously dangerous from a national security and economic standpoint. America had to do something. Republicans asked for a three tiered approach to the problem: (1) Conserve; (2) Exploit nonrenewable sources of energy; (3) increase research on renewable sources of energy, all being done within the free market system with appropriate government assistance. The Democrats' approach to the same problem was revolutionary: "[T]he federal government has an important role to play in insuring the nation's energy future." To hammer the point home it also stated that "realities are that rising energy prices, falling domestic supply, increasing demand, and the threat to national security of growing imports, have not been contained by the private sector." The Democratic platform in effect declared the private sector to be a failure and announced its intention to control the energy problem from Washington. In a succession of sentences it explained how oil and gas prices would be controlled; it predicted how the economy would positively respond to a new system of central planning.

SCHOOL PRAYER AND ABORTION

Democrats were silent on school prayer. Republicans favored a constitutional amendment to permit nonsectarian, voluntary prayer in public schools. Democrats supported Supreme Court decisions that legalized abortion. Republicans supported a constitutional amendment "to restore protection of the right to life for unborn children." According to polls,[11] Carter had a small edge on the abortion issue (46–44 percent, proabortion), but the prayer issue may have eliminated his advantage on social matters.

CRIME

Both parties agreed that crime was a problem that needed more attention, and that drugs, gun control and juvenile delinquency were major elements of the problem. Republicans supported the possession of firearms as stated in Amendment Two of the Constitution; Democrats supported gun control. The parties essentially agreed on law and order goals and differed in ways to achieve them. Republicans focused on assisting local law enforcement; Democrats sought to become a part of it. Nothing said by either party would substantially change the attitudes of their natural constituencies; but given the turbulent times, the party with the tougher reputation for law enforcement, the Republicans, had the advantage.

WAR AND PEACE

Republicans wanted to rebuild American military superiority: "In constant dollars, the present defense budget will no more than match the defense budget of 1964.... In 1975 Soviet defense programs exceeded ours in investment by eighty-five percent, exceeded ours in operating costs by twenty-five percent, and exceeded ours in research and development by sixty-six percent. The issue is whether our forces will be adequate to future challenges." With that as their predicate, Republicans promised to modernize all sections of the military establishment and, in selected areas, to increase its size. Democrats approached the subject of defense spending with caution: "[It will be enough] to meet the real security needs of the American people." Another example of their tentative approach in military spending is as follows: "[M]odern, well-equipped and highly mobile land forces are more important than large numbers of sparsely-equipped infantry divisions." Such truisms appeared throughout the Democratic plank on defense. And it was not unusual to find a moral tone within the defense plank. For example, there is the following: "Covert action must be used only in the most compelling cases where the national security of the U.S. is vitally involved; assassination must be prohibited." The Republican plank on defense bristles with energy; the Democratic plank pursues safety at the lowest possible cost, a relatively timid approach to national defense. In a more normal economic climate, this issue would have been a huge win for Ford; under the existing circumstances (post–Vietnam and the economy), it wasn't.

THE ECONOMY

Both parties agreed to rigidly enforce antitrust laws. Beyond that, they had little in common. Republican comments were mostly warnings about what would happen if Democrats won and implemented their party platform. Government controls, higher taxes and higher spending would be the result, they claimed; inflation ("the number one destroyer of jobs") would follow and the "integrity of our money" would be compromised. To end high unemployment, they said, freedom must reign, inflation must not take place and the value of the dollar must be protected. Democratic plans for the economy began by establishing a crisis atmosphere and by raising doubts about the ability of Republicans to address it: "Today, millions ... are unemployed. Our industrial capacity is ... wastefully under-utilized. There are houses to build, urban centers to rebuild.... Something is wrong when there is work to be done, and the people ... willing to do it are without jobs."

Before making proposals, Democrats took one more wallop at the quality of Republican economic leadership: "During the past twenty-five years, the American economy has suffered five major recessions, all under Republican administrations. During the past eight years, we have had two costly recessions with continuing unprecedented peacetime inflation."

Having defined a mountainous problem Democrats then proposed their mountainous solution, which included: (1) A planned economy — targets for employment, production and prices; central control of the money market; direct federal control over prices and wages; (2) Federal coordination of interest rates and credit policies, especially in low-income markets; (3) Establishment of laws that facilitate union organizing and amendment of laws that restrict it. The misery index was at its highest in 1976,[12] which gave Carter a huge advantage, especially since it came on the heels of Watergate and the exit from Vietnam. But the solution proposed by Democrats was so draconian that some observers wondered if fear of government could overcome fear of a troubled economy. The Democratic agenda had by this time become pure progressivism, a road that can lead to socialism.

TAX POLICY

Both parties acknowledged the need for tax reform but beneath that simple phrase hid total disagreement on what constitutes reform. In their platform, Republicans sought to simplify and clarify; Democrats wanted adjustments that facilitated their goal of income redistribution, which they regarded as social justice. Republicans introduced fear when they noted that full implementation of Democratic plans would significantly raise taxes or, failing that, increase debt and worsen inflation. Democrats did not explain how they would fund new programs, or the expanded old ones, except to suggest that their idea of tax reform would generate more income from high-end taxpayers, who, in effect, would carry the new load. Republicans dropped a toe delicately into the waters of the welfare state when they proposed tax credits for college training, technical training and child care expenses for working parents. These were additions to the menu of social benefits coming from Washington that were hidden from view as such by making them part of tax policy — a small hypocrisy. History gives Republicans an edge on tax issues; for that reason Ford is given the edge. But the "soak the rich" approach to taxation of Democrats was growing in appeal to a public that was becoming more class conscious than ever before in modern American history — it had begun under FDR, and the 1976 Democratic platform showed that the same approach to taxation was alive and well.

DEFICITS AND DEBT

Complexity equals boredom in politics. For that reason, issues like national debt seldom get much attention in presidential elections despite their importance. But properly handled (especially during hard times when the antenna of the electorate is finely tuned to pick up anything that deals with money) it can have more impact than usual. The reaction of the parties to growing debt was completely different. Republicans related mushrooming debt to uncontrolled spending and used language like "Every dollar spent by government is a dollar earned by you. Government must always ask: ... Can we afford it? [The] Democrat-controlled Congress that has been unwilling to discipline itself to live within our means. No nation can spend its way into prosperity; a nation can only spend its way into bankruptcy." They were firm in their resistance to constant borrowing, and in their defense of an independently operated Federal Reserve: "The number one cause of inflation is the government's expansion of the nation's supply of money ... needed to pay for deficit spending.... The independence of the Federal Reserve System must be preserved." Democrats, on the other hand, blamed the recession and the free market for rising debt: "The depressed production and high unemployment rates ... have produced federal deficits totaling $242 billion." They promised debt relief in the form of changes in budget procedure, as long as those changes didn't interfere with social goals: "The Democratic Party is committed to the adoption of reforms such as zero-based budgeting ... and sunset laws which do not jeopardize the implementation of basic human and political rights." And the Democrats sought to bring the Federal Reserve System into the loop of the national planning system mentioned above: "The Federal Reserve must be made a full partner in national economic decisions and become responsive to the economic goals of Congress and the President."

(Ford exercised his veto power sixty-six times [more than Nixon and less than Eisenhower][13] but was otherwise powerless to control the spending of the Democratic Congress. Nevertheless, he was associated with the deficits and Carter was not. By default — because of the simple accounting formula according to which each president is blamed for whatever happens on his watch — Ford loses points on this issue and Carter gains.*)

*Growing debt is not caused by recessions, but by deficits in the federal budget. Deficits are caused by mushrooming costs, plunging federal receipts, or both. Social service costs constantly grew throughout

Civil Rights

Both party platforms expressed concern over the possibility that modern communication technology could compromise the right of citizens to protect the privacy of their lives. They agreed on the need to add protections for women's rights and that a discrimination-free marketplace must be maintained in education, housing, government and business. The primary areas of disagreement were: (1) Forced busing to achieve integration: Republicans protected the right to attend neighborhood schools and they supported a constitutional amendment to forbid forced busing. Democrats approved of forced busing; (2) Quotas (hiding as affirmative action): Republicans sought fairness, but approached affirmative action warily. Democrats promoted it with gusto, using such language as the following: "[W]e pledge vigorous federal programs and policies of compensatory opportunity to remedy for many ... the generations of injustice and deprivation"; (3) Inner City Problems: Race and war riots during the height of the civil rights and Vietnam War protests were lessening, but the attention they drew to the condition of the nation's large cities remained.

Both parties were attentive to this issue in their platforms in language that gave voters a clear choice. Republicans favored solutions developed and administered at the local level, assisted by federal funds, and their platform had devastating things to say about the Democratic approach to the problem. They said, for example, "All this has happened during the years that the number of federal urban programs has increased almost tenfold: from 45 in 1946 to 435 in 1968; and expenditures have increased ... from $1 billion to $30 billion." Undeterred by criticism, Democrats proposed no cutbacks in existing programs and added more, such as federal funds for economic development, health care, education and environment; funds to offset the impact of inflation; housing and mortgage loan subsidies. Mostly based on the historical record, Carter wins this issue by default.

But as implementation of new civil rights laws spread across the nation, fears developed over methods being employed to achieve equity in all aspects of American life. For example, some people feared forced busing; others wondered if affirmative action programs would morph into quotas and demands for reparation payments from an innocent generation. Such concerns chipped away at the Democratic advantage on this issue.*

the Nixon and Ford administrations; revenue failed to grow in one year (1971). During the eight-year period, deficits amounted to $194 billion, which was added to national debt and $166 billion of it (86 percent) was caused by excessive social spending. Source: The National Debt of the United States, 1941-2008, Robert E. Kelly.

*(1) Republicans were repelled by ideas of intergenerational guilt followed by proposals for "remedies." They believed that eliminating current discrimination was enough; Democrats sought more. (2) Direct aid is more attractive to inner city voters than calls for volunteerism, self-control and local programs that are partially supported by federal funds. But some voters were uncomfortable with a huge federal presence in local problems and the expansion of it that accompanies a larger federal reach.

SOCIAL PROGRAMS

Since the presidency of LBJ, social programs had gotten lots of space in party platforms. Specific program ideas were presented by both parties, but the underlying dispute was about the proper role of the federal government in national affairs—limited, as originalists believed, or expansive, as progressives held. Republican comment in its platform attempted to educate the public about the legitimacy and affordability of Democratic programs. Democrats took legitimacy for granted and added a laundry list of expanded or new programs. Their attitude toward such things is captured in a few words: "We do pledge a government that will be committed to a fairer distribution of wealth, income and power." Some citizens feared the influence of the growing federal government; others supported it.

FOREIGN POLICY

Hundreds of words were used by both parties to explain their foreign policy vision. "More of the same" would have been adequate, with some modest exceptions such as the following: (1) The language used by Republicans was typically more muscular and focused; Democratic words were more outreaching and global; (2) Democrats pledged to use more blacks when dealing with African issues and they had more to say about that part of the world. Otherwise, both agreed to bargain from a position of strength, to maintain traditional alliances, to bargain with the Soviet Union and China, and to support those who sought freedom. Nixon had faults, but he was a good foreign policy president and Ford did nothing to negate his better policies. Carter, inexperienced in such matters, could not present his views as persuasively as Ford. Ford, however, lost some (perhaps all) of this edge during a television debate in which he flubbed a basic question.

LEADERSHIP

Ford, a likable man, was not personally involved in Watergate. He presented to voters an impressive resume. He emphasized his experience in national and international affairs and pointed to his opponent's lack of same. Carter, a successful ex–naval officer, businessman and state politician with a spotless personal reputation had an agreeable way about him. He emphasized his proven background as a public administrator and the need to change the Washington way of doing business. The Democratic platform was not timid in its description of Republican leadership: "Two Republican Administrations have both misused and mismanaged the powers of national government, obstructing the pursuit of economic and social opportunity, causing needless hardship and despair among millions of our fellow citizens." The appetite for change was in the air. Polls predicted Carter would win by fifteen points.[14]

So ends the analysis of party platforms. Watergate, Vietnam and the weak economy constituted such a heavy load for Ford that few expected him to win and many expected him to be trounced.

Top Candidates

Vice President Ford and Gov. Jimmy Carter were the nominees, the former a long-time Washingtonian with a well-known background, the latter a mystery man ("Jimmy Who?") from Georgia who had surprised the entire political world by defeating in the primaries many high profile luminaries in his party.

GERALD R. FORD, REPUBLICAN

Born: 1913; **Education:** University of Michigan, Yale University Law School; **Wife:** Elizabeth Bloomer; **Children:** Four; **Died:** 2006.[15]

Leslie Lee Lynch, Jr., born in Nebraska, was brought up in Michigan where his mother, Dorothy, divorced her alcoholic husband and married Gerald Rudolph Ford, owner of a paint store. The boy, Leslie, did not know about his biological father until his high school years. He retained his original name until he graduated from college, at which time he officially changed it to Gerald R. Ford, Jr.

Ford, an excellent student in high school (top 5 percent), was also popular and talented enough as a football player to attract the notice of recruiters from the University of Michigan. His profile remained steady in college; he was a good student and his team's most valuable football player. The Detroit Lions and the Green Bay Packers offered him contracts, but he turned them down to enter law school.

Yale University was open to him because they needed an assistant football coach and he also coached boxing. With these jobs as leverage, plus his academic record in high school, Ford entered the law school in 1938 and graduated third in his class four years later. He returned to Michigan to practice law.

The man who was later to be classified by many in the media as clumsy and slow-minded was in fact one of America's most athletically gifted presidents with a leadership and academic record that could compare with the best. Law practice led to politics and, among other things, Ford worked in Wendell Willkie's unsuccessful 1940 campaign against Roosevelt. When World War II broke out, he was in the middle of a local battle for control of the Republican Party against the entrenched interests.

The service record of many politicians of that day is more cosmetic than substantial. Not so with Ford; he was a genuine, battle-tested veteran who served in the South Pacific as an officer on the *Monterey*, a light aircraft carrier. He took part in major naval engagements against the Japanese, earning in the process ten battle stars. Few Washington politicians had a more impressive military career; fewer still received less credit from the media for his military and political service. After four years of service, he was honorably discharged.

Law practice beckoned again after the war, as did marriage to Elizabeth Bloomer, whom he married in the midst of his 1948 campaign for the House of Representatives. The primaries were Ford's biggest problem because opposition was stiff, but the combination of tough campaigning plus his military record and a sensible message carried him through. During the subsequent election contest, he easily disposed of his Democratic opponent, and his career in Washington began.

Ford won repeated elections to the House and became especially known for his muscular ideas on how to confront the challenge to the world posed by communist China and the Soviet Union. His rise to power within the House was steady. As the leader of the "Young Turks," a group of younger representatives, he became chairman in 1963 of the Republican Conference; two years later he successfully challenged the minority leader, and won. He was the most powerful Republican in the House. Such was his prestige that President Johnson named him to serve on the Warren Commission, which was charged to investigate the Kennedy assassination.*

Presidential politics of the time featured a split in the Republican Party between conservatives, led by Goldwater, and liberals, led by Rockefeller. Ford leaned toward Goldwater, but not so far as to ruin his reputation as a centrist. He supported the Eisenhower campaign and approved of the choice of Nixon as a running mate (and stood by Nixon during his darkest days). In the 1964 campaign (Johnson/Goldwater), he nominated his friend from Michigan, George Romney, but when his candidate failed, he gave full support to Goldwater.

Since Democrats had the votes to pass whatever they wanted in the House, Ford as a Republican leader had little practical power. But to the extent that he had it, he used it to thwart LBJ's spending agenda. And he became one of Washington's most effective critics of the president's war policies in Vietnam. He was one of many from the "fight it, or quit it" school that regularly advised the president to fight the war more vigorously.

Ford supported Nixon's presidential runs in 1968 and 1972 and his policies thereafter. Retirement was on his mind when, to everybody's surprise, Vice President Spiro Agnew in 1973 was forced to resign (charged with accepting bribes). Ford was offered the position, according to some, because he could easily be confirmed by the Senate, a high qualification to Nixon, who had been flattened by Watergate charges and who didn't want to add to his woes by having to fight a confirmation battle.

Eight months later, Nixon's misdeeds caught up with him. He resigned

*Ford agreed with the conclusion of the Warren Commission: Oswald did it, unassisted.

and Ford became president. One month later, Ford granted a full pardon to Nixon.[16]

Two attempts were made in 1975 to assassinate Ford. Lynette "Squeaky" Fromme, a follower of the infamous killer Charles Manson, tried to shoot him and was stopped and apprehended by a secret service agent. Less than a month later, Sara Ann Moore also tried and failed.[17]

JIMMY CARTER, DEMOCRAT

Born: 1924; **Education:** Georgia Southwestern College, Georgia Institute of Technology, United States Naval Academy; **Wife:** Eleanor Smith; **Children:** Four.[18]

James Earl Carter was the first of four children parented by James (a farmer) and Lillian (a nurse). During his early years, James helped his father on the farm and saved his wages until he was able to buy a house in the price-deflated depression market. He accumulated five properties before he was through, an early demonstration of the talent and aggressiveness that was to characterize his career. He rented the houses to people he knew in his hometown of Plains, Georgia. Jimmy's father was a stern man; his mother nurtured the mind of her bright son. Carter had an uncle in the navy who regularly sent postcards from various ports in the world. These contacts struck a chord with the boy and, before he went to high school, he announced that one day he would be in the navy.

School was no problem for the intelligent young man, and he graduated from high school as class valedictorian. After high school, he wanted to go to Annapolis, but patriotic fervor was high in the early years of World War II and he had to get into the long line of applicants. Disappointed but undeterred, Carter went to college in Georgia, graduated in 1942, entered Annapolis a year later and graduated in 1946 in the top 10 percent of his class. Shortly thereafter, he married Rosalynn Smith.

Carter selected submarines as his area of interest at a time when the navy was in the early phase of building a nuclear fleet. The project was headed by Captain Hyman Rickover, a brilliant and demanding leader. Carter was assigned to him and later said that, next to his father, Rickover had more influence on his life than any other man. Toward the end of Carter's naval career, he taught nuclear engineering to the elite crew of one of the first two nuclear submarines, the *Seawolf.*

Carter's father died of cancer in 1953 and the danger was real that the family farm would be lost, leaving Carter's mother, Lillian, in desperate straits. Carter resigned from the navy and returned to manage the farm. This was not a pleasant decision for Carter's wife, who preferred the security and the travel associated with military life.

Profits from the farm were small when Carter took over, and the South was changing rapidly in ways that sometimes made life more difficult for him. The recent Supreme Court decision that made segregated schools illegal had upset southerners, including those in Plains; additional pressures were ongoing to eliminate segregation everywhere. Groups were formed, united in their protest against such things. Carter was the only white male in Plains to stay clear of the protests. His neighbors were angered by this and his business suffered.

Over time, racial pressures subsided, and by 1959 Carter was running a prosperous farm. This permitted him to become more active in community affairs. He served on the boards of schools and libraries and became a church deacon and Sunday school teacher. Inevitably, this led to an election that made Carter chairman of the board of education. A successful run for the state senate followed, where he served two terms and earned the reputation of being a fiscally responsible politician who would resist segregation at every turn.

Political experience fueled Carter's ambitions for higher office. He ran an unsuccessful campaign in 1966 for governor, losing badly to Lester Maddox, one of the South's most outspoken segregationists. Bitterly disappointed, Carter was back in the race in 1970, this time more appreciative of the racial sentiments of the electorate. He moved principle to the closet, minimized his appearances before blacks, campaigned against forced busing and otherwise reduced his image as a civil rights warrior, making himself more pleasing to those who feared integration. The strategy worked; he won in a squeaker with 49 percent of the votes. This is one of countless examples of how the practice of politics in the United States can corrupt the participants.

Almost as if to make up for his campaign tactics, Carter returned to form after the election. He called for an end to segregation in his inauguration speech; he ran his administration in an open and fair way; he increased substantially the number of black workers in government. He also demonstrated the organizational acumen that came from his naval and business background. On the downside, he showed signs of weakness that would later disturb his presidency — an arrogant, morally superior attitude that infuriated opponents and turned away many Democrats who were inclined to support him. Carter was admired but he wasn't loved.

Presidential politics in the Democratic Party were in disarray around this time. Richard Nixon destroyed George McGovern in the 1972 race, and the 1976 nomination seemed to be up for grabs. "Why not me?" is the thought that must have occurred to the relatively inexperienced Carter, who never suffered from a loss of self-esteem. The rest is history.

Election Tone

Gerald Ford was sixty-three years old, healthy and vigorous, when he ran for president in 1976; Carter was a sturdy fifty-two. If Ford lost it was likely he would retire from public life; if Carter lost, his public career could continue if he competed well and did nothing to dishonor himself. Since the two men hardly knew each other, there was no personal animus between them. Unless something unforeseen changed, the campaign would deal with issues more than personalities.

Some of those issues were provided by Supreme Court decisions made since the last close election in 1968. Supreme Court justices Earl Warren (1954–69) and Warren Burger headed the Court assisted by fourteen associate justices.[19] As a team they made controversial decisions, some of which rocked the nation:

- 1969: The possession of obscene materials is constitutional; the distribution of them is not (*Stanley v. Georgia*).
- 1969: The "fairness doctrine," which requires broadcasters to present a balanced presentation of public issues, is constitutional (*Red Lion Broadcasting Co. v. FCC*). This decision was reversed in 1974 (*Miami Herald Publishing Co. v. Tomillo*).
- 1969: A jury system that discriminates against blacks violates the equal protection clause of Amendment Fourteen (*Alexander Holmes v. County Board of Education*).
- 1971: Federal courts are constitutionally authorized to oversee and create remedies for mandated desegregation (*Swann v. Charlotte-Mecklenburg Board of Education*).
- 1971: State laws permitting the funding of salaries and supplies in nonpublic schools (mostly Catholic), which are related to nonreligious education, are unconstitutional (*Lemon v. Kurtzman*).
- 1972: State laws that restrict the distribution of contraceptives to married couples are unconstitutional (*Eisenstadt v. Baird*).
- 1972: Execution as a sentence for a crime is constitutional, but it must be used with discretion; the punishment must fit the crime (*Furman v. Georgia*).
- 1973: A woman has a right to an abortion (*Roe v. Wade*).
- 1974: The presidential right to "executive privilege" is not unqualified. It is customarily restricted to military and diplomatic affairs (*United States v. Nixon*).
- 1974: Desegregating a dual school system does not require any particular racial balance in the schools, grades or classrooms (*Miliken v. Bradley*).
- 1975: The availability of abortion services can be constitutionally advertised (*Bigelow v. Virginia*).
- 1975: A student must be given notice and some form of hearing before they are suspended (*Goss v. Lopez*).
- 1976: A state law requiring spousal approval for an abortion is unconstitutional (*Planned Parenthood v. Danforth*).

The day of a remote federal government was clearly over. With its laws and its Supreme Court decisions, the government had found its way into the most remote corners of the public sector. These decisions provoked anger and applause and they had significant impact on voter attitudes during the subject election. These rulings of the Court during the Nixon and Ford years were a reflection of the chaotic times, when all standards were being challenged, when the mores of the nation were being shaken and when families were being torn apart by rebellious youngsters and their mentors. And they were forming voters' minds about loyalty to political party. Most certainly, in an incalculable way, they affected the tone of both conventions and, later, the election itself.

In all elections, the hottest issues often emerge from the handling of affairs during the previous administration. It was no different in 1976. The campaign was mostly a referendum on the record of the Nixon/Ford administration.

Ford, for example, was held responsible by most of the press and by the public for the domestic policies of his own administration, even though it was Congress, not he, who formulated most of them. But this was not to the advantage of Carter to the degree one might expect because robust criticism on his part could ricochet to Ford's advantage. It would reveal that domestic policy was largely the construction of the Democratic Party, Carter's party. With minor exceptions, Democrats had controlled Congress from Roosevelt to Ford, mostly by veto-proof margins.[20] But without getting into cause and effect details, Carter could and did point to the budgetary consequences of those policies. So, indirectly, he leveled the accusatory finger of responsibility at Ford.

This was troubling for Ford. The four-year deficits, which occurred mostly under his watch, were the highest to that point in American history,[21] despite sharp cutbacks in military costs and personnel.[22] But the fundamental cause of deficits was, by this time, built into the federal budget. The government's heart was bigger than its pocketbook — 82 percent of the four-year deficit was caused by the excessive cost of social programs over which Ford had zero control. Another 11 percent of it was caused by excessive interest expense, most of it related to debt inherited from previous administrations that had been similarly afflicted.[23] Persistent and avoidable federal deficits were a new phenomenon that began with the redefinition of government's fundamental role during the 1932 to 1968 era. Given the circumstances (oil prices and a recession caused by them), it's fortunate deficits were not even larger. Ford was not a bad money manager; he was required to handle a difficult situation and did a better job of it than the numbers imply he did. By 1976, there had been ample warning that the financing of social programs needed restructuring.

The top income tax rate was 70 percent; the corporate rate 52 percent. Capital gains taxes gradually increased from 25 to 39 percent.[24] Ford could not brag about tax policy, but neither could Carter criticize it except for claims of unfairness and the usual "soak the rich" proposals. These were some of the aspects of the Nixon/Ford administration that in 1976 Ford had to defend or explain: huge deficits, a dollar under attack, high taxes, a miserable end to an unpopular war and trouble on the streets.

No wonder Carter had such a broad smile on his face throughout the campaign. The supply of things to attack was endless. Ford, no matter how innocent in fact, was guilty of this mess unless he could prove himself innocent.

TELEVISION DEBATES

The first series of television debates was in 1960, during which Vice President Richard Nixon, an experienced debater, and Sen. John Kennedy, a relatively unknown quantity, faced off. Nixon was burned badly in the first debate and was at least singed in the others, not because of content but because Kennedy was relatively better looking and more personable. The era of personality politics began with that first debate, and with it a new set of qualifications for the job was born — wit, charm, appearance and a memory good enough to absorb intense coaching. What one appeared to be had become as important as what one was. Many past presidents would have failed that test (the cold and reserved Thomas Jefferson and the blunt and somewhat imperious John Adams come to mind), as Nixon did in 1960, some say to an extent that cost him the presidency. But it is here to stay, something to be dealt with.

It is the common tendency of the best known contenders to avoid debates, just as it is the common tendency for the lesser known to demand them. Today, it would probably be a political mistake for a candidate to refuse to debate because the public and the media expect it, and would likely think poorly of the candidate who deprives them of the chance to appraise them in that format. Johnson (1964) and Nixon (1968 and 1972) successfully avoided the march of time. Both were keenly aware of what debates did in 1960; they weren't about to take the same risk and they were well-known enough to get away with it.

Perhaps Ford could have done the same. He was better known and far more tested than the one-term governor of Georgia, Jimmy Carter. Why then did he agree to debate? The answer is simple. The Nixon/Ford administration had been so troubled that he was far behind in the polls (in June 1976 his approval rating was 45 percent). Three debates were scheduled: September 23 in Philadelphia; October 6 in San Francisco; October 22 in Williamsburg.[25]

- Debate #1: Moderator, Edwin Newman, *Baltimore Sun*; Panelists, Frank Reynolds, ABC; James Gannon, *Wall Street Journal*; Elizabeth Drew, *New Yorker*. Domestic affairs were the essential subject matter. Carter, the critic, was aggressive. Ford, he said, was a poor leader who, aside from avoiding another major scandal, was a do-nothing president with no new programs. He, of course, talked about the mess in Washington that he would clean up; tax policy needed redoing because it undertaxed corporations, benefited the rich and penalized the poor. Ford, the defender, was also aggressive. Carter was inexperienced, he said, and lacked perspective and distorted or misunderstood the facts. Alert to problems in the economy, Ford said he would reduce taxes, cut spending and lower unemployment by expanding the private sector. He defended the pardon of Nixon as a step toward the healing of a divided nation, as an appropriate step for a man who, by his resignation in disgrace, had been punished enough, as a necessary step so that Ford could concentrate on governing the nation.

- Debate #2: Moderator, Pauline Frederick, National Public Radio; Panelists, Richard Valeriani, NBC; Henry Trewitt, *Baltimore Sun*; Max Frankel, *New York Times*. Foreign affairs were the essential subject matter, and Ford was expected to dominate. Carter, the aggressor, again attacked Ford's leadership, claiming that Henry Kissinger, not Ford, was running foreign affairs, and doing it badly: the U.S. was too weak and had lost international respect. Ford defended himself adequately against Carter's attacks until he made the blunder that cost him the debate and, perhaps, the presidency. In response to a question posed by Max Frankel, Ford said, "There is no Soviet domination of Eastern Europe, and there never will be under a Ford administration." In response to a follow-up question, he elaborated on his initial response, saying that Yugoslavia, Romania and Poland were not dominated by the Soviet Union. Carter jumped on those comments and said that he'd like to see Ford persuade the Poles, Czechs and Hungarians in America that their homelands were not under the Soviet boot behind the Iron Curtain. Ford's comments reverberated across the nation and diminished him as an experienced leader of foreign policy. A post-debate poll showed Carter ahead by six points—up from his previous lead of two points.[26]
- Debate #3: Moderator, Barbara Walters, ABC; Panelists, Joseph Kraft, columnist; Jack Nelson, *Los Angeles Times*; Robert Maynard, *Washington Post*. Subject matter covered a variety of national and defense issues. The aggressive, attacking tone of the first two debates did not continue into this one. It was subdued and cordial. Watergate still lured some panelists, who grilled Ford about his resistance to a deeper probe into the matter when he was in the House. He was questioned as well about his "rotten" and "hopeless" record on economic and environmental issues. Two specifics mentioned by Ford were more money for defense and lower spending so that a tax decrease for the middle class could be considered. Carter was asked to explain why he had lost so much of his early lead in the polls.[27] The panelists were also curious about how his largely Georgian staff would work in Washington. Carter was vague about his specific remedies for unemployment, but they included strong leadership, meeting with labor and business leaders and voluntary price restraints. Both candidates were asked questions about inner cities, appointments to the Supreme Court, minority issues, etc. It was a relatively quiet and undramatic exchange of views.

Despite his major blunder in the second debate, Ford's decision to engage in debate seemed a good one. Carter, by consensus, won the debates, but at the end, Ford was closer than he was at the beginning. In August, Carter had been ahead 50 to 37 percent; at the end of the second debate, Ford's worst, Carter's lead was down to six points; when the debates ended, Ford was even. Those who claim that Ford lost the election because of his gaffe during the second debate should be cautioned by these numbers.[28]

THE MCCARTHY FACTOR

Eugene McCarthy served in the House (1949) and the Senate (1959–71). He made his first foray into presidential politics in 1968 when he announced his opposition to the Vietnam War. He was determined to end the war policies of LBJ by winning the Democratic nomination.[29] McCarthy demonstrated vote-getting ability in the early primaries to a degree that, many believe, led to the resignation of LBJ from presidential politics.

Being against LBJ, however, was not the same for a voter as being for McCarthy. Instead, Vice President Hubert Humphrey's decision to enter the race proved to be the end of McCarthy's surge. He drew passionate support up to, and including, the wild Democratic convention of that year; but he did not have the delegate strength to overcome Humphrey's dominance.

McCarthy had tried before (1972) to win the Democratic nomination, but he did poorly in the primaries and dropped out. Now here he was at it again in 1976, running as an Independent on a platform that promised full employment (by shortening the work week) and nuclear disarmament. He took a stand against the two-party dominance in American politics and argued for easier access to the electoral system for third party candidates. His efforts to compete in 1976 eased the way for future candidates.

McCarthy appeared on the ballot in thirty states, and he attracted almost 1 percent of the vote, which, in a tight election, made him an important player. He never again approached a position of similar influence.

Presidential Campaigns

The preliminaries were over and the adversaries were in starting position. The time had arrived for each man to make his case to the American people.

Ford's primary problem was to separate himself from the memory of the Nixon administration and all that it meant to the voters (Vietnam, Watergate, etc.) with such effectiveness that he emerged as a candidate running on his own credentials. Carter's primary problem was no longer anonymity but the need to persuade Americans that he was experienced enough to lead the nation out of the Nixon morass and into a fresher, cleaner world.

FORD CAMPAIGN

Few men entered a political campaign with more negative things on his political back than Gerald Ford carried — recessions, inflation, unemployment, My Lai, the weak-kneed end of the endless war. Yet he did so, bravely, and, in most respects, well.[30]

He ran against a one-term governor from one of the smaller states. Against this he offered a deep political career, which included executive experience at the vice presidential level, plus his own sterling reputation for personal integrity, bolstered by his appointment to the Warren Commission by the father of the welfare state, Lyndon Johnson. To make his case, Ford had to maintain his dignity throughout the campaign and demonstrate, in scheduled debates and otherwise, that he was far more experienced and qualified than his opponent. His spotless personal record was sufficient to assure voters that there would be no more Watergates.

Ford's need for respect faced difficulties, some self-caused, that hindered his progress: (1) He had an unfortunate proclivity to live his most embarrassing moments in public. For example, one of his drives on a golf course hit a spectator on the head. This plus a few stumbles at the wrong place and at the wrong time activated his second problem, the media. (2) Perhaps as likable a man as has ever entered the White House — a man of intellectual capability as demonstrated by his scholastic, legal and political careers, an athlete of considerable skill as shown by football honors he accumulated in college — Ford was nevertheless assaulted by a campaign of ridicule that was based upon his mishaps. He was slow-witted, clumsy and without social grace, said the press; Chevy Chase lampooned him on *Saturday Night Live*; LBJ, who had thought enough of Ford to appoint him to the Warren Commission, once said of Ford, "He couldn't fart and chew gum at the same time."[31] Such minimization of his personal abilities struck at the heart of Ford's campaign and considerably added to the difficulty of reaching his goal.

Then he added another fillip of his own: During the second debate with Carter he announced in response to a question by a panelist that Eastern European countries were not under the control of the Soviets. The reporter pressed on with a follow-up question. Ford was obdurate — the Soviets did not control Eastern Europe, nor would they, he said, in a Ford administration. The press gleefully jumped on this response and kept it in the category of hot news because Ford refused to agree that he had made a mistake in the debate. This faux pas diminished one of Ford's major claims to superiority — foreign policy experience. Some hold that this error cost Ford the election. There is reason to doubt this facile explanation. Polls indicated he was well behind Carter after the conventions and had caught up by the time the debates ended.[32]

The economy was another cross Ford had to carry, but he was not totally without weapons. Yes, inflation and unemployment rates were high, but they were coming down.[33] And if the Democratic Congress would approve his tax cuts, improvements would accelerate. It wasn't a strong case, but it was something real and current that invited voters to look ahead, not behind.

Ford's campaign was primarily and necessarily defensive in nature, but it also had a primary aggressive theme: Carter was an inexperienced liberal who would expand the size of government and add more social programs and taxes. In a better time, it might have been a winning theme. But with Watergate and Vietnam on everybody's mind, it wasn't a better time.

CARTER CAMPAIGN

"I will never lie to you."[34] That brief quotation of Carter's captured the spirit of his campaign. Images of Vietnam and Watergate popped up every time he said that, or anything like it. The simple utterance of the words was more effective than any direct attack against Ford.

Carter had several hurdles to leap before he would be accepted as an electable candidate. As a single-term governor from a small southern state, he was inexperienced, especially in foreign affairs; in terms of presidential politics, his national recognition rating was low; he was a southerner whose ability to attract northern voters was in doubt: "Jimmy Who?" This was an oft quoted question that presented Carter's principal problem concisely. He had to escape anonymity.

Carter, aware of such things, had carefully built a career to address them: Chair of the Governors Campaign Committee (1972); chair of the Democratic National Committee (1974). Such positions moved him into the public eye, and the publication of *Why Not the Best?*, his biography, was also helpful. It was well received and defined him as a man who was different, one who could restore dignity to the once-revered White House.[35] Finally, his success in the primaries that led to his nomination helped. But he still needed something dramatic, after the nomination, to build his image to a presidential dimension, something like national debates.

A popular Republican nominee with a clean record behind him would have ignored requests for a nationally televised debate. But that wasn't Ford's situation. He had lots of things to explain, and he was confronted by an inexperienced opponent who was charging him with Nixon's misdeeds. Debates could give him a chance to display his wholesomeness, his primary defense against attempts to link him with Nixon. And he agreed because he was behind in the polls[36]; he needed exposure as much as Carter. On the other hand, his agreement to debate also gave to Carter the "something" he badly needed — intense national exposure.

Carter made the most of his opportunity, waiting for anything to happen that could turn the event into a large asset for him. Ford provided it with his incorrect comments about the scope of Soviet influence in Eastern Europe.

Ford's mistake about the Soviet's sphere of influence, Carter's intelligent response to it and the treatment given to it by a press that was well-disposed toward Carter stripped away—in the minds of many voters—the vice president's alleged superiority in foreign affairs.

The last debate was held on October 22, 1976.[37] Thereafter—no doubt with increased confidence—Carter pressed his constant themes: To elect Ford would be to reelect Nixon; Washington was a mess and he, an outsider, would clean it up. When voters lose confidence in an administration they want to believe the challenger; their critical faculties are not as sharp as usual. They wanted to believe Carter; they wanted to forget Vietnam and Watergate. Ford's debating mistake made it easier for some of them to forget Carter's inexperience. Carter's comparative anonymity became to many people an asset for him instead of a liability. Maybe an outsider was needed to wipe the slate clean and begin again.

Carter's appeal to voters was simple and consistent. He indirectly pinned Ford with Nixon's failures, recession and scandals; he called for a government "as honest and decent and fair and competent and truthful and idealistic as are the American people." Carter began his race to the top with a huge lead in the polls. On the day he cast his vote, it was a horse race.[38]

Election Results, 1976

The election of 1976 featured the lowest voter turnout (54 percent) since World War II. The results were razor thin by any measurement.[39]

Election Results 1976

Candidates	EV	%	Pop. (000)	Pop. %	Pop. %
Carter	297	55.2	40,831	50.1	51.0
Ford	240	44.6	39,148	48.0	49.0
McCarthy		757	.9		
Other	1	.2	820	1.0	
Total	538	100.0	81,556	100.0	100.0

Notes: EV=electoral vote; Pop. = popular vote; Ronald Reagan received one electoral vote.

Source: NY Times Almanac 2009, p. 132

Had Ford won all of the third party-type popular votes, Carter would have marginally prevailed. Further analysis is needed to measure the importance of the minority vote.

Minority voters over the years have been left of center, antiestablishment types—Greenback, Prohibition, Union Labor, Social Democrat, Socialist, Progressive, Independent, etc. It is reasonable to assume that most minority voters in 1976, if turned loose, would have preferred Carter, who ran as the antiestablishment candidate, over Ford. Ford took California in 1976. Carter was penalized by minority voters. Absent their competition, he might have won the state.

Election Results 1976
States with 15+ Electoral Votes
Winning Percent

Candidates/ Votes	CA 45	IL 26	MI 21	NJ 17	NY 41	OH 25	PA 27	TX 26
Carter	47.6	48.1	46.4	47.9	52.0	48.9	50.4	51.1
Ford	49.4	50.1	51.8	50.1	47.5	48.7	47.7	48.0
Total	**97.0**	98.2	98.2	98.0	99.5	**97.6**	98.1	99.1

EV=electoral vote; Pop. = popular vote; Bold type = fringe vote had theoretical impact in that state.

Source: http://uselectionatlas.org/RESULTS/

Carter won Ohio by a whisker. It is likely his margin would have been larger absent the third party competition.

Based on the above analysis, Carter, not Ford, was punished by minority competition in larger states. Had their votes been restricted to the major candidates, it is likely he would have done better, that a doable victory in California would have put him beyond the reach of any Ford comeback. Carter's margin of victory was less than 2 percent in four states: Oklahoma (8), Oregon (6), South Dakota (4) and Virginia (12)[40]—a total of thirty electoral votes. Ford lost the election by fifty-seven electoral votes. Had he won all of the above states it would not have been enough.

The overall conclusion is this: The election was close but decisive. The minority vote did not create Carter's victory; it stole votes from him. Decisive though it was, the popular vote indicated that the nation was still divided. Predictably, governing would be a problem. Carter won the South and the industrial northeast (organized labor, minorities, urban liberals and southerners—the New Deal coalition)—twenty-three states. Ford took the West (except Hawaii), some New England states and the upper Midwest—twenty-seven states.[41]

More broadly, advocates for a larger, activist government once more won the ideological battle. Progressivism (now called liberalism) had begun under Wilson, was fanned by FDR and became intensive under LBJ. For good or for ill, the nation was bending left, headed for a political harbor unintended by the Founders, a process intimidating to many Americans and comforting to others.

The Carter Cabinet

The choice of cabinet members is a serious business. Balance must be struck between the rewarding of friends, competence and personality. At the end of the process, a president must have the best men in the most critical positions—State, Defense and Treasury—who can work collegially with the members of his inner circle, and competent men in the other positions who can be depended on to follow presidential policy. Carter's selections were[42]: **Vice President:** Walter Mondale, Minnesota; **Secretary of State:** Cyrus Vance, Virginia (1977–80), Edmund Muskie, Maine; **Secretary of Defense:** Harold Brown, New York; **Secretary of Interior:** Cecil D. Andrus, Idaho; **Secretary of Commerce:** Juanita Kreps, Kentucky, (1977–79), Philip Klutznick, Missouri; **Secretary of Health, Education and Welfare:** Joseph A. Califano, New York (1977–79), Patricia R. Harris, Illinois; **Secretary of Transportation:** Brock Adams, Georgia (1977–79), Neil Goldschmidt, Oregon; **Secretary of Treasury:** W. Michael Blumenthal, Germany, California, New Jersey (1977–79), G. William Miller Oklahoma, California, New York; **Attorney General:** Griffin Bell, Georgia (1977–79), Benjamin Civiletti, Maryland; **Secretary of Agriculture:** Robert Bergland, Minnesota; **Secretary of Labor:** F. Ray Marshall, Louisiana; **Secretary of Education:** Shirley Hufstedler, Colorado (1980–81); **Secretary of Urban Development:** Patricia R. Harris, Illinois (1977–79), Moon Landrieu, Louisiana; **Secretary of Energy:** James R. Schlesinger, New York (1977–79), Charles Duncan, Jr. (1979–81), Texas.

Carter's cabinet was diverse racially and geographically. Most had impressive resumes. The surprise choice was Schlesinger as the first secretary of energy, not because of his qualifications, which were stellar, but because he was a Republican from the controversial Nixon White House. Carter had considerable difficulty in forming a workable team out of his cabinet members, especially in the area of foreign affairs, a flaw that affected his decisions and added to his reputation of being indecisive. Turnover in cabinet positions does not necessarily mean a lack of harmony. But Carter did have deep divisions within his cabinet.

The Carter Congress

The presidential election, after analysis, indicated that Carter had won decisively but marginally from a geographical and a popular-vote point of view.

The congressional elections told a different story. Democrats were returned to the House and Senate in veto-proof numbers. They ruled Washington during Carter's first two years with the same iron hand that had prevailed under Kennedy and Johnson, and almost as powerfully during his last two years.

Pro-Administration Congressional Power

Congress	Year	President	House %	Senate %
94	1975	Ford	**33**	**38**
95	1977	Carter	67	61
96	1979	Carter	64	58

Appendix 1.1, 1.2

Bold type=minority position

A presidential election is a reflection of the national mind. Based on the 1976 election, control in Congress should have been marginally in favor of Democrats. That wasn't the case. Congressional control continued at Johnsonian levels and didn't reflect national mood as measured by the Carter vote. This was especially surprising in the House, where members must stand for reelection every two years. When any election disgorges extremely unbalanced results, it's time to look at it critically in search of weaknesses that inordinately protect (as in this case) or weaken the position held by officeholders. The need for such an examination was palpable in 1976 and 1978.

Evidence suggests that Carter was the weakness—he underachieved. It seems likely that another, more experienced Democrat would have won by a larger margin.

"Tip" O'Neil (MA) led the House during Carter's term. He had risen to the position of speaker during the Nixon/Ford years. Robert Byrd (WV), Senate leader during the Carter presidency, was as experienced and as capable as his counterpart, O'Neil, was in the House.[43]

Given such majorities in Congress, Carter, despite his marginal victory, could expect a super-efficient presidency in terms of accomplishment. Nothing stood in his way — except himself.

The Carter Supreme Court

Carter was sworn in by Chief Justice Warren Burger, who had been appointed by Richard Nixon. Nine justices served during Carter's term, eight of them appointed by Republican presidents.[44]

Supreme Court Justices, 1977–80

Judge	Began	Appointed by	Ended
Warren Burger (MN)	1969	Nixon	1986
William Brennan (NJ)	1956	Eisenhower	1990
Potter Stewart (OH)	1958	Eisenhower	1981
Byron White (CO)	1962	Kennedy	1993
Thurgood Marshall (MD)	1967	Johnson	1991
Harry Blackmun (MN)	1970	Nixon	1994
Lewis Powell (VA)	1972	Nixon	1987
William Rehnquist (WI)	1972	Nixon	1986
John Stevens (IL)	1975	Ford	

Source: Oyez, http://www.oyez.org/— Members of the Supreme Court,[45] http://www.supremecourtus.gov/about/members.pdf; *Men in Black*, Mark Levin, p. 8

Thurgood Marshall became indifferent to his duties in his later years. *People* magazine called him a television addict in 1982. He kept his seat for as long as his likely replacement was a conservative. "If I die, prop me up and keep on voting," he told his clerks. Concerning the Constitution he observed, "I [do not] find the wisdom, foresight or sense of justice exhibited by the framers particularly profound."[46]

The Burger court was activist and rendered some of most controversial in Supreme Court history.[47]

The United States was still suffering the side effects of having lived through some difficult national spasms. The counterculture, the endless war in Vietnam, street protests and riots, the oil embargo and Watergate had all stirred emotions that left the nation politically divided. Then, on the legal front, came the barrage of Supreme Court decisions dealing with pornography, free speech as it related to religious behavior, and abortion. Such things left the nation morally bewildered and divided.

And, from a legal standpoint, the "shock and awe" rulings of the Supreme Court continued during the Carter years. A review of a few cases makes the point[48]:

BEAL V. DOE (1977)

The facts: A state law forbade the funding of non-therapeutic abortions under the Medicaid program.

The issue: Does the state law violate Title XIX of the Social Security Act?

The decision: No, 6–3. But the Court made it equally clear that, if they wanted to, states could fund voluntary abortions. The Court was not asked to rule on what the state could do. Such comments on states' rights were gratuitous and constituted a backhanded approval of voluntary abortions. Abortion lobbies were in hot pursuit of federal funds for voluntary abortions under Medicaid and were repeatedly turned back by the Court: *Maher v. Roe* (1977); *Poelker v. Doe* (1977); *Harris v. McRae* (1980).

REGENTS V. BAKKE (1978)

The facts: The University of California Medical School, under its affirmative action program, reserved 16 percent of its admissions to qualified minorities. Bakke, a white man, twice applied for admission and was twice refused. His qualifications exceeded those of any minority who had been accepted during the same time period. He contended the refusal to accept him was based upon race.

The issue: Was the policy of the university in this case in violation of the Fourteenth Amendment (equal protection clause) and the Civil Rights Act of 1964?

The decision: No and yes. In a remarkable showing of intellectual cowardice, there was no majority opinion. Four justices (Burger, Blackmun, Rehnquist, Stevens) regarded the university's affirmative action program to be a quota system in disguise, which violated the Civil Rights Act; four justices (Brennan, Stewart, White, Marshall) ruled that the use of race as a criterion in admission decisions was constitutionally proper. The deciding opinion, cast by

Justice Powell, agreed with both groups: Racial quotas are wrong, but the use of race as a permissible criterion was constitutional. Out of this pool of indecisiveness came the only thing of importance to Bakke — he was admitted. Failure to be definitive in this case was an invitation to get more of them. The issue is still being debated, and "weasel" words continue to characterize the Court's decisions. The inference, right or wrong, is obvious: The Court is being guided by public opinion, an uncomfortable thought to those who believe in a government by law.

UNITED STEELWORKERS V. WEBER (1979)

The facts: A union and a company agreed on an affirmative action program that was designed to improve the number of skilled black workers: half of those selected for training positions were to be blacks. Weber, a qualified white, was passed over because, he said, of reverse discrimination.

The issue: Does the affirmative action program violate Title VII of the 1964 Civil Rights Act, which forbids discrimination based upon race?

The decision: No, 5–2. The Act "did not intend to prohibit the private sector from taking effective steps" to implement the goals of Title VII. The program seeks to eliminate patterns of racial segregation and does not prohibit white employees from advancing. Burger and Rehnquist wrote dissenting opinions; Powell and Stevens did not participate. Few issues have been more disturbing to citizens than affirmative action. Justice demands some form of accelerated progress for modern-day blacks who have been penalized because of long-standing patterns of behavior; the same justice insists that modern whites should not be penalized for the sins of their forefathers. Most Americans accept compassionate, intelligent affirmative action. The questions: To what degree and how much longer?

FULLILOVE V. KLUTZNICK (1980)

The issue: A federal law required that at least 10 percent of federal funds allocated for public works programs be awarded to minority companies. Fullilove claimed the law discriminated against him and others. Klutznick was the secretary of commerce.

The facts: Does the 10 percent clause violate the Fourteenth Amendment?

The decision: No, a 6–3 decision. The set-aside program under the law was a legitimate exercise of congressional power. Congress is not required to act in a "color-blind" fashion. Stewart, Rehnquist and Stevens dissented. This was another affirmative action case under a different name. In this case it was Congress and its power to establish numerical quotas that was being questioned.

Basic issues battered the legal system, their numbers a testimony to the instability of the national psyche. Abortion activists persisted in their attempts to legalize the federal funding of voluntary abortions; the attempt to create fairness in the marketplace created other problems; the insistence of blacks for equal rights brought similar claims from other groups and the list of hyphenated Americans grew longer each year, each one seeking its special slice of the American pie.

Confronted by such a sea of faces with such a variety of demands, for how long could the nation remain reasonably unified?

Domestic Affairs Relative to Current Political Issues

The future looked rosy. True, Carter won the election minimally, which seemed to foretell, at the least, a troubled administration. But that theoretical conclusion was contradicted by the reality of congressional elections. Although the people by their votes had said they were not wild about Carter, you'd never know it by the type of Congress they gave to him. He had the veto-proof power that usually accompanies an unusually popular president. Given this political gift, it was reasonable to expect that what Jimmy wanted, Jimmy would get. But that wasn't the case.[49]

DOMESTIC EVENTS

Carter began dramatically. He pardoned draft dodgers from the Vietnam War. Then he blocked the funding for a favorite Pentagon project — building the B-1 bomber. Apart from the sensibleness of the latter decision, it was popular with the war weary public and the antiwar clique. The trans–Alaska oil pipeline was completed in 1977, and oil was pumping before the year was finished.[50] After the Iranian revolution (1978–79), oil prices doubled and waiting lines at gas stations became commonplace.[51] Carter ordered all imports from Iran discontinued, and all Iranian assets seized (a response to the hostage crisis). Iran and the hostage crisis, topics that defined the Carter administration, had a powerful impact on Americans at home. The price of oil in 1974 was $41 per barrel, in 1979 $74 per barrel, in 1980 $98 per barrel (Iran/Iraq war).[52] Such cost surges burned a hole in the pocketbooks of Americans.

LEGISLATIVE EVENTS

Legislative events result from, among other things, human interaction. But Carter had other ideas on how to go about things. He was determined to lead by example. He would be honest and clear; he would never lie; he would expect similar behavior in return.

He was tested by Congress early in his administration with "pork barrel" projects, which he labeled as corrupt and useless spending. And he earned enemies in return. Carter's support in the nation was shallow, which meant his power over Congress was minimal. Party leaders knew this, and a series of bouts between the executive and the legislative branches of the government commenced. Congress rejected some Carter initiatives; Carter vetoed congressional projects. What should have been clear legislative weather for Carter, and for Democrats, turned out to be the opposite. What Carter got, he struggled for, and he got less than one in his position should have gotten.

Most of Carter's significant legislative accomplishments occurred in his first two years, as follows[53]:

- The Community Reinvestment Act (1977) was a law designed to prevent "red-lining," the systematic denial of credit to people living in certain areas.*
- The Department of Energy Organization Act (1977) established the Department of Energy — a response to oil embargoes — a consolidation of all energy efforts under one roof. Carter did good work in energy. America's dependence on oil diminished during his administration. The value of this was overlooked because of the publicity given to the shortage and the higher price of oil due to the hostage crisis and the Iran/Iraq War.
- The Foreign Corrupt Practices Act (1977) addressed corruption. Bribery is a way of life in some foreign countries. Because of Watergate, a wave of Puritanism swept over Washington, and Carter was the perfect president to take a stand on the issue. No bribes were to be paid by American companies to get business. Some claimed the act harmed American business. But over time, attempts to eliminate corrupt global business practices have broadened and penalties on Americans have become less severe.
- The International Emergency Economic Powers Act (1977) provides the president with the power to confiscate assets of, or to otherwise hurt the interests of, any nation or person who has acted in such a way as to cause a national emergency.
- The Ethics in Government Act (1978) was a response to the Watergate scandal. Under its terms federal employees must make public financial disclosures; some activities of ex-employees after they retire are prohibited; other rules governing gifts, etc., were put in place.
- The Civil Service Reform Act (1978) was also a response to Watergate. During the campaign, Carter promised to reform the system and eliminate the possibility of abuses allegedly caused by Nixon. With this act, he delivered what he pledged to do.

*The original intent of this legislation was to improve the quality of banking services to poor neighborhoods. In 1989 it was updated with regulations that, in effect, lowered lending standards. An impact of this was the housing crisis of 2008 when millions of people couldn't afford the mortgages on homes that were losing value daily.

- The Foreign Intelligence and Surveillance Act (1978) addressed a problem that needed solving: How to monitor dangerous activities without, at the same time, opening the door to levels of unconstitutional invasions of privacy. This act attempted to draw the fine line between legitimate and illegitimate snooping. This sensitive problem was still being debated as part of the homeland security issue in 2010.
- The Nuclear Non-Proliferation Act (1978) had as its basic purpose the control of the exportation of any processes or devices that could be used to develop nuclear weapons, and to assist the United Nations, and other countries, to do the same.
- The National Energy Conservation Policy Act (1978) was an all-out attempt to conserve energy at home, in business and in government and was another response to the oil embargo of the 1970s.

Tax policy remained essentially unchanged under Carter.[54]

The Carter administration and techniques employed by Carter and his men have been much maligned. Objectively appraised, however, he had a substantial legislative record, especially in his first two years, that has had an enduring impact on domestic affairs.

ECONOMIC GROWTH

The recession under Ford, which lasted sixteen months,[55] ended in the summer of 1975. Thereafter, the economy rebounded and did well under Carter until, in late 1980, it once again slid into a short recession that ended in July.[56]

Gross Domestic Product, Public Debt

Year	GDP (bil)	% Growth	Public Debt (bil)	% PD/GDP
1976	1,738.8	11.4	477.4	27.5
1977	1,974.4	13.5	549.1	27.8
1978	2,218.3	12.4	607.1	27.4
1979	2,502.4	12.8	640.3	25.6
1980	2,725.4	8.9	711.9	26.1

Source: Historical Tables 2010, 1.2,7.1.

The misery index under Carter skyrocketed to 36.0, featuring inflation of 13.6 percent. With such an inflation rate, comparative growth figures in GDP lose all meaning until adjusted, as follows:

Gross Domestic Product, Inflation Adjusted
1976–80

Year	GDP (bil)	Growth %	Year	GDP (bil)	Growth %
1976	4,414.4		1979	5,125.8	4.4
1977	4,664.3	5.6	1980	5,132.6	0.0
1978	4,909.9	5.3			

Source: Historical Tables 2010, 10.1

The trend line is the same, but the results in the real world were far different. Carter began with a strong economy that consistently weakened until, in 1980, it was flat.

Those who take comfort from the debt/GDP ratio have much to learn by studying the Carter administration. For all practical purposes, the ratio stayed about even — not too good and not too bad, from that isolated standpoint. On the other hand, public debt increased by $235 billion, and interest expense in 1980 was almost 40 percent as expensive as national defense. Except for national defense and Social Security it was the most expensive line item in the 1980 federal budget.[57]

Carter left behind a weak economy and the worst misery index in history[58]:

Misery Index 1980

Interest	Inflation	Unemployment	Total
15.3	13.6	7.2	36.1

Note: The Federal Reserve policy of fighting inflation with high interest rates helped to create Carter's miserable misery index.

On its face, the misery index made a clear political statement, to wit: A Democrat would not be elected in 1980 — Ronald Reagan won the 1980 election with a ten-point margin.

Foreign Affairs Relative to Current Political Issues

Carter never lacked confidence during the first two years of his presidency. Despite his lack of foreign policy experience, he approached international problems head-on and made significant decisions.[59]

THE PANAMA CANAL TREATY, 1977

Under the terms of the Panama Canal Treaty Panamanians would have, by 2000, control of the canal.[60] This resolved long-standing differences with Panama, which had made it clear since the 1960s that they wanted the United States out of their country. LBJ tried and failed to get a deal acceptable to both sides. Nixon made more headway, but Watergate got in the way of further progress. Now it was Carter's time to handle the hot political issue. The final treaty preserved America's right to use the canal and permitted it to defend it. The decision to abandon American sovereignty in Panama was opposed by Republicans, especially Ronald Reagan.

CAMP DAVID ACCORDS, 1978

The accords were signed after twelve days of intense negotiation between Egyptian president Sadat and Israel prime minister Begin; the process was monitored by Carter at Camp David.[61] As a result of this commendable effort, normal relations between the two nations were established and other details that affected the region were agreed to. The accords did not by any means solve long-term enmity between the Jews and Arab states, but they represented a step forward that has not been outdone by any agreement made since. This was the crown jewel of Carter's work in foreign policy, a major achievement with long-lasting positive consequences, something of which the often criticized Carter can be justly proud.

CHINA

Carter's actions toward China were dramatic and controversial. He granted formal recognition in 1979 to the communist regime. By itself, this was controversial, made more so by the fact that he also withdrew recognition of the Republic of China (Taiwan) and unilaterally revoked the Mutual Defense Treaty with that nation that had been approved by, and was defended by, the Eisenhower/Nixon administration.

Recognition of China significantly reduced tensions in East Asia that since have matured into a healthy commercial relationship between the two nations. As a balm to Taiwan, America continued to supply it with arms with which it could defend itself against an aggressive China. Republicans opposed this treatment of Taiwan and tested, all the way to the Supreme Court, Carter's unilateral power to abrogate the peace treaty with that nation. Barry Goldwater led the charge and lost.

SOVIET UNION

There is much to admire in the idea of an outsider bringing new and fresh ideas to Washington. Having said that, it is also true that inexperience can be dangerous, especially in foreign affairs as experience is needed in many situations.

Those waiting for Carter's inexperience to show were rewarded in his handling of the Soviet Union, America's most formidable and aggressive enemy. For example, in Ethiopia, the Marxist regime was involved in a territorial dispute with Somalia. The Soviets, assisted by Cuba, helped the Marxists with men and materials. Carter's key advisers on such matters could agree only on the need for a response, but they disagreed on the type of response. Carter couldn't form an independent view that would pull his advisers together. He ended up giving a foreign policy speech in which he agreed with both points of view (hard line vs. diplomacy). The speech revealed him for what he was on the issue—confused and indecisive.

Regarding the SALT treaties, Carter approached the idea of arms limitation idealistically. He wanted sharp reductions on both sides. Through his aides, he announced his objectives before the talks began. Negotiations failed; the eventual treaty was much like the old one and was never approved by Congress. As a result, Carter and his team appeared inept.

The presence of Cuban troops working with the Soviets in Ethiopia alarmed the White House and led to a more detailed examination of that nation's activities. The intelligence services, it was learned, had failed to report that thousands of Soviet troops had remained in Cuba since the standoff between the two nations in the 1960s. Alarm bells were sounded. The issue was deeply studied by a panel of peerless examiners. They decided the few troops in Cuba were no threat. Crisis ended! Again, the administration looked incompetent.

NEUTRON BOMB

There was interest in 1977 in further development of a nuclear weapon. Carter signed on to the project, more reluctantly than his associates knew. As the project progressed it was learned that there were objections to the deployment of the weapon in Europe. At that point, Carter's reluctance to do anything not cleared by allies became apparent and he canceled the project.[62] This on again, off again approach to an issue of such significance was a major embarrassment for the United States.

HOSTAGE CRISIS, 1979–80

Iranian students broke into the American embassy in Tehran and held sixty Americans hostage for 444 days. It soon became apparent that the Iranian government, not the students, was behind the deed.

Carter's credibility as a leader, already sinking rapidly, deteriorated more as every day of irresolution passed. The hostages were taken in the first place partly because of the decision made by Carter to allow the shah of Iran, who had been deposed, to come to America for medical treatment, a courtesy that enraged Shah-hating Iranians.

Carter could not get National Security Adviser Brzezinski and Secretary of State Vance to agree on a course of action, and he lacked the personal conviction that might have brought them together. After months of inaction, a rescue attempt was organized; it failed dismally. Carter, and the United States, looked like a powerful bull with no horns. Secretary of State Vance, constantly at odds with National Security Adviser Brzezinski, was kept out of the planning for the rescue mission. He resigned shortly after its failure.

Carter did have foreign policy successes, notably the agreement between Egypt and Israel. But the combination of his inexperience and ego got him into big trouble to an extent that far outweighed his accomplishments. He was a poor — almost dangerous—foreign policy president.

Conclusion

Why was the election of 1976 so close? Some close elections would have had the opposite result, if this or that group of states had shifted from one candidate to the other — if luck had switched partners. That wasn't the case in this election. The statistical results reflected reality. Carter and Ford were almost equally popular and the close electoral vote was a fair reading of popular sentiment. No realistic rearrangement of state victories would have changed the result; the absence of third-party competition would not have benefited Ford.

Given the condition of the nation in 1976, and the reputation of the Nixon/ Ford presidency, the Democratic candidate should have won in a romp. Why wasn't that the case seems to be the more proper question. The answer: Probably because Democrats fielded, from a professional standpoint, the wrong candidate. Carter's vigorous primary campaign took the initiative away from insiders and put the party in a position where it had to choose him, a relative unknown. Arguably, one of the other well known men who were outmaneuvered by Carter during the primaries would have beaten Ford by a larger margin.

12

2000: George W. Bush vs. Albert A. Gore

(Electoral Votes 538; Majority 270)

Introduction

The last presidential election analyzed in this book was the 1976 race between Vice President Ford and Jimmy Carter, the surprise Democratic nominee who was a relative unknown to Washington politics and to politicians. Carter won, then at the end of his only term left behind an economy in shambles and a stand-off with Iran that had for months paralyzed foreign policy.

Before the next close election, between Gov. George W. Bush and Vice President Albert Gore, Presidents Ronald W. Reagan, in two terms, George H.W. Bush, in a single term, and William J. Clinton, in two terms, had their chances to handle national affairs. Each man contributed something substantial to the ongoing debates during the 2000 election.

Ronald Reagan,[1] had inherited the worst misery index in modern history.[2] Interest and inflation rates were going through the roof; unemployment was over 7 percent. National debt was out of control because spending on entitlement programs continued at an unaffordable pace.[3] The threat of national bankruptcy loomed. The Cold War was getting hotter; Carter had failed to free the American hostages in Iran. America badly needed an effective president who would deal with the immediate problems and set America off on a more promising course. At the end of Reagan's eight years, the misery index was 50 percent lower, the threat of national bankruptcy was gone, the Cold War was over, and the Iran hostages were home. Debt continued to be a major problem; the entitlement programs, untouched, were still in place. The expansion of them was stopped under Reagan, but he couldn't reduce or restructure them because he didn't have the congressional wallop to do so.

Reagan was the only conservative Republican president in the twentieth century. His influence was enormous. It became, for example, fashionable again to cite balanced budgets as being a useful goal, to point to high debt as a danger and to relate it to overspending. He became to Republicans what FDR has been to Democrats. He was the leading advocate for small government, free enterprise, personal responsibility and the Constitution created by the Founders, just as FDR was the leading proponent of a large activist government, controlled enterprise, community responsibility and a living Constitution that bent to the needs of the day, as interpreted by the judges of the day. Both were the flesh and blood symbols of the foundational difference between the two major parties. Reagan's influence has been palpable in every Republican convention since he retired.

In terms of the 2000 election, George H.W. Bush[4] is remembered positively for his expert handling of the Kuwait War.[5] He overcame Democratic resistance, he organized an impressive array of international allies, including Arabian nations, and he, with the use of America's remarkable military, brought the war to a quick and convincing close (1990–91). On the downside, he is remembered as the man who broke his word on taxation. Confronted by a slowdown in the economy, he did what he had promised he would never do. He raised taxes, a decision, some believe, that led to his failure to win a second term. (It is far more likely that the decision of Ross Perot to run as an Independent did him in.) Bush was not an inspirational influence in 2000, but he was (and remains) one of the best liked men to hold the Oval Office.

William J. Clinton[6] arguably became president because Ross Perot's ambition prevented George H.W. Bush from defeating him in 1992. Clinton won by two electoral votes with 43 percent of the popular vote. A young man when elected (46), he represented a departure from the past and a fresh voice in Washington. By virtue of age, personality and intelligence he had the potential for greatness. And he had his accomplishments. But in terms of the 2000 election, he was remembered for two things: (1) A budget surplus in his second term that actually reduced public debt, a rare event in modern politics; (2) His sexual appetites smeared the White House and was the remote cause of his impeachment (which he survived).

Analysis reveals that the budget surplus was manufactured by non-repeatable machination; but in the public eye (which has little patience with analysis), that record accrues to his benefit and provided a comfort zone for the Democratic nominee. On the other hand, Clinton's sexual behavior split the nation emotionally. Young supporters and other groups from the left continued to embrace him (his approval rating was 66 percent when he retired[7]), but other voters were viscerally opposed to him and to anything related to him. His behavior and what it did to the reputation of the presidency was the Republican's strongest weapon in the 2000 elections.

History in 2000 was decidedly in the Republicans' corner. Their candidate would invoke Clinton's name at every opportunity, subtly perhaps but persistently. Democrats had to run away from the past, apologize as best they could and shift the conversation, as soon as possible, to the future.

Conventions

The spirit of every convention is to some extent influenced by the experiences of previous presidents, which give to each party something to brag about, or to hide from. Democrats could always hold up a picture of John Kennedy and get a cheer. He didn't do much during his abbreviated presidency, but the Kennedy public relations machine had turned him into a Democratic icon. They couldn't talk much about LBJ because of Vietnam, and reaching back to FDR for a whiff of prestige was getting to be a tired method of developing enthusiasm. Now they had the administration just ended to deal with. Was Clinton an asset or a liability? They didn't know for sure. The polls said he was an asset; his record said he wasn't. In short, nostalgia wasn't going to be on the front burner with Democrats in 2000. The future had to be the focus.

Republicans were in better shape. Hoover was forgotten; Nixon was out of the news for good; and Reagan was the political colossus that hung over the convention hall. The mere mention of his name would evoke a cheer from the delegates. And it didn't hurt to mention George H.W. Bush either as most everybody seemed to like him. No doubt about it, Republicans had the bragging rights in the 2000 election year.

Convention time is always exciting, especially so at the end of a two-term controversial president. Clinton's outgoing poll numbers were surprisingly high,[8] but there was no doubt he was considered controversial by some voters because of his record of personal behavior and because of the way he had politicized the White House. But he was also loved, especially by blacks, for his compassionate and caring ways. To the end, Bill Clinton was a charmer.

These dual qualities hung over both conventions. Republicans wanted someone — anyone — who was nothing like Clinton and who would restore dignity to the White House. Democrats wanted someone who would continue their progressive initiatives, which had been frustrated by six years of Republican control in Congress.

DEMOCRATIC CONVENTION

The Democratic national convention was held in Los Angeles during the second week in August.[9] Sen. Bill Bradley gave Vice President Al Gore modest competition for the nomination during early primaries, but the contest was over by March and, as expected, Gore was the man.

Would President Clinton and his wife attend the convention? Would they speak? These turned out to be the most dramatic questions in a convention that was otherwise a routine affair. Clinton spoke on the first night, saying, "I made one of the best decisions of my life, asking Al Gore to be my partner." Hillary Clinton was also a featured speaker at the convention.[10]

Gore was the only man nominated. His selection of Sen. Joe Lieberman

(CT) as his running mate, the first Jew to be so honored, drew attention, but otherwise the proceedings were cool. Democrats left the convention in a confident mood, with but one dark cloud to worry about — Clinton's behavior while he was in office. Otherwise, the facts were: A budget surplus was achieved during Clinton's last term; the economy seemed strong; there were no major wars. What better environment could a Democratic candidate ask for?

But there was that dark cloud to consider. Yes, polls looked good in August, but how good would they look in November after Clinton's past behaviors were once more trotted before the public eye? Clinton's difficulties involving women; using the White House as a vote-getting tool; lying; the impeachment were enough to give Gore insomnia.

The major elements in the Democratic platform appear later in this chapter.

REPUBLICAN CONVENTION

The Republican national convention was held in Philadelphia during the first week in August.[11] Gov. George W. Bush (TX) was the easy winner, but his road to victory was much more strenuous than Gore's. To begin with, he had five competitors, Sen. John McCain (AZ), Ambassador Alan Keyes, Steve Forbes, Gary Bauer and Sen. Orin Hatch (UT). Hatch lasted for one primary, Bauer for two and Forbes for three.[12]

Keyes and McCain competed in all twenty-three primaries. Keyes mostly attracted the religious right, and his vote was a subtraction from the Bush vote. But the size of his vote in any state turned out to have zero influence on the outcome. From the beginning, it was a contest between Bush and McCain. Bush's appeal was to the conservative voter; McCain's to the liberal Republican and the crossover voter. It was a replay of Goldwater versus Rockefeller Republicans, with McCain (a westerner) surprisingly filling the progressive mold that the New York governor once symbolized.

Bush took the early lead in Iowa. McCain replied with a surprise win in New Hampshire (with the crossover vote). Then Bush took Delaware and South Carolina, but McCain replied with Arizona and Michigan. Then Bush took charge. Except for the New England states, he swept the rest of the primaries.[13] McCain, a bitter man at the end of the campaign, was a thorn in Bush's side throughout his eight-year presidency. The selection of Bush was historic. If successful in his bid for the presidency, he would be the first son to succeed a presidential father since John Quincy Adams.

He was cautious about the selection of a running mate and when his nomination seemed secure he asked Dick Cheney, a former associate of his father, to conduct a search for him. During the interplay between the two men it occurred to Bush that he was looking at the man he wanted, Cheney himself. And so the marriage was sealed. Many heralded the decision as a wise one; others said it was a sign that the inexperienced Bush would rely too much on the old guard.

The convention ended on a positive note. Republicans weren't intimidated by Gore and relished the chance to run against the reputation of Clinton. Time would show that their own candidate wasn't exactly squeaky clean; but he was a figure Republicans were proud to offer to the public.

Republican and Democratic Platforms

Party platforms are usually ignored by all but activist insiders and political junkies. One look at the size of them, which seems to get bigger as time goes on, provides the reason for this indifference. In 2000, it took Democrats 24,000 words to explain what they stood for, Republicans 35,000 words.[14]

Democrats are wordy because they view the presidency as an opportunity to make life better for everybody, a self-imposed duty for government that can't be explained in a few words: They will, if possible, get you in a union, find you a job, raise your pay, improve your working conditions, get you promoted without discrimination, secure your private pensions, give you a government pension, increase your unemployment insurance, cover your health program, provide breakfasts for your children, subsidize their lunches, assure their promotion through the grades, guide them into college, provide grants/loans/tax deductions for their educations and keep your taxes low, etc., while they pass the bill along to the "rich." They assume responsibility for peace and justice in places like Bosnia and Kosovo, for hunger in the world, for the spread of HIV/AIDS and other diseases, for Middle East peace, for such things as international human rights, equality for women and international labor standards while, at the same time, they deal with the real-time problems in Russia, China, Iraq, Iran, OPEC, etc. Republicans are also wordy, but for a different reason. Their appetite for scope is not so grand. Instead they use verbal expansion to explain how they will do things better — Social Security, Medicare, Energy, Defense, Environment, etc.* As a simplification, one might say the Democratic platform is a blueprint for how a perfect world can be created, and the Republican platform is a recitation of what has to be done to fix current problems and to establish a new period of growth and prosperity.

Despite colorful phrases and the endless number of platform planks in over 50,000 words of political language, there are only a few key issues that

*Moderate progressives, the controlling wing of the Republican Party in 2000, instead of resisting the progressive agenda concentrated on managing its programs more efficiently and, in so doing, gave tacit approval to their existence. The conservative wing (opposed to progressivism) had been ineffective since the political demise of Goldwater until it was given new life by Reagan. George H.W. Bush, a moderate progressive, was a step back for conservatives. Clinton's progressive aims were substantially minimized by the rise of Republican power in Congress. The growing influence of conservatives was reflected in the party platform. It can be fairly said that their position in the Republican Party in 2000 was the same as the progressives vis-à-vis the 1912 Democratic Party.

turn voters one way or another: Government, war and peace, the economy (the misery index), tax policy, budget/debt, civil rights, social programs, foreign policy and leadership. But as is often the case, there were special issues of importance to this election: The behavior of the Clintons in the White House, terrorism and immigration. The contrasting positions of the candidates on these issues will be examined below:

THE CLINTON FACTOR

Nothing negative or apologetic about Clinton appeared in the Democratic platform, which is understandable. Only positive aspects of the record during his presidency were discussed. Republicans in their platform made no specific references to Clinton's behavior, but one phrase seemed to make the point. It referred to the need for the "rule of law," and it pointed to the dangers of an administration "that lives by evasions, cover-up, stonewalling and duplicity." Other than that, in a document of humungous length, Republicans did not exploit the Clinton factor, their political instincts no doubt somewhat blunted by his still high standing in the polls.[15] Nobody could be more different from Clinton than Gore. Yet, there was a residual after-odor attached to the Clinton presidency, which unfairly clung to Gore and was impossible to measure. It would hurt him. On the other hand, Clinton's popularity would help him. Which would be stronger?

TERRORISM

Terrorism was a characteristic of the time that should have influenced the defense budget. The record demonstrates that Democrats considered terrorists to be international criminals who should be captured and brought to trial in American courts. In this way they caught and punished the bombers of the World Trade Center. To them, Osama bin Laden was Public Enemy Number One because he was associated with the largest terrorist activities. Democrats also supported additional protections from possible attack against the nation's computers and against the Internet. And while moving to protect America they warned of the dangers of stereotyping and stepping on civil liberties. Republicans were not as subtle. They referred to terrorism as a "quickly evolving threat." They noted that current attacks were bombings, that future ones could involve chemical, biological or even nuclear weapons, and that "we must prepare for all." They proposed four principles to guide future behavior: (1) No concessions to terrorists; (2) punish state sponsors of terrorists; (3) punish terrorists; 4) assist others who are attacked. The WTC bombing and the attack on the USS *Cole* in Yemen brought the terrorist threat to the front of the American mind, which for eight years was not thrilled by Clinton's behavior as commander in chief. The Democratic plank was weak, the Republican robust.

IMMIGRATION

Democrats supported a reorganization of the Immigration and Natural- ization Service (INS) designed to shorten waiting times for applicants. They supported improved border control and harsher punishment for employers who hire illegals. They opposed guest worker programs and continued to support the family unification principle as the cornerstone of the immigration system. Republicans had little to say about immigration or border control. They pro- posed total reform in INS and believed family unification should be narrowed to wives and children. They opposed a national ID card and believed that English should be made the common language of the nation. Neither plank was strong. Illegal immigration, especially over the southern border, had become a national disgrace. The issue of immigration had become so politicized since the 1960s that neither party had the courage to take the stand that was good for the nation for fear of alienating prospective voters.

ENVIRONMENT

The Democratic approach to the environment was global, symbolized by the desire to ratify the Kyoto Treaty, which would commit the United States to an international agreement of pollution reduction. Republicans specifically stated that environmental concerns must move forward in harness with eco- nomic concerns. They too supported pollution reduction but did not approve the Kyoto approach, which they regarded as ineffective and an invasion of Amer- ican sovereignty. Environmentalists made considerable progress during Clin- ton's administration, a fact that was not met with universal approval. Bush's balanced approach seemed more fitting and more consistent with the indepen- dent American character.

EDUCATION

Both political parties publicly recognized that education in America was in trouble. The difference between them was political and philosophical. Democrats were heavily supported by unions, especially teachers' unions, whose views influenced Democratic policy and opinions on such things as federal involvement, federal spending, teacher education, teacher testing, student test- ing, class size, curriculum, etc. Republicans had no similar alliances. On the philosophical level, Democrats typically see an active roll for the federal gov- ernment in public education problems (school lunches, preschool programs, etc.); Republicans tend to stand back and allow state and local government do the work. This is an example of preaching to the choir. Neither platform said anything that would steal voters from the other.

LAW AND ORDER

Democrats were proud of gun control bills they passed; they wanted a drug czar and tougher enforcement of drug laws. They opposed racial profiling and sought tougher punishment for crimes committed against women and children. Republicans were a better bet to protect gun owners and had a better record of dealing with crime. Democrats were seldom regarded as tough policemen because their enforcement policies became entangled with their political alliances.

ABORTION

Democrats unequivocally supported abortion; Republicans just as firmly opposed it. This had been a nation-dividing issue since the Supreme Court rendered its decision on *Roe v. Wade* (1973). There was little or nothing that could be said on either side to change the status quo. Polls on the issue favored Bush.[16]

WAR AND PEACE

Clinton slashed the size of the military during a period when the terrorist threat was growing, nuclear arms were proliferating, and the Middle East was typically on the edge of war. In the face of the actual record, the Democratic pledge to "develop a modern military force" and "to introduce new high-tech weapons" and to equip our forces to resist "unconventional attack" rang hollow. Republicans pointed to the downsized military that had been overused, the equipment that was as tired as the men and the 25 percent of the combat units that, for one reason or another, were unfit for combat duty. Defense spending as a percent of GDP was at its lowest since before Pearl Harbor. Service morale was low because of enforced social experimentation; such things Republicans promised to change. This was not the time for a downsized military and, arguably, there might never again be such a time if America is to survive. Military action approved by Clinton got, at best, mixed reviews. It was a time for strong leadership. Gore's relationship with Clinton hurt him in all things military.

THE ECONOMY

Unemployment remained stubbornly high, but it was lower than the rate Democrats inherited. Clinton ended up with a lower misery index than he inherited.[17] But there was a current-day pain that dimmed the bloom on this economic rose. The price of crude oil nearly doubled in 2000[18] and prices at the pump jumped by one-third,[19] bringing wails of dismay from America's drivers. Higher oil prices also tended to exacerbate another growing difference between the political parties: How shall America be powered in the future?

ENERGY

It is by itself informative that Democrats had no energy plank in their platform statement. "Protecting Our Environment" was the heading under which energy was discussed, as if the production of energy was a hurdle to overcome to protect nature. The language used dramatizes the nation's responsibility to be "the stewards of God's creation" and the need to ratify "a strong international treaty to combat global warming."

Democrats bragged they had stopped "drilling and mining" on America's "wild places." Their guiding principle was "We have to do what's right for our Earth because it is the moral thing to do." Their more direct solutions to the energy crisis included more efficient automobiles and the use of technology to clean up the nation's present consumption of fossil fuels—oil, gas and coal. Republicans pointed to the drop in domestic production, the closing of refineries, the refusal to build nuclear plants, the neglect of hydro power and the road-blocking of new development projects as the fruit of Democratic policy, informed by out-of-control environmentalists, which Republicans claimed was the core of the energy problem. They proposed to seek energy from all national sources until dependence on foreign oil was reduced to acceptable levels; to invest in renewable forms of energy and to sponsor conservation. The rise in the cost of gasoline in 2000 was a reminder to drivers of what OPEC had done to America in the past and provided a contemporary edge to the Republican argument.

TAX POLICY/BUDGET/DEBT

Democratic spending proposals were intimidating; Republican tax cuts and reorganization notions had followers. This issue was not a slam dunk for Democrats. They could show good numbers, but taxes, gasoline and unemployment were high.[20] On the substantive side, there was merit to the argument that Clinton had ridden on the crest of the Reagan boom, which had only sputtered for a few months under President George H.W. Bush. The Clinton surplus during his last four years in office was created by maneuvers that could not be repeated (but it was a political reality).[21]

CIVIL RIGHTS

The time of daily battles over civil rights was passed. The era of full implementation began in the 1960s and was continuing. Progress of blacks in all phases of American life was significant. Education was the current problem of major significance. Unfortunately, it could not be attacked on those grounds alone. The black family as an institution had collapsed. Poor performance in schools was a by-product of this. Solving this problem was the challenge of the future. (The disintegration of the black family and the need for a total overhaul of the immigration system were inextricably linked with the education problem.)

SOCIAL PROGRAMS

The average voter has no idea abut how much his government has changed since Great Society programs were introduced in the 1960s. Thereafter the gap between defense spending and the cost of the welfare state steadily narrowed until, in 1971, it was 1.2 times more expensive to pay for it than it was to pay for the defense of the nation (in 2000, it was 3.8 times more expensive). What the voters did know, however, was this: Social Security and Medicare programs were in significant financial trouble and payroll taxes would not long support payment obligations. Democrats had a record of protecting these programs, both of which were aimed at the elderly, which could explain why they gave such terse treatment to the subject, satisfying themselves with a promise to modernize, protect and improve them. Republicans pointed out financial weaknesses of both programs and laid out detailed solutions, which involved personal savings and investment accounts, more personal freedom and responsibility and less government dependence. Republican observations about the vulnerability of the programs were accurate, but their proposed solutions did not hit senior minds as powerfully as Democratic arguments hit their fears. Younger voters should have paid more attention.

FOREIGN POLICY

(1) Russia would lead the list of foreign policy concerns for as long as it held so many nuclear weapons. Democrats worked well at arms reduction with the Russians and promised more of the same. Republicans promised to do likewise. Democrats did it; voters will give them the credit for it. (2) Both parties seemed to be feeling their way toward a sensible relationship with the emerging powerhouse of China. Nothing startling was said on either side. Developing an enduring relationship with China would take time and patience. There was some political mileage for Republicans here because of their clear stand over Taiwan and because under Nixon and Kissinger relations with China had been first established. (3) In Iraq it was American policy, formed by Clinton, to remove Saddam Hussein from power. Democrats pledged again in 2000 to do so, using force "as necessary." Saddam was still in power in 2000 and refusing to allow inspectors to investigate his weapons of mass destruction (WMD) capabilities. He was also still financing terrorists in Palestine. It was generally believed he had chemical and biological weapons. Republicans promised to rebuild the coalition that was used in the Kuwait War to bring Saddam to heel and to take immediate action if signs appeared that he had, or was developing,

nuclear weapons. Democrats had their chance to defang Saddam and failed. (4) Both parties agreed that Iran was seeking nuclear weapons and shouldn't have them, and that he was supporting terrorists in Palestine and elsewhere and should stop. Democrats had been ineffective in controlling Iran. (5) Both parties agreed to continue the negotiating process involving Israel. Although Clinton failed to make a deal, he tried hard to do so and came close. He was given credit for making a strong effort. (6) OPEC nations bumped the price of oil in 2000, demonstrating once more the vulnerability of the American economy to foreign whim. This is the American energy problem in Arab guise. Neither party in their platforms addressed how to deal with the OPEC nations; both dealt with the problem as an energy question. The quickest way to get away from Arab control is to become energy independent; the fastest way to independence is to turn the American energy industry loose on developing as much energy from natural resources as possible and to rapidly decrease the amount of gasoline needed by American vehicles. Democrats resisted attempts to develop fossil fuels and nuclear energy; Republicans supported both. Conservation and the long-term development of renewable sources of energy (water, hydro, etc.) were approved by both, but timing and degree of each party were different. (7) If North Korea had the nuclear bomb or was close to it in 2000, it meant they had cheated on the treaty they had signed several years earlier. Democrats didn't admit the existence of the bomb and promised to watch the situation closely. Republicans said the bomb existed and was symptomatic of the growing pro-liferation problem. North Korea was cheating but evidence was not conclusive, and a treaty did exist. The fears of the day favored Republicans on all national defense issues. (8) The idea was supposed to be to reduce the proliferation of nuclear weapons in the interests of world survival. India and Pakistan became nuclear powers on Clinton's watch, and perhaps North Korea as well. Iran was on the hunt; Iraq had the brainpower to get moving as soon as the world turned its back. Not a good record. And Republicans pointed to it.

LEADERSHIP

There was no question about the experience and the apparent competency of Gore; tangential questions concerning his ethics did not appear to be very damaging. Questions about competency were better addressed to Bush, who had never held a federal position and who had no experience in international affairs. Added to this was the decision of the major media and the liberal community to portray him as a buffoon because he was not a glib public speaker. He overcame most of this bias by his performance during the debates and by the naturalness of his character that voters could see during the campaign.

Those who view party platforms to be irrelevant aspects of the political scene are the same observers who like to say that there isn't a dime's worth of difference between the two political parties once they get into power. The danger of that statement is that there is enough truth in it to convince many people of its validity. Neither party, once in charge, normally governs as it would like. The requirement to accommodate forces both sides toward the center and develops the appearance of sameness.

But the instinct to do otherwise is powerfully evident in party platforms, a fact worthy of note for one simple reason: Sometimes the need for accommodation isn't present because the party in power has such a majority in Congress that it can do anything it wishes. In such an instance, the party platform becomes a blueprint for action — a clear warning of what lies ahead. Democrats under FDR and LBJ had such power, and in both cases the nation lurched radically to the left. Nobody who read the party platforms during those years was surprised.

The ultimate protection of the people from tyranny is the Constitution. When a single political party controls the executive and legislative branches of government with veto-proof majorities, only the Supreme Court can stop a president who has the support of his party from becoming a dictator. If Supreme Court justices believe in and support the Constitution, the freedom of the people in such a case has a powerful protector. If on the other hand the Court is not devoted to the Constitution but instead substitutes logic that is "suitable for the times," freedom is at risk. The lesson of history is: Fight for the Constitution and against those who would weaken it.

Party platforms for the year 2000 were extraordinarily long, but in terms of their general substance they fit the familiar mold. Democrats, since Wilson in the election of 1912, had pursued the perfect society. Where possible, they had created a network of cradle to grave programs designed to ease the way of citizens through life. Theirs was a paternalistic approach to government; their tendency was to think of Americans in terms of groups (men/women, black/white, rich/poor, etc.); they favored an activist Supreme Court. Republicans supported some progressive ideas and programs, but continued to espouse such things as individual freedom, liberty and responsibility in a free market system. They believed in a small, tightly controlled federal government, states' rights and a Supreme Court manned by judges who interpret law but do not make it.

The Democratic Party of 2000 was focused, most members being devoted to its progressive principles. The Republican Party was fractured, with one segment eager to adopt the popular progressive ideas that seemed to win elections and those who believed the nation had strayed too far from its roots. The party barely clung together during elections in order to remain competitive. Republicans faced a bleak future if its members could not once more agree on the viability of the Constitution as a governing document for modern society.

The party platforms made it abundantly clear that two parties with different visions were being presented to the people. Their choice would either affirm the progressive approach to governance offered by Democrats, or they would choose to follow the ideas of a new leader with more conventional ideas.

Thumbnail Sketches of Top Candidates

Vice President Al Gore was the obvious heir apparent to the controversial Clinton presidency. George W. Bush, the governor of Texas, was the history-making nominee of the Republican Party who, if elected, would be the second man in history to follow his father into that high office. Gore was a lifelong politician with a deep political pedigree; Bush was the latest member of one of America's great political families to offer his services to the public.

Gore was known as a prolific speaker and a prodigious debater. Bush was a straight talking Texan who came straight to the point using words that, the press learned, were not always the correct ones. In an understated way, he had performed well in Texas debates, being cool under fire. It shaped up as an interesting race between opposites—the polished professional politician versus the good old boy from Texas.

ALBERT A. GORE, DEMOCRAT

Born: 1948; **Education:** Harvard and Vanderbilt universities; **Wife:** Mary Aitcheson; **Children:** Four.[22]

Al Gore was born in Washington, D.C., but grew up on the family farm in Carthage, Tennessee. He spent plenty of time in Washington because his father was a U.S. senator; his mother, the second woman to graduate from Vanderbilt law school, was also a busy professional. Due to his parents' careers, the Thompson family managed the family farm and had a large influence on Gore as a young man. Gore entered Harvard at age seventeen where he majored in government. And it was during those years that he met a professor for geophysics and oceanography, Roger Reveille, who stimulated in him a lifelong curiosity—the impact of CO_2 emissions on global temperature.

Gore was opposed to the Vietnam War and in correspondence with his father referred to America's anticommunism as "a National obsession" and a "psychological illness." He was a full-fledged pot-smoking member of the anti-war movement of the 1960s.

Gore graduated from Harvard in 1969 and, despite his opposition to the war, he enlisted in the army in 1970 to avoid the embarrassment his father — who was running for reelection (he lost)—would have to bear if he refused to serve. While in the army, he married Mary "Tipper" Aitcheson in a ceremony at the magnificent Washington Cathedral.

Gore did not have what one could call a bloody, rugged military experience. The Vietnam War took place between 1955 and 1975. Gore was sixteen when it started. He was eighteen in 1966 and twenty-two when in 1970 he joined the army and served as an army journalist in Vietnam from Christmas until May 1971—about five months. There are those who question the authenticity of some of Gore's "war stories."

From 1971 to 1976, Gore studied at Vanderbilt (theology and law) and Harvard (law) during the course of which he conducted a series of investigations that, according to him, sent many crooked politicians to jail, a claim that was later to be shown as another of his now-famous embellishments.

Politics! It had been his father's life and it beckoned to him as the irresistible lure that took him from his rather wandering lifestyle to one of service and purpose. He ran for a seat in the House of Representatives in 1976 and won. He was twenty-eight years old. Gore remained in the House until 1985, at which time he moved into the seat formerly held by his father, a U.S. senator from Tennessee. But this wasn't enough—Gore's ambition was in high gear. He sought the Democratic nomination in 1988 and won seven primaries and caucuses, but it wasn't enough to stop the bid of Gov. Michael Dukakis (MA).

Throughout his career, Gore's passionate interest in the relationship between CO_2 emissions and global warming never waned, and it intensified during his years in the Senate. He published a book on the subject in 1992 that has been translated into thirty-two languages.

Then came the election of 1992, when he was forty-four. He was not ready for another run at the gold ring. But when Bill Clinton came calling with his invitation to join him on the Democratic ticket for that year, he agreed to participate, and he did so effectively. Gore had important duties with Clinton and his influence was seen early when, in addition to supporting Clinton's huge tax increase, he proposed and Clinton backed a CO_2 tax designed to punish polluters and move investment capital toward renewable sources of energy. The entire energy industry rebelled and eventually the proposal was pulled back. But Gore was now close to the top where great power lived. His zeal to curb carbon dioxide emissions grew by the day, and he would keep the issue of his life alive.

Gore was an effective vice president. He helped the president diplomatically (e.g., Ukraine); he defanged Ross Perot, one of the administration's harshest critics on NAFTA, in a television debate; he gave parents control over sex and violence on television with his V-chip; he advised the president on Washington politics; he led the movement to shrink the payroll of the federal government, etc. Reelection in 1996 over the weak candidacy of Sen. Bob Dole (KS) was a cakewalk for Clinton and Gore. Both men were tainted, however, because of the suspicious origins of campaign funds.

Gore made another bid for recognition of his environmental concerns with his support of the Kyoto Treaty. The president backed him, but nobody else in town did. Consensus was that the shock to the U.S. economy would be too severe, and the effort would be fruitless because major polluters like China and India refused to cooperate.

Gore was not involved in Clinton's romantic diversions. He remained far removed from the scandal and emerged unscathed, as he should have. Guilt by association, however, is never totally stamped out. As he pondered the value of the still popular Clinton to his presidential race, he measured as well the downside of embracing a colleague with a noxious personal background.

GEORGE W. BUSH, REPUBLICAN

Born: 1946; **Education:** Yale; Harvard (MBA); **Wife:** Laura Welch; **Children:** Two.[23]

George Bush was born in New Haven, Connecticut, while his father, a naval hero of World War II, was a sophomore at Yale. He and his parents, George and Barbara, lived for a time in apartments provided for returning veterans and their families. But it was Westward Ho for the Bushes when father George moved to seek his fortune in the Texas oil boom. He was successful commercially and, as he put it, they lived the American dream: "High school football on Friday night; little league and the neighborhood barbecue." But there was tragedy too: their daughter, Robin Bush, died of leukemia before her fourth birthday, an event that left a permanent mark on the family.

There are those who point to faults in their parents or dark chapters in their childhood to explain quirks or flaws in their character. George isn't one of them. His parents are warm, exceptional people and Midland, Texas, was "an idyllic place to grow up," according to a close friend of Bush's. Bush, who still has a close relationship with his parents, expressed it another way: "I'd like to be buried in Midland." To him it was, is and always will be home.

Bush, like his father, is a baseball addict, not as talented, but just as devoted and aggressive, according to those who knew him at San Jacinto Junior High School, where he also played football (quarterback) and served as class president. After San Jacinto, Bush settled firmly into his father's footsteps and moved to Phillips Academy in Andover, Massachusetts. He played some sports, mostly basketball, but the level of competition finally overcame his limited skills and they occupied less of his time. He was popular at Andover and did well. Yale was next. It wasn't comfortable for him and he didn't do as well, by his own admission.[24]

Bush grew up in a Republican family and was himself a Republican when he went to Yale. But he soon learned the Yale his father graduated from was not the Yale he was attending. Since Vietnam, it — like many universities — had swung left. To some extent, he was the proverbial fish-out-of-water during his undergraduate years. For example, during a conversation with the university chaplain, Bush, a freshman, mentioned his father, who had just been defeated in a close race for the Senate. The chaplain replied, "Oh, yes, I know your father. And frankly, he was beaten by a better man." Bush never forgot the tactless remark.

Bush is easy to underrate because of his laid back manner, and because he allows media to put him down, often without comment. Others see more. For example, a former special counsel to President Clinton and adviser to Al Gore,

Lanny Davis, said, "This notion of intellectual lightness is totally missing the point.... George coasted through Yale courses.... But don't mistake that for not being intellectually acute. My memory of him is that he was an astute observer of people ... and had an incredible talent for getting along with them. I tell my fellow Democrats not to underestimate him."

Bush graduated in 1968 (majoring in history) during the height of the Vietnam War and qualified for flight school in Georgia, where he trained for a year. Thereafter he served in the states as a flying (F-102) member of the Texas National Guard until his discharge in 1973. At various times, he was granted leaves of absence to participate in political campaigns. As a member of the Guard, Bush had to have a minimum number of flying hours per year. During the latter part of his reserve career he was grounded for lack of training time, which made him eligible for the draft. But the war by that time was winding down; he was not called and he was honorably discharged.

Bush was twenty-seven when the war was over and he headed for Harvard Business School. Apparently exposure to one prestigious liberal eastern college did not blind him to the benefits attached to attending another. He was older than many of the students and his ambitions were entirely different from most of them. They dreamt of careers on Wall Street; he sat at the back of the class and made his plans for a career in his beloved Texas.

The oil industry beckoned to Bush as it had to his father. He returned to Midland with his MBA degree from Harvard. He married Laura in 1977, and in 1978, now a settled businessman, he formed Arbusto Energy, which later (1982) became Bush Exploration. In 1984, Bush Exploration merged with Spectrum 7, with Bush serving as chairman and CEO; in 1986, the company was sold to Harken Energy. Bush, now forty years old, was out of the oil business with a pocketful of money. His father was vice president to Ronald Reagan from 1981 to 1988. With no intention to downplay Bush's accomplishments as a businessman, it is worth noting that having such a powerful father is not exactly a liability.

Politics always fascinated Bush, probably because of his father's career and his lifelong involvement in it. Whatever the reason, the sale of the oil business gave Bush the freedom to engage in his first political race. He ran for Congress in 1978 and won the nomination of his party but lost in the final election. The defeat sent him back to the world of business and gave him the chance to reignite one of the flames of his life — baseball. He formed a syndicate, bought the Texas Rangers, organized public financing, built a state-of-the-art ballpark and, with himself as CEO, made the franchise a profit maker that eventually ballooned his $600,000 investment into a return of $15 million.

George Bush had a "thing" for then Gov. Ann Richards of Texas. He does not take kindly to those who aim personal insults at his father, which he believes Richards did when she said at the 1988 Democratic national convention about his father: "He can't help it if he was born with a silver foot in his mouth." She also referred to him as "shrub" and as "some jerk running for public office." Apart from political satisfaction, George Bush must have personally relished sending Gov. Ann Richards to the political boneyard when he challenged and defeated her in the 1994 gubernatorial race in Texas with almost 54 percent of the vote. His brother Jeb ran for governor of Florida in the same year and lost. (He returned in 1988 and won.)

Bush had a successful first term despite the fact that Congress was dominated by Democrats. His ability to pull people together was such that it was difficult to find anyone to run against him in 1998. He won 94 percent of the counties and about 45 percent of the Latino vote. The overwhelming size of his victory immediately drew the attention of party leaders, activists and money men. He was an automatic presidential candidate — perhaps the frontrunner. Bush formed a presidential exploratory committee in October 1999. He was in the game.

Election Tone

In every election, one party usually has the historical advantage, in the sense that one candidate's antecedents carry more current political wallop than the others. In this case, Bush had Reagan and his father to brag about; Gore had Clinton. No contest. Bush had the bragging rights. Presumably out of deference to his father, he didn't make as much of the Reagan legacy as he could have.

Al Gore was fifty-two, Bush fifty-four. Both were in the prime of their lives; both were in good condition. They had met, because both had spent considerable time in Washington. But the relationship wasn't a close one, nor would it have been under normal circumstances. They were dissimilar personalities— Gore reserved, aloof and formal, and Bush open, accessible and friendly. To the extent that personality would lure votes in the election, Bush would be the winner.

The lack of animus between the candidates does not mean that the election was low key, or boring —far from it. And Supreme Court rulings were one of the reasons for this. The Court in those years was led by Supreme Court justices Warren Burger (1969–86) and William Rehnquist, who were assisted by fourteen assistant justices.[25]

Many of the most controversial decisions made by the Court had taken place during previous years, but new issues arose and the old ones were rehashed over and over. A sample of the cases heard — that had continuing impact in 2000 — since the last close election in 1976 follows:

- 1977: State law forbidding nontherapeutic abortions under Medicaid is constitutional (*Beal v. Doe*).

- 1978: The use of race as a principal criterion for admission to college is constitutional (*Regents v. Bakke*).
- 1979: An affirmative action program in a factory that seeks to eliminate patterns of segregation is constitutional if it does not prohibit white employees from advancing (*United Steelworkers v. Webber*).
- 1980: Congress has the power to establish set-aside programs designed to provide work for minority companies (*Fullilove v. Klutznick*).
- 1985: It is unconstitutional for teachers to conduct prayer services during the day (*Wallace v. Jaffree*).
- 1987: A state mandate to teach "creation science" is unconstitutional (*Edwards v. Aguillard*).
- 1989: The display of a crèche inside a courthouse is unconstitutional (*Allegheny County v. ACLU*).
- 1989: A state may withhold access to its facilities for the purpose of elective abortions (*Webster v. Reproductive Health Services*).
- 1989: A citizen has a First Amendment right to burn the American flag as a sign of protest against public policy (*Texas v. Johnson*).
- 1989: A requirement to award a fixed percent of all civic contracts to minority companies represents an unconstitutional quota (*Richard v. J.A. Croson Co.*).
- 1990: If a school permits some school clubs, it must permit Christian clubs (*Westside School District v. Mergens*).
- 1990: Congress does not have the power to make flag burning illegal as it is protected speech (*U.S. v. Eichman*).
- 1992: State law that requires a woman to inform her husband before having an abortion is unconstitutional (*Planned Parenthood v. Casey*).
- 1993: If school property is made available to nonreligious groups, it must also be available to religious groups (*Center Moriches School District v. Lamb's Chapel*).
- 1995: When a school provides funding for student publications, it cannot withdraw it solely on the grounds that the content is religious or manifests a particular belief (*Rosenberger v. Univ. of Virginia*).
- 1997: There is no constitutional right to assisted suicide (*Washington v. Glucksburg*).
- 2000: Partial-birth abortions are protected by the Fourteenth Amendment (*Stenberg v. Carhart*).
- 2000: Prayers recited before sporting events are unconstitutional (*Santa Fe v. Doe*).

There were two other decisions of importance that had little or no impact on the tone of the election campaigns: (1) A serious attempt by Congress to mandate reductions in the costs of government programs was ruled unconstitutional by the Court (*Bowsher v. Synar*, 1986)—to accomplish such an end would take a constitutional amendment; (2) the Supreme Court ended the legal war between Bush and Gore over the Florida vote, and the presidency. This ruling made Bush haters out of many Democrats that lasted for eight years.

Abortion, prayer of any kind and affirmative action were issues that kept returning to the Court in slightly modified form. With every ruling on such sensitive issues, a life was affected, an attitude was formed and a vote was influenced. Just as it was true that proponents of the progressive ideology had changed government since the early decades of the twentieth century, so had the Supreme Court — mostly since the 1960s — changed the mores and the behavior of Americans. It is likely that every voter in 2000, to some degree, acted as they did because of something the Court decided.

THE CANDIDATES FROM A DEMOCRATIC PERSPECTIVE

Clinton, with all of his personal faults, was still the popular representative of the modern generation. Dissimilar though Gore was, he carried the flag of the same cause. And his high energy supporters were determined he would succeed.

Bush, a product of the same generation, was regarded by Gore supporters as a deserter. He was not just the political opposition; he had sold out to the older generation that opposed their attitudes toward welfare, education, religion, abortion, sex, drugs, homosexuality, marriage, etc. If he wasn't defeated, America would be headed back toward the stone age.

THE CANDIDATES FROM A REPUBLICAN PERSPECTIVE

Gore himself wasn't an issue, but he symbolized the continuation of Clinton and the progressive agenda. The president's sexual antics in the White House, the politicization of the nation's most revered home, the scandalous pardons at the end of Clinton's regime, etc., had caused a feeling among activist Republicans that was akin to hate, that went beyond political competition. They wanted him and everything that reminded them of him out of sight, including Gore. They wanted to purify the White House with the presence of a decent president and first lady. This was not a political goal; this was a mission. Bush had an impressive professional record. He had lived a decent life with his wife, Laura, and their two daughters. They subscribed to conventional values. The Republicans believed George and Laura Bush would re-dignify the White House and George would operate an efficient government.

This was the typical liberal versus conservative imbroglio made more piquant by the flaws in the Democratic icon, Bill Clinton. As usual, the happenings during past administrations, especially the most recent one, provided most of the fodder for the current campaign. The slant of the candidates on current issues, and their personal foibles, present and past, rounded out the subject matter of the contest.

Regarding the personal lives and characteristics of the candidates, a few items loomed that might have been, but were not, destructive:

- Gore's youthful behavior: The aloof, proper, remote Gore observed on the campaign trail had been a pot-smoking, anti-everything college student who didn't straighten out until he entered politics.
- Gore's military record: Gore was antimilitary during the Vietnam War and ended up as an army journalist only because he didn't want to embarrass his father, who was fighting for political survival. His military career lasted for five months.
- Bush's youthful behavior: Bush once said, "When I was young and foolish, I was young and foolish." He was right. A heavy drinker, he settled down to a life of sobriety when he married Laura.
- Bush's military record: Bush served in the Texas National Guard as a fighter pilot, which required him to maintain his skills by flying a minimum number of hours per year. He met his standards until the final months of the war when he was grounded for failing to comply. The war was almost over and so he was given an honorable discharge.

The issues of youthful peccadilloes and military records never rose to the level of major concern for the candidates, probably because Gore didn't want to talk about it and Bush didn't feel apologetic. But some in the media did their best to make it otherwise.

Those who follow politics keep their eyes on news reports during the final ten days of the campaigns. This is stiletto time, the period when those who are so inclined release the stab in the back — a late-breaking story of a scandalous nature against a candidate. So it was on November 3, 2000, when Alison Mitchell of the *New York Times* uncovered the news that Gov. Bush had been arrested for drunken driving twenty-four years before. The advisability of rushing such an election-influencing story into the news is subject to question; its impact on voters will never be known. But it shows how "little" things can become big things if the press wants them to be. George Bush admitted the accuracy of the charge. He stopped drinking in 1986.

Bush was also a sitting target for those who measure intelligence by one's command of rhetoric, a skill that did not come with the Bush genes. He provided some beauties to ridicule him with: "This thaw took a while to thaw — it's going to take a while to unthaw." "Anyone engaging in illegal transactions will be caught and persecuted." "And they have no disregard for human life."[26] There's no question these are beauties, and repeating them was the method used by Bush's opponents to suggest that he had the brain of a walnut. It was a clever, effective and durable insult.

From the outset, it was clear the election was going to be close. According to a *New York Times* story in September, "The race is so competitive ... that the difference in support between Mr. Gore and Mr. Bush is statistically insignificant."[27] Polls suggested that voters found both men equipped to lead. The question with Bush was readiness; with Gore, it was likeability.

The Kennedy/Nixon race had firmly established the principle that how much a candidate was liked was, to many voters, as important as how much he was admired for his ability to lead. This was not lost on Gore's handlers, who were very much aware of the cold exterior of their charge and of his tendency to become pedantic, and they did their best to package him as a warmer man. Likewise, Bush's handlers were aware of their advantage, and they scheduled their man to appear in settings where his natural warmth was projected.

As the campaigns continued it became apparent that the readiness issue had become a central one and that the debates would probably settle it as well as it could be settled. Whether to have them and how many to have were among the most important subjects discussed during the early weeks. The Gore camp saw them as their opportunity to crush the nincompoop from Texas and ride to victory by a wide margin. The Bush camp, who knew their man was underrated (he had done well in Texas debates against the charismatic Ann Richards), saw the debates as the vehicle that would establish Bush's readiness to serve as the nation's president. Three debates in October were agreed upon.[28]

The other issues were a matter of thrust and parry, with neither candidate moving the needle on the polls by much. Gore bragged about the economy: Bush reminded voters that except for a few months under his father, Clinton and Gore had ridden the wave of the Reagan boom. Gore said that the answer to the energy problem was to move away from fossil fuels, tax CO_2 emissions, promote renewable sources of energy and join the world in fighting global warming. Bush replied that reliance on foreign oil had to be broken, that natural resources and renewable sources should be developed, all of it to be done in an environmentally responsible way. *New York Times* column headings of September 30, 2000, sum up the arguments nicely: "Bush ... Endorses New U.S. Drilling to Curb Prices"; "Gore Says Bush Plan will Cause Lasting Damage to the Environment."

The candidates' solutions to Medicare took more of their time than they gave to Social Security. Concerning the latter, Bush had no effective response to Gore's claim that Bush intended to raid the (nonexistent) Social Security lockbox. Fear to older citizens was a more powerful motivator than Bush's arguments for reform. Without going into the details, it's sufficient to say that Gore's solution to Medicare was more federal control; Bush wanted less federal control and more personal savings accounts of various kinds.

But behind the issues, there was the Clinton factor. It was difficult to find someone he hadn't offended by some aspect of his behavior — sexual, political use of the White House, questionable campaign contributions, perjury, scandalous pardons, etc. On the other side, he was a charismatic man. He carried the torch of his generation; the flaws within him did not project externally (as they did with Nixon), and he had been the president during some good times, which, for many, was a sign of competence. These were offsets to the misdeeds. The net effect on voters can never be known.

Television Debates

Three debates were scheduled: October 3, 11, and 17, 2000. Instead of the usual panel, there was to be one moderator, Jim Lehrer of PBS. The first debate was held in Boston, the second in Winston-Salem, North Carolina, and the third in St. Louis.[29]

Debate 1

The moderator could ask questions and he allowed time to each candidate to question the other. The primary subject matter was supposed to be oil and energy policy. But the format guaranteed that subject matter would roam. And it did: Bush's experience, Medicare, energy, abortion, the selection of Supreme Court judges, foreign policy (Yugoslavia), when to use military power, how to use our new-found prosperity, tax policy, education, government's role during a crisis, Social Security, campaign finance reform,

There was no personal animosity between the candidates since they only casually knew each other. But Gore was the physical manifestation of what has herein been referred to as the Clinton factor, and Bush reflected the attitude of many of his supporters with some of his responses to Lehrer's questions: (1) "It's time for a fresh start. It's time for a new look. It's time for a fresh start after a season of cynicism.... I don't know the man [Gore] well, but I've been disappointed about how he and his administration have conducted the fundraising affairs. You know, going to a Buddhist temple and then claiming it wasn't a fundraiser isn't my view of responsibility." (2) "You know, this man has no credibility on the issue [campaign finance reform]. As a matter of fact, I read in the *New York Times* where he said he co-sponsored the McCain-Feingold Campaign Fundraising Bill. But he wasn't in the Senate with Senator Feingold. And so, ... what you need to know about me is I will uphold the law, I'm going to have an attorney general that enforces the law. The time for campaign funding reform is after the election. This man has outspent me and the special interests are outspending me. And I am not going to lay down my arms in the middle of the campaign for somebody who has got no credibility on the issue." Gore, it seems, was not on Bush's list of "most admired" men.

Debate 2

The format was that of a conversation. Topics covered included priorities, America's international image, America's international obligations, the Middle

East, Iraq, Yugoslavia, use of the military, Rwanda, racial profiling, discrimination, gay marriage, gun control, Medicare/health care, tax policy, and the environment. The discussion on environment and global warming was special because of the enduring interest in those topics during the years that followed. Gore said, "We must make the rescue of our environment the central organizing principle for civilization and there must be a wrenching transformation to save the planet." Bush said, "But I don't think we know the solution to global warming yet. And I don't think we've got all the facts.... I tell you one thing ... I'm not going to let the United States carry the burden for cleaning up the world's air. Like Kyoto Treaty would have done. China and India were exempted from that treaty."

Debate 3

Questions came from voters in the audience who were introduced by the moderator. Only the moderator could ask follow-up questions. Topics included health, cost of drugs, nationalized health care, education, taxes, Medicare, the Middle East, use of the military, gun control, family farms, inheritance tax, morality in the nation, voter apathy, diversity, capital punishment. This debate was filled with softball questions that candidates easily answered.

PBS did a post-debate analysis of the debate, hosted by Gwen Ifill, that featured Paul Gigot (conservative) and Mark Shields (liberal). A summary of their views on the first debate follows[30]: Gigot opined, "I think he [Bush] did show that he could go toe to toe with Gore." Shields said, "I think that George Bush did meet a threshold tonight." Neither man claimed a knockout for their candidate.

From there, it was all uphill for Bush. According to Gallup polls, he trailed Gore by eights points when the debates began; when they finished, he was four points ahead — a turnaround of twelve points. This was the largest turnaround in the forty-year history of such polls.[31]

Going into the debates, it was the objective of the super-confident Gore to demolish his opponent and go on to a decisive victory. The Gallup poll said he missed his mark by a wide margin; it was Bush's objective to erase the concerns of voters about his readiness to lead. The Gallup poll said he proved his point.

The Nader Factor

Ralph Nader headed the Green Party. He had no chance to win the election, and he knew it. Some people saw him as the evil presence who stole the election from Al Gore. The reason for that position is clear. The election turned on who won Florida. Bush won the state by the thinnest of margins; more than ninety-seven thousand Floridians voted for Nader, a left of center politician. Absent his presence on the ballot, it is reasonably theorized that the same voters would have chosen Gore, which would have made him the clear winner.

Nader, born in 1934, has been an anticorporate advocate for consumerist causes since the late 1950s. He first ran for the presidency in 1996, and he's been at it ever since. He has yet to win an electoral vote. As Winston Churchill once observed, democracy is a sloppy process. To a great extent, this is due to the freedom of speech that is permitted. It is a blessing to have it as a right, but sometimes it does more harm than good. Gore might agree that the Nader candidacy of 2000 was such a case.

Presidential Campaigns

The media to a great extent establishes the tone of any campaign. It is they who pounce upon facts of their selection and make them major news, in so doing fixing the minds of voters on the things that they themselves consider important.

Poll after poll has shown the media to be predominantly liberal.[32] From this it becomes understandable why, from the beginning, Bush was labeled a dunderhead. And to make the point, the media had his malapropisms to giggle over, verbal ammunition he regularly supplied and they gleefully used. Imagine their shock in October 2000 when incoming polls showed that the guy who couldn't put his socks on by himself had demolished their liberal genius in the debates. Needless to say, the "stupid" approach to the campaign had lost much — if not all — of its thunder, as had the issue of readiness. The Texan had shown a surprising grasp of a variety of issues in wide-ranging debates.

The only baggage Gore carried into the campaign was Clinton. His leadership wasn't questioned, nor was his ability to lead. He had a good economy at his back; the nation was not involved in major warfare. But the Clinton factor gnawed at him. It had embarrassed him in the debates. Should he use the still popular Clinton in his campaign or keep him in the rear?

GORE CAMPAIGN

Gore, like many before and after him in the political arena, found himself moving away from principles of conviction to those of political convenience.[33] When he ran for president in 1988 he opposed federal funding for abortion, he supported a moment of silent prayer in schools and the interstate sale of handguns. In 2000, he was a different man. He promised to nominate judges who supported abortion rights, gay rights and a clear separation between religion and government.

He had an aggressive gay agenda. Clinton had appointed 150 homosexuals to government posts. Gore implied he would continue that policy and would also lift the "don't ask, don't tell" policy of the military toward homosexuals. His outreach also included a promise to support hate crimes legislation.

Gore had expected to be on the offensive throughout the presidential campaign, but gradually the opposite became the case. First, of course, there was the Clinton factor and the direct or indirect charges that he was personally tied to the habits and practices of his predecessor. But in addition to this, Bush's taunt during the debates ("this man has no credibility") nipped at his heels, supported by his past exaggerations, and his fund-raising practices. In short, on a personal basis, he had to contend with two streams of incoming fire, one that required him to defend Clinton and the other to defend himself. Gore had no response to the shots against Clinton's personal record, and few effective responses to explain his own fund-raising missteps.

Finally, he had the personality issue to contend with. Bush was likable; Gore wasn't. His handlers did their best to warm him up, but try as they might he inevitably came across as exciting as yesterday's prunes. The hope finally became that experience and competence would overcome dullness. Just as personal issues put him on the defensive, so did the debate on the issues, once one of his greatest strengths. Bush's credibility had grown; Gore's ascendancy on issues shrank, especially after the debates. He was no longer the master giving lessons to a presidential wannabe; he was in the political fight of his life with a surprisingly capable man from Texas.

One of Gore's most critical campaign decisions was how to handle Clinton. Perhaps the most direct way of explaining his decision is to say that he decided to run on his own record. Clinton was obvious by his absence. Gore has been criticized for this. Nobody can prove if he was right or wrong. There is strong evidence to support his decision.

He got almost fifty-one million votes, more than Bush and more than any president in history up to that time except for Ronald Reagan (1984). It's difficult to criticize the candidate who got more votes than his opponent. He lost the election because he didn't win the state of Florida, not because of the absence of Bill Clinton — or so the argument goes.

BUSH CAMPAIGN

"I have no stake in the bitter arguments of the last few years," Bush said in his nomination acceptance speech. "I want to change the tone of Washington to one of civility and respect."[34] There's little doubt that Bush was sincere when he made that statement, and he probably believed he could pull it off. After all, he had dealt with a Democratic power structure in Texas. Why not Washington? Time would tell. There is a depth to partisanship in the capital city that has made cynics out of many idealists.

A campaign without emotion is a campaign headed nowhere. And the emotion in this campaign was supplied by the man who wasn't there — Bill Clinton. And, to a lesser extent, Gore supplied some of it because he had troublesome credibility issues.[35]

"Dignity and honor" were themes that Bush hammered during the early months of his campaign. He felt the pain of his supporters and he pledged to make them proud once more of the highest office in the land, and the house of all Americans.

Not enough can be said about how much the debates meant to Bush. He had the resume and demeanor of a leader, but the readiness question had haunted him until he put it to rest in the debates. With that behind him, he could and did engage Gore on the issues.

His credibility grew as time moved on and — especially after the debates — he lowered the frequency of his references to the past and hit the issues of the day head-on, some of them the so-called untouchable ones: Social Security and Medicare, both of which were headed for financial collapse. It probably surprised both candidates that Medicare became such a hot issue as well as health care in general. Democrats saw federal solutions; Republicans saw private solutions. It is ever thus.

Bush's tone changed. Early in the campaign, when discussing issues, he just laid out his own programs, the idea being that he needed to build credentials with the public. Now, with weeks of campaigning and the debates behind him, he pointed out contrasts between his approach and Gore's. He began to challenge the so-called expert. He did this in town hall settings that brought him close to people and brought out the more attractive aspects of his character and personality. His program of tax relief and government reorganization was a bold one. The media continued to exploit Bush's verbal mistakes, but he laughed it off, often making jokes about himself and his tongue twisters.

The difference between the two candidates was clear. All other things being equal, the election of Bush would send America off on a different direction, if he had congressional support.

As Election Day neared, it was apparent it would be a close race as Bush led by less than 2 percent in the polls. He had established himself as a credible candidate; Gore, competent and experienced, had run a good race. Now the people would speak.

Election Results, 2000

The election of 2000 seemed unique at the time, but as this book has shown, it was only one of many close or disputed elections in the history of the United States, some of which had characteristics that were somewhat similar, for example[36]:

- 1824: The two strongest candidates were John Quincy Adams and Andrew Jackson. But two minority candidates, William Crawford and Henry Clay, were strong enough to deprive the winner (Jackson) of a majority of the electoral vote, which threw the election into the House for the final decision. As a result of backroom dealing with Clay, Adams emerged the winner. The House almost became the referee in the 2000 election.

- 1876: Samuel Tilden (Democrat) and Rutherford Hayes (Republican) were the contenders. The electoral vote was razor thin and in dispute in three states, South Carolina, Florida and Louisiana. A commission of sixteen men was formed to decide the winners in those states, five from the House, five from the Supreme Court, five from the Senate and one independent. The independent later resigned and a Republican replaced him. The commission did its duty and in each of the three states, Hayes was declared the winner. Under the law that established it, the decision could be challenged by both houses of Congress. The House challenged; the Senate didn't. Hayes won. The honesty of the process was in question in 1876. The same thing occurred in 2000.

- 1888: Grover Cleveland, the Democratic president, was running for a second term against Republican Benjamin Harrison. Cleveland, like Gore, won the popular vote but lost the electoral vote. After the 1888 election, Democrats railed against the electoral system; they did the same in 2000.

But no election was any closer than the 2000 contest, as is shown below:

Election Results 2000

Candidates	EV	%	Pop. (000)	Pop. %	Pop. %
Bush	271	50.5	50,455	47.9	49.7
Gore	266	49.5	50,992	48.4	50.3
Nader			2883	2.7	
Other			1067	1.0	
Total	537	100.0	105,397	100.0	100.0

EV=electoral vote; Pop. = popular vote; One elector from D.C. abstained
Source: NY Times Almanac 2009, p. 134

The vote couldn't have been much closer. Florida was ultimately the difference maker, but there were other states that were very close as well:

State	EV	Gore	Bush
Iowa	2	48.6	48.2
New Hampshire	7	46.8	48.1
New Mexico	5	47.9	47.9
Oregon	7	47.0	46.5
Wisconsin	11	47.8	47.6
Total	32		

Source: http://uselectionatlas.org/RESULTS/

One can rest assured that loyalists from the Republican Party were searching for ways to mine electoral votes (or to protect what they had) in these marginal states while the attention of the rest of the country was fastened on Florida.

Election Results 2000
States with 15+ Electoral Votes
Winning Percent

Candidates /Votes	CA 54	FL 25	IL 22	MI 18	NJ 15	NY 33	OH 21	PA 23	TX 32
Bush	41.7	48.9	42.6	46.1	40.3	35.2	50.0	46.4	59.3
Gore	53.5	48.8	54.6	51.3	56.1	60.2	46.5	50.6	38.3
Total	95.2	97.7	97.2	97.4	96.4	95.4	**96.5**	97.0	97.3

EV=electoral vote; Pop. = popular vote; Bold type = fringe vote had theoretical impact in that state.

Source: http://uselectionatlas.org/RESULTS/

It is difficult to win a presidential election in the United States without the support of the highly populated states. There are two other ways to complete that sentence:

- ...without the support of minority groups, which tend to congregate in large cities.
- ...without the support of the major media, which tend to locate in the most populous cities.

Despite this, Bush did it. He lost in six of the nine largest states: California, Illinois, Michigan, New Jersey, New York and Pennsylvania. The major media supported Gore. Bush got about one-third of the Latino vote[37] and practically none of the black vote.

Ultimately, the drama settled in Florida. It began on Election Day, November 7, 2000, and, in effect, ended with a Supreme Court decision on December 12, 2000. The days in between contained the fiercest political battle that has ever been waged in the United States, summarized as follows[38]:

- Nov. 7: At 7:50 P.M. the Associated Press (AP) declared Gore the winner in Florida; within ten minutes, the major television networks agreed. By 10:00 P.M. the networks began to back away from their call as additional votes favoring Bush were counted.
- Nov. 8: Shortly after 2:00 A.M., the networks called Bush the winner by a wide margin; shortly thereafter, Gore called Bush and conceded. An hour later, when reports suggested that Bush's lead had vanished, the networks retracted their projection. Gore called Bush again and retracted his concession. At this point the Bush lead was 1,784 votes; voting irregularities were charged, especially in Palm Beach County (punch card ballots). The margin of victory for Bush was less than .05 percent, so a full machine count of the Florida vote was ordered. Gov. Jeb Bush recused himself from the process.
- Nov. 9: Gore won the preliminary nationwide popular vote. Neither candidate had enough electoral votes to be declared the winner. The Gore

team requested a hand recount in four strong Democratic counties. Sixty-four of the state's sixty-seven counties completed their recount; Bush's lead was down to 362 votes.

- Nov. 12: Palm Peach and Volusia counties were still counting.
- Nov. 13: Florida secretary of state Kathleen Harris did not extend the deadline date for certifying election results.
- Nov. 14: Bush's lead was down to 300 votes.
- Nov. 15: Harris, in a petition to the Florida supreme court, asked the justices to order all counties to end manual recounts. The Bush camp joined Harris in the petition. The Florida court denied the requests.
- Nov. 16: The Bush team submitted arguments to the U.S court of appeals in Atlanta to end recounts in Florida. The Gore team filed opposing arguments. The Florida supreme court ruled that Palm Beach County could proceed with its recount.
- Nov. 17: A Leon County circuit judge upheld Harris' decision to reject late vote tallies resulting from manual recounts. The Florida supreme court barred Harris from certifying the presidential election "until further order of the court." The U.S. court of appeals in Atlanta denied the Bush request to stop recounts on constitutional grounds.
- Nov. 18: After overseas votes were tabulated, Bush's lead grew to 930 votes.
- Nov. 20: The Florida supreme court heard arguments from both sides on the question of whether Harris should consider hand recounts before she certified.
- Nov. 21: The Florida supreme court in a unanimous decision ruled that hand recounts must be considered by Harris. A certification date of November 26 was established.
- Nov. 22: The Bush team filed a petition with the U.S. Supreme Court to review the ruling of the Florida supreme court. Miami-Dade County voted to halt its manual recount.
- Nov. 23: The Gore team requested the Florida supreme court to force Miami-Dade to resume the recount. The court rejected the request.
- Nov. 24: The U.S. Supreme Court agreed to hear arguments on the Florida supreme court ruling that selective manual recounts must be included in the state's final vote count.
- Nov. 26: Harris certified Bush as the winner in Florida. His final margin of victory was 537 votes.
- Nov. 27: The Gore team contested the results. A flurry of legal activity continued during the day.
- Nov. 28: Legal action was centered in Tallahassee over 14,000 disputed ballots. The judge ordered the ballots and a sample of the voting booth and voting machines brought to his court.
- Nov. 30: A truck with more than 450,000 presidential ballots from Palm Beach was in transit to Tallahassee. The Gore team filed papers with the Florida

supreme court asking them to order a recount of 14,000 disputed ballots (all seven judges on the court were Democrats).

• Dec. 1: The Florida supreme court refused to order the recount of the 14,000 votes. The U.S. court of appeals agreed to hear two cases that challenged the Florida hand count.

• Dec. 2: The Gore team continued its legal pressure on the 14,000 contested ballots in a circuit court.

• Dec. 4: Legal action continued. Gore continued to lose ground. Judge Sauls ruled that recounts weren't warranted — the votes would stand in Palm Beach, Miami-Dade and Nassau counties

• Dec. 6: The Atlanta court denied Bush's appeal to ignore recounts.

• Dec. 7: The Gore team appealed the Sauls ruling to the Florida supreme court. The court heard arguments from both sides.

• Dec. 8: The Florida supreme court ruled (4–3) in favor of Gore on the Sauls issue and ordered a statewide recount of undervotes. (When a voter, by their selections on the ballot, is obviously engaged but mysteriously does not vote for either presidential candidate, an undervote (oversight) is created.) Attempts by the Gore team to have absentee and overseas ballots thrown out were rejected.

• Dec. 9: Florida began a statewide recount of undervotes. The U.S. Supreme Court issued a stay of the recounts.

• Dec. 11: The U.S. Supreme Court heard arguments on the recount issue in Florida.

• Dec. 12: The U.S. Supreme Court ruled (7–2) that the Florida court's decision on recounts was unconstitutional: "It is obvious that the recount cannot be conducted in compliance with the requirements of equal protection and due process."

• Dec. 13: Gore conceded.

Bush attempted to bring to Washington the cooperative attitude that had made him successful in Texas. But many Democrats openly accused him of stealing the election, and they were in a hardball frame of mind. The wall of partisanship that dated back to the beginning of the progressive era that began with Theodore Roosevelt and Woodrow Wilson haunted the Bush presidency from beginning to end.

The Bush Cabinet

Washington had been managed for eight consecutive years by a Democratic administration. Clinton and Gore had little trouble mingling with eastern culture, but Bush, a Texan from head to toe despite his Harvard and Yale education, brought his western ways with him. It was a social and political jolt for Washington.

Bush himself was no rookie at this game, having been at his father's side through many campaigns, plus his own experiences as governor. And he had ready access to the professionals who worked with his father and to the faithful people, like Karl Rove and Karen Hughes, who had been with him throughout his political career. With such advisers to call upon, it was expected that an outstanding cabinet would emerge.[39]

Bush's selections were: **Vice President:** Dick Cheney, Wyoming; **Secretary of State:** Colin L. Powell, New York; **Secretary of Defense:** Donald H. Rumsfeld, Illinois; **Secretary of Interior:** Gale Ann Norton, Colorado; **Secretary of Commerce:** Don Evans, Texas; **Secretary of Health and Human Services:** Tommy G. Thompson, Wisconsin; **Secretary of Transportation:** Norman Y. Mineta, California; **Secretary of Education:** Rod Paige, Texas; **Secretary of Homeland Security:** Tom Ridge, Pennsylvania; **Secretary of Treasury:** Paul H. O'Neil (2001–02); John W. Snow; **Attorney General:** John Ashcroft, Missouri; **Secretary of Agriculture:** Ann H. Venerman, California; **Secretary of Labor:** Elaine Chao, New York; **Secretary of Housing and Urban Development:** Melquíades Martínez, Florida (2001–03), Alphonso Jackson, Texas; **Secretary of Energy:** Spencer Abraham, Michigan; **Secretary of Veteran's Affairs:** Anthony Principi, California

Cheney and Rumsfeld were political heavyweights, and Secretary of State Powell had served at the highest level of government for years. The only misfit was Paul O'Neil at Treasury, an unfortunate place to have a weakness because, as things turned out, the economy tanked as soon as Bush took office and there was a great need for strength and coordination in that position.

Civil rights groups were noticeably silent about the high positions given to women and minorities during the Bush administration.[40]

The Bush Congress

Citizens typically overstate the power of the president. They vote for this candidate or that because they want change. But, especially in fiercely partisan times when patriotism so often gives way to party loyalty, voters do not elect a man when they choose their president; they elect the symbol of a group. In most cases, he will do what the group permits him to do. That being the case, Bush could have all the best intentions in the world about restoring civility to the political dialogue, but recent history said he would not get too much cooperation unless he had plenty of congressional wallop. And he didn't have it. Just as his election was a sign of a split nation, so were the congressional elections.

Postelection Republicans ended up with marginal control of the House. The House speaker was Dennis Hastert (R-MI), who succeeded Newt Gingrich (R-GA), the political live wire who led Republicans back to power in the 1994 election. The same was true in the Senate, which was led by Trent Lott (R-MS).

This minimum margin of control was no recipe for power; it was a recipe for haggling, Washington's highest skill.

Pro-Administration Congressional Power

Congress	Year	President	House %	Senate %
106	1999	Clinton	**49**	45
107	2001	Bush	51	50
108	2003	Bush	53	51

Appendix 1.1, 1.2

Bold type=minority position

How a nation spends defines what a nation is. And in many ways, it provides insight into the character of the president himself. For example, one fact and two numbers tell a large amount of history:

- On September 11, 2001, four planes were highjacked by Islamist terrorists shortly after takeoff from American airports. One was destined to crash into the White House or the Capitol in Washington, D.C., but, because of the bravery of a few passengers, it was retaken and crashed in a Pennsylvania field. Two planes crashed into the twin tower buildings at the World Trade Center in New York City. The third plane crashed into the Pentagon building in Washington, D.C. War did not immediately follow, but from that day forward, the Bush administration was at war against terrorists.
- Defense spending in 2000 — when the threat of terrorists was apparent and had been manifested in many bloody ways — was low. Clinton had cut it to $294 billion; in 2004 under Bush, it was $456 billion, an increase of 55 percent. Those numbers say something about both presidents.
- In 2000, the cost of the welfare state was $1.1 trillion; in 2004, it was $1.5 trillion, an increase of 36 percent. During a time of war, when the nation was expanding its military might, Congress stubbornly refused to face a budget reality: The nation could not afford the array of social programs as they were presently financed.

As usual, the president, because of budget deficits, emerged from these four years with the reputation as a spender. Actually, he was revenue starved because of the recession[41]; he had to rebuild a weakened military and the costs of carrying the welfare state were not reduced by Congress.

The Bush Supreme Court

Bush was sworn in by Chief Justice William Rehnquist, who served with eight other justices during Bush's first term.[42] Seven of the nine justices had been nominated by Republican presidents, three of them originalists (Rehnquist, Scalia, Thomas),[43] two of them wild cards (Kennedy, O'Connor) and two of them activists (Stevens and Souter) who usually joined Clinton appointees Ginsburg and Breyer, who wrote opinions that would, it was hoped, lure either Kennedy or O'Connor into their camp and result in a 5–4 opinion.

Supreme Court Justices, 2001–2004

Judge	Began	Appointed by	Ended
William Rehnquist (WI)	1972	Nixon	2005
John Stevens (IL)	1975	Ford	
Sandra Day O'Connor	1981	Reagan	2006
Antonin Scalia	1986	Reagan	
Anthony M. Kennedy	1988	Reagan	
David H. Souter	1990	Bush	2009
Clarence Thomas	1991	Bush	
Ruth Bader Ginsburg	1993	Clinton	
Steven G Breyer	1994	Clinton	

Source: Oyez, http://www.oyez.org/—Members of the Supreme Court,[44] http://www.supremecourtus.gov/about/members.pdf

A sample of cases heard during Bush's first term provides insight into the concerns of the time.[45]

BOARD OF EDUCATION V. EARLS (2002)

The facts: A high school district required that all students who participated in extracurricula activities consent to a urinalysis testing for drugs. Two students and their parents brought suit.

The issue: Does school policy violate the Fourth Amendment (the right of people to be secure in their persons ... against unreasonable searches and seizures)?

The decision: No, 5–4. The policy reasonably served the school's interest in preventing drug use among its students. Stevens, O'Connor, Souter and Ginsberg dissented. The impact of the drug culture was finding its way to the Court.

ELK GROVE UNIFIED SCHOOL DISTRICT V. NEWDOW (2002)

The facts: Newdow's daughter attended a school that recited the pledge of allegiance. He objected to the phrase "under God," claiming it violates the First Amendment. He was divorced; his wife had custody.

The issue: Does the father have standing on the issue? If so, does the subject phrase violate the First Amendment?

The decision: No, 8–0. Newdow does not have custody and therefore does not have standing. The constitutional question languished and the church/state arguments continued.

GRUTTER V. BOLLINGER (2003)

The facts: Barbara Grutter, a well-qualified white woman, applied for admission to the University of Michigan Law School. She was denied under a system that admittedly uses race as a factor in making decisions because it serves a compelling interest in developing diversity in the student body. The district court supported Grutter; the appellate court overruled.

The issue: Is the admissions procedure constitutional?

The decision: Yes, 5–4. The admission procedure is constitutional because race is only one of many factors examined, it does not constitute a quota system and it does not "unduly" harm other applicants. Rehnquist, Scalia, Kennedy and Thomas dissented. The Supreme Court has been kicking this affirmative-action ball back and forth for years.

GRATZ V. BOLLINGER (2003)

The facts: Jennifer Gratz applied to the University of Michigan School of Literature. She was denied admission. The university has a policy of admitting almost all applicants from three minority groups: African Americans, Hispanics and Native Americans. Because of the Grutter decision, Gratz pressed her claim for admission, arguing that the policy when she applied was not "narrowly tailored."

The issue: Was school policy as applied to Gratz constitutional?

The decision: No, 6–3. The policy as applied was unconstitutional — a violation of the equal protection clause. Stevens, Souter and Ginsberg dissented.

The interesting impression that emerges from this review is that the Court has no idea of what to do with the affirmative action question that has been coming at them from different directions for decades, standing shoulder to shoulder with abortion as the issue that must keep them up nights more than any others.

Domestic Affairs Relative to Current Political Issues

Seldom if ever has an incoming president been confronted by a world that was so much different from the one he planned for. The prosperity that was to fuel the great plans Bush had for entitlement reform went up in a puff of smoke; the peace he needed to focus attention on national needs disappeared during a single morning in September; the private sector he looked to as the source of continuing wealth became entangled in an evil web of corruption and scandal.

DOMESTIC EVENTS

The first bad news in 2001 was the noticeable decline in federal tax receipts that eventually resulted in a total for the year that was 2 percent lower than the baseline receipts of 2000.[46] In a budget environment laden with entitlement programs that always go up and never down, this spelled trouble. Then came the wallop of wallops—the attack of September 11, 2001. Almost three thousand people were killed in New York and Washington. Millions were spent reestablishing the American financial system. Some experts say the airlines have never fully recovered.[47]

Clinton's peace was gone. It had always been a wispy thing. Terrorism had morphed into a frightening, well organized force. An old familiar friend, Osama bin Laden, soon took credit for planning the deed. It is alleged that bin Laden was offered to Clinton but, since Clinton approached terrorism as a criminal matter, he did not take him in because he did not "have enough evidence to indict him"[48]

The world changed on 9/11; Bush's agenda changed on 9/11. Prior to that time, he was dedicated to the restructuring of America into a form that was both affordable and compassionate. After 9/11, he was primarily a wartime president, ever mindful of his oath to protect the nation and, right or wrong, increasingly convinced that America was involved in the most important long-term fight for its life in its history.

He didn't have to work hard to stay on his toes. Evidence popped up everywhere reminding Bush of the dangers in play. For example, a string of letters containing anthrax infected twenty-two people, killed five and terrorized the nation (two U.S. senators received letters, Tom Daschle and Patrick Leahy[49]); Bush received serious intelligence about the possibility of a "dirty" nuclear bomb being detonated in a major American city.[50] Revenue disappearing and war appearing in an instant, one would think, would be enough to consider over morning coffee. Then the other shoe dropped, one that lingered and served to make the pain even worse. It comes under the heading of "corporate scandals,"[51]—another name for fleecing the public. A few of the more prominent ones follow: In October 2001 Enron went bankrupt. Executives were eventually jailed for filing false profits; bribing officials and manipulating energy markets. In November Arthur Andersen, Enron's auditor was found guilty of obstruction of justice. Its credibility was destroyed and the entire profession was stained. In February 2002 Global Crossing went bankrupt. It had inflated its revenue falsely. In April Adelphi Communications' founding family and executives were arrested for fraud.

The last thing an economy and recession need that have just been hit with a surprise military attack that sends a shock through the nation is a series of corporate scandals that shakes investor confidence in the free market. But that's what it got. And Bush paid for it.

Tax receipts for the next three years were never as large as Clinton's revenue in 2000.[52] Prior to Bush, the average president since Eisenhower's second term, had enjoyed a 35 percent increase in revenue over the previous four years. Clinton was the highest with 37 percent. With Bush, it was 5 percent.[53]

Historically, modern presidents confront recessions in either of two ways, which may be categorized as the FDR way or the Reagan way. The FDR way is to get the unemployed back to work by engaging in massive public spending. This requires that tax rates be kept at least as high or, in most cases, higher for the "rich." The FDR approach benefits unemployed construction workers or civil servants. But public works projects do little for the unemployed accountant, architect, salesman, factory worker or waitress. The Reagan way is to downsize government and provide incentives for the private sector to expand, invent, rehire and grow. This requires lower taxes for all, especially on investment income, and tax breaks on anything that stimulates investment.

Bush chose the Reagan way. He lowered taxes in 2001 and 2003. During his second term, the growth in his tax income was 30 percent — almost normal.

If the FDR way and the Reagan way of handling recessions both have the support of well-regarded economists (and they do), history must become the teacher of last resort. Did the FDR way pull the nation out of the Great Depression? Did the Reagan way pull the nation out of the Carter recession? Did the Reagan way work under Bush? Will the FDR way work for President Obama in 2010?

ECONOMIC GROWTH

During its final year, the Clinton administration showed a 6.4 percent growth in GDP, which adjusted for inflation reduced it to a respectable 4.3 percent. This is the economic climate Bush expected to deal with. It is not what he got.

Gross Domestic Product 2000–04

Year	GDP (bil)	Adjusted GDP (bil)*	Real Growth	Debt (bil)	Debt/GDP**
2000	9,708.4	9,708	4.3	3,409.8	35.1
2001	10,059.8	9769	.1	3,319.6	33.0
2002	10,378.4	9948	1.8	3,540.4	34.1
2003	10,803.7	10,151	2.0	3,913.4	36.2
2004	11,503.7	10,535	3.8	4,295.5	37.3

Source: Historical Tables 2010, 10.1

*In 2000 dollars; **unadjusted

The idea of the Bush tax cuts was to stimulate growth in GDP and, because of that, growth in jobs, profits, and, ultimately, in federal income. It turned out that way. GDP growth was almost back to normal in 2004; tax revenue, for the first time since he became president, was on the rise — up more than 5 percent from the previous year.[54]

National debt was a problem born under LBJ. Its primary cause, unaffordable social programs, was allowed to continue. Future presidencies were contaminated and an unending series of deficits followed.[55] And so it was under Bush. The deficit soared, primarily due to a lack of revenue. But the core problem remained untouched and debt zoomed once again. America was on the path to self destruction that had begun four decades earlier.

Legislative Events

The work of the U.S. Congress may be altered by such things as wars and economic calamities, but it never stops. And important laws and resolutions were passed, during Bush's first term that still reverberate today. Highlights appear below[56]:

- USA Patriot Act (2001): When national security is threatened, tension builds up in a democracy between the need to protect and the right to be free. This act responded to the 9/11 threat in a variety of ways—enhanced domestic security against terrorism, enhanced surveillance, enhanced border protection, etc. Civil liberty activists jumped all over this bill when it was passed and continued to do so while Bush was in office.
- No Child Left Behind (2001): This was the idealistic Bush at work before he realized that his Texas charm would get him nowhere in partisan Washington. He teamed with the most partisan Democrat of all, Sen. Ted Kennedy (MA), to pass an education bill that established accountability standards for schools (including standardized testing in reading and mathematics) and teachers. Federal funding was substantially increased. Teachers' unions opposed this reform from the beginning. The quality of public school education in the nation continues to be a major problem.[57]
- Born Alive Infants Protection Act (2002): This law extends human rights to any child who is born alive, including those who survive abortion.
- Department of Homeland Security Act (2002): This act consolidated the activities of twenty-two existing agencies under one head (a cabinet position) whose focus would be to prevent attacks within the nation, minimize damage, assist in recovery, monitor drug connections with terrorists, etc. The department became active in early 2003.

The aforementioned tax cuts were also passed in 2001.

On September 18, 2001, a joint resolution was passed giving Bush the power to use "all necessary and appropriate force against those nations, organizations or persons he determines planned, authorized, committed or aided the terrorist attacks that occurred on September 11, 2001, or harbored such organizations or persons, in order to prevent any future acts of international terrorism against the United States by such nations, organizations or persons."[58]

IMMIGRATION

Legal immigration in the 1990s was more than double the rate in the 1970s,[59] and illegal immigrants were pouring over the southern border. Americans had two basic concerns: (1) Immigrants were not as interested in assimilation as they once were, and the broad acceptance of multiculturalism in the nation had made Americans less inclined to help aliens to assimilate. Cultural fears, as a consequence were on the rise. (2) America was at war. Leaky borders are a risk. Many American's were bewildered by Bush's attitude toward this problem because in most cases, he was rock-solid on defense matters. His leanings toward illegal immigrants were regarded by many as a tendency toward amnesty, which adversaries regarded as an invitation to more illegal crossings. Supporters for his position came mostly from the other side of the aisle.

Foreign Affairs Relative to Current Political Issues

Following 9/11, there was a national surge of patriotism, a phenomenon that resulted in the aforementioned joint resolution that permitted Bush to exercise his duties as commander in chief. It lasted for a few weeks, but for the rest of Bush's term he got no Democratic support during the war, and he was demonized by Democratic leaders and the major media. The endless chant was: He is the liar who led us into an unnecessary war. About half the country believed it; the other half didn't.

Bush went to war in Iraq based upon information handed down from the Clinton administration and upon intelligence estimates from around the world and the U.N., all of which assumed that Saddam Hussein had weapons of mass destruction in chemical and biological form and had at least the capacity to build nuclear weapons and the missile systems to deliver them. Saddam was generally regarded as a menace to the world.[60] Either the intelligence was wrong or Saddam sent his inventory of weapons to Syria (which Israel believes), because no weapons were found when U.S. troops finally arrived in Baghdad. Many presidents from Adams to Bush have had to make serious security decisions based on incomplete evidence. As usual, history will be the final judge.

In his January 2002 State of the Union speech Bush evoked memories of Reagan's comments about an "evil empire" (the Soviet Union) when he described his modern day "axis of evil": Iraq, Iran and North Korea. The world took notice.

AFGHANISTAN

Afghanistan is where it all began, and it was Bush's first point of attack. The reason was simple. Osama bin Laden was the brains behind the 9/11 attack.

He had established training camps for terrorists in Afghanistan under the protection of the governing group known as the Taliban, Sunni Muslims of the Wahhabi wing of Islam. The U.S. asked the Taliban to give up bin Laden. They refused. The U.S. attacked, drove the Taliban and bin Laden over the border into Pakistan and established a shaky government in Kabul. NATO troops were brought in; NATO money was organized to help the new government.

Once the Taliban was chased into Pakistan, nation-building began and the military operation bumped into a serious roadblock. They couldn't invade a sovereign state to route the Taliban, and Pakistan had little control over the section of its land in which the Taliban took residence. At the end of Bush's' first term, Afghanistan was more civilized than before, but the military action was in limbo.*

IRAQ

American policy under Clinton was that Saddam Hussein had to go as the leader of Iraq; he was a destabilizing force who, it was generally believed, at the least, had chemical and biological weapons of mass destruction (WMD) and the intellectual organization and the wealth to quickly become a nuclear power. He had never abided by the agreement that followed the war with Kuwait; he refused to allow full inspection of his facilities by UN inspectors, who suspected nuclear development. He cost America and its allies billions per year to supervise Iraq from the air; he was providing financial aid to the Palestinian terrorists.

Bush and others believed reports about Saddam actual and incipient arsenal of WMD and considered him a threat to the national security of the United States.[61] Iraq was no nuclear threat, but chemical and biological weapons are simple to hide, and the possibility that someone as antagonistic to the U.S. as Saddam would make them available to a terrorist organization was a real one. In his State of the Union address in January 2003, Bush announced he was ready to attack Iraq even without a UN mandate. In February, secretary of state Colin Powell presented to the UN the American case for war against Iraq.[62] In March, the war began.

The formal resistance of the Iraqi military was quickly defeated. The difficulty of organizing the Shia, Sunni and Kurds into one nation was, however, underestimated. Long-subdued hatreds and rivalries broke out. The possibility of civil war a constant fear and the difficulty of establishing a central government was severe.

At the end of 2004, the future of the Iraq venture still in doubt, America was divided on its necessity, importance and relevance. The president was under siege.

Pakistan is a nuclear power. If it loses control to the terrorists, the terrorists become a nuclear power.

IRAN

Iran seemed to be the Iraq experience reborn. Negotiations accomplished nothing. Iran claimed it wanted to develop nuclear energy (despite the fact that it had huge oil reserves). The world believed its real purpose was to become a nuclear power.[63] It had successfully experimented with long-range missiles. Combined with its lust for a nuclear bomb, this was a potentially lethal combination.

Iran openly stated that Israel should be destroyed.[64] Some of its fanatics appeared to welcome the Armageddon that would follow if they attempted to vaporize Israel. The stakes, apart from Israel, were high. Iran is mostly Shia; the rest of the Arab world is mostly Sunni. There is great animosity between those two branches of Islam. If Iran got the bomb, it would proliferate throughout the region. The danger of a world-changing war loomed.

Bush, accused by opponents for his "going it alone" style of diplomacy, left it up to the Europeans to bargain sense into Iran's leaders. They failed. The same problem was four years older in 2004 and Iran was four years closer to the bomb.

NORTH KOREA

North Korea promised the Clinton administration it would discontinue its development of a nuclear weapon. It lied. Negotiations began again, this time with China, Russia, Japan and South Korea at the table.[65] The negotiations were about as fruitful as those with Iran.[66]

North Korea had tested missiles for years. It was generally believed it had nuclear weapons, although there was dispute over the sophistication of its delivery capability. The difference between the North Korean threat to the United States and the Iranian threat was distance. North Korea is within shooting distance; Iran is far away.

RUSSIA

Since the dissolution of the Soviet Union, Russia had struggled with its so-called freedom. Its citizens weren't accustomed to it. Some preferred the cradle-to-grave mediocrity of communism to the risk and rewards of capitalism. Others were just confused. The leaders, of course, preferred to give orders rather than seek votes. The result had been a government that was a mixture of the old and the new, with a tendency to slip back to the old because of the prominence of such leaders as ex–KGB agent Vladimir Putin.

Putin and Bush got along well personally. But some say that relations between the two nations reached a postwar low under Bush.[67] The American press lays this at the feet of Bush. And that may be correct. But it's also correct to note that Bush favored such things as the expansion of NATO,[68] and he disapproved of Russia's handling of the Chechens.[69] Putin resented both positions, which might have had something to do with the formal coolness between the nations. Russia tends to be cool toward firm American presidents.

CHINA

The Bush administration's attitude toward China was pragmatic.[70] In some cases America would compete; in others, it would cooperate. The Bush team was more open in its support of Taiwan than Clinton's—but it continued to oppose independence for it.[71]

The relationship remained useful to both, but undramatic. If a solution to the North Korean problem was to be found, China would be a key player.

Conclusion

Why was the election of 2000 so close? First of all, based on the factual record, it shouldn't have been. Peace and good times should have added up to a Gore win, with the only drag being Clinton's reputation. But he was gone; Gore was clean.

True, there was nothing extraordinary about Gore. He told tall tales about himself; his past money-raising practices raised an eyebrow or two. But such traits are not strange in a politician. It's also true his was a ponderous personality, more inclined to induce yawns than applause from his listeners. But if windbags are competent, voters are inclined to favor the brain and forget the wind. Overall, such failings might have gained Gore as many votes as they cost him.

Perhaps truth is easier to find if approached from the other direction. Gore, after all, did attract the largest popular vote in history to that point except for Reagan's big win in 1984. He did his job. The more interesting question is: Why did Bush get so many votes? Bush was an attractive candidate running against what appeared to be a successful record. He offered change. But why change when the nation was at peace and the budget was in surplus? These were, to a certain extent, illusory accomplishments, but in most cases the public didn't know that and they were enough to draw votes. Gore was a good-looking candidate, smart, experienced, and had a good wife. Why vote for Bush?

The answer offered here is one word: Clinton! His downside was more powerful than expected. Many voters wanted him, and everything related to him, out. And Bush was the vehicle to resolve their wishes.

Conclusion

This has been a long journey, to go from page one to this place in this book. And, like all books of this type, it has been a pleasure to write, especially because the period of history featured herein not only covers the dozen closest presidential elections but also because it tells the history of the beginning, but not yet the end, of two great movements, which for purposes of convenience will be referred to as the Political Movement and the Judicial Movement.

The Political Movement

Political movements are initially the weeds in what appears to be a healthy garden. They sprout up because something about the current political scene becomes sufficiently unpleasant to attract a recognizable group of followers.

The industrial revolution in the nineteenth century produced many wonders and mountains of riches. It also brought attention to the inequities of millions of poor people whose annual earnings were still below the poverty line as late as the 1930s. In addition to serving as the justification for labor unions, this circumstance in industry had political consequences:

- 1840s–1900s: The Liberty, Abolitionist, Free Soil, Constitutional, Union, Greenback, Union Labor, Populist, Prohibition, Social Democrat and Socialist parties appeared in presidential contests and rarely took more than 10 percent of the popular vote and never won an electoral vote, except in 1869, 1892 and 1896. Before discounting these movements completely, we must remember as an example that Amendment Eighteen was ratified in 1919 and Prohibition began. Over time, prohibitionists developed power.
- 1900s: The Prohibition, Social Democrat and Socialist parties were active on the heels of a promising beginning from Populists. But the issue that had invigorated that movement (unlimited coinage of silver) died, and with it, the party. The remaining groups had little impact on presidential races.
- 1910s: Dissident groups that consolidated issues and reappeared in 1912 as

the Progressive Party fortuitously drew a leader of national stature, Theodore Roosevelt, who drew them and their issues into the mainstream of American politics. The Socialist Party also competed in that race; together, they took one-third of the popular vote and won eighty-eight electoral votes. In 1916, with Roosevelt back under the Republican canopy from which he had strayed, Wilson and the Democrats adopted the Progressives, and that independent party disappeared into the innards of both major political parties, one branch following Roosevelt and the other following Wilson.

That is the genesis of the progressive movement that has dominated American politics ever since. It was born in the discontent of the industrial revolution; its aim was to form a more just society. Its general impact was to turn government away from the attitude that had governed the behavior of earlier presidents— manage America and ensure the nation's safety — to one that added one insignificant letter to the job description of the president — manage Americans and ensure the nation's safety.

The modern political system that has emerged from this political revolution is not the one envisaged by the Founders. It may be better or worse, depending on your point of view. But two things are clear: the modern system is different and it is expensive. Given the flow of public debt described in these pages, it is also too expensive.

The Judicial Movement

Progressives dislike the handcuffs placed on federal action imposed by the Constitution and prefer the "living document" theory that allows for various interpretations depending on varying circumstances as viewed by varying jurists. This made possible a more active government in the affairs of the people and the private sector.

Modern America is different from what it was, say, in the 1950s partly because the Supreme Court has made it so. It is not the purpose here to review the sample of cases already analyzed in these pages. A few comments on a few topics will make the point:

- Sex: Abortion was illegal and rare; today it is legal and frequent; sex out of marriage took place, but was frowned upon. Today it is taken for granted with no penalties except those imposed by disease or unwanted pregnancies.
- Family: Control of children was accepted as being the right and responsibility of parents until, because of abusive behavior, the state had to step in. This is no longer the case.
- Pornography: This was once a back-street, brown paper-wrapped industry

that was policed by people, cities and states. Today, porn is an accepted, flourishing business.
- Religion: America from its beginnings was an openly religious nation. Today it is not. Prayer and any mention of a Supreme Being have been stripped from schools. Religious symbols are under attack everywhere, etc., all of this because of the modern interpretation of Amendment One of the Constitution.

Supreme Court decisions on such matters do much to establish the moral tone of the culture. Modern America may be better off or worse off than it was, say, in 1950. But this much is sure — it is different.

(History tells us that a number of associate justices to the Supreme Court have served beyond the time when their capabilities were unchallenged. This should never happen. The Chief Justice should be required to report once a year on the physical and mental condition of his associates to Congress for appropriate action.)

The Closest Elections

In this book we have recalled words of some of the greatest men this nation and the world have ever known. In writing about them it has been a humbling experience to vicariously use, for a short time, the reasoning power and the eloquence of the Founders, who created a government never before seen and so aptly described by Lincoln at Gettysburg: "of the people, by the people, for the people."

The Founders, especially Washington and Adams, had a deep aversion for the concept of political parties, which they believed would split the nation into factions. But when Washington, the-man-against-whom-nobody-would-run, resigned and competition appeared, it was only a matter of time before opponents began to identify themselves with names that eventually became political parties. And with their rise came the possibility of the close elections that are the subject matter of this book.

After the defeat of Adams in 1800, the party of Jefferson and Jackson dominated Washington except for short presidential interludes with Presidents Harrison and Tyler, and Taylor and Fillmore. The close election during this period took place in 1824 (John Quincy Adams vs. Andrew Jackson). Democratic-Republicans (as they were then known) had no opposition party to contend with, so four men from the same party slugged it out.

During and after the Civil War, the Republican era began with Lincoln (1860) and ended with Garfield/Arthur (1865–88). This period produced three close elections, 1876 (Hayes vs. Tilden), 1880 (Garfield vs. Hancock) and 1884 (Cleveland vs. Blaine).

The presidency went back and forth between the parties from 1884 to 1896, featuring the battles of Cleveland and Harrison, who had the normal issues to contend with plus rapid expansion to the West. McKinley (1896) was the first of a string of presidents who won elections by reasonably comfortable margins that ended with Wilson (1913–20). America was tired of war in 1920 and another period of Republican rule began that lasted until the election in 1932 of Franklin Roosevelt (FDR). No close elections took place in this relatively prosperous period that, ironically, ended up in the stock market crash of 1929 and the ensuing Great Depression.

Democrats dominated the political scene from 1933 to 1952, mostly under FDR, followed by Truman. President Eisenhower (1953–60) served as a relief station for progressives as they gained steam for their big push under Kennedy and Johnson (1961–68). The Kennedy/Nixon race in 1960 was one of the close ones.

From 1968 to 2008, the presidency went back and forth, producing three of the close contests, 1968 (Nixon/Humphrey), 1976 (Carter/Ford) and 2000 (Bush/Gore). The Bush/Gore race, one of the most thrilling, was made so because Gore won the popular vote. On the surface the decisive figure in that race wasn't running and that was Bill Clinton. Some unknown portion of the Bush vote — probably the decisive one — was an anti–Clinton vote from people who, irrespective of party, wanted everything related to him out of the White House, so noxious to them was his behavior. And Gore, a good-living man, paid the price.

Gore went home a bitterly disappointed man. So it is in a competitive society, and may it always be so. There is risk involved with liberty but the rewards are great. Beware of those who would take the lumps out of the road — at a price. Welcome the challenges that give us the winners and give the rest of us the chance to win.

So this book ends. The Constitution is still venerated, in the sense that we admire the works of the masters from afar, something we bow to as we go about our modern lives too often under the new and changing laws of changing people, freed from the sturdy bedrock of the document that once harbored our principles and guided our actions.

We still refer to ourselves as a Democratic Republic, because it is self-satisfying or politically useful to do so. But in our hearts, we know this is a different place with different rules made by people who have turned many constitutional clauses to mush. The modern political system resembles European socialism more closely than it does the Republic that, for the most part, still existed in the 1950s in America. That is a condition that pleases some and frightens others.

What is the future? Long-term social eruptions such as those that America has experienced over the last five decades have a natural end. They tend to create something quite grand, which was the end product of the Colonial revolt and the Revolutionary War, or they tend to collapse into something quite painful was the end product of communism that created the Soviet Union, which in less than a century devolved into the confused and seriously weakened Russia that exists today.

The fate of America is still in the balance. The public is deciding: Go left? Go right? Elections will probably remain close, waiting for leaders to take the nation to its final resting place as a great one grown strong because of adversity overcome or a weak one that, due to inaction or misdirected leadership, is a shadow of what it once was.

Appendices

1.1 Washington Power Structure:
House of Representatives, 1789–2001

Con.	Term	House Speaker	PA	AA	O	ALL	President
1	1789–91	Muhlenberg (F)	37	28	0	65	Washington (F)
2	1791–93	TrumbullJ (F)	39	30	0	69	"
3	1793–95	Muhlenberg (F)	**51**	54	0	106	"
4	1795–97	Dayton (F)	**47**	59	0	106	"
5*	1797–99	"	57	49	0	106	Adams (F)
6	1799–01	Sedgwick (F)	60	46	0	106	"
7*	1801–03	Macon (DR)	68	38	11	107	Jefferson (DR)
8	1803–05	"	103	39	0	142	"
9	1805–07	"	114	28	0	142	"
10	1807–09	Varnum (DR)	116	26	0	142	"
11	1809–11	"	92	50	0	142	Madison (DR)
12	1811–13	Clay (DR)	107	36	0	143	"
13	1813–15	"	114	68	0	182	"
13	1815	Langdon C (-R)					"
14	1815–17	Clay (DR)	119	64	0	183	"
15	1817–19	"	146	39	0	185	Monroe (DR)
16	1819–21	"	160	26	0	186	"
16	1821	Taylor (R)					"
17	1821–23	Barbour (R)	155	32	0	187	"
18	1823–25	Clay (DR)	72	141	0	213	"
19*	1825–27	Taylor (R)	109	104	0	213	Adams JQ (I)
20	1827–29	Stevenson (D)	**100**	**113**	0	213	"
21	1829–31	"	136	72	5	213	Jackson (D)
22	1831–33	"	126	66	21	213	"
23	1833–35	"	143	63	34	240	"
23	1835	Bell (W-D)					"
24	1835–37	Polk (D)	143	75	24	242	"
25	1837–39	"	128	100	14	242	Van Buren (D)
26	1839–41	Hunter (W)	125	109	8	242	"
27	1841–43	White (W)	142	98	2	242	Harrison/Tyler (W)
28	1843–45	Jones (D)	72	147	4	223	Tyler (W)
29	1845–47	Davis (D)	142	79	6	228	Polk (D)
30	1847–49	Winthrop (W)	**110**	**116**	4	230	"

Bold type indicates that the resident president had a minority position in Congress.

301

Con.	Term	House Speaker	PA	AA	O	ALL	President
31	1849–51	Cobb (D)	**108**	**113**	12	233	Taylor/Fillmore (W)
32	1851–53	Boyd (D)	85	**127**	21	233	Fillmore (W)
33	1853–55	"	157	71	6	234	Pierce (D)
34	1855–57	Banks, (R)	**83**	**100**	51	234	"
35	1857–59	Orr (D)	132	90	15	237	Buchanan (D)
36	1859–61	Pennington (R)	**83**	**116**	39	238	"
37	1861–63	Grow (R)	108	44	31	183	Lincoln (R)
38	1863–65	Colfax (R)	86	72	27	184	"
39	1865–67	"	136	38	19	193	Lincoln/Johnson (R)
40	1867–69	"	173	47	6	226	Johnson (R)
40	1869	Pomeroy (R)					"
41	1869–71	Blaine (R)	171	67	5	243	Grant (R)
42	1871–73	"	136	104	3	243	"
43	1873–75	"	199	88	5	292	"
43	1875	Kerr (D)					"
44	1875–77	Randall (D)	**103**	**182**	8	293	"
45*	1877–79	"	**136**	**155**	2	293	Hayes (R)
46	1879–81	"	**132**	**141**	20	293	"
47*	1881–83	Keifer (R)	151	128	14	293	Garfield/Arthur (R
48	1883–85	Carlisle (D)	**117**	**196**	12	325	Arthur (R
49*	1885–87	"	**182**	**141**	2	325	Cleveland (D
50	1887–89	"	167	152	6	325	"
51*	1889–91	Reed T (R)	179	152	1	332	Harrison (R
52	1891–93	Crisp (D)	**86**	**238**	8	332	"
53	1893–95	"	218	124	14	356	Cleveland (D
54	1895–97	Reed (R)	**93**	**254**	10	357	"
55	1897–99	"	206	124	27	357	McKinley (R)
56	1899–01	Henderson (R)	187	161	9	357	"
57	1901–03	"	200	151	6	357	McKinley/Roosevelt (R)
58	1903–05	Cannon (R)	207	176	3	386	Roosevelt
59	1905–07	"	251	135	0	386	"
60	1907–09	"	223	167	1	391	"
61	1909–11	"	219	172	0	391	Taft (R)
62	1911–13	Clark (D)	**162**	**230**	2	394	"
63	1913–15	"	291	134	10	435	Wilson (D)
64	1915–17	"	230	196	9	435	"
65	1917–19	"	**214**	**215**	6	435	"
66	1919–21	Gillett (R)	**192**	**240**	3	435	"
67	1921–23	"	302	131	2	435	Harding (R)
68	1923–25	Gillett 62% support in the House	225	207	3	435	Harding/Coolidge (R)
69	1925–27	Longworth (R)	247	183	5	435	Coolidge (R)
70	1927–29	"	238	194	3	435	"
71	1929–31	"	270	164	1	435	Hoover (R)
72	1931–33	Garner (R)	218	216	1	435	"
73	1933–35	Rainey (D)	313	117	5	435	Roosevelt (D)
74	1935–37	Byrns (D)	322	103	10	435	"
74	1937	Bankhead (D)					"
75	1937–39	"	334	88	13	435	"

Con.	Term	House Speaker	PA	AA	O	ALL	President
76	1939–41	"	262	169	4	435	"
77	1941–43	Rayburn (D)	267	162	6	435	"
78	1943–45	"	222	209	4	435	"
79	1945–47	"	242	191	2	435	Roosevelt/Truman (D)
80	1947–49	Martin (R)	188	246	1	435	Truman (D)
81*	1949–51	Rayburn (D)	263	171	1	435	"
82	1951–53	"	235	199	1	435	"
83	1953–55	Martin (R)	221	213	1	435	Eisenhower (R)
84	1955–57	Rayburn (D)	203	232	0	435	"
85	1957–59	"	201	234	0	435	"
86	1959–61	"	153	283	1	437	"
87*	1961–63	McCormack (D)	263	174	0	437	Kennedy/Johnson (D)
88	1963–65	'	259	176	0	435	Johnson (D)
89	1965–67	"	295	140	0	435	"
90	1967–69	"	247	187	1	435	"
91*	1969–71	"	192	243	0	435	Nixon (R)
92	1971–73	Albert (D)	180	255	0	435	"
93	1973–75	"	192	242	1	435	Nixon/Ford (R)
94	1975–77	"	144	291	0	435	Ford
95*	1977–79	O'Neil (D)	292	143	0	435	Carter (D)
96	1979–81	"	277	158	0	435	"
97	1981–83	"	192	242	1	435	Reagan (R)
98	1983–85	"	166	269	0	435	"
99	1985–87	"	182	253	0	435	"
100	1987–89	Wright (D)	177	258	0	435	"
101	1989–91	"	175	260	0	435	Bush GHW (R)
102	1991–93	Foley (D)	167	267	1	435	"
103	1993–95	"	258	176	1	435	Clinton (D)
104	1995–97	Gingrich (R)	204	230	1	435	"
105	1997–99	"	206	228	1	435	"
106	1999–01	Hastert (R)	211	223	1	435	"

http://clerk.house.gov/art_history/house_history/index.html

PA=pro-administration; AA=anti–administration; O=other; F=Federalist; DR=Democrat-Republican; I = Independent; W = Whig; D=Democrat; R=Republican
*Presidential dogfights

1.2 Washington Power Structure: Senate, 1789–2001

Con.	Term	Majority Leader	PA	AA	O	ALL	President
1	1789–91	None	18	8	0	26	Washington (F)
2	1791–93	"	16	13	1	30	"
3	1793–95	"	16	14	0	30	"
4	1795–97	"	21	11	0	32	"
5*	1797–99	"	22	10	0	32	Adams (F)
6	1799–01	"	22	10	0	32	"
7*	1801–03	"	17	15	2	34	Jefferson (DR)
8	1803–05	"	25	9	0	34	"
9	1805–07	"	27	7	0	34	"
10	1807–09	"	28	6	0	34	"

Con.	Term	Majority Leader	PA	AA	O	ALL	President
11	1809–11	"	27	7	0	34	Madison (DR)
12	1811–13	"	30	6	0	36	"
13	1813–15	"	28	8	0	36	"
14	1815–17	"	26	12	0	38	"
15	1817–19	"	30	12	0	42	Monroe (DR)
16	1820–21	"	37	9	0	46	"
17	1821–23	"	44	4	0	48	"
18	1823–25	"	17	31	0	48	"
19*	1825–27	"	**22**	**26**	0	48	Adams JQ (I)
20	1827–29	"	**21**	**27**	0	48	"
21	1829–30	"	25	23	0	48	Jackson (1)
22	1830–32	"	24	22	2	48	"
23	1832–35	"	20	26	2	48	"
24	1835–37	"	26	24	2	52	"
25	1837–39	"	35	17	0	52	Van Buren (D)
26	1839–41	"	30	22	0	52	"
27	1841–43	"	29	22	1	52	Harrison/Tyler (W)
28	1843–45	"	29	23	0	52	Tyler (W)
29	1845–47	"	34	22	2	58	Polk (D)
30	1847–49	"	38	21	1	60	"
31	1849–51	"	25	**35**	2	62	Taylor/Fillmore (W)
32	1851–53	"	**23**	**36**	3	62	Fillmore (W)
33	1853–55	"	38	22	2	62	Pierce (D)
34	1855–57	"	39	21	1	62	"
35	1857–59	"	41	20	5	66	Buchanan (D)
36	1859–61	"	38	26	2	66	"
37	1861–63	"	31	15	4	50	Lincoln (R)
38	1863–65	"	33	10	9	52	"
39	1865–67	"	39	11	4	54	Lincoln/Johnson (R)
40	1867–69	"	57	9	2	68	Johnson (R)
41	1869–71	"	62	12	0	74	Grant (R)
42	1871–73	"	56	17	1	74	"
43	1873–75	"	47	19	8	74	"
44	1875–77	"	46	28	2	76	"
45*	1877–79	"	40	35	1	76	Hayes (R)
46	1879–81	"	**33**	**42**	1	76	"
47*	1881–83	"	37	37	2	76	Garfield/Arthur (R)
48	1883–85	"	38	36	2	76	Arthur (R)
49*	1885–87	"	**34**	**42**	0	76	Cleveland (D)
50	1887–89	"	37	39	0	76	"
51*	1889–91	"	51	37	0	88	Harrison (R)
52	1891–93	"	47	39	2	88	"
53	1893–95	"	44	40	4	88	Cleveland (D)
54	1895–97	"	**40**	**44**	6	90	"
55	1897–99	"	44	34	12	90	McKinley (R)
56	1899–01	"	53	26	11	90	"
57	1901–03	"	56	32	2	90	McKinley/Roosevelt (R)
58	1903–05	"	57	33	0	90	Roosevelt (R)

*Bold type indicates that the resident president had a minority position in Congress.

Con.	Term	Majority Leader	PA	AA	O	ALL	President
59	1905–07	"	58	32	0	90	"
60	1907–09	"	61	31	0	92	"
61	1909–11	"	60	32	0	92	Taft (R)
62	1911–13	"	52	44	0	96	"
63	1913–15	"	51	44	1	96	Wilson (D)
64	1915–17	"	56	40	0	96	"
65	1917–19	"	54	42	0	96	"
66	1919–21	"	47	49	0	96	"
67	1921–23	"	59	37	0	96	Harding (R)
68	1923–25	Curtis (R)	53	42	1	96	Harding/Coolidge (R)
69	1925–27	"	54	41	1	96	Coolidge (R)
70	1927–29	"	48	46	2	96	"
71	1929–31	Watson (R)	56	39	1	96	Hoover (R)
72	1931–33	"	48	47	1	96	"
73	1933–35	Robinson (D)	59	36	1	96	Roosevelt (D)
74	1935–37	"	69	25	2	96	"
75	1937–39	Robinson/Barkley (D)	76	16	4	96	"
76	1939–41	Barkley (D)	69	23	4	96	"
77	1941–43	"	66	28	2	96	"
78	1943–45	"	57	38	1	96	"
79	1945–47	"	57	38	1	96	Roosevelt/Truman (D)
80	1947–49	White (R)	45	51	0	96	Truman (D)
81*	1949–51	Lucas (D)	54	42	0	96	"
82	1951–53	McFarland (D)	49	47	0	96	"
83	1953–55	Taft/Knowland (R)	48	47	1	96	Eisenhower (R)
84	1955–57	Johnson (D)	47	48	1	96	"
85	1957–59	"	47	49	0	96	"
86	1959–61	"	35	65	0	100	"
87*	1961–63	Mansfield (D)	64	36	0	100	Kennedy/Johnson (D)
88	1963–65	"	66	34	0	100	Johnson (D)
89	1965–67	"	68	32	0	100	"
90	1967–69	"	64	36	0	100	"
91*	1969–71	"	43	57	0	100	Nixon (R)
92	1971–73	"	44	54	2	100	"
93	1973–75	"	42	56	2	100	Nixon/Ford (R)
94	1975–77	"	38	60	2	100	Ford
95*	1977–79	Byrd (D)	61	38	1	100	Carter (D)
96	1979–81	"	58	41	1	100	"
97	1981–83	Baker (R)	53	46	1	100	Reagan (R)
98	1983–85	"	54	46	0	100	"
99	1985–87	Dole (R)	53	47	0	100	"
100	1987–89	Byrd (D)	45	55	0	100	"
101	1989–91	Mitchell (D)	45	55	0	100	Bush GHW (R)
102	1991–93	"	44	56	0	100	"
103*	1993–95	"	57	43	0	100	Clinton (D)
104	1995–97	Dole/Lott (R)	48	52	0	100	"
105	1997–99	Lott	45	55	0	100	"
106	1999–01	"	45	55	0	100	"

http://www.senate.gov/artandhistory/history/common/briefing/Majority_Minority_Leaders.htm#4 http://www.senate.gov/pagelayout/history/one_item_and_teasers/partydiv.htm

PA=pro-administration; AA=anti–administration; O=other; F=Federalist; DR=Democrat-Republican; I = Independent; W = Whig; D=Democrat; R=Republican

Democrats first elected a Senate Leader in 1920; Republicans, in 1925.

*Presidential Dogfights

2. Sequence of Admission of States to the Union

	State	Date Admitted to Union
1	Delaware	December 7, 1787
2	Pennsylvania	December 12, 1787
3	New Jersey	December 18, 1787
4	Georgia	January 2, 1788
5	Connecticut	January 9, 1788
6	Massachusetts	February 6, 1788
7	Maryland	April 28, 1788
8	South Carolina	May 23, 1788
9	New Hampshire	June 21, 1788
10	Virginia	June 25, 1788
11	New York	July 26, 1788
12	North Carolina	November 21, 1789
13	Rhode Island	May 29, 1790
14	Vermont	March 4, 1791
15	Kentucky	June 1, 1792
16	Tennessee	June 1, 1796
17	Ohio	March 1, 1803
18	Louisiana	April 30, 1812
19	Indiana	December 11, 1816
20	Mississippi	December 10, 1817
21	Illinois	December 3, 1818
22	Alabama	December 14, 1819
23	Maine	March 15, 1820
24	Missouri	August 10, 1821
25	Arkansas	June 15, 1836
26	Michigan	January 26, 1837
27	Florida	March 3, 1845
28	Texas	December 29, 1845
29	Iowa	December 28, 1846
30	Wisconsin	May 29, 1848
31	California	September 9, 1850
32	Minnesota	May 11, 1858
33	Oregon	February 14, 1859
34	Kansas	January 29, 1861
35	West Virginia	June 20, 1863
36	Nevada	October 31, 1864
37	Nebraska	March 1, 1867
38	Colorado	August 1, 1876
39	North Dakota	November 2, 1889

	State	Date Admitted to Union
40	South Dakota	November 2, 1889
41	Montana	November 8, 1889
42	Washington	November 11, 1889
43	Idaho	July 3, 1890
44	Wyoming	July 10, 1890
45	Utah	January 4, 1896
46	Oklahoma	November 16, 1907
47	New Mexico	January 6, 1912
48	Arizona	February 14, 1912
49	Alaska	January 3, 1959
50	Hawaii	August 21, 1959

3. Misery Index, 1950–2000:
Interest Rate+Inflation Rate+Unemployment Rate

President	Year	Interest	Inflation	Unemployment	Total
Roosevelt	1932	2.6	-10.3	23.6	15.6
Roosevelt	1936	1.5	1.0	16.9	19.4
Roosevelt	1940	1.5	.7	14.6	16.8
Roosevelt	1944	1.5	1.6	1.2	4.3
Truman	1948	1.8	7.7	3.4	12.9
Truman	1952	3.0	2.3	2.7	8.0
Eisenhower	1956	3.8	1.5	3.8	9.1
Eisenhower	1960	4.8	1.5	6.6	13.1
Johnson	1964	4.5	1.3	5.0	10.8
Johnson	1968	6.3	4.3	3.4	13.9
Nixon	1972	5.3	3.3	5.2	13.7
Ford	1976	6.8	5.8	7.8	20.4
Carter	1980	15.3	13.6	7.2	36.1
Reagan	1984	12.0	4.3	7.3	23.6
Reagan	1988	9.3	4.1	5.3	18.7
Bush	1992	6.3	3.0	7.4	16.7
Clinton	1996	8.3	2.9	5.4	16.6
Clinton	2000	4.3	3.4	5.4	12.4

Interest 1932–48, Bond Yields & Interest Rates, http://www.nber.org/palmdata/erp/b73.html#Primeratechargedbybanks%3Cahref=%27#N_5%27%3E\5\%3C/a%3E

Interest, 1952–08, *The National Debt of the United States*, Robert E. Kelly 2008, McFarland, NC

Inflation 1932–08, Historical Inflation Rate: Inflationdata.com.

Unemployment, Historical Statistics, Colonial to 1957, p. 73

Unemployment 1960–08, U.S. Unemployment rate, http://www.miseryindex.us/urbymonth.asp

4. National Debt/GDP, 1864–2008

Year	President	Public Debt (bil)	GDP (bil)	Debt/GDP
1864	Lincoln	1.8	9.5	19
1868	Johnson	2.6	8.2	32
1872	Grant	2.3	8.2	28
1876	Grant	2.2	8.3	27
1880	Hayes	2.2	10.4	21
1884	Arthur	1.8	11.8	15
1888	Cleveland	1.7	13.9	12
1892	B. Harrison	1.6	16.4	10
1896	Cleveland	1.8	15.5	12
1900	McKinley	2.2	20.6	11
1904	T. Roosevelt	2.3	25.7	9
1908	T. Roosevelt	2.6	30.0	9
1912	Taft	2.9	37.4	8
1916	Wilson	3.6	49.6	7
1920	Wilson	26.0	88.4	29
1924	Coolidge	21.2	86.9	24
1928	Coolidge	17.6	97.4	18
1932	Hoover	19.5	58.7	33
1936	F. Roosevelt	33.8	83.8	40
1940	F. Roosevelt	42.8	96.8	44
1944	R. Roosevelt	184.8	209.2	88
1948	Truman	216.3	256.0	84
1952	Truman	214.8	348.6	62
1956	Eisenhower	222.2	427.2	52
1960	Eisenhower	236.8	517.9	46
1964	Johnson	256.8	640.4	40
1968	Johnson	289.5	866.6	33
1972	Nixon	322.4	1178.3	27
1976	Ford	477.4	1736.5	27
1980	Carter	711.9	2726.7	26
1984	Reagan	1307.0	3840.2	34
1988	Reagan	2051.6	5008.6	41
1992	G.H.W. Bush	2999.7	6239.9	48
1996	Clinton	3734.1	7694.1	49
2000	Clinton	3409.8	9709.8	35

National debt 1864–1888: http://chestofbooks.com/reference/Bepler-Handy-Manual-Of-Knowledge/National-Debt-Of-The-United-States.html

National debt 1892–1936: http://www.usgovernmentspending.com/federal_debt_chart.html1900–1939: http://www.treasurydirect.gov/govt/reports/pd/histdebt/histdebt_histo3.htm

GDP/National Debt 1940–2008, Historical Tables 2010

Note: National debt = public debt only; interagency debt is excluded

5. Active Military

Year	President	Active (000)	Events
1789	Washington	718	1785–1900
1795	"	5,296	
1799	Adams	5,438	
1801	Jefferson	7,108	
1802	"	3,220	
1810	Madison	11,554	
1812	"	12,631	War of 1812–15
1815	"	40,885	
1820	Monroe	15,113	
1828	J.Q. Adams	11,431	
1830	Jackson	11,942	
1840	Van Buren	21,616	
1844	Tyler	20,919	Mexican 1846–48
1848	Polk	60,308	
1850	Fillmore	20,824	
1856	Pierce	25,867	
1860	Buchanan	27,958	Civil 1861–65
1864	Lincoln	1,031,724	
1868	Johnson	66,412	
1870	Grant	50,348	
1880	Hayes	37,894	
1884	Arthur	39,400	
1888	Cleveland	39,035	
1890	B. Harrison	38,666	
1896	Cleveland		
1898	McKinley	235,785	Spanish 1898
1900	"	139,344	
1915	Wilson	174,112	
1917	"	643,833	WWI 1917–18
1919	"	1,172,602	
1920	"	343,303	
1930	Hoover	255,648	
1940	F. Roosevelt	458,365	
1941	"	1,801,101	WWII 1941–46
1942	"	3,858,791	
1943	"	9,044,745	
1944	F. Roosevelt	11,451,719	
1945	"	12,123,455	
1946	Truman	3,030,088	
1950	Truman	1,460,261	Korea
1952	"	3,635,912	
1955		2,935,107	
1960	Eisenhower	2,476,435	
1964	Johnson	2,687,409	Vietnam 1964–73
1968	Johnson	3,547,902	
1970	Nixon	3,066,294	
1975	Ford	2,128,120	
1980	Carter	2,050,627	
1985	Reagan	2,151,032	

Year	President	Active (000)	Events
1990	G.H.W. Bush	2,043,705	Iraq-1990–91
1991	"	1,989,555	
1992	"	1,807,177	
1993	Clinton	1,705,103	
1994	"	1,610,490	
1995	"	1,518,224	
1996	"	1,471,722	
1997	"	1,438,562	
1998	"	1,406,830	
1999	"	1,385,703	
2000	"	1,384,338	Afghanistan 2001–

Sources: http://www.legendsofamerica.com/na-indianwartime
line.html; N.Y. Time Almanac 2009, p 167; http://www.info
please.com/ipa/A0004598.html; http://www.history.army.mil/
books/amh-v1/ch05.htm; 1918-almost 3 million, http://www.pbs.
org/fmc/book/11government5.htm

6. Historical Interest Rates and Unemployment Rates, 1791–1950

Year	President	Interest Rate	Unemp Rate	Year	President	Interest Rate	Unemp Rate
1791	Washington	3.13		1891	"	2.40	5.40
1795	"	3.94		1892	Cleveland	1.44	3.00
1800	Jefferson	4.07		1893	"	1.71	11.70
1898	McKinley	2.09	12.40	1894	"	1.67	18.40
1899	"	2.02	6.50	1904	T. Roosevelt	1.12	5.40
1810	Madison	5.37		1909	Taft	1.90	5.10
1815	"	5.75		1910	"	1.78	5.90
1820	"	5.63		1913	Wilson	1.91	4.30
1825	J.Q. Adams	5.20		1914	"	1.91	7.90
1830	Jackson	3.91		1915	"	1.91	8.50
1840	Harrison	4.37		1916	"	1.91	5.10
1845	Polk	6.93		1917	"		4.60
1850	Fillmore	6.00		1918	"		1.40
1855	Pierce	6.42		1919	"	2.43	1.40
1860	Lincoln	4.89		1920	Coolidge	4.19	5.20
1861	"	4.40		1921	"	4.16	11.70
1862	"	2.51		1922	"	4.31	6.70
1865	"	2.89		1925	"	4.30	3.20
1866	"	4.80		1929	Hoover	4.01	3.20
1870	Grant	5.21		1930	"	4.07	8.70
1871	"	5.34		1931	"	3.64	15.90
1874	"	4.75		1932	F. Roosevelt	3.07	23.60
1879	Hayes	4.68		1935	"	2.57	20.10
1884	Cleveland	2.98		1940	"	2.42	14.60
1889	Harrison	2.50		1941	"	2.27	9.90
1890	"	2.28	4.00	1942	"	1.74	4.70

Year	President	Interest Rate	Unemp Rate	Year	President	Interest Rate	Unemp Rate
1943	"	1.32	1.90	1946	"	1.75	3.90
1944	"	1.30	1.20	1950	"	2.24	5.30
1945	Truman	1.40	1.90				

Source: http://www.mall-net.com/wsnutri/natdebt.html

7.1 Immigration by Decade and Year, 1820–2000

Decade	Amount (000)	Decade	Amount (000)
1820–30	151.8	1831–40	599.1
1841–50	1713.3	1851–60	2598.2
1861–70	2314.8	1871–80	2812.2
1881–90	5246.6	1891–00	3687.6
1901–10	8795.4	1911–20	5735.8
1921–30	4107.2	1931–40	528.4
1941–50	1035.0	1951–60	2515.5
1961–70	3321.7	1971–80	4493.3
1981–90	7338.1	1991–00	9095.4
		Total	66089.4

Source: 1820–2000, *N.Y. Times Almanac 2008*, p. 300; Source: 2000–06, Federation for American Immigration Reform, http://www.fairus.org/site/PageServer?pagename=research_research 9605#ins

7.2 Immigration as a Percentage of Total Population Growth, 1901–2000

Period	%	Period	%
1901–10	39.6	1911–20	17.7
1921–30	15.0	1931–34	-.1
1935–39	3.2	1940–44	7.4
1945–49	10.2	1950–54	10.6
1955–59	10.7	1960–64	12.5
1965–69	19.7	1970–80	19.4
1981–90	32.8	1991–00	27.8

Source: N.Y. Times Almanac 2008, p.300

7.3 Foreign-Born Population
by Source, 1850–2003

Year	Total (mil)	Europe/ Canada %	Latin America %	Other %
1850	2.2	99.0	1.0	Minor
1870	5.6	97.6	1.0	1.4
1890	9.2	97.4	1.2	1.4
1900	10.3	97.3	1.6	1.1
1910	13.5	96.3	2.8	.9
1920	13.9	93.8	4.2	2.0
1930	14.2	92.2	5.6	2.2
1940	11.6	NA	NA	NA
1950	10.3	NA	NA	NA
1960	9.7	84.3	9.3	6.4
1970	9.6	68.1	18.8	13.1
1980	14.1	42.6	31.1	26.3
1990	19.8	25.8	42.5	31.7
2000	28.4	17.1	50.8	32.1
2003	33.5	13.7	53.3	33.0

Source: N.Y. Times Almanac 2008, p. 300

8.1 Inflation Rate, December 1950–2000

Year	1950	1960	1970	1980	1990	2000
0	5.9	1.4	5.6	12.5	6.1	3.4
1	6.0	1.0	3.3	8.9	3.1	1.6
2	1.0	1.3	3.4	3.8	2.9	2.4
3	1.0	1.6	8.7	3.8	2.8	1.9
4	-1.0	1.0	12.3	4.0	2.7	3.3
5	.0	1.9	6.9	3.8	2.5	3.4
6	3.0	3.4	4.9	1.1	3.3	2.5
7	2.9	3.0	6.7	4.4	1.7	4.0
8	1.8	4.7	9.0	4.4	1.6	0.0
9	1.7	6.2	13.3	4.7	2.7	

Source: http://inflationdata.com/inflation/Inflation_Rate/Histor
icalInflation.aspx?dsInflation_currentPage=0

8.2 Unemployment Rate, 1950–2000

Year	1950	1960	1970	1980	1990	2000
0	5.3	5.5	4.9	7.1	5.6	4.0
1	3.3	6.7	5.9	7.6	6.8	4.7
2	3.0	5.5	5.6	9.7	7.5	5.8
3	2.9	5.7	4.9	9.6	6.9	6.0
4	5.5	5.2	5.6	7.5	6.1	5.5
5	4.4	4.5	8.5	7.2	5.6	5.1
6	4.1	3.8	7.7	7.0	5.4	4.6
7	4.3	3.8	7.1	6.2	4.9	4.6
8	6.8	3.6	6.1	5.5	4.5	5.8
9	5.5	3.5	5.8	5.3	4.2	

Source: http://stats.bls.gov/cps/cpsaat1.pdf

Chapter Notes

Introduction

1. *The Founders' Almanac* (Washington, DC: Heritage Foundation, 2001), 206.
2. *Ibid.*
3. *Ibid.*, 205.
4. *Ibid.*, 207.
5. Abraham Lincoln Quotes, http://think exist.com/quotes/Abraham_Lincoln/.

Chapter 1

1. Appendix 2.
2. U.S. Dept. of State, http://www.state.gov/r/pa/ho/time/nr/14318.htm.
3. U.S. Dept. of Treasury, http://www.us-treas.gov/education/history/events/1600-1799.shtml.
4. Achieving Early America, http://www.earlyamerica.com/earlyamerica/milestones/whiskey/.
5. U.S. History, http://www.u-s-history.com/pages/h480.html.
6. *Ibid.*, h443.
7. President Elect Articles, http://www.presidentelect.org/art_before12.html.
8. Federalists, http://www.u-s-history.com/pages/h375.html.
9. Citizendium, http://en.citizendium.org/wiki/Democratic-Republican_Party.
10. David McCullough, *John Adams* (New York: Simon & Schuster, 2001), 499.
11. Miller Center, http://millercenter.org/academic/americanpresident/adams.
12. PBS, http://www.pbs.org/wgbh/amex/adams/peopleevents/e_diploma.html.
13. *Britannica,* http://www.britannica.com/EBchecked/topic/334521/Arthur-Lee.
14. President Elect, http://www.president-elect.org/e1789.html.
15. U.S. Congress, http://bioguide.congress.gov/scripts/biodisplay.pl?index=P000357; Wikipedia, http://en.wikipedia.org/wiki/List_of_United_States_political_families_%28P%29.

16. Answers.com, http://www.answers.com/topic/aaron-burr.
17. *New York Times Almanac 2009,* 125.
18. Oyez, http://www.oyez.org./.
19. Appendix 2.
20. Answers.com, http://www.answers.com/topic/ratification-of-the-constitution.
21. Larry Sabato and Howard Ernst, *Encyclopedia of American Political Parties and Elections* (New York: Checkmark, 2007), 298–299.
22. *Ibid.*, 150, 151.
23. U.S. Senate, http://www.senate.gov/art andhistory/history/common/generic/VP_Thom as_Jefferson.htm.
24. McCullough, *John Adams,* 462–63.
25. *Ibid.*
26. Sabato and Ernst, *Encyclopedia of American Political Parties and Elections,* 298–299.
27. *Ibid.*
28. McCullough, *John Adams,* 465.
29. The American Presidency, http://www.presidency.ucsb.edu/showelection.php?year=1796.
30. PBS, http://www.pbs.org/wgbh/amex/adams/sfeature/sf_qa.html#sf_qa_06.
31. PBS, http://www.pbs.org/wgbh/amex/adams/sfeature/sf_qa.html#sf_qa_03.
32. Miller Center, http://millercenter.org/academic/americanpresident/adams.
33. First Federal Congress, 1789–91, http://www.gwu.edu/~ffcp/exhibit/p1/members/.
34. The Speaker's House, http://www.speakershouse.org/history.html.
35. Connecticut State Library, http://www.cslib.org/gov/trumbullj.htm.
36. Biographies, http://www.let.rug.nl/usa/B/dayton/dayton.htm.
37. Appendices 1-1, 1-2.
38. Appendix 1-1.
39. Oyez, http://www.oyez.org/.
40. John Rutledge, http://www.history.army.mil/books/RevWar/ss/rutledge.htm.
41. *Ibid.*
42. Wm. J. Brennan, http://www.michaelariens.com/ConLaw/justices/brennan.htm.

43. Mark R. Levin, *Men in Black* (Washington, DC: Regnery, 2005), 2.

44. Miller Center, http://millercenter.org/academic/americanpresident/adams.

45. Benjamin Franklin Bache, p. 8, http://www.libraries.psu.edu/digital/pahistory/folder_3/page_1.html.

46. Major Acts of Congress, http://www.enotes.com/major-acts-congress.

47. Debate on a Standing Army, http://www.shsu.edu/~his_ncp/Starmy.html.

48. Miller Center, http://millercenter.org/academic/americanpresident/adams.

49. *Ibid.*

50. Infoplease, http://www.infoplease.com/ce6/history/A0852911.html.

51. Miller Center, http://millercenter.org/academic/americanpresident/adams.

Chapter 2

1. *New York Times Almanac 2009,* 125.

2. Historic Valley Forge, http://www.ushistory.org/valleyforge/served/hamilton.html.

3. *New York Times Almanac 2009,* 125.

4. From Revolution to Reconstruction, http://www.let.rug.nl/~usa/B/ccpinckn/ccpinckn.htm.

5. See discussion in chapter 1 of this book.

6. Thomas Jefferson, http://sc94.ameslab.gov/TOUR/tjefferson.html.

7. *The Founders' Almanac* (Washington, DC: Heritage Foundation), 205.

8. Whiskey Rebellion, http://www.globalsecurity.org/military/ops/whiskey_rebellion.htm.

9. *New York Times Almanac 2009,* 125.

10. The Presidential Election of 1800, Joanne B. Freeman, p. 1,

11. http://www.historynow.org/historian4.html.

12. *New York Times Almanac 2009,* 125.

13. McCullough, *John Adams,* 537.

14. *Ibid.*

15. Answers.com, http://www.answers.com/topic/judiciary-act-of-1801.

16. Answers.com, http://www.answers.com/topic/fries-s-rebellion.

17. Miller Center, http://millercenter.org/academic/americanpresident/adams.

18. Alien & Sedition Acts 1798, http://www.earlyamerica.com/earlyamerica/milestones/sedition/.

19. Joanne B. Freeman, *The Presidential Election of 1800,* http://www.gilderlehrman.org/historynow/09_2004/historian4.php

20. http://www.historynow.org/historian4.html.

21. Thomas Jefferson Encyclopedia, http://wiki.monticello.org/mediawiki/index.php/James_Callender.

22. Richard N. Rosenfeld, *American Aurora* (New York: St. Martin's, 1997).

23. Timothy Pickering, http://www.nps.gov/history/museum/exhibits/revwar/image_gal/indeimg/pickering.html.

24. James McHenry, http://www.history.army.mil/books/RevWar/ss/mchenry.htm.

25. Seth Kaller, Inc., http://www.sethkaller.net/catalogs/39-revolutionary-war/62-john-adams-attacks-alexander-hamiltons-treachery-and-discusses-prospect-of-war-with-england-or-fr.

26. CNN, http://www.cnn.com/2008/LIVING/wayoflife/08/22/mf.campaign.slurs.slogans/index.html.

27. Thomas Jefferson timeline, http://www.monticello.org/jefferson/timeline.html.

28. Miller Center, http://millercenter.org/academic/americanpresident/jefferson.

29. President Elect, http://www.presidentelect.org/e1800.html#state.

30. Electoral Vote 1800, http://www.usconstitution.net/ev_1800.html.

31. David Lieb's Atlas, http://uselectionatlas.org/RESULTS/.

32. Miller Center, http://millercenter.org/academic/americanpresident/jefferson.

33. Oyez, http://www.oyez.org/.

34. Samuel Chase, http://colonialhall.com/chase/chase4.php.

35. Oyez, http://www.oyez.org/.

36. Infoplease, http://www.infoplease.com/ipa/A0101289.html.

37. *Times* Online, http://www.timesonline.co.uk/tol/news/world/us_and_americas/us_elections/article5055404.ece?token=null&offset=0&page=1.

38. Miller Center, http://millercenter.org/academic/americanpresident/keyevents/jefferson.

39. *Ibid.*

40. Stanford, http://ai.stanford.edu/~csewell/culture/laws.htm.

41. Miller Center, http://millercenter.org/academic/americanpresident/keyevents/jefferson.

42. Major Acts of Congress, http://www.enotes.com/major-acts-congress.

43. Miller Center, http://millercenter.org/academic/americanpresident/adams.

Chapter 3

1. U.S. Government Revenue, http://www.usgovernmentrevenue.com/federal_revenue.

2. Appendix 4.

3. Appendix 5.

4. *Ibid.*

5. *New York Times Almanac 2009*, 168.
6. U.S. Government Revenue, http://www.usgovernmentrevenue.com/federal_revenue.
7. Appendix 4.
8. U.S. Government Revenue, http://www.usgovernmentrevenue.com/federal_revenue.
9. U.S. History, http://www.u-s-history.com/pages/h277.html.
10. Appendix 5.
11. Answers.com, http://www.answers.com/topic/missouri-compromise.
12. Answers.com, http://www.answers.com/topic/rush-bagot-treaty.
13. Answers.com, http://www.answers.com/topic/adams-on-s-treaty.
14. Appendix 2.
15. *New York Times Almanac 2008*, 112.
16. Miller Center, http://millercenter.org/academic/americanpresident/jqadams.
17. Miller Center, http://millercenter.org/academic/americanpresident/jackson.
18. *Georgia Encyclopedia*, http://www.georgiaencyclopedia.org/nge/Article.jsp?id=h-2488.
19. Men Who Ran for President, http://www.juntosociety.com/othercandidates/henryclay.html.
20. Wikipedia, http://en.wikipedia.org/wiki/Henry_Clay.
21. Answers.com, http://www.answers.com/topic/henry-brockholst-livingston.
22. Answers.com, http://www.answers.com/topic/samuel-chase.
23. Junto Society, http://www.juntosociety.com/vp/thomkins.html.
24. *Portland (ME) Eastern Argus*, October 18, 1824 (American Historical Newspapers, Boston Public Library).
25. *Trenton (NJ)Federalist*, August 8, 1824.
26. *Haverhill (MA) Gazette*, November 20, 1824.
27. Sabato and Ernst, *Encyclopedia of American Political Parties and Elections*, 307.
28. Election of 1824, http://www.u-s-history.com/pages/h262.html.
29. Miller Center, http://millercenter.org/academic/americanpresident/jqadams/essays/biography/3.
30. David Lieb's Atlas, http://uselectionatlas.org/RESULTS/.
31. Miller Center, http://millercenter.org/academic/americanpresident/jqadams.
32. *Ibid.*
33. Miller Center, http://millercenter.org/academic/americanpresident/jqadams/essays/biography/3.
34. *Ibid.*
35. Infoplease, http://www.infoplease.com/biography/us/congress/taylor-john-w.html.
36. Wikipedia, http://en.wikipedia.org/wiki/John_W._Taylor_(politician).

37. Infoplease, http://www.infoplease.com/biography/us/congress/stevenson-andrew.html.
38. Wm. J. Brennan, http://www.michaelariens.com/ConLaw/justices/brennan.htm.
39. Oyez, http://www.oyez.org/.
40. Miller Center, http://millercenter.org/academic/americanpresident/jqadams.
41. Appendices 1-1, 1-2.
42. Miller Center, http://millercenter.org/academic/americanpresident/jqadams.
43. *Ibid.*
44. Appendix 5.
45. Encyclopedia.com, http://www.encyclopedia.com/doc/1G2-3406400922.html.
46. Appendix 2.
47. Manifest Destiny, http://www.civics-online.org/library/formatted/texts/manifest_destiny.html.
48. Miller Center, http://millercenter.org/academic/americanpresident/jqadams.
49. U.S. Congress, http://bioguide.congress.gov/scripts/biodisplay.pl?index=c000044.
50. *New York Times Almanac 2009*, 279.
51. Appendix 7.
52. Miller Center, http://millercenter.org/academic/americanpresident/jqadams.
53. White House, http://www.whitehouse.gov/about/presidents/johnquincyadams/.
54. Probert Encyclopedia, http://www.probertencyclopaedia.com/cgi-bin/res.pl?keyword=John+Quincy+Adams&offset=0.

Chapter 4

1. *New York Times Almanac 2009*, 125–28.
2. *Times* Online, http://www.timesonline.co.uk/tol/news/world/us_and_americas/us_elections/article5055404.ece?token=null&offset=0&page=1.
3. Miller Center, http://millercenter.org/academic/americanpresident/jackson.
4. *New York Times Almanac 2009*, 127.
5. Miller Center, http://millercenter.org/academic/americanpresident/vanburen.
6. U.S. History, http://www.u-s-history.com/pages/h967.html.
7. Miller Center, http://millercenter.org/academic/americanpresident/harrison.
8. *New York Times Almanac 2009*, 125–127.
9. Miller Center, http://millercenter.org/academic/americanpresident/tyler.
10. Miller Center, http://millercenter.org/academic/americanpresident/polk.
11. Miller Center, http://millercenter.org/academic/americanpresident/taylor.
12. Miller Center, http://millercenter.org/academic/americanpresident/fillmore.
13. Answers.com, http://www.answers.com/topic/compromise-of-1850.

14. Miller Center, http://millercenter.org/academic/americanpresident/pierce.
15. The History Place, http://www.history place.com/lincoln/kansas.htm.
16. Miller Center, http://millercenter.org/academic/americanpresident/buchanan.
17. Miller Center, http://millercenter.org/academic/americanpresident/johnson.
18. Miller Center, http://millercenter.org/academic/americanpresident/lincoln,
19. Miller Center, http://millercenter.org/academic/americanpresident/grant.
20. U.S. Government Revenue, http://www.usgovernmentrevenue.com/.
21. Rep/Dem. Convention History, http://www.poynter.org/column.asp?aid=68171&id=49.
22. U.S. History.org., http://www.ushistory.org/gop/convention_1856.htm.
23. Republican Convention, http://www.loc.gov/rr/main/republican_conventions.pdf.
24. U.S. Congress, http://bioguide.congress.gov/scripts/biodisplay.pl?index=W000585.
25. James G. Blaine, http://www.u-s-history.com/pages/h726.html.
26. U.S. Congress, http://bioguide.congress.gov/scripts/biodisplay.pl?index=W000585.
27. White House, http://www.whitehouse.gov/about/presidents/RutherfordBHayes/.
28. U.S. Congress, http://bioguide.congress.gov/scripts/biodisplay.pl?index=W000341.
29. Party Platforms, http://www.presidency.ucsb.edu/platforms.php.
30. Democratic Convention, http://www.loc.gov/rr/main/democratic_conventions.pdf.
31. Specie Resumption Act, http://www.u-s-history.com/pages/h719.html.
32. Party Platforms, http://www.presidency.ucsb.edu/platforms.php.
33. Miller Center, http://millercenter.org/academic/americanpresident/hayes.
34. Samuel J. Tilden, http://www.u-s-history.com/pages/h397.htm.
35. Aug. 27, 1876.
36. U.S. History, http://www.u-s-history.com/pages/h213.html.
37. Oyez, http://www.oyez.org/.
38. Levin, *Men in Black*, preface.
39. David Lieb's Atlas, http://uselectionatlas.org/RESULTS/.
40. Sabato and Ernst, *Encyclopedia of American Political Parties and Elections*, 324.
41. David Lieb's Atlas, http://uselectionatlas.org/RESULTS/.
42. Sabato and Ernst, *Encyclopedia of American Political Parties and Elections*, 325.
43. U.S. History, http://www.u-s-history.com/pages/h397.html.
44. Miller Center, http://millercenter.org/academic/americanpresident/hayes.

45. Miller Center, http://millercenter.org/academic/americanpresident/hayes/essays/biography/4.
46. Roscoe Conkling, http://www.u-s-history.com/pages/h706.html.
47. Sabato and Ernst, *Encyclopedia of American Political Parties and Elections*, 324.
48. Appendix 1-1.
49. Judiciary Act 1869.
50. Oyez, http://www.oyez.org/.
51. Exploring Constitutional Law, Doug Linder, http://www.law.umkc.edu/faculty/projects/ftrials/conlaw/reynoldsvus.html.
52. U.S. Supreme Court Center, http://supreme.justia.com/us/99/130/.
53. Miller Center, http://millercenter.org/academic/americanpresident/hayes.
54. Roscoe Conkling, http://www.u-s-history.com/pages/h706.html.
55. Miller Center, http://millercenter.org/academic/americanpresident/arthur.
56. Miller Center, http://millercenter.org/academic/americanpresident/hayes.
57. *Ibid.*
58. Business Cycles, http://www.nber.org/cycles.html.
59. Ohio History, http://www.ohiohistorycentral.org/entry.php?rec=503.
60. Wikipedia, http://en.wikipedia.org/wiki/Timeline_of_labor_issues_and_events #1870s.
61. U.S. History, http://www.u-s-history.com/pages/h171.html.
62. Appendix 7.
63. Miller Center, http://millercenter.org/academic/americanpresident/hayes.
64. *Ibid.*
65. National Archives, http://www.archives.gov/locations/finding-aids/chinese-immigration.html.
66. Chinese-American Experience, http://immigrants.harpweek.com/ChineseAmericans/2KeyIssues/BurlingameTreaty1868.htm.
67. Samuel J. Tilden, http://www.samueltilden.com/.
68. Sabato and Ernst, *Encyclopedia of American Political Parties and Elections*, 326.

Chapter 5

1. Democratic Conventions, http://www.loc.gov/rr/main/democratic_conventions.pdf.
2. Republican Conventions, http://www.loc.gov/rr/main/republican_conventions.pdf.
3. History Central, http://www.historycentral.com/elections/Conventions/1880Rep.html.
4. *New York Times Almanac 2008*, 114.
5. Democratic Conventions, http://www.loc.gov/rr/main/democratic_conventions.pdf.

6. The Political Graveyard, http://political graveyard.com/parties/D/1880/index.html.

7. Party Platforms, http://www.presidency. ucsb.edu/ws/index.php?pid=25836.

8. American Presidency Project, http:// www.presidency.ucsb.edu/platforms.php.

9. Miller Center, http://millercenter.org/ academic/americanpresident/garfield.

10. *New York Times Almanac 2008*, 113,

11. James Garfield Quotes, http://www. brainyquote.com/quotes/authors/j/james_a_ garfield_2.html.

12. U.S. Presidential Election 1880, http: //www.absoluteastronomy.com/topics/United _States_presidential_election_1880.

13. Answers.com, http://www.answers.com/ topic/winfield-scott-hancock#Early_life_and_ family.

14. *Ibid.*

15. *Ibid.*

16. *Ibid.*

17. Sabato and Ernst, *Encyclopedia of American Political Parties and Elections*, 327.

18. U.S. History, http://www.u-s-history. com/pages/h212.html.

19. Wikipedia, http://en.wikipedia.org/ wiki/James_Weaver.

20. David Leip's Atlas, http://uselectionat las.org/RESULTS/.

21. *Ibid.*

22. Miller Center, http://millercenter.org/ academic/americanpresident/arthur.

23. Miller Center, http://millercenter.org/ academic/americanpresident/garfield.

24. U.S. Congress, http://bioguide.congress. gov/scripts/biodisplay.pl?index=K000048.

25. U.S. Congress, http://bioguide.congress. gov/scripts/biodisplay.pl?index=C000152.

26. Oyez, http://www.oyez.org/.

27. Miller Center, http://millercenter.org/ academic/americanpresident/garfield.

28. ClassBrain.com, http://www.classbrain. com/artteenst/publish/article_130.shtml.

29. History Central, http://www.historycen tral.com/rec/IndustrialAge/PendletonAct.html.

30. Bob's World, http://www.bobsuniverse. com/BWAH/21-Arthur/18820801a.pdf.

31. U.S. Census Bureau, http://www.census. gov/population/www/documentation/twps00 56/twps0056.html.

32. Appendix 7.

33. Appendix 2.

34. Miller Center, http://millercenter.org/ academic/americanpresident/Arthur.

35. *Ibid.*

Chapter 6

1. Republican Conventions, http://www. loc.gov/rr/main/republican_conventions.pdf.

2. Miller Center, http://millercenter.org/ academic/americanpresident/arthur.

3. Socialist Alternative, http://www.sa.org. au/index.php?option=com_content&task= view&id=1041&Itemid=106.

4. *Britannica*, http://www.britannica.com/ EBchecked/topic/396208/Mugwump.

5. U.S. History, http://www.u-s-history. com/pages/h706.html.

6. Democratic Conventions, http://www. loc.gov/rr/main/democratic_conventions.pdf.

7. Miller Center, http://millercenter.org/ academic/americanpresident/cleveland.

8. NNDB, http://www.nndb.com/people/ 235/000050085/.

9. Miller Center, http://millercenter.org/ academic/americanpresident/bharris.

10. Miller Center, http://millercenter.org/ academic/americanpresident/cleveland.

11. Sabato and Ernst, *Encyclopedia of American Political Parties and Elections*, 328.

12. *Ibid.*

13. *Ibid.*

14. U.S. History, http://www.u-s-history. com/pages/h726.html.

15. *Ibid.*

16. *Ibid.*, 329.

17. Religious Liberty Archive, http://www. churchstatelaw.com/historicalmaterials/8_11. asp.

18. *Ibid.*, http://churchstatelaw.com/state-constitutions/index.asp.

19. Oyez, http://www.oyez.org/.

20. *Catholic Encyclopedia*, http://www.new advent.org/cathen/08677a.htm.

21. *Wheeling (WV) Register*, August 2 and 12, 1884 (American Historical Newspapers, Boston Public Library).

22. Sabato and Ernst, *Encyclopedia of American Political Parties and Elections*, 328.

23. U.S. History, http://www.u-s-history. com/pages/h738.html.

24. *Ibid.*, http://www.u-s-history.com/pages/ h262.html.

25. American Presidency Project, http:// www.presidency.ucsb.edu/showelection.php ?year=1884.

26. David Lieb's Atlas, http://uselectionat las.org/RESULTS/index.html.

27. Miller Center, http://millercenter.org/ academic/americanpresident/cleveland.

28. U.S. Congress, http://bioguide.congress. gov/scripts/biodisplay.pl?index=H000493.

28. Oyez, http://www.oyez.org/.

30. Miller Center, http://millercenter.org/ academic/americanpresident/cleveland.

31. *Ibid.*

32. Miller Center, http://millercenter.org/ academic/americanpresident/cleveland/essays/ biography/4.

33. National Bureau of Economic Research, http://www.nber.org/cycles.html.

34. Miller Center, http://millercenter.org/academic/americanpresident/cleveland.

35. Suite101.com, http://americanhistory.suite101.com/article.cfm/president_clevelands_first_term.

36. Answers.com, http://www.answers.com/topic/dawes-act.

37. Encarta, http://encarta.msn.com/encyclopedia_761554156_3/grover_cleveland.html.

38. National Women Suffrage Assoc., http://memory.loc.gov/ammem/naw/nawstime.html.

39. U.S. History, http://www.u-s-history.com/pages/h744.html.

40. Miller Center, http://millercenter.org/academic/americanpresident/cleveland.

41. Appendix 7.

42. *Ibid.*

43. AFL-CIO, http://www.aflcio.org/aboutus/history/history/timeline.cfm.

44. Wikipedia, http://en.wikipedia.org/wiki/Timeline_of_labor_issues_and_events.

45. American Presidency Project, http://www.presidency.ucsb.edu/platforms.php.

46. U.S. Dept. of Labor, http://www.dol.gov/OPA/ABOUTDOL/LABORDAY.HTM.

47. AFL-CIO, http://www.aflcio.org/aboutus/history/history/gompers.cfm.

48. American Presidents, http://www.american-presidents.com/grover-cleveland.

49. Infoplease, http://www.infoplease.com/ipa/A0801767.html#.

50. Appendix 2.

51. Miller Center, http://millercenter.org/academic/americanpresident/cleveland.

52. *Ibid.*

53. *Ibid.*

54. *Ibid.*

55. Mt. Holyoke, http://www.mtholyoke.edu/acad/intrel/gc26.htm.

56. Miller Center, http://millercenter.org/academic/americanpresident/cleveland.

Chapter 7

1. See chapter six of this book.

2. Democratic Conventions, http://www.loc.gov/rr/main/democratic_conventions.pdf.

3. Republican Conventions, http://www.loc.gov/rr/main/republican_conventions.pdf.

4. NNDP, http://www.nndb.com/people/235/000050085/.

5. Miller Center, http://millercenter.org/academic/americanpresident/bharrison/.

6. Party Platforms, http://www.presidency.ucsb.edu/platforms.php.

7. Miller Center, http://millercenter.org/academic/americanpresident/harrison.

8. Larry Sabato and Howard Ernst, *Encyclopedia of American Political Parties and Elections* New York: Checkmark), 330.

9. *Ibid.*

10. Ancestry.com, http://freepages.genealogy.rootsweb.ancestry.com/~lthurman/allen/allen.html.

11. Cleveland Chronicles, http://www.angelfire.com/il/ClevelandFamilyChron/Prez2.html.

12. Miller Center, http://millercenter.org/academic/americanpresident/cleveland.

13. Sabato and Ernst, *Encyclopedia of American Political Parties and Elections,* 330.

14. Appendix 6.

15. David Leip's Atlas, http://uselectionatlas.org/RESULTS/.

16. Appendix 2.

17. David Leip's Atlas, http://uselectionatlas.org/RESULTS/.

18. *Ibid.*

19. *Ibid.*

20. Miller Center, http://millercenter.org/academic/americanpresident/harrison.

21. The Making of a Nation, Election 1888, http://www.tingroom.com/voa/5/Making/18710.html.

22. Oyez, http://www.oyez.org/.

23. Wikipedia, http://en.wikipedia.org/wiki/Yick_Wo_v._Hopkins.

24. Miller Center, http://millercenter.org/academic/americanpresident/bharrison.

25. *Ibid.*

26. Oyez, http://www.oyez.org/.

27. Miller Center, http://millercenter.org/academic/americanpresident/bharrison.

28. *Ibid.*

29. Major Acts of Congress, http://www.enotes.com/major-acts-congress.

30. *Ibid.*

31. Miller Center, http://millercenter.org/academic/americanpresident/bharrison.

32. U.S. History, http://www.u-s-history.com/pages/h762.html.

33. U.S. Citizenship and Immigration Services, http://www.uscis.gov/portal/site/uscis.

34. Appendix 7.

35. *Ibid.*

36. Global Security.org, http://www.globalsecurity.org/military/systems/ship/scn-1889-harrison.htm.

37. Appendix 5.

38. Appendix 2.

39. Global Security.org, http://www.globalsecurity.org/military/systems/ship/scn-1889-harrison.htm.

40. Miller Center, Key Events, http://millercenter.org/academic/americanpresident/bharrison.

41. U.S. History, http://www.u-s-history.com/pages/h768.html.

42. Department of Commerce, http://www.commerce.gov/.

Chapter 8

1. *New York Times Almanac 2009*, 129–31.
2. *Times* Online, http://www.timesonline.co.uk/tol/news/world/us_and_americas/us_ele ctions/article5055404.ece?token=null&offset =0&page=1.
3. Miller Center, http://millercenter.org/academic/americanpresident/cleveland.
4. Miller Center, http://millercenter.org/academic/americanpresident/mckinley.
5. Miller Center, http://millercenter.org/academic/americanpresident/taft.
6. Miller Center, http://millercenter.org/academic/americanpresident/harding.
7. Infoplease, http://www.infoplease.com/ce6/history/A0848032.html.
8. Miller Center, http://millercenter.org/academic/americanpresident/coolidge.
9. Miller Center, http://millercenter.org/academic/americanpresident/roosevelt.
10. Claremont Institute, http://www.clare mont.org/publications/precepts/id.83/precept _detail.asp.
11. Claremont Institute, http://millercenter.org/academic/americanpresident/hoover.
12. Miller Center, http://millercenter.org/academic/americanpresident/fdroosevelt.
13. FDR: The Economic Bill of Rights, http://www.worldpolicy.org/projects/globalrights/econrights/fdr-econbill.html.
14. Miller Center, http://millercenter.org/academic/americanpresident/truman.
15. Appendix 2.
16. Museum of Broadcast Communications, http://www.museum.tv/archives/etv/P/htmlP/presidential/presidential.htm.
17. Smithsonian, http://www.smithsonian mag.com/history-archaeology/1948-democra tic-convention.html.
18. History of Presidential Primaries, http://jjb.yuku.com/topic/215542/t/History-of-pres idential-primaries.html.
19. History of Presidential Primaries, http://www.plunderbund.com/2007/12/28/history-of-presidential-primaries/.
20. University of Alabama, http://www.ala bamamoments.alabama.gov/sec54.html.
21. Democratic Convention 1948, http://www.loc.gov/rr/main/democratic_convent ions.pdf.
22. Miller Center, http://millercenter.org/academic/americanpresident/truman.
23. The Civil Rights Legacy of Harry S Truman, http://millercenter.org/.
24. Miller Center, http://millercenter.org/academic/americanpresident/truman.

25. *Ibid.*
26. U.S. History, http://www.ushistory.org/gop/convention_1948.htm.
27. *Ibid.*
28. Smithsonian, http://www.smithsonian mag.com/history-archaeology/1948-democra tic-convention.html.
29. Republican Conventions, http://www.loc.gov/rr/main/republican_conventions.pdf.
30. The Great Truman Surprise, http://www.kennesaw.edu/pols/3380/pres/1948.html.
31. States' Rights Convention, http://www.alabamamoments.alabama.gov/sec54.html.
32. Smoking Gun Archive, http://www.the smokinggun.com/archive/dixiecrat1.html.
33. Progressive Party 1948, http://www.lib.uiowa.edu/spec-coll/Bai/epstein.htm.
34. Progressive Party Platform, http://www.davidpietrusza.com/1948-party-platforms.html.
35. Miller Center, http://millercenter.org/academic/americanpresident/truman.
36. Sabato and Ernst, *Encyclopedia of American Political Parties and Elections*, 350–51.
37. Wikipedia, http://en.wikipedia.org/wiki/Thomas_E._Dewey#Early_life_and_family.
38. Internet Accuracy Project, http://www.accuracyproject.org/cbe-Dewey,Thomas.html.
39. Strom Thurmond Institute, http://www.strom.clemson.edu/strom/bio.html.
40. Absolute Astronomy, http://www.abso luteastronomy.com/topics/Henry_A._Wallace #encyclopedia.
41. U.S. Department of Commerce, *Historical Statistics Colonial Times to 1957*, p. 710.
42. Oyez, http://www.oyez.org/.
43. *Ibid.*
44. Smithsonian.com, http://www.smithso nianmag.com/history-archaeology/1948-de mocratic-convention.html.
45. Miller Center, http://millercenter.org/academic/americanpresident/truman.
46. Harry Truman's 1948 Comeback Campaign, http://politics.usnews.com/opinion/ar ticles/2008/10/30/past — present-harry-trum ans-1948-comeback-campaign.html
47. Miller Center, http://millercenter.org/academic/americanpresident/truman.
48. Harry S. Truman Library, http://www.trumanlibrary.org/teacher/campaign.htm.
49. The Great Truman Surprise, http://www.kennesaw.edu/pols/3380/pres/1948.html.
50. Strom Thurmond Institute, http://www.strom.clemson.edu/strom/bio.html.
51. The Great Truman Surprise, http://www.kennesaw.edu/pols/3380/pres/1948.html.
52. The Experts Got It Wrong, http://www.austincc.edu/lpatrick/his1302PCM/WhenAllT heExperts2.html.

53. The Great Truman Surprise, http://www.kennesaw.edu/pols/3380/pres/1948.html.
54. *Ibid.*
55. *Ibid.*
56. Harry Truman's 1948 Comeback Campaign, http://politics.usnews.com/opinion/articles/2008/10/30/past — present-harry-trumans-1948-comeback-campaign.html
57. The Great Truman Surprise, http://www.kennesaw.edu/pols/3380/pres/1948.html.
58. Harry S. Truman Library, http://www.trumanlibrary.org/teacher/campaign.htm.
59. History News Network, http://hnn.us/articles/1166.html.
60. Gallup, http://www.gallup.com/poll/7444/gallup-brain-strom-thurmond-1948-election.aspx.
61. U.S. News, 12/15/02, http://www.kennesaw.edu/pols/3380/pres/1948.html.
62. University of Alabama, http://www.alabamamoments.alabama.gov/sec54.html.
63. American Heritage, http://www.americanheritage.com/articles/magazine/ah/1989/2/1989_2_92.shtml.
64. Sabato and Ernst, *Encyclopedia of American Political Parties and Elections,* 350–51.
65. David Liep's Atlas, http://www.uselectionatlas.org/.
66. *Ibid.*
67. Miller Center, http://millercenter.org/academic/americanpresident/truman.
68. U.S. Senate, http://www.senate.gov/artandhistory/history/common/generic/People_Leaders_McFarland.htm.
69. Oyez, http://www.oyez.org/.
70. Justia, http://supreme.justia.com/us/339/637/.
71. History, http://www.ssa.gov/history/1950.html.
72. Office of Budget and Management, Historical Tables 2010, 3.1.
73. Major Acts of Congress, http://www.enotes.com/major-acts-congress/central-intelligence-agency-actngress.
74. HUD, http://www.hud.gov/offices/adm/about/admguide/history.cfm#1940.
75. U.S. Dept. of Labor http://www.dol.gov/esa/minwage/coverage.htm.
76. History, http://www.ssa.gov/history/1950.html.
77. Federal Civilian Defense Act, http://www.enotes.com/major-acts-congress/federal-civil-defense-act.
78. History, http://history.sandiego.edu/GEN/filmnotes/kefauver.html.
79. History Central, http://www.historycentral.com/documents/McCarran.html.
80. Eleanor Roosevelt Historic, http://www.nps.gov/archive/elro/glossary/huac.htm.

81. Appendix 5.
82. Historical Tables 2010, 3.1.
83. Historical Tables, http://www.enotes.com/major-acts-congress/export-import-bank-act.
84. Major Acts of Congress, http://www.enotes.com/major-acts-congress/united-nations-participation-act — enabled U.S. to join U.N.
85. Truman Library, http://www.trumanlibrary.org/teacher/berlin.htm.
86. *New York Times Almanac 2008,* 444.
87. Major Acts of Congress, http://www.enotes.com/major-acts-congress/atomic-energy-acts.
88. U.S. Dept. of State, http://www.state.gov/r/pa/ho/time/cwr/82210.htm.
89. *Ibid.,* http://www.enotes.com/major-acts-congress/mutual-security-act.
90. Ranking Presidents, http://falcon.arts.cornell.edu/govt/courses/F04/PresidentialRankings.pdf.

Chapter 9

1. Miller Center, http://millercenter.org/academic/americanpresident/truman.
2. WSJ, http://online.wsj.com/public/resources/documents/info-presapp0605-31.html.
3. Office of Budget and Management, Historical Tables 2010, 3.1.
4. Infoplease, http://www.infoplease.com/ce6/people/A0861642.html.
5. Miller Center, http://millercenter.org/academic/americanpresident/eisenhower.
6. Historical Tables 2010, 1.2.
7. *Historical Statistics Colonial Times to 1957,* p. 721.
8. *Ibid.,* 710.
9. *Times* Online, http://www.timesonline.co.uk/tol/news/world/us_and_americas/us_elections/article5030539.ece.
10. 1960 Republican Convention, http://www.loc.gov/rr/main/republican_conventions.pdf.
11. Gary Allen, *The Rockefeller File,* chapter 13, http://www.reformation.org/rockefeller-file.html.
12. The 1960 Republican Convention, http://www.chicagohs.org/history/politics/1960.html.
13. Cold War Museum, http://www.coldwar.org/Articles/60s/u2_incident.asp.
14. The 1960 Republican Convention, http://www.chicagohs.org/history/politics/1960.html.
15. *Ibid.*
16. *The Atlantic* Online, http://www.theat

lantic.com/past/docs/issues/95dec/conbook/co
nbook.htm.
17. The 1960 Republican Convention, http:
//www.chicagohs.org/history/politics/1960.
html.
18. *Ibid.*
19. Democratic Conventions, http://www.
loc.gov/rr/main/democratic_conventions.
pdf.
20. U.S. Congress, http://bioguide.congress.
gov/scripts/biodisplay.pl?index=h000953.
21. U.S. Congress, http://bioguide.congress.
gov/scripts/biodisplay.pl?index=s001136.
22. Miller Center, http://millercenter.org/
academic/americanpresident/lbjohnson..
23. Miller Center, http://millercenter.org/
academic/americanpresident/kennedy.
24. America, http://www.america.gov/st/
usg-english/2007/September/20070917120019
ndyblehs0.1648523.html.
25. Sabato and Ernst, *Encyclopedia of American Political Parties and Elections*, 356.
26. *Ibid.*, 357.
27. Sean J. Savage, *JFK, LBJ, and the Democratic Party*. Albany: State University of New
York Press, 2004.
28. Eleanor Roosevelt Papers, http://www.
gwu.edu/~erpapers/mep/displaydoc.cfm?doc
id=jfk41.
29. *Washington Post,* http://www.washing
tonpost.com/wp-dyn/content/article/2005/06/
21/AR2005062101632.html.
30. American Presidency Project, http://
www.presidency.ucsb.edu/platforms.php.
31. Economic Bill of Rights, http://www.
worldpolicy.org/projects/globalrights/econ-
rights/fdr-econbill.html.
32. Miller Center, http://millercenter.org/
academic/americanpresident/nixon; Nixon Library, http://www.nixonlibrary.gov/.
33. U.S. Congress, http://bioguide.congress.
gov/scripts/biodisplay.pl?index=V000118.
34. Miller Center, http://millercenter.org/
academic/americanpresident/kennedy.
35. Suite 101.com, http://americanhistory.
suite101.com/article.cfm/woodrow_wilson_
and_white_supremacy.
36. *Ibid.*, http://millercenter.org/academic/
americanpresident/eisenhower.
37. Oyez, http://www.oyez.org/.
38. Levin, *Men in Black,* preface.
39. Oyez, http://www.oyez.org/.
40. MBC (Museum of Broadcast Communications), http://www.museum.tv/eotvsection.
php?entrycode=kennedy-nixon.
41. Nixon vs. Kennedy 9/26/60, http://www.
youtube.com/watch?v=QazmVHAO0os.
42. Kennedy-Nixon Debates, http://www.
museum.tv/archives/etv/K/htmlK/kennedy-
nixon/kennedy-nixon.htm.
43. Miller Center, http://millercenter.org/
academic/americanpresident/kennedy.
44. The Second Nixon-Kennedy debate,
http://www.archive.org/details/SecondCam
paignDebateNixon-kennedy1960.
45. 1960 debates, http://www-cgi.cnn.com/
ALLPOLITICS/1996/debates/history/1960/.
46. Today in History, http://memory.loc.
gov/ammem/today/oct21.html.
47. Political Party Platforms, http://www.
presidency.ucsb.edu/platforms.php.
48. *Los Angeles Times,* http://latimesblogs.
latimes.com/thedailymirror/2010/01/nixon-
leads-kennedy-in-poll.html.
49. The Road to Camelot, http://www.ken
nesaw.edu/pols/3380/pres/1960.html.
50. Appendix 3.
51. Political Party Platforms, http://www.
presidency.ucsb.edu/platforms.php.
52. The Road to Camelot, http://www.ken
nesaw.edu/pols/3380/pres/1960.html.
53. Wikipedia, http://en.wikipedia.org/
wiki/United_States_presidential_election,_
1960#Campaign_promises.
54. *New York Times,* http://www.nytimes.
com/2000/06/18/opinion/l-nixon-and-eisen
hower-794201.html.
55. 1960 Road to Camelot, http://www.ken
nesaw.edu/pols/3380/pres/1960.html.
56. Infoplease, http://www.infoplease.com/
ce6/history/A0851502.htmlPlease.
57. Miller Center, http://millercenter.org/
academic/americanpresident/kennedy.
58. *New York Times Almanac 2009,* 130.
59. NPR, http://www.npr.org/templates/
story/story.php?storyId=16920600.
60. Absolute Astronomy, http://www.abso
luteastronomy.com/topics/Lyndon_B._John
son#encyclopedia.
61. Road to Camelot, http://www.kenne
saw.edu/pols/3380/pres/1960.html.
62. Appendix 3.
63. King Center, http://www.thekingcen
ter.org/DrMLKingJr/Chronology.aspx.
64. Savage, *JFK, LBJ, and the Democratic
Party,* p. 63.
65. President Johnson, http://www.reforma
tion.org/president-lyndon-johnson.html.
66. David Leip's Atlas, http://uselectionat
las.org/RESULTS/.
67. Probable Cause, http://roswell.fortune
city.com/angelic/96/pctime.htm.
68. Infoplease, http://www.infoplease.com/
ce6/history/A0851502.htmlPlease.
69. Bnet, http://findarticles.com/p/articles/
mi_m0BDW/is_15_42/ai_73409412/.
70. Miller Center, http://millercenter.org/
academic/americanpresident/lbjohnson.
71. TV Guide, http://www.tvguide.com/
celebrities/rebekah-johnson/264915.

72. LBJ Military Service, http://www.lbjlib. utexas.edu/johnson/archives.hom/FAQs/mili tary/military.asp.

73. Abe Fortas, http://www.absoluteastron omy.com/topics/Abe_Fortas#encyclopedia.

74. Miller Center, http://millercenter.org/ academic/americanpresident/lbjohnson.

75. Heller, *Kennedy Cabinet, America's Men of Destiny,* 5.

76. Appendix 1-1.

77. Answers.com, John McCormack, http:// www.answers.com/topic/john-william-mccor mack.

78. Answers.com, John Garner, http:// www.answers.com/topic/john-nance-garner.

79. U.S. Congress, http://bioguide.congress. gov/scripts/biodisplay.pl?index=M000113.

80. Wm. J. Brennan, http://www.michaelar iens.com/ConLaw/justices/brennan.htm.

81. Mark R. Levin, *Men In Black* (Washington, DC: Regnery, 2005), preface, 5, 6.

82. Oyez, http://www.oyez.org/.

83. Miller Center, http://millercenter.org/ academic/americanpresident/kennedy.

84. Robert E. Kelly, *The National Debt of the United States, 1941–2008* (Jefferson, NC: McFarland, 2008), 95–110.

85. Savage, *JFK, LBJ, and the Democratic Party,* 110–115.

86. Housing Act 1961, http://www.presi dency.ucsb.edu/ws/index.php?pid=8216.

87. U.S. Dept. of Labor, http://www.dol. gov/oasam/programs/history/mono-mdta text.htm.

88. ARC, http://www.arcmass.org/jfk/tab id/635/Default.aspx.

89. U.S. E.E.O.C., http://www.eeoc.gov/epa/ anniversary/epa-40.html.

90. Major Acts of Congress, http://www.e notes.com/major-acts-congress.

91. U.S. Peace Corps, http://multimedia. peacecorps.gov/multimedia/pdf/policies/ms101 .pdf.

92. Answers.com, http://www.answers.com/ topic/arms-control-and-disarmament-act-1961-and-amendments.

93. Major Acts of Congress, http://www.e notes.com/major-acts-congress/foreign-assis tance-act.

94. Cuban Missile Crisis, http://library. thinkquest.org/11046/days/bay_of_pigs.ht ml.

95. Space Races.com, http://www.thespace race.com/timeline/.

96. *Ibid.*

97. JFK Library, http://www.jfklibrary.org/ Historical+Resources/JFK+in+History/Nu clear+Test+Ban+Treaty.htm.

98. Miller Center, http://millercenter.org/ academic/americanpresident/kennedy.

Chapter 10

1. Robert E. Kelly, *The National Debt of the United States, 1941–2008* (Jefferson, NC: McFarland, 2008), 123.

2. Historical Tables 2010, 3.1

3. *Ibid.*

4. *Ibid.,* 7.1

5. *Ibid.*

6. Historical Tables 2010, 1.1, 7.1.

7. Appendix 7.

8. All Politics, http://www.cnn.com/ALL POLITICS/1996/conventions/chicago/facts/ chicago68/index.shtml.

9. Nobel Prize, http://nobelprize.org/nobel _prizes/peace/laureates/1964/king-bio.html.

10. Answers.com, http://www.answers.com topic/robert-f-kennedy.

11. *Ibid.,* http://www.answers.com/topic/ george-mcgovern.

12. Bio, http://www.biography.com/arti cles/Abbie-Hoffman-9341100.

13. This Day in History, http://www.his tory.com/this-day-in-history.do?action=Artic le&id=52776.

14. Political Graveyard, http://politicalgrave yard.com/parties/R/1968/index.html.

15. Our Campaigns, http://www.ourcam paigns.com/RaceDetail.html?RaceID=47022.

16. Nixon Quotations, http://www.brainy quote.com/quotes/quotes/r/richardmn116455. html.

17. *New York Times Almanac 2009,* 132.

18. Miller Center, http://millercenter.org/ academic/americanpresident/nixon.

19. Wikipedia, http://en.wikipedia.org/wiki/ George_C._Wallace#1968_third_party_presid ential_run.

20. *Ibid.,* http://en.wikipedia.org/wiki/Geo rge_Wallace#Democratic_presidential_prim aries_of_1964.

21. *Ibid.,* http://en.wikipedia.org/wiki/Geo rge_Wallace.

22. Bio, http://www.biography.com/arti cles/Jackie-Robinson-9460813.

23. American Presidency Project, http:// www.presidency.ucsb.edu/index.php.

24. Appendix 3.

25. American Independent Party Platform, http://www.aipca.org/platform.html.

26. LBJ Library, http://www.lbjlib.utexas. edu/johnson/archives.hom/FAQs/humphrey/ HHH_home.asp.

27. Miller Center, http://millercenter.org/ academic/americanpresident/nixon.

28. Biography, http://www.biographybase. com/biography/Wallace_George.html; Wiki pedia, http://en.wikipedia.org/wiki/George_ Wallace.

29. See chapter10 of this book.

30. American Thinker, http://www.ameri canthinker.com/2009/07/walter_cronkite_vietnam_and_th_1.html.

31. Oyez, Oyez.com.

32. *Ibid.*

33. *Washington Post,* http://www.washing tonpost.com/wp-dyn/content/article/2008/11/03/AR2008110302609.html.

34. Timeline 1968, 1968, http://www.stg.brown.edu/projects/1968/reference/timeline.html.

35. Center for Public Integrity, http://www.buyingofthepresident.org/index.php/the_hanna_project/election_year/1968_nixon_vs_humphrey/.

36. Real Clear Politics, http://www.realclear politics.com/articles/2007/11/nixon_1968_clin ton_2008.html.

37. Wikipedia, http://en.wikipedia.org/wiki/United_States_presidential_election,_1968#Campaign_strategies.

38. Larry J. Sabato, *Encyclopedia of American Political Parties and Elections* (New York: Checkmark, 2007), 359–61.

39. Gallup, http://www.gallup.com/poll/9457/election-polls-vote-groups-19681972.as px.

40. Center for Public Integrity, http://www.buyingofthepresident.org/index.php/the_hanna_project/election_year/1968_nixon_vs_humphrey/.

41. Wikipedia, http://en.wikipedia.org/wiki/George_Wallace#Democratic_presidential_pri maries_of_1964; George Wallace quotes, http://thinkexist.com/quotes/george_wallace/; Brainy Quotes, http://thinkexist.com/quotes/george_wallace/.

42. Miller Center, http://millercenter.org/academic/americanpresident/nixon.

43. *Ibid.*

44. Wikipedia, http://en.wikipedia.org/wiki/United_States_presidential_election,_1968#Results.

45. Miller Center, http://millercenter.org/academic/americanpresident/nixon.

46. Oyez, http://www.oyez.org/.

47. Wikipedia, http://en.wikipedia.org/wiki/Warren_E._Burger.

48. Wm. J. Brennan, http://www.michaelar iens.com/ConLaw/justices/brennan.htm.

49. Oyez, http://www.oyez.org/.

50. Wikipedia, http://en.wikipedia.org/wiki/Fairness_Doctrine.

51. Open Jurist, http://openjurist.org/405/us/625.

52. Miller Center, http://millercenter.org/academic/americanpresident/nixon.

53. Historical Tables 2009, 1.1, 1.2.

54. Historical Tables 2009, 1.1.

55. Wikipedia, http://en.wikipedia.org/wiki/List_of_recessions_in_the_United_States#Great_Depression_to_present.

56. Historical Tables 2010, 10.1.

57. Historical Tables 2010, 1.1.

58. Appendix 3.

59. Robert E. Kelly, *The National Debt of the United States* (Jefferson, NC: McFarland, 2008), 353.

60. Miller Center, http://millercenter.org/academic/americanpresident/nixon.

61. Appendix 3.

62. Historical Tables 2010, 3.1.

63. *Ibid.*

64. Center on Budget Priorities, http://www.cbpp.org/cms/?fa=view&id=512.

65. Miller Center, http://millercenter.org/academic/americanpresident/nixon.

66. Kent May 4 Center, http://www.may4.org/; Jackson State, http://www.may41970.com/Jackson%20State/jackson_state_may_1970.htm.

67. PBS, http://www.pbs.org/wgbh/amex/vietnam/trenches/my_lai.html.

68. Biography, Wm. Calley, http://www.law.umkc.edu/faculty/projects/ftrials/mylai/myl_bcalleyhtml.htm.

69. Wikipedia, http://en.wikipedia.org/wiki/United_States_presidential_election,_1968#Results.

Chapter 11

1. Republican Conventions, http://www.loc.gov/rr/main/republican_conventions.pdf; Political Graveyard, http://politicalgraveyard.com/parties/R/1976/index.html; Wikipedia, http://en.wikipedia.org/wiki/Republican_Party_%28United_States%29_presidential_primaries,_1976#Prim.

2. Spark Notes, http://www.sparknotes.com/biography/reagan/section6.rhtml.

3. *Ibid.*

4. Miller Center, http://millercenter.org/academic/americanpresident/ford.

5. *Time,* http://www.time.com/time/mag azine/article/0,9171,879612,00.html.

6. Miller Center, http://millercenter.org/academic/americanpresident/ford.

7. Democratic National Conventions, http://www.loc.gov/rr/main/democratic_conventio ns.pdf.

8. American Elections, http://www.geo cities.com/Athens/Agora/8088/ElectPandC.html.

9. Source: American Presidency Project, http://www.presidency.ucsb.edu/index.php.

10. *New York Times Almanac 2009,* 159–60.

11. Life Site News, http://www.tldm.org/News12/PercentageOfAmericansApprovingAbortionDrops.htm.

12. Appendix 7.

13. Presidential Vetoes, http://www.infoplease.com/ipa/A0801767.html.

14. Ann Coulter, http://scottthong.wordpress.com/2008/10/22/ann-coulter-researches-the-pro-democrat-poll-bias-through-8-presidential-elections/.

15. Miller Center, http://millercenter.org/academic/americanpresident/ford.

16. The History Place, http://www.historyplace.com/speeches/ford.htm.

17. USA Presidents, http://www.usa-presidents.info/ford.htm.

18. Miller Center, http://millercenter.org/academic/americanpresident/carter.

19. Oyez, http://www.oyez.org/.

20. Appendices 2.1, 2.2.

21. Robert E. Kelly, *The National Debt, 1941–2008* (Jefferson, NC: McFarland, 2008), Appendix 1.

22. *Ibid.*, Appendices 7, 2, 8.3.

23. *Ibid.*, Appendix 1-1.

24. Historical Tax Rates, http://www.huppi.com/kangaroo//TaxTimeline.htm.

25. 1976 debates, http://www-cgi.cnn.com/ALLPOLITICS/1996/debates/history/1976/.

26. Gallup, http://www.freerepublic.com/focus/news/2086652/posts.

27. *Ibid.*

28. *Ibid.*

29. Wikipedia, http://en.wikipedia.org/wiki/Eugene_McCarthy#Presidential_campaigns_1972_and_1976; U.S. Congress, http://bioguide.congress.gov/scripts/biodisplay.pl?index=M000311.

30. Miller Center, http://millercenter.org/academic/americanpresident/ford.

31. Simonsez, http://symonsez.wordpress.com/2010/03/12/this-model-was-ford-tough/.

32. Gallup, http://www.freerepublic.com/focus/news/2086652/posts.

33. Appendix 3.

34. Miller Center, http://millercenter.org/academic/americanpresident/carter.

35. Jewish Press, http://www.jewishpress.com/pageroute.do/41398/.

36. Gallup, http://www.freerepublic.com/focus/news/2086652/posts.

37. All Politics, http://www-cgi.cnn.com/ALLPOLITICS/1996/debates/history/1976/.

38. Gallup, http://www.freerepublic.com/focus/news/2086652/posts.

39. U.S. Presidential Elections, http://uselectionatlas.org/RESULTS/.

40. David Liep's Atlas, http://uselectionatlas.org/RESULTS/.

41. *Ibid.*

42. Miller Center, http://millercenter.org/academic/americanpresident/carter.

43. Appendix 1-1, 1-2.

44. Oyez, http://www.oyez.org/.

45. Wm. J. Brennan, http://www.michaelariens.com/ConLaw/justices/brennan.htm.

46. Mark R. Levin, *Men in Black* (Washington, DC: Regnery, 2005), 5–9.

47. Oyez, http://www.oyez.org/.

48. *Ibid.*

49. Miller Center, http://millercenter.org/academic/americanpresident/carter.

50. Oil Timeline, http://timelines.ws/subjects/Oil.HTML.

51. Miller Center, http://millercenter.org/academic/americanpresident/carter.

52. Historical Cruse Oil Prices, http://www.inflationdata.com/inflation/Inflation_Rate/Historical_Oil_Prices_Table.asp.

53. Major Acts of Congress, http://www.enotes.com/major-acts-congress.

54. Marginal Tax Rates, http://www.truthandpolitics.org/top-rates.php.

55. National Bureau of Economic Research, http://www.nber.org/cycles.html.

56. *Ibid.*

57. Historical Tables 2010, 3.1.

58. Appendix 3.

59. Miller Center, http://millercenter.org/academic/americanpresident/carter.

60. Answers.com, http://www.answers.com/topic/panama-canal-treaty.

61. Camp David Accords, http://www.britannica.com/EBchecked/topic/91061/Camp-David-Accords.

62. Wikipedia, http://en.wikipedia.org/wiki/Neutron_bomb.

Chapter 12

1. Miller Center, http://millercenter.org/academic/americanpresident/reagan.

2. Appendix 3.

3. Robert E. Kelly, *The National Debt of the United States, 1941–2008* (Jefferson, NC: McFarland, 2008), 335.

4. Miller Center, http://millercenter.org/academic/americanpresident/bush.

5. Gulf War, http://www.indepthinfo.com/iraq/kuwait.html.

6. Miller Center, http://millercenter.org/academic/americanpresident/clinton.

7. About.com, http://uspolitics.about.com/od/polls/l/bl_historical_approval.htm.

8. *Ibid.*

9. Democratic National Conventions, http://www.loc.gov/rr/main/democratic_conventions.pdf.

10. Wikipedia, http://en.wikipedia.org/wiki/2000_Democratic_National_Convention#Notable_speakers.

11. Republican National Conventions, http://www.loc.gov/rr/main/republican_conventions.pdf.

12. Wikipedia, http://en.wikipedia.org/wiki/Republican_Party_%28United_States%29_presidential_primaries,_2000#Results_breakdown_by_state.

13. *Ibid.*

14. American Presidency Project, http://www.presidency.ucsb.edu/platforms.php.

15. About.com, http://uspolitics.about.com/od/polls/l/bl_historical_approval.htm.

16. Wikipedia, http://en.wikipedia.org/wiki/Abortion_in_the_United_States.

17. Appendix 7.

18. Historical Crude Oil Prices, http://www.inflationdata.com/inflation/Inflation_Rate/Historical_Oil_Prices_Table.asp.

19. Reason.com, http://reason.com/archives/2007/03/23/gasoline-prices-conspiracy-or.

20. Appendix 7.

21. Kelly, *The National Debt of the United States, 1941–2008*, 283–85.

22. Miller Center, http://millercenter.org/academic/americanpresident/clinton; Al Gore Center, http://www.algoresupportcenter.com/aboutal.html.

23. Miller Center, http://millercenter.org/academic/americanpresident/gwbush; Wikipedia, http://en.wikipedia.org/wiki/George_W._Bush.

24. Buzzle.com, http://www.buzzle.com/editorials/6-10-2005-71385.asp.

25. Oyez, http://www.oyez.org/.

26. About.com, http://politicalhumor.about.com/library/blbushisms.htm.

27. *New York Times,* http://www.nytimes.com/2000/10/03/us/2000-campaign-poll-candidates-given-high-marks-poll-fitness-lead.html?pagewanted=1.

28. Comission on Presidential Debates, http://www.debates.org/index.php?page=2000-debates#oct-3-2000.

29. Television Debates, http://www.presidency.ucsb.edu/debates.php.

30. PBS, http://www.pbs.org/newshour/bb/politics/july-dec00/sgend_10-3.html.

31. Gallup, http://www.gallup.com/poll/110674/presidential-debates-rarely-gamechangers.aspx.

32. Media Bias Basics, http://www.mediaresearch.org/biasbasics/biasbasics1.asp.

33. Absolute Astronomy, http://www.absoluteastronomy.com/topics/Al_Gore_presidential_campaign,_2000.

34. Miller Center, http://millercenter.org/academic/americanpresident/gwbush.

35. Center for Public Integrity, http://www.buyingofthepresident.org/index.php/the_hanna_project/election_year/1996_clinton_vs_dole/.

36. History Central, http://www.historycentral.com/elections/Disputedelections.html.

37. *Washington Post,* http://www.washingtonpost.com/wp-dyn/articles/A26119-2004Dec25.html.

38. David Liep's Atlas, http://www.uselectionatlas.org/INFORMATION/ARTICLES/pe2000timeline.phpl.

39. Miller Center, http://millercenter.org/academic/americanpresident/gwbushl.

40. Democratic Underground, http://www.democraticunderground.com/discuss/duboard.php?az=view_all&address=103x390391.

41. Historical Tables, 1.1

42. Oyez, http://www.oyez.org/.

43. Wm. J. Brennan, http://www.michaelariens.com/ConLaw/justices/brennan.htm.

44. Oyez, http://www.oyez.org/.

45. *Ibid.*

46. Historical Tables, 1.1.

47. *U.S. News,* http://www.msnbc.msn.com/id/14959937.

48. *National Review,* http://www.nationalreview.com/interrogatory/interrogatory091103b.asp.

49. Wikipedia, http://en.wikipedia.org/wiki/2001_anthrax_attacks.

50. Carl C. Hodge, *U.S. Presidents and Foreign Policy* (Santa Barbara, CA: ABC-CLIO, 2007), 381.

51. Forbes, http://www.forbes.com/2002/07/25/accountingtracker.html.

52. Historical Tables 2010, 1.1.

53. Kelly, *The National Debt of the United States, 1941–2008.*

54. Historical Tables 2010, 1.1.

55. Kelly, *The National Debt of the United States, 1941–2008.*

56. Major Acts of Congress, http://www.enotes.com/major-acts-congress.

57. About.com, http://usliberals.about.com/od/education/i/NCLBProsCons.htm.

58. Online News Hour, http://www.pbs.org/newshour/bb/military/terroristattack/joint-resolution_9-14.html.

59. Appendix 7.

60. Iraq and WMD, http://www.gwu.edu/~nsarchiv/NSAEBB/NSAEBB80/.

61. *Ibid.*

62. CommonDreams.org, http://www.commondreams.org/headlines03/0811-09.htm.

63. YNetnews, http://www.ynetnews.com/articles/0,7340,L-3159691,00.html.

64. *Ibid.*

65. BBC, http://news.bbc.co.uk/2/hi/asia-pacific/4732091.stm.

66. Arms Control Association, http://www.armscontrol.org/factsheets/dprkchron.

67. *Time,* http://www.time.com/time/world/article/0,8599,1728451,00.html.

68. Timeline, NATO, http://timelines.ws/countries/NATO.HTML1.

69. Wikipedia, http://en.wikipedia.org/wiki/Second_Chechen_War.

70. On The issues, http://www.ontheissues.org/Celeb/George_W__Bush_China.htm.

71. East-West Center, http://www.eastwestcenter.org/fileadmin/stored/pdfs/BushAsia.pdf.

Bibliography

American Historical Newspapers, Boston Public Library.

Crocker, H.W. *Politically Incorrect Guide to the Civil War*. Washington, DC: Regnery, 2008.

DeGregorio, William A. *The Complete Book of U.S. Presidents*. New York: Wings, 1991.

Diner, Steven J. *A Very Different Age*. New York: Hill & Wang, 1998.

Folsom, B., Jr. *New Deal or Raw Deal*. New York: Simon & Schuster, 2008.

Heller, Deane Fons, and David Heller. *The Kennedy Cabinet; America's Men of Destiny*. Biography index reprint series. Freeport, N.Y.: Books for Libraries Press, 1969.

Historical Statistics of the United States, Colonial Times to 1957, U.S. Department of Commerce.

Historical Tables 2010. Office of Management and Budget.

Hodge, Carl C. *U.S. Presidents Foreign Policy*. Santa Barbara, CA: ABC-CLIO, 2007.

Irons, Peter. *God on Trial*. New York: Penguin, 2008.

_____. *The People's History of the Supreme Court*. New York: Penguin, 2006.

Kelly, Robert E. *The National Debt of the United States, 1941–2008*. Jefferson, NC: McFarland, 2008.

Kirk, Russell. *The Conservative Mind, from Burke to Santayana*. Chicago: H. Regnery, 1978.

Levin, Mark R. *Men in Black*. Washington, DC: Regnery, 2005.

Link, Arthur S. *Woodrow Wilson and the Progressive Era, 1910–17*. New York: Harper & Row, 1954.

McCullough, David. *John Adams*. New York: Simon & Schuster, 2001.

New York Times Almanac 2009.

Past and Present: Harry Truman's 1948 Comeback Campaign, U.S. News, 10/30/08.

Portland (ME) Eastern Argus, October 18, 1824.

Rosenfeld, Richard N. *American Aurora*. New York: St. Martin's, 1997.

Sabato, Larry J. *Encyclopedia of American Political Parties and Elections*. New York: Checkmark, 2006.

Savage, Sean J. *JFK, LBJ, and the Democratic Party*. SUNY series on the presidency. Albany: State University of New York Press, 2004.

Spalding, Matthew. *The Founders' Almanac A Practical Guide to the Notable Events, Greatest Leaders & Most Eloquent Words of the American Founding*. Washington, D.C.: Heritage Foundation, 2002.

Statistical Abstract of the United States 2008.

Steadman, Charles W. *The National Debt Conclusion*. Westport, CT: Praeger, 1993.

Wheeling (WV) Register, August 2 and 12, 1884. — American Historical Newspapers, Boston Public Library.

Wright, Benjamin J., ed. *"The Federalist": The Famous Papers of the Principles of American Government (by Alexander Hamilton, James Madison, John Jay)*. New York: Barnes & Noble, 1996.

Internet Sources

Abe Fortas, http://www.absoluteastronomy.com/.

About.com, http://www.about.com/.

Absolute Astronomy, http://www.absoluteastronomy.com/.

Achieving Early America, http://www.earlyamerica.com/.

AFL-CIO, http://www.aflcio.org/.

Al Gore Center, http://www.algoresupportcenter.com/.

Alien & Seditions Acts 1798, http://www.earlyamerica.com/.

All Politics, http://www-cgi.cnn.com/.

America, http://www.america.gov/.

American Elections, http://www.geocities.com/.

American Heritage, http://www.americanheritage.com/.

American Independent Party Platform, http://www.aipca.org/.

American Presidents, http://www.american-presidents.com/.

American Thinker, http://www.americanthinker.com/.

Ann Coulter, http://scottthong.wordpress.com/.2008/10/22/ann-coulter-researches-the-pro-democrat-poll-bias-through-8-presidential-elections/.

Answers.com, http://www.answers.com/.

ARC, http://www.arcmass.org/.

Arms Control Association, http://www.armscontrol.org/.

Associated Content, http://www.associatedcontent.com/.

Atlantic Online, http://www.theatlantic.com/.past/docs/issues/95dec/conbook/conbook.htm.

BBC, http://news.bbc.co.uk/.

Benjamin Franklin Bache, http://www.libraries.psu.edu/digital/pahistory/folder_3/page_1.html.

Biographies, http://odur.let.rug.nl/~usa/B/index.htm.

Biography.com, http://www.biography.com/.

Biography Base, http://www.biographybase.com/.

Biography, Wm. Calley, http://www.law.umkc.edu/.

Bnet, http://findarticles.com/.

Bob's World, http://www.bobsuniverse.com/.

Britannica, http://www.britannica.com.

Business Cycles, http://www.nber.org/.

Buzzle.com (Kerry/Bush) http://www.buzzle.com/.

Camp David Accords, http://www.britannica.com/.

Catholic Encyclopedia, http://www.newadvent.org/.

Center for Public Integrity, http://www.buyingofthepresident.org/.

Center on Budget Priorities, http://www.cbpp.org/.

Chinese-American Experience, http://immigrants.harpweek.com/.

Citizendium, http://en.citizendium.org/.wiki/.

The Civil Rights Legacy of Harry S Truman, http://millercenter.org/.

Civil Service Reform, http://www.classbrain.com/.

Cleveland Chronicles, http://www.angelfire.com/.

CNN, http://www.cnn.com/.

Cold War Museum, http://www.coldwar.org/.

Commission on Presidential Debates, http://www.debates.org/.

CommonDreams.org (Iraq), http://www.commondreams.org/.

Connecticut State Library, http://www.cslib.org/.

Conservapedia, http://www.conservapedia.com/.

Cuban Missile Crisis, http://library.thinkquest.org/.

David Leip's Atlas, http://uselectionatlas.org/.

Debate on a Standing Army, http://www.shsu.edu/.

Democratic Convention, http://www.loc.gov/.

Democratic Underground, http://www.democraticunderground.com/.

Department of Commerce, http://www.commerce.gov/.

East-West Center, http://www.eastwestcenter.org/.

Economic Bill of Rights, http://www.worldpolicy.org/.projects/globalrights/econrights/fdr-econbill.html.

Eleanor Roosevelt, http://www.nps.gov/elro/

Eleanor Roosevelt Papers, http://www.gwu.edu/.

Election of 1824, http://www.u-s-history.com/.

Electoral Vote 1800, http://www.usconstitution.net/.

Encarta, http://encarta.msn.com/.

The Experts Got It Wrong, http://www.austincc.edu/lpatrick/his1302PCM/.WhenAllTheExperts2.html.

Exploring Constitutional Law, Doug Linder, http://www.law.umkc.edu/.

FDR's Economic Bill of Rights, http://www.worldpolicy.org/.projects/globalrights/econrights/fdr-econbill.html.

First Federal Congress, 1789–91, http://www.gwu.edu/.

Forbes, http://www.forbes.com/.

From Revolution to Reconstruction, http://www.let.rug.nl/.

Gallup, http://www.gallup.com/.poll/.

George Wallace Quotes, http://thinkexist.com/.

Georgia Encyclopedia, http://www.georgiaencyclopedia.org/.

Global Security.org, http://www.globalsecurity.org/.

The Great Truman Surprise, http://www.kennesaw.edu/.

Grover Cleveland, http://www.mtholyoke.edu/.

Gulf War, http://www.indepthinfo.com/.

Harry S. Truman Library, http://www.trumanlibrary.org/.

Haverhill (MA) Gazette, November 20, 1824.

Historic Valley Forge, http://www.ushistory.org/.

Historical Crude Oil Prices, http://www.inflationdata.com/.

Historical Tax Rates, http://www.huppi.com/.kangaroo//TaxTimeline.htm.

History Central, http://www.historycentral.com/.

History (Kefauver), http://history.sandiego. edu/.

History News Network, http://hnn.us/articles/.

History of Presidential Primaries, http://www. cqpolitics.com/.

The History Place, http://www.historyplace. com/.

History (Social Security), http://www.ssa.gov/.

Housing Act 1961, http://www.presidency.uc sb.edu/.

HUD, http://www.hud.gov/.

Infoplease, http://www.infoplease.com/.

Internet Accuracy Project, http://www.accura cyproject.org/.

Iraq and WMD, http://www.gwu.edu/.

Jackson State, http://www.may41970.com/.

James G. Blaine, http://www.u-s-history.com/.

James Garfield Quotes, http://www.brainy quote.com/.

James McHenry, http://www.history.army.mil/ books/.

Jewish Press, http://www.jewishpress.com/.

John F. Kennedy Library, http://www.jfklibra ry.org/.

John Rutledge, http://www.history.army.mil/ books/.

Judiciary Act 1869, http://judgepedia.org/in dex.php/Judiciary_Act_of_1869.

Junto Society, http://www.juntosociety.com/.

Justia, http://supreme.justia.com/.

Kennedy-Nixon Debates, http://www.muse um.tv/archives/.

Kent May 4 Center, http://www.may4.org/.

King Center, http://www.thekingcenter.org/.

Los Angeles Times, http://latimesblogs.latimes. com/.thedailymirror/2010/01/nixon-leads-kennedy-in-poll.html.

Lyndon B. Johnson Library, http://www.lbjlib. utexas.edu/.

Major Acts of Congress, http://www.enotes. com/.

The Making of a Nation, Election 1888, http:// www.tingroom.com/.

Manifest Destiny, http://www.civics-online. org/.

Marginal Tax Rates, http://www.truthandpol itics.org/.

MBC (Museum of Broadcast Communica-tions), http://www.museum.tv/eotvsection. php?entrycode=kennedy-nixon.

Media Bias Basics, http://www.mediaresearch. org/.

Men Who Ran for President, http://www.jun tosociety.com/.

Miller Center, http://millercenter.org/.

Mt. Holyoke, http://www.mtholyoke.edu/ac ad/intrel/gc26.htm.

Museum of Broadcast Communications, http: //www.museum.tv/archives/.

National Archives, http://www.archives.gov/.

National Bureau of Economic Research, http: //www.nber.org/.

National Review, http://www.nationalreview. com/.

National Women Suffrage Association, http:// memory.loc.gov/.

Nelson Rockefeller, http://www.reformation. org/.rockefeller-file.html.

1976 debates, http://www-cgi.cnn.com/.

1960 debates, http://www.debates.org/.

1960 debates, http://www.cgi.cnn.com/.

The 1960 Republican Convention, http://www. chicagohs.org/.history/politics/1960.html.

Nixon Quotes, http://www.brainyquote.com/.

Nixon vs. Kennedy 9/26/60, http://www.you tube.com/.

NNDB, http://www.nndb.com/.people/.

Nobel Prize, http://nobelprize.org/.

NPR, http://www.npr.org/.

New York Times, http://www.nytimes.com/. nixon-and-eisenhower-794201.html.

Ohio History, http://www.ohiohistorycentral. org/.

Oil Timeline, http://timelines.ws/subjects/Oil. HTML.

On the Issues, http://www.ontheissues.org/.

Online News Hour, http://www.pbs.org/.

Open Jurist, http://openjurist.org/.

Our Campaigns, http://www.ourcampaigns. com/.

Oyez, http://www.oyez.org/.

Party Platforms, http://www.presidency.ucsb. edu/.

PBS, http://www.pbs.org/.ewshour/bb/poli.

Political Graveyard, http://politicalgraveyard. com/.

President Elect Articles, http://www.presiden telect.org/.

President Johnson, http://www.reformation. org/.

The Presidential Election of 1800, http://www. gilderlehrman.org/historynow/09_2004/his torian4.php

Presidential Vetoes, http://www.infoplease. com/.

Probable Cause, http://roswell.fortunecity.com/.

Probert Encyclopedia, http://www.proberten cyclopaedia.com/.

Progressive Party 1948, http://www.lib.uiowa. edu/.

Progressive Party Platform, http://www.david pietrusza.com/.

Ranking Presidents, http://falcon.arts.cornell. edu/govt/courses/F04/PresidentialRanki ngs.pdf/.

Real Clear Politics, http://www.realclearpoli tics.com/.

Reason.com, http://reason.com/.

Religious Liberty Archive, http://www.church statelaw.com/.

Republican/Democratic Convention History, http://www.poynter.org/.

Republican Convention, http://www.loc.gov/rr/main/republican_conventions.pdf.

Richard M. Nixon Library, http://www.nixonlibrary.gov/.

Roper, http://www.ropercenter.uconn.edu/.

Road to Camelot, http://www.kennesaw.edu/.

The Rockefeller File, Gary Allen, http://www.whale.to/b/allen_b.htm.

Roscoe Conkling, http://www.u-s-history.com/.

Samuel Chase, http://colonialhall.com/.

Samuel J. Tilden, http://www.samueltilden.com/.

Samuel J. Tilden, http://www.u-s-history.com/.

The Second Nixon-Kennedy debate, http://www.archive.org/.details/SecondCampaignDebateNixon-kennedy1960.

Seth Kaller, Inc., http://www.sethkaller.net/.

Simonsez, http://symonsez.wordpress.com/.

Smithsonian, http://www.smithsonianmag.com/.

Smoking Gun Archive, http://www.thesmokinggun.com/.

Space Races.com, http://www.thespacerace.com/.

Spark Notes, http://www.sparknotes.com/.

The Speaker's House, http://www.speakershouse.org/.

Stanford, http://ai.stanford.edu/.

States' Rights Convention, http://www.alabamamoments.alabama.gov/.

Strom Thurmond Institute, http://www.strom.clemson.edu/.

Suite101.com, http://americanhistory.suite101.com/.

Television Debates, http://www.presidency.ucsb.edu/.

ThinkExist.com (G. Wallace), http://thinkexist.com/.

This Day in History, http://www.history.com/.

Thomas Jefferson Encyclopedia, http://wiki.monticello.org/.

Thomas Jefferson, http://sc94.ameslab.gov/.

Thomas Jefferson Timeline, http://www.monticello.org/.

Time Online, http://www.timesonline.co.uk/.

Time, http://www.time.com/.

Timeline 1968, http://www.stg.brown.edu/.

Timeline, NATO, http://timelines.ws/countries/.

Timothy Pickering, http://www.nps.gov/.

Today in History, http://memory.loc.gov/.

Trenton NJ Federalist, August 8, 1824.

Tripolitan War, http://www.u-s-history.com/.

TV Guide, http://www.tvguide.com/.celebrities/rebekah-johnson/264915.

U.S. Census Bureau, http://www.census.gov/.

U.S. Citizenship and Immigration Services, http://www.uscis.gov/.

U.S. Congress, http://bioguide.congress.gov/.

U.S. Department of Labor http://www.dol.gov/.

U.S. Department of State, http://www.state.gov/.

U.S. Department of Treasury, http://www.ustreas.gov/.

U.S. EEOC, http://www.eeoc.gov/.

U.S. Government Revenue, http://www.usgovernmentrevenue.com/.

U.S. History, http://www.u-s-history.com/.

U.S. History, http://www.ushistory.org/.

U.S. News, December 15, 2002, http://www.kennesaw.edu/.

U.S. News, http://www.msnbc.msn.com/.

U.S. Peace Corps, http://multimedia.peacecorps.gov/.

U.S. Presidential Elections, http://uselectionatlas.org/.

U.S. Presidents, http://www.usa-presidents.info/.

U.S. Senate, http://www.senate.gov/.

U.S. Supreme Court Center, http://supreme.justia.com/.

University of Alabama, http://www.alabamamoments.alabama.gov/.

Washington Post, http://www.washingtonpost.com/.

Washington Post, http://www.washingtonpost.com/.wp-dyn/content/article/2005/06/21/AR2005062101632.html.

Whiskey Rebellion, http://www.globalsecurity.org/.

White House, http://www.whitehouse.gov/.

Wikipedia, http://en.wikipedia.org/.

Wm. J. Brennan, http://www.michaelariens.com/.

WSJ, http://online.wsj.com/.

Woodrow Wilson, http://www.claremont.org/.

YNetnews, http://www.ynetnews.com/.

Index